Passageways: An Interpretive History of Black America
Volume II: 1863–1965

HARCOURT BRACE

soon to become

A Harcourt Higher Learning Company

Soon you will find Harcourt Brace's distinguished innovation, leadership, and support under a different name . . . a new brand that continues our unsurpassed quality, service, and commitment to education.

We are combining the strengths of our college imprints into one worldwide brand: Harcourt Our mission is to make learning accessible to anyone, anywhere, anytime—reinforcing our commitment to lifelong learning.

We'll soon be Harcourt College Publishers. Ask for us by name.

One Company
"Where Learning Comes to Life."

Passageways: An Interpretive History of Black America
Volume II: 1863–1965

Colin A. Palmer
City University of New York
Graduate School

Harcourt Brace College Publishers

Fort Worth   Philadelphia   San Diego   New York   Orlando   Austin   San Antonio
Toronto   Montreal   London   Sydney   Tokyo

973.0496 P173p v. 2

Palmer, Colin A., 1942-

Passageways

Publisher	Earl McPeek
Acquisitions Editor	David Tatom
Product Manager	Steven K. Drummond
Developmental Editor	Margaret McAndrew Beasley
Project Editor	Angela Williams Urquhart
Production Manager	Annette Dudley Wiggins
Art Director	Candice Johnson Clifford

Cover Image: Jacob Lawrence, *The Migration of the Negro,* panel no. 23, tempera on masonite, 12" × 18", The Phillips Collection, Washington, DC. Courtesy of the artist and Francine Seders Gallery, Seattle, WA.

ISBN: 0-15-502483-3

Library of Congress Catalogue Number: 97-74864

Copyright © 1998 by Holt, Rinehart and Winston

All rights reserved. No part of this publication may be reproduced or transmitted in any form or by any means, electronic or mechanical, including photocopy, recording, or any information storage and retrieval system, without permission in writing from the publisher.

Requests for permission to make copies of any part of the work should be mailed to: Permissions Department, Harcourt Brace & Company, 6277 Sea Harbor Drive, Orlando, Florida 32887-6777.

Special acknowledgments of copyright ownership and of permission to reproduce works (or excerpts thereof) included in this edition begin on page 295 and constitute an extension of this page.

Address for Orders
Harcourt Brace & Company, 6277 Sea Harbor Drive, Orlando, FL 32887-6777
1-800-782-4479

Address for Editorial Correspondence
Harcourt Brace College Publishers, 301 Commerce Street, Suite 3700,
Fort Worth, TX 76102

Web site address:
http://www.hbcollege.com

Printed in the United States of America

0 1 2 3 4 5 6 039 10 9 8 7 6 5 4 3

Preface

The proliferation of scholarship since the 1960s on various aspects of the history of black Americans provides the raison d'être for this synthesis. It is a daunting challenge because of the vast and changing literature and the inherent difficulty of interpreting a people's past. Unlike previous syntheses, the two volumes that comprise this work center blacks in their own history. The story is told from the standpoint of the volumes's subjects; blacks are not viewed through the lens of America's white majority, nor do I recount their history in terms of their roles in the making of the United States. Rather, I emphasize how a people made and remade themselves over time. Black Americans are shown as the principal architects of their struggles. The work is intended for a diverse audience of specialists, students, and the general public.

Volume I begins on the African continent, the ancestral societies of black Americans. It recounts the Africans's social, political, and cultural arrangements prior to their forced migration to America, emphasizing the centrality of their cultures in the new lives they fashioned. The ways in which these pioneering Africans and their progeny laid the foundations of black America constitute the primary focus of the volume. It is a poignant tale of a people's travail, their struggles, and ultimately their survival. The black American odyssey under slavery is not unique, however. Other black societies in the Americas experienced, in varying degrees, a similar trajectory. Consequently, Volume I, in particular, is a contribution to the larger history of the African diaspora.

Volume II addresses the struggles by black Americans to realize themselves in the aftermath of slavery and in succeeding years. Building upon the first volume, and drawing upon the extensive secondary literature, it focuses on the enormous societal challenges they confronted after 1863, the myriad ways with which they responded to them, the institutions they created, and the creative energies they unleashed. As in the first volume, the story is told from the standpoint of the subjects; black Americans are the principal actors in their struggles and attempts to achieve their possibilities.

FEATURES OF THE TWO VOLUMES

The publication of *Passageways* marks the first appearance in many years of a major new general work on the history of African Americans. The two-volume work is distinguished by the following features.

Passageways
- situates African Americans at the core of their own history
- depicts African Americans actively constructing their own paths through hostile times and environments
- reflects current scholarship and fresh interpretation on the black past
- incorporates voices of the people through speeches, prayers, poems, and jokes
- combines chronological structure with thematic perspectives
- provides authoritative narrative and engaging illustrations
- includes an extensive bibliographic essay

IN APPRECIATION

This book builds upon the work of several scholars and I gratefully acknowledge my dependence on them. I have tried to limit my use of footnotes at times, but the list of recommended readings highlights additional works that have been indispensable in the preparation of the book.

I began the preliminary work on this volume while I was in residence at the Stanford Humanities Center in 1992–1993. I thank everyone associated with the Center for the privilege of working there. My thanks also go to the University of North Carolina at Chapel Hill and the Graduate School of the City University of New York for their invaluable support. I also benefited a great deal from the comments of those who read the manuscript for the press, although I did not always agree with them. Erica Ball and Kelvin Sealey of the CUNY Graduate School provided detailed criticisms of the manuscript, for which I am deeply grateful. Graduate students in my course, Social Movements in the African Diaspora, read the manuscript and offered useful suggestions for its improvement. Peter Vellon and Michael Yudell of the CUNY Graduate School assisted in the identification of illustrative materials and I thank them. James Sweet, a doctoral candidate at the CUNY Graduate School, deserves a very special thanks. He typed the several drafts of the manuscript, deciphering my handwriting, pointing out errors, identifying sources, and offering critical advice. The manuscript is much the better for his efforts.

I am also grateful to the following reviewers who gave their time to read and provide suggestions on an early draft of this volume:

Edna Greene Medford, Howard University

Rick Moniz, Chabot College

Gerald L. Smith, University of Kentucky

Robert C. Watson, Hampton University

Undoubtedly, errors may remain in this work and I take full responsibility for them.

Contents

Introduction   x

Chapter 1
Constructing Freedom, 1863–1879   1

Chapter 2
Maintaining White Supremacy: From the Compromise to 1917   33

Chapter 3
Struggling for Direction after 1879   47

Chapter 4
Uplifting the Race: 1879–1917   66

Chapter 5
Constructing an Identity: From Turner to Garvey   82

Chapter 6
The Generation of 1917   106

Chapter 7
Intellectual and Cultural Life: From Emancipation to the Harlem Renaissance   130

Chapter 8
A People in Motion, 1915–1955   156

Chapter 9
Building Organizations, Weathering Storms before and after Garvey   184

Chapter 10
Looking Outward: World War I to the Civil Rights Movement   202

Chapter 11
Claiming Equal Rights, 1917–1954   219

Chapter 12
Forcing Change: 1955–1965   239

Further Reading   279
Photo Credits   295
Literary Acknowledgments   296
Index   300

Introduction

This book, the second of a three-volume work, is an interpretation of the history of black Americans since the signing of the Emancipation Proclamation in 1863. It ends in 1965, the year that marked the conclusion of the effective stage of the civil rights movement. Its twelve chapters focus on the principal currents in black life during a period of rapid internal transformations, the years when a people tried to achieve their human possibilities and claim their rightful place in the land of their birth. As I indicated in the first volume, the metaphor *passageways*, characterizes the myriad ways that blacks have had to construct and navigate their path through the racial minefields that impeded them.

As should be clear from the narrative that follows, this book is the history of a people, not the history of a nation state. A people's internal trajectory, particularly that of an oppressed, marginalized group, and one that did not enjoy full citizenship rights, is not coterminous with the political history of the state. There may be occasions on which the two coincide and there is obviously a dialectical relationship, but the markers that define the history of a nation seldom reflect the inner lives and history of specific groups, viewed on their own terms and through their own lens. None of this means that the history of blacks can, at all levels, be isolated from the study of others in American society. I simply stress that our first task is to center our subjects in their own lives.

Such a task is not easily accomplished, and it requires a rethinking of what is, or what is not, black history. For example, a reading list in African American history since 1865 prepared for doctoral students at one American university arranged the books under such headings as, "Reconstruction," "Post-Reconstruction Order, North and South," "Early Twentieth Century," and "Depression and World War II." Similarly, as this introduction was being written, a major university advertised a vacancy for a specialist in "colonial, early national, and antebellum African American history." It is clear from these two egregious examples, which are by no means isolated ones, that the experiences of blacks as a people are simply slotted into the traditional national periodization with no recognition of the inner motions of the group or the defining moments that are peculiar to them. To do so is to view a people primarily through an external lens and to ignore the worlds they created for themselves. It is, to use a rough analogy, as if the markers for the history of women derive from the experiences of men or the watersheds in the history of gays and lesbians emanate from those of heterosexuals. This is absurd. We must first situate a group of people in their own worlds before we can begin to place them in larger contexts. Historians and teachers must always ask the question: "Whose history are we writing and teaching?" The answer to this question is the essential starting point for any exploration of a group or a people's past.

Rejecting the traditional and nation-state centered watersheds that historians have employed in their histories of black Americans, I have organized this volume around defining moments that reflect the trajectory of the people who are the subjects of this work. I fully expect these watersheds to be controversial, but I will have achieved my purpose if scholars and students alike begin to grapple with the imperative to identify markers that are rooted primarily in a people's internal experiences, their sinews, and deep structures.

The Emancipation Proclamation ended slavery in most places in 1863 and seemingly inaugurated new opportunities for the liberated peoples. Two years later, the Thirteenth Amendment to the Constitution formally terminated the institution everywhere. With freedom's arrival, blacks assumed the arduous and daunting challenge of constructing new lives and creating the organizations that would meet their own needs. Although slavery had ended, most whites had not changed their attitudes toward blacks and sought to confine them to subordinate places in society, even introducing labor systems in the former Confederacy that were nothing more than forms of modified slavery. Freedom conveyed a different meaning to many whites than it did to blacks. As blacks struggled to command their future, sometimes with the assistance of Republican-led federal administrations, they confronted myriad obstacles at the local levels.

When the federal government abandoned its experiment in the reconstruction of the former Confederacy in 1877, the newly freed were left to confront the power of the still entrenched white supremacists. By 1879, the emancipated peoples had realized that freedom had not brought fundamental changes in their lives and had not altered power relationships in the South. Several thousands made the fateful decision to abandon the South, leaving for the promise of a better life in Kansas. The Kansas Fever exodus, as this movement was called, was a defining moment in black life. It meant an end to the post-emancipation period, dramatized the recognition that freedom was in many respects an illusion, and started the large scale migration from the South that would be an important feature of black life for much of the twentieth century. Accordingly, the exodus must be seen as inaugurating a new and important phase and direction in the history of blacks as a people.

The years after 1879 saw a continuation of the struggle by blacks for self-definition. They debated the direction of the race, established a plethora of organizations, engaged in programs of economic and social uplift, and participated in the nation's life, albeit as junior partners. By 1917, however, an identifiably new mood emerged in black America. Slavery had ended formally half a century earlier and a new generation born to parents who had never been enslaved had come to maturity. The decision of these people (and their parents too), who I have called the Generation of 1917, to stand their ground and confront white violence in the social disturbances of 1917, 1919, and 1921 and later, suggested a markedly aggressive direction in the black struggle and reflected the maturation of the changes that were occurring in the structure of black life since 1863. The rise of the movement led by Marcus Garvey and its assertion of a confident blackness constituted a second shift; the literary, artistic, and cultural flowerings called the Harlem Renaissance represented a third development, and the great migration from the South to the North and to the West formed a fourth. All of these motions that appeared circa 1917, or at least during the second decade of the twentieth century, constituted the second watershed in a people's history since 1863, reflecting new initiatives, new energies, and a multifaceted struggle for their rights.

There was, accordingly, a noticeable acceleration in the pace of change in black America during the first half of the twentieth century. Increasingly, blacks had become a national presence as many left the South for the Northeast, the Midwest, and, to a lesser extent, the West. They became more urbanized and an industrial proletariat began to be forged. A smaller proportion found employment in the agricultural sector as opportunities became available in the industrial arenas, but at the lower rungs of the ladder. Literacy levels improved, self-help organizations flourished, and there was a heightening of political consciousness. Organizations such as the National Association for the Advancement of Colored People led the campaign against white violence, as epitomized by lynchings, and they also contested racial segregation in the South.

The third watershed since 1863 must be seen, therefore, as the culmination of these inner transformations that began before 1917 but quickened thereafter. In 1955, blacks began a sustained challenge to segregation, demanding their civil rights.

Beginning with a bus boycott in Montgomery, Alabama, in December 1955, blacks were able to force the larger society to remove some of the racially inspired barriers that stood in their way. The ability to launch and sustain such a struggle tells us that blacks as a people had developed the institutions, political will, and the capacity to wage an aggressive assault on an oppressive societal order. Under the circumstances, the Montgomery boycott both reflected and charted new directions in black life.

This energy survived with varying degrees of intensity and achieved notable successes over a ten-year period. The movement for civil rights achieved its last major legislative victory with the passage of the Voting Rights Act in 1965, a year that I argue marked an end to one phase of the struggle and ushered in another. Not only did the movement head North after 1965, but it broadened its focus to include a demand for economic justice. Consequently, I see this shift in strategy and goals, as well as the end of the period of legislative successes, as representing a fourth watershed. The book will not address the period after 1965 because this will become the subject of a third volume. The watersheds that I propose, then, are as follows: (1) 1863–1879; (2) 1879–circa 1917; (3) 1917–1955; (4) 1955–1965. I should emphasize that watersheds are not watertight periods. The processes that we seek to identify should be fitted into discrete moments only with the utmost caution. Similarly, the chapters that follow in this volume are only loosely organized according to time lines, more for the convenience of the reader and less an indication that the motions we address had temporal boundaries.

Overall, this volume describes and discusses a people in constant struggle and motion. It tries to capture the spirit of those men and women who, in ways large and small, spectacular and unspectacular, claimed their own human spaces and fought to surmount societal oppression. In order to tell their story as much as possible from their standpoint, I have included their voices to the degree that space allowed. Thus, I have tried to incorporate their speeches, prayers, poems, and jokes into the narrative. I could not, of course, address all of the developments and issues in black life since 1863 in a work of this nature. It was not my intention to sacrifice analysis for detail. Some readers will undoubtedly question the choices that I made and my emphases, but interpretive works, as opposed to traditional narrative histories, seek to identify the principal currents in a people's history and often treat them in broad strokes. Still, many if not most issues are treated here in greater depth than in similar volumes.

Because this is intended to be the internal history of a people, I do not focus on developments in the larger society except to the degree to which they impacted the course of black life, for good or ill. As such, individual whites are not central to the story. I do emphasize, however, the ways in which a changing racial ideology operated to control the nation's institutions, exposed blacks to mob violence, and denied them their right to full citizenship. A systemic racism diminished blacks as much as it did whites, but not in the same ways.

Passageways is not an exercise in hagiography, although I do identify with the people and the struggles that I describe. Nor is it to be perceived as falling within the genre of a contributionist history that views blacks as playing a supporting role in the making of America. Scholars who approach the writing of black history from such a perspective may well be justified in doing so, but that is not the book I attempted to write. Above all, this is a book about a resilient people making themselves, a task that as of this writing, remains unfinished.

Constructing Freedom, 1863-1879

"Thank God," exulted an old black woman as she hugged the mule of one of the black soldiers who triumphantly entered Charleston, South Carolina, in February 1865. The soldier held aloft a banner that was at once gratifyingly expressive and filled with a delicious promise. The word LIBERTY, which it boldly proclaimed, was one of the most emotional and sacrosanct in the black vocabulary. A second woman in the welcoming parade, unrestrained by her sixty-nine years, danced and chanted as she greeted Liberty's arrival:

> Ye's long been a-comin'
> Ye's long been a-comin'
> Ye's long been a-comin'
> For to take the land.[1]

Liberty's tardy arrival did not temper this woman's enthusiasm and her embrace of what its coming and presence portended. But neither she nor those whose sentiments she voiced understood that the realization of freedom's promise would pose new challenges and invite new frustrations.

The adoption of the Thirteenth Amendment to the U.S. Constitution in 1865 formally ended slavery everywhere. The Emancipation

Proclamation that President Abraham Lincoln had issued on January 1, 1863, was a pragmatic response to the North's difficulties in the Civil War, the pressure of the abolitionists, and the efforts of the enslaved who punctured the institution from within. Ideally, the Thirteenth Amendment enlarged the possibilities of the newly freed and those who had escaped slavery's chains before the war. Between the issuance of the Emancipation Proclamation in 1863 and the exodus to Kansas in 1879, blacks wrestled with the meanings of freedom, responded to the challenges of their new legal condition, and fought for their birthright. While there were measurable successes, they also experienced disillusionment and failure. By 1879, many had begun to abandon the South, signaling an end to the euphoric promise of emancipation and effecting a fundamental break with the past.

The Civil War had an enormously transforming effect on blacks–slaves and free people–as well as on whites. Free blacks had watched anxiously as a divided white population fought to determine the future of the nation state. At the outbreak of the war, the Union rebuffed the efforts of the black men who wanted to enlist, and its leaders proclaimed that it was not a war about slavery. Southern secessionists were not given to any such claims, since they knew all along that they were fighting to preserve their way of life, and a racialized slavery was at its core. Recognizing the potential of the war as an instrument of emancipation, most free blacks never wavered in their support of the Union's cause and greeted slavery's end as the removal of the shackles that they too had borne. The 180,000 free black men who eventually enlisted anticipated receiving all the rights of citizenship and the attendant opportunities. Black men and women everywhere embraced notions that freedom meant the withering away of racial barriers to their advancement. Blacks, freed from the crippling burden of slavery's existence and the demands of opposing it, found that freedom presaged new challenges and responsibilities.

For the 4 million newly freed persons, this was a time of boundless possibilities. Freedom was more than the absence of legal bondage. Fundamentally, it meant a new way of perceiving themselves, for they were no longer defined as human property. The psychological leap from slavery to freedom was, for some, immediate. Abandoning their masters, thousands had claimed themselves free during the war. The Emancipation Proclamation and the Thirteenth Amendment laid the legal groundwork for the transition to freedom, but the deeper changes occurred within each individual. Throwing off habits of obedience and deference to former owners and other whites would pose a challenge to all. The experience of the war and the emerging reality of the weakness of their masters, vis-à-vis the invading forces, had created a sense of their own possibilities. No one who saw the war up close or had participated in it escaped its transforming impact. As the conflict became a war for emancipation, the slaves, at least those who knew what was at stake, must have begun to prepare themselves mentally for the time when they would be free.

To many, freedom brought its own indescribable exhilaration. Some were uncomprehending at first, doubting that the moment had arrived. Others recognized the daunting challenges, reacting with uncertainty and fear. These emotions were not mutually exclusive; all slaves felt the tug of freedom and the countervailing pull of doubt and apprehension. Slavery's impact upon its victims was nothing if not varied, and the responses to emancipation were neither uniform nor fixed. While the desire for freedom was almost universal, much was tempered by the security of the known and the tenacity of old habits and understandings. Uncle Eph, who labored on a Virginia plantation, chose to leave after the Emancipation Proclamation declared him free. Upon his return after a few days, the old man confessed, "I jes wanter see whut it feel lak tuh be free." But Uncle Eph had stronger pulls and ties. "I wanter to go back to Ole Marster's plantation whar I was born. It don' look de same dar, an' I done see nuff uh freedom," the freedman added.[2]

The varied, hesitant, and sometimes contradictory responses of the newly freed to their changed legal reality were perfectly understandable. At one level, slavery had been legally destroyed, but this did not mean that the former bondmen could immediately transform their lives even if they so desired. Lacking land, capital, access to the sources of power, and the broader networks of associations that could make the difference between success and failure, freed persons understood the enormity of the challenges they confronted. Although they faced similar challenges everywhere, not all of the newly freed shared the same liabilities, at least not to the same extent. A few, by dint of their own initiatives, had acquired modest amounts of capital prior to their emancipation. Such persons would have enjoyed an economic head start in their struggle to make freedom work for them. Others who had escaped to join the Union army before or after the Emancipation Proclamation had acquired certain advantages that would serve them well. Those who served in the army and had saved their wages enjoyed a measure of economic independence when they returned home.

Most of the newly freed, however, possessed nothing of material consequence. Freedom, to them, had a more restrictive meaning. Although they were liberated from slavery's chains, they were hardly in a position to embrace many of the possibilities of their new legal condition. Once the euphoria of emancipation had waned, countless decisions about the future had to be made almost simultaneously and without any clear indication that the former slaves could control their lives. They had to decide whether to remain and work with their former owners or to abandon the sites of their oppression. This was one of the most important decisions that these persons had to make in their lives. In addition to their lack of material resources, many had an emotional attachment to the land upon which they had been born, experienced life's joys and burdens, and grown to maturity. The graves of family members and friends reinforced these deep ties. Understandably, the decision to leave was as difficult as the one to stay; the one inaugurated a courageous leap into the unknown and the other reflected an accommodation to the security of familiar terrains and relationships.

The emancipation of the slaves presented enormous national challenges also. President Lincoln was cognizant of the need to protect the interests of the newly freed and to readmit the secessionist states to the Union. In outlining his policy on admission of the states when he issued his "Proclamation of Amnesty and Reconstruction" on December 8, 1863, Lincoln promised a full pardon to the rebels and a return of their property, excepting slaves. In order to qualify, the rebels would have to swear their loyalty to the Union and endorse the emancipation of the slaves. As soon as the number of those taking the oath in a particular state reached 10 percent of those who had voted in the election of 1860, a new state government could be organized. Lincoln also promised: "Any provision which may be adopted by such State government in relation to the freed people of such State, which shall recognize and declare their permanent freedom, provide for their education, and which may yet be consistent, as a temporary arrangement, with their present condition as a laboring, landless, and homeless class, will not be objected by the national Executive."[3]

Seen narrowly, the president wanted to reestablish civil authority in the rebel states, literally a process of reconstruction. His offer to restore the confiscated lands of the rebels angered those abolitionists who wanted emancipation to produce changes in the economic order of the South. In order for freedom to be meaningful for blacks, abolitionists thought such a reconstruction of society "must be primarily economical and industrial; it must commence by planting a logical population in the South, not only as its cultivators but as its rightful and actual owners. . . . No such thing as a free, democratic society can exist in any country where all lands are owned by one class of men and cultivated by another."[4] Such a fundamental change in Southern society frightened those unable to embrace the vision of a polity where blacks and whites possessed equal rights and shared economic and political power. The competing visions of the place of blacks and whites in a reconstructed South were never satisfactorily resolved and became the source of much debate and conflict.

RECONSTRUCTING THE UNION

In order to understand the process of reconstructing the South and the principal developments in the lives of blacks after Emancipation and ending with the exodus to Kansas in 1879, we shall first discuss briefly the main currents in white opinion and the policies and programs that were implemented at the federal and state levels. This will provide a necessary understanding of the larger political and ideological contexts within which the motions in black life in the South took place and the ways in which they were enhanced, thwarted, or limited by them.

Among the most important and early federal attempts to aid the freed people was the creation of the Freedmen's Bureau. Authorized by Congress in March 1865, the bureau was responsible for "the supervision and management of all abandoned lands, and the control of all subjects relating to refugees and freedmen from rebel states."[5] In effect, the bureau assumed responsibility for overseeing the relationship between the freed people and whites and to protect their interests. It established branches in the former Confederacy, and its agents sought to balance the competing needs and interests of the two groups of people. White Southerners often distrusted these agents, since they interfered in their relationships with the former slaves.

The pace and nature of the new societal order in the making, presided over by the Freedmen's Bureau, was made more complicated by the assassination of President Lincoln in April 1865. The new president, Andrew Johnson, did not seek retribution against the former secessionist states. Like his martyred predecessor, Johnson believed that individuals were culpable in the secession, but legally, the states had not left the Union. A former Tennessee slaveowner, President Johnson never repudiated the doctrine of white supremacy, nor did he embrace civil equality for blacks. In his annual message to Congress in 1867, the president maligned blacks by claiming that they demonstrated less "capacity for government than any other race of people. No independent government of any form has ever been successful in their hands. On the contrary," the president said, "wherever they have been left to their own devices they have shown a constant tendency to relapse into barbarism."[6] In his plan of Reconstruction, which he issued in May 1865, Johnson pardoned the Southern rebels and returned their confiscated property, excepting slaves, once they swore allegiance to the Union. A number of persons, including high-ranking officials of the Confederacy, had to seek individual pardons. The president also named a new provisional governor of North Carolina, empowering him to call an election to choose delegates to a constitutional convention. The franchise would be restricted to white men. Johnson later extended this order to six other states.

Johnson's conciliatory policy toward the white South pleased some Republicans, but it displeased others who supported more punitive measures and black suffrage as well. Southern whites who gathered at the constitutional conventions ignored the question of black suffrage. "This is a white man's government, and intended for white men only.... The

Supreme Court of the United States [in the Dred Scott decision] has decided that the negro is not an American citizen," declared the provisional governor of South Carolina.[7] White northerners as a whole were not necessarily more predisposed to guaranteeing the suffrage for black male citizens. In the fall of 1865, the voters of Wisconsin, Connecticut, and Minnesota rejected constitutional amendments that would have ensured and protected that right.

Recognizing that President Johnson had given them breathing space to reconstruct antebellum society essentially as they saw fit, white Southerners introduced a series of draconian measures aimed at creating a modified form of racial slavery. Not only did they intend to maintain white supremacy and a hierarchical racial order, but also they wanted to ensure that they had a coerced and dependable black labor force. Accustomed to extracting forced labor services from blacks, former slaveowners were certain that the freed people would never work on their own volition. Such perceptions also rested on racist beliefs that blacks were naturally indolent. George Fitzhugh, one of the white South's prominent ideologues, expressed the view, "A great deal of severe legislation will be required to compel Negroes to labor as much as they should . . . we must have a Black Code."[8] Frances Butler Leigh, a white woman, believed, "No Negro will work if he can help it, and is quite satisfied just to scrape along doing an odd job . . . to earn money to buy a little food."[9]

Such assessments of the freed persons' character and will to work were not only erroneous but perversely self-serving. Nevertheless, they served to legitimize the introduction of a range of measures designed to limit the freedom of blacks, to ensure their continued subordination to whites, and to perpetuate their status as a servile labor force. Known collectively as the Black Codes, these statutes were reminiscent of the slave laws that emancipation had seemingly made obsolete. South Carolina and Mississippi pioneered this legislative effort to undermine the meanings of freedom and maintain the racial status quo. The Mississippi code stipulated that all blacks should sign labor contracts in January each year. Failure to do so could result in a charge of vagrancy. Blacks who broke their contracts lost their wages and were liable to arrest by any white person. Whites who enticed black workers away from their employers in order to hire them were subjected to fines. In order to restrict the economic choices of the freed persons, the law prohibited them from renting land in areas considered urban. There were similar oppressive measures in South Carolina. That state made it illegal for blacks to pursue any occupation save those of farmer or servant. Individuals who could afford to pay a tax of up to $100 avoided such restrictions. Given the economic situation of most freed persons, very few of them would have been in a position to exercise this option.

These and other racially restrictive legislation proliferated in the moribund Confederacy in 1865 and 1866. The states, in general, adopted provisions punishing blacks who exercised their new right not to work for whites and to withdraw from the labor market. In Louisiana and Texas, the law sought to force black women who abandoned field work to return to it. The labor contracts, the legislation said, "shall embrace the labor of all the members of the family able to work." The laws permitted black orphans to be seized and apprenticed to whites, thereby rendering coerced and unpaid labor. Convicts could be parceled out to white farmers, who competed for their services, and an accusation of vagrancy became the excuse to assign blacks to work for the planters.[10] Never the protector of blacks anywhere before 1865, the laws and the judicial system functioned as the ally of the planters after emancipation, and the courts were used to help undo that which was lost during the war. In the process, the laws and the courts became the surrogates of an intransigent white majority, unable or unwilling to recognize that blacks were no longer property to be controlled and disposed of at will.

The agents of the Freedmen's Bureau and the army frequently protested against the most oppressive legislation and stayed their enforcement. Abolitionists and progressive northern Republicans were dismayed at the adoption of the Black Codes and the brazen ways in which white Southerners attempted to circumscribe the freedom of blacks. Such behavior convinced many Republicans—known as Radicals—that the suffrage was a necessary corollary of black freedom. It also made them realize that Congress had to play a more aggressive role in the reconstruction of the South. On February 13, 1866, the Republican-dominated Congress passed a civil rights bill proclaiming blacks to be citizens and striking down the Black Codes. The bill recognized the right of blacks to "full and equal benefit of all laws and proceedings for the security of person and property as is enjoyed by white citizens." President Andrew Johnson vetoed the bill on the grounds that it discriminated against whites by providing "for the security of the colored race safeguards which go infinitely beyond any that the General Government has ever provided for the white race." This assertion was not only disingenuous; it showed a lack of moral leadership at the highest levels of the nation. Johnson's decision was popular among those whites who did not view blacks as fellow citizens. One newspaper wondered how long it would be before Congress "will say the negro shall vote, sit in the jury box, and intermarry with your families?"[11]

Congressional disenchantment with the president's veto led to the adoption of the Fourteenth Amendment, granting citizenship to blacks and all other persons born in the country. States that denied any of its citizens the right to vote would have their congressional representation reduced. The Congressional election in the fall of 1866 was, in many respects, a referendum on the Fourteenth Amendment. Republicans won a clear majority, as the mostly northern electorate declined to endorse President Johnson's opposition to it. Digging in their heels, southern legislatures rejected the Fourteenth Amendment, further alienating its northern proponents. Congress responded, after much acrimonious debate, with the Reconstruction Act of 1867.

The act established five military districts in the Confederate states. All of these states, with the exception of Tennessee, were placed under the jurisdiction of a commander charged with the power to use the army to bolster his authority. The states were required to write new constitutions, establishing manhood suffrage. These constitutions had to be ratified by the electorate. In addition, the states had to adopt the Fourteenth Amendment. The Reconstruction Act was unquestionably a victory for radical Republicans and blacks, but its implementation would be another story. In many respects, the act's promise for blacks was essentially hollow; it introduced no fundamental changes in economic and political power arrangements in the South. The freed people, who needed land as their economic lifeline, were promised none. The military occupation was a temporary expedient, and black suffrage was to be guaranteed only in the former Confederate states. Most of all, the passage of the Reconstruction Act did not mean that most whites had changed their attitudes toward blacks, and without such a change in majority opinion and in the deeper structures of society, the black condition could hardly have improved significantly.

White supporters of the former Confederacy had lost the Civil War, but they had not been vanquished. With President Andrew Johnson opposed to the Reconstruction Act and ostensibly on the side of the old order, the challenge to reconstruct the South was nothing if not forbidding. White Republicans in the South, benefiting from the support of the freed persons, however, sought to make reconstruction work. At the end of voter registration in the ten unreconstructed states in 1867, there were 635,000 whites on the rolls and 735,000 blacks. Many whites had declined to participate in the process, and others had been disqualified by some of the terms of the Reconstruction Act. Black voters, accordingly, constituted a majority in South Carolina, Louisiana, Florida, Mississippi, and Alabama. When the votes were counted for the constitutional conventions, blacks had won 30 percent of the seats, southern whites 45 percent, and northern whites who had relocated in the South, 25 percent. Of the ten state conventions, blacks formed a majority in Louisiana and South Carolina.

The constitutions that emerged from the conventions were, for the most part, enlightened. Southern-born white Republicans, however, joined white Conservatives to oppose any provisions that would mandate racial integration in the schools. The constitutions generally remained silent on provisions that would have led to "social equality," a prospect that frightened whites regardless of their party affiliation. These constitutional silences were ominous; in later years the laws that sanctioned segregation would confine blacks to subordinate places in the social system. Still, these new constitutions adopted provisions mandating universal male suffrage, systems of public education, a variety of social reforms, and measures guaranteeing the civil rights of black citizens. Most constitutions either allowed former Confederates to vote with no restrictions or disenfranchised them for a time. No constitution sanctioned the confiscation of land belonging to the rebels. By early 1870, the ten states had been readmitted to the Union, and a new chapter in the American experience had begun.

We are not concerned here with the details of that chapter, but only with its broad contours. The presidential election of 1868 demonstrated that the nation's wounds were still bleeding profusely and that issues of race and the place of blacks in the polity remained central factors. While Republicans promoted black franchise in the South, their national platform maintained that the "question of suffrage in all the loyal States properly belongs to the people of those States."[12] Such contradictions were contemptible; it was a strategy that pandered to white racism in the North. Their presidential candidate, former Union general Ulysses S. Grant, spoke of peace, but the Democrats were relentless in their assaults on the Reconstruction Act, promising to save the white South from "barbarous" blacks and to restore their "birthrights." During the interim between Grant's election to the presidency and his inauguration, Republicans resolved their contradiction on the question of the franchise for blacks by getting Congress to adopt the Fifteenth Amendment. The amendment, which was ratified in 1870, prohibited the states and the federal government from denying the franchise to male citizens on the basis of color, race, or past condition.

Southern Democrats, in particular, were outraged by the Amendment, and many disgruntled whites used extralegal means to keep blacks away from the polls, uphold white supremacy, and avenge a variety of perceived wrongs. A number of vigilante groups already existed in the region, preaching the gospel of white supremacy and attacking blacks and their white Republican allies. The most notorious of these groups was the Ku Klux Klan. Formed in Tennessee in 1866, the Klan represented a barbaric form of white power. Its murderous assaults against its imagined enemies were frequently done under the cover of dark and with the connivance of the authorities.

The times required outstanding leadership given the seeming intractability of the nation's problems and the enormity of the challenges. But America was served by a series of mediocre presidents after Lincoln's death, men unable or unwilling to inspire the nation to reach its promise or to keep faith with its founding ideology. Apart from the race question, the nation's leaders had to grapple with civil service reform, labor unrest, extralegal violence, tariff reduction, the monetary system, economic growth, and other pressing issues. Disenchantment with President Grant led some liberal Republicans to join the Democrats in opposing his reelection in 1872. Their controversial candidate, the newspaperman

Horace Greeley of New York, failed to generate much enthusiasm, and Grant won easily. Black voters remained staunchly Republican. The veteran leader Frederick Douglass denounced the coalition that supported Greeley, maintaining that the Republican party "has within it the only element of friendship for the colored man's rights."[13] During the waning moments of the Forty-Third Congress in 1875, the legislators under Republican leadership adopted a civil rights bill. The Civil Rights Act of 1875 prohibited discrimination in public transportation and accommodation as well as in the selection of juries.

This was the last gasp of Republican rule in Congress and of the Reconstruction of the South. Southern Republicans as a whole had never been without their internal divisions, and their administrations were often tainted by scandal and corruption. The majority of southern whites either opposed or barely tolerated the changes in their society that the reconstructed regimes had introduced. Northern white Republicans, removed as they were from the realities of life in the South, eventually grew tired of their abstract commitment to the rights of blacks. One Washington newspaper was rather honest in its conclusion in 1874: "People are becoming tired of . . . abstract questions, in which the overwhelming majority of them have no direct interest. The negro question, with all its complications, and the reconstruction of the Southern States with all of its interminable embroilments, have lost much of the power they once wielded."[14] The truth of the matter was that the radical Republicans who fought to transform the South and promote the rights of blacks were unrepresentative of white attitudes and opinions. Had the majority of northern Republicans, or northern whites as a whole, been driven primarily by principle, as opposed to the need to punish their Southern kin, their commitment to racial justice would not have been so fickle, and it would not have expired after a decade.

The signs that many whites had grown tired of the challenges and frustrations of Reconstruction were evident in the results of the 1874 Congressional election. Democrats gained control of the Forty-Fourth Congress, among other successes, and the Republicans realized that they had to remove the black and Southern albatrosses if they were to retain the presidency in 1876. Southern white Democrats and their allies in the terrorist organizations scared black voters away from the polls, and white Republicans were made to look like traitors to the cause of white supremacy. As a result of these tactics, Republican weariness with Reconstruction, and the effects of the economic depression of 1873, Democrats captured all but three state governments in the South by 1876. Only South Carolina, Louisiana, and Florida stood apart from the tidal wave of white reaction.

But there were other ominous signs. Controlled by the Democrats, the U.S. Congress reduced the appropriations for the Department of Justice, undermining its ability to monitor and enforce the Reconstruction

Act. In two groundbreaking decisions issued in 1876, the Supreme Court narrowed the reach of the Fourteenth and Fifteenth Amendments. In *United States* v. *Reese,* the Court held that the Fifteenth Amendment did not guarantee access to the franchise. It merely "prevents the states or the United States . . . from giving preference . . . to one citizen of the United States over another on account of race, color, or previous condition of servitude," the Court concluded. This decision gutted the amendment and with it the meaning of the franchise for the new black citizens. In *United States* v. *Cruikshank,* the Court maintained that the amendments passed after the war granted the federal government the power to intervene only in cases where states violated the rights of blacks. It was the responsibility of the states themselves to guarantee the protection of the victim when his rights were violated by other individuals.[15] This decision, in effect, abandoned blacks to the mercy of the states, where their rights were likely to be circumscribed or abrogated at will.

The hotly contested presidential elections of 1876 resulted in the coup de grâce for Reconstruction. The Democrats were committed to ending the experiment in Reconstruction and to withdrawing federal troops from the South. The Republicans were more divided on the matter, but there was every indication that no matter who emerged the victor, there would be enormous changes in Southern policy. The polling, particularly in South Carolina, Florida, and Louisiana, was characterized by an appalling degree of intimidation and fraud. The election results remained in doubt for some time while investigations continued and Democrats and Republicans worked out "deals." In the end, Rutherford B. Hayes, a Republican from Ohio, assumed the presidency but not before agreeing to withdraw the troops from the South and to provide funds for several projects in a number of states. Known as the Compromise of 1877, this agreement allowed the former Confederate states to manage their own affairs in accordance with their own desires. The federal government retreated from its responsibility and promise to protect the freed people and to supervise the transition from slavery to freedom. Reconstruction, to be sure, could not have lasted indefinitely, but its end once more exposed the freed people to the will of the former slaveowners, revealing the societal and racial wounds that had never been healed. Delivering a eulogy at the end of Republican rule and of Reconstruction, the African Methodist Episcopal minister and politician Henry McNeal Turner intoned, rather cynically:

> It is with unusual pain, we are compelled to chronicle the sad news, that the great Republican Party, hero of many battles and author of National Sovereignty, American Freedom, Civil and Political rights and many other world renowned and heaven approved works, was slaughtered in the house of his friends, April 24, 1877. He had been

indisposed for several years, being seriously afflicted by Negro haters, office seekers, dough faces, weather cocks, time servers, and large numbers of political hypocrites, false pretenders, and unprincipled vagabonds. Such a number of wounds and diseases all preying upon his system at once was too much to be resisted, and the political giant of the 19th century had to succumb to the inevitable.[16]

MAKING FREEDOM WORK

The attitudes and activities of whites in the public and private spheres constitute only one aspect of the post–Civil War history of the nation in general, and the South in particular. In fact, the term "Reconstruction," which has been used to characterize the decade 1867–1877, should be used with great caution when discussing the woof and warp of black history during those turbulent years. The freed people were actually seeking to *construct* new lives and to claim their spaces as American citizens. For most, slavery had no nostalgic appeal and there was no desire to return to their legal status as the property of whites. They were not trying to reconstruct the past. The dynamic process of constructing new lives in freedom did not end in 1877; its fundamental drives were hardly dictated by what whites did or did not do. The primary impetus came from within, reflecting the human imperative to create the means of survival and to develop the mechanisms of sustenance.

Not all of the freed people had the same immediate needs and not all embraced the same vision of the future. As we have already indicated, much depended on a number of variables, including age, the possession of marketable skills, literacy levels, material circumstances when freedom came, and the degree of political consciousness. The opportunities for the young and those in the prime of their lives were potentially greater than for their older brethren. Similarly, those who were literate or possessed specialized skills of one sort or another in artisanal or agrarian pursuits faced better employment possibilities. The few who had acquired modest amounts of capital during their enslavement had some breathing space, while those who were more acutely aware of their rights would be less obsequious to whites and more insistent in their demand for change of any stripe. The war had had a politically transforming effect on many, and freedom, with its promise and ultimate disappointments, would further enhance that process.

The newly freed had needs that were immediate and no different from those of white citizens. They needed land, jobs, and a measure of economic security. But they were also entitled to the full panoply of rights that white Americans, particularly men, took for granted. The defining and animating principle of black life in those heady years was how to make the economic and political machinery of the society respond to a people's just needs, all the while creating their own passageways in the face of white intransigence. There was also a pervasive desire on the part of many people to create a new and better nation out of the ashes of the war, one where racial, gender, and class differences would be of little consequence. The black writer and lecturer, Frances Ellen Watkins Harper expressed such a view at the Eleventh National Woman's Rights Convention, held in 1866:

> We are all bound up together in one great bundle of humanity and society cannot trample on the weakest and feeblest of its members without receiving the curse in its own soul. . . . The grand and glorious revolution which has commenced, will fail to reach its climax of success, until throughout the length and breadth of the American Republic, the nation shall be so color blind, as to know no man by the color of his skin or the curl of his hair. It will then have not privileged class, trampling upon and outraging the underprivileged classes, but will be then one great privileged nation, whose privilege will be to produce the loftiest manhood and womanhood that humanity can attain.17

Slavery's end meant, at least in theory, that blacks had become members of civil society and were no longer excluded from its benefits, responsibilities, and challenges. Some persons, as we noted in the case of Uncle Eph, tested their new freedom by simply leaving the site of their former oppression for a while. Booker T. Washington recalled, "After the coming of freedom, there were two points upon which practically all the people on our place were agreed, and I find that this was generally true throughout the South: that they must change their names, and that they must leave the old plantation for at least a few days or weeks in order that they might really feel sure that they were free."[18] One white resident of Florida was rather perspicacious in noting, "The negroes don't seem to feel free unless they leave their old homes just to make it sure they can go when and where they choose."

Some freed people left for a few days; others stayed away much longer. Many did not return at all, leaving uncomprehending whites to adjust to the new order. One white woman in Virginia complained that the newly freed "are all anxious to leave home and many that seemed perfectly contented in slavery are now dissatisfied, and many humane kind masters, who owned large numbers of servants, have been left without a single one."[19] Exercising their right to freedom of movement, these people visited relatives or moved to cities or towns or even to another state. Such movement, whether it meant a temporary or permanent abandonment of their former residences, constituted an assertion of independence and a psychologically liberating venture into the unknown. Using humor to celebrate their freedom and independence, blacks told the following story:

Slave Owner: Ah, dear, faithful, loyal Uncle Tom! Lincoln has forced you to accept freedom—against my wishes, and, I am sure, against yours. Dear old friend and servant, you need not leave this plantation. Stay here with us; kindly, gentle, self-sacrificing Uncle Tom!

Uncle Tom: Thank you, deah, kine, lovin', gen'rous Massa. I reckon I'll leave. But befo' I go I wants you ter know I will allus 'membuh you ez de son uv a bitch you is an' allus wuz![20]

Many freed persons also moved for very practical reasons. Some left because their former masters required them to do so. Others went in search of jobs and better economic opportunities, and still others began a quest for relatives from whom they had been separated during slavery or by the war. Ignoring the admonitions of white planters, many blacks streamed into the cities and towns of the South, rejecting labor on the plantations and farms and the past that it symbolized. By 1870, cities such as Montgomery, Selma, Richmond, Memphis, and Charleston had large black populations. For some, the trek to the cities was fraught with disappointment as they confronted unemployment, hostile white authorities, poor housing, and a generally unwelcoming atmosphere. Some would return to the familiar plantations to nurse their shattered dreams.

The movement from rural areas to the city and back again, as well as the migration from one rural location to another, manifested both the promise of freedom and the magnitude of its failures. Charlie Davenport, a freed person who had lived in Mississippi, recalled:

> I was right smart bit by de freedom bug for a while. It sounded pow'ful nice to be tol': "You don't have to chop cotton no more. You can th'ow dat hoe down an' go fishin' whensoever de notion strikes you. An' you can roam 'roun at night an' court gals jus as you please. Aint no master g'wine a-say to you, 'Charlie, you's got to be back when the clock strikes nine.'" I was fool 'nough to b'lieve all that kin' o' stuff.[21]

Seen from the outside, such a construction of freedom was undoubtedly unrealistic, but it was real enough for Charlie Davenport and the many who were groping with the meanings of freedom for the first time. Violet Guntharpe captured the tremendous gulf between the optimism about the future that most felt and their stark circumstances. "Us had no education, no land, no mule, no cow, not a pig, nor a chicken, to set up housekeeping," she lamented. "De birds had nests in de air, de foxes had holes in de ground, and de fishes had beds under de great falls, but us colored folks was left widout any place to lay our heads." [22]

Under the circumstances, black mobility was not only one measure of a people's desire to transform their condition, but it was also a reflection of the obstacles that impeded the realization of freedom's possibilities. Throughout the 1860s and for much of the 1870s, many blacks, as seems to be the case with migrants in general, moved short distances and in stages. Some rejected the South entirely, seeking their fortunes in the North. The North was not yet the beacon of southern black hopes and aspirations that it would become in the first decades of the twentieth century, but 68,000 relocated to these states during the 1870s. Most had been residents of the Upper South and border states. Traveling under the aegis of the American Colonization Society, 2,394 blacks abandoned the country for Liberia between 1865 and 1869, and about 100 left annually during the 1870s.[23]

Former slaves who left the sites of their oppression were making an obvious physical break with the past. But this belied the inner changes that were occurring, the new identities that were being forged. For many, the names that they had acquired during their enslavement were signifiers of a debased past. For others, particularly those who had been named by parents or family members, their names bore no such badge of degradation. We can never know how many of the freed people changed their names as one means of exorcising the past and creating a new identity. But the practice was sufficiently widespread to invite white derision and sometimes anger. Troubled by the desire of the former slaves to change their names and "to throw off that badge of servitude," one white woman, Eliza Frances Andrews, confessed: "All these changes are very sad to me, in spite of their comic side. There will soon be no more mammies or daddies, no more uncles and aunties. Instead of "maum Judy" and "uncle Jacob," we shall have our "Mrs. Ampey Tatoms," and our "Mr. Lewis Williamses."[24] Eliza Andrews was correct. By choosing new names, these blacks were symbolically burying the past, asserting new identities and altering the traditional social relations between themselves and whites.

The desire to formalize marriage unions in the wake of emancipation also symbolized new beginnings. Although many slaves had participated in marriage ceremonies, such unions lacked legal sanction. With freedom came the opportunity to renew their vows and validate the marriage. For those persons whose children, or spouses, or siblings had been separated from them during slavery, the anxious search for them was one of the most poignant features of emancipation. Hawkins Wilson epitomized this painful desire to be reunited with family members. As a young man of sixteen, he had been sold by his Virginia master to someone in Texas. In 1867, twenty-four years after this traumatic event, he wrote to the Freedmen's Bureau seeking assistance in finding his sisters:

> I am anxious to learn about my sisters, from whom I have been separated many years–I have never heard from them since I left Virginia twenty four years ago–I am in hopes that they are still living and I am anxious to hear how they are getting on–I have no other one to apply to but you and am persuaded that you will help one who stands in need of

your services as I do—I shall be very grateful to you, if you oblige me in this matter—One of my sisters belonged to Peter Coleman in Caroline County and her name was Jane—Her husband's name was Charles and he belonged to Buck Haskin and lived near John Wright's store and in the same county—She had three children, Robert, Charles, and Julia, when I left—Sister Martha belonged to Dr. Jefferson, who lived above Wrights' store—Sister Matilda belonged to Mrs. Botts, in the same county. My dear uncle Jim had a wife at Jack Langley's and his wife was named Buck and they all belonged to Jack Langley—These are all my dearest relatives and I wish to correspond with them with a view to visit them as soon as I can hear from them. . . . You will please send the enclosed letter to my sister Jane, or some of her family if she is dead. . . .

[Enclosure]

Dear Sister Jane, Your little Brother Hawkins is trying to find out where you are and where his poor old mother is—Let me know and I will come to see you—I shall never forget the bag of biscuits you made for me the last night I spent with you—Your advice to me to meet you in Heaven has never passed from my mind. . . . I have learned to read and write a little. . . . When I meet you, I shall be as much overjoyed as Joseph was when he and his father met after they had been separated so long. . . . Thank God that now we are not sold and torn away from each other as we used to be—we can meet if we see fit and part if we like. . . .[25]

Whether or not Hawkins found his relatives is, unfortunately, not known. But his letters revealed that slavery had never destroyed the bonds of kith and kin; the trauma of forced separation had not obliterated the capacity to love and to remember. Some of these searches ended successfully; others were protracted failures. Time had taken its relentless toll. Some persons died before they could be found; for others, no credible leads existed, no traces of their loved ones' existence. Many had acquired new names, complicating the search, and physical features had changed over time. For the persistent, the search never ended, at least until death intervened. The wounds that slavery had inflicted upon its victims were etched in their souls, the memories of atrocities had not receded, but the passionate desire to reunite families showed that the core of the enslaved person's humanity remained inviolate.

That being said, the freed persons still needed the resources to sustain themselves and ultimately improve the quality of their lives. With a handful of exceptions, the former slaves owned nothing and were starting new lives politically powerless and economically disadvantaged. Thaddeus Stevens, a Radical Republican, said it well:

We have turned, or about to turn, loose four million slaves without a hut to shelter them or a cent in their pockets. The infernal laws of slavery have prevented them from acquiring an education, understanding the commonest laws of contract, or of managing the ordinary business of life. This Congress is bound to provide for them until they can take care of themselves. If we do not furnish them with homesteads, and hedge them around with protective laws; if we leave them to the legislation of their late masters, we had better have left them in bondage.[26]

Few of the newly freed would have disagreed with this judgment. Most had spent their lives in rural environments working in agrarian activities, and when freedom came they aspired to be landowners. Landownership, and the independence that it symbolized, was to be their primary means of entry into the economic worlds of freedom. To own cultivable and productive land was, at least potentially, to claim a secure place in the economy of the region and to improve one's fortunes. A Louisiana man revealed his dreams to Frederick Law Olmstead just before the war began. "If I was free, massa; if I was free," the man offered, "I would go to work for a year, and get some money for myself,– den–den–den–den, massa, dis is what I do–I buy me, fus place, a little house, and a little lot of land."[27] Statements such as these, heartfelt and poignant, reveal the pain of slavery and the anguished longing for freedom's possibilities.

Similarly, a black soldier spoke for many when he reported, "Every colored man will be a slave, & feel himself a slave, until he can raise him own bale of cotton & put him own mark upon it & say dis is mine!" But land ownership had meanings that went beyond the economic. The former slaves had developed an emotional attachment to the soil where many were born and raised, or had labored and buried their dead. One resident of Port Royal Island asked a visiting teacher from the North to "tell Linkum [Lincoln] dat we wants' land–dis bery land dat is rich wid de sweat ob we face and de blood ob we back. We born here; we parents' grave here; we donne oder country; dis yere our home."[28]

Many slaves seemed to have embraced the illusion that they would be given land when the war ended and freedom came. There were widespread rumors to that effect, and some of the actions of the federal officials fed those expectations. In some cases, the officials had turned a blind eye to the occupation by the slaves of land owned by their masters. Some Northern soldiers assured the slaves that they would receive land at the end of the war. In January 1865, Union general William Tecumseh Sherman issued his Special Field Order Number 15, which set aside parcels of land for the freed persons. A representative of the Freedmen's Bureau even told a gathering of blacks, "They must not only have freedom, but homes of their own, thirty or forty acres with mules, cottages and school houses."[29] The freed persons were convinced that they had earned the right to the land, having worked as unpaid workers to enhance the nation's prosperity. Bayley Wyatt articulated his people's claim to land:

> We has a right to the land where we are located. For why? I tell you. Our wives, our children, our husbands, has been sold over and over

again to purchase the lands we now locates upon; for that reason we have a divine right to the land. . . . And den didn't we clear the land, and raise the crops ob corn, ob cotton, ob tobacco, ob rice, ob sugar, ob everything. And den didn't them large cities in the North grow up on de cotton and de sugars and de rice that we made? . . . I say they has grown rich, and my people is poor.[30]

Such sentiments, no matter how justified or widespread, did not translate into the acquisition of land by the majority of blacks anywhere. Black aspirations collided with the determination of white Southerners to keep them landless and dependent. Those blacks who took possession of land without the sanction of the authorities or the approval of the owners were invariably evicted. Southern whites declined to sell land to blacks who could afford it, and few could obtain credit to fund their purchases. Most whites whose land was confiscated during the war had it returned to them, denying the freed persons access to it. There was very little support for confiscation among those white Republicans who wanted blacks to become landowners. To them, confiscation violated the rights of private property, which was deemed to be sacrosanct. Adding its voice to the opponents of confiscation, the *New York Times* warned, "An attempt to justify the confiscation of Southern land under the pretense of doing justice to the freedmen, strikes at the root of all property rights."[31] Emancipation had, of course, shattered that principle. Slaves were human property, and freedom without compensation amounted to an act of confiscation. The *New York Times* and those who shared its position knew that the acquisition of land by blacks would ultimately alter the power relationships in the South, providing more autonomy for blacks and a greater range of choices. The implications of this were too troubling for many whites, regardless of their class position and regional location, and difficult to contemplate.

In spite of the obstacles they confronted, a small number of freed persons became property owners during the 1860s and the 1870s. Some accomplished this as a consequence of their own efforts; others received the assistance of missionaries, philanthropists, and even the federal authorities. In 1866, Congress passed the Southern Homestead Acts, which set aside land for the freed persons. Much of this land was of poor quality, but by 1869 about 4,000 persons had applied to take advantage of the act. Most blacks who acquired real estate, however, drew upon their own paltry resources, sometimes benefiting from the postwar decline in land prices. In the rural Deep South, 16,161 blacks owned real estate in 1870. In comparison to whites' tracts, theirs were generally quite small. In South Carolina, one black family in 21 owned some land; in Georgia, the ratio was one in 36, Mississippi one in 43; and in Alabama, one in 51.

The rate of property ownership in the rural Upper South was somewhat better. Overall, one black family in 21 owned some real estate in

1870. In Kentucky, it was one in 15, North Carolina one in 29, and Virginia one in 34.[32] This process of property accumulation continued in the two regions during the 1870s and later. Black women, in contrast to women of mixed racial ancestry, joined the ranks of property owners, although their number was relatively small. By 1870, the value of the estates owned by 9,362 free black women was $5,569,000.[33] Prior to the end of slavery, most female property owners in the region had been racially mixed and were more likely to live in South Carolina and Louisiana. Some of these persons lost their property during the war and their slaves were freed as well. It must be emphasized, however, that most blacks remained propertyless and economically marginal. Still, those who purchased land, regardless of its size, demonstrated an admirable resourcefulness and a capacity to rise from the ashes.

Freed from bondage and lacking in real estate, the overwhelming majority of Southern blacks had only their labor to sell. With the death of 260,000 white men in the war and the maiming of many others, a severe labor shortage existed throughout the South, but particularly in Florida and the Southwest. In a market economy, such a situation would have unquestionably benefited workers; the competition for their services would have brought higher wages, and they would have been able to exercise the right of choice. But nothing was normal in the American South in the aftermath of emancipation. As we have already seen, Southern whites restricted black freedom by introducing a battery of repressive legislation and manipulated the judicial system to meet their labor needs. The Freedmen's Bureau and northern opinion tempered the worst excesses of these laws, and many freed persons voted with their feet.

The bottom line, of course, was that most freed people had to find jobs or enter into other arrangements with the planters in order to support themselves and their families. This was simply a matter of survival, an assumption of responsibility for themselves. But freed persons, as a group, were never the passive victims of white economic power. Understanding their own needs and sensitive to planter dependence on their labor, they tried to bend the system in their direction as best they could. It was at bottom a struggle between capital and labor, the privileged and the dispossessed. Our examination of the ways in which the freed people sought to create new labor relations and the limited breathing space that some achieved should not lead the modern reader to minimize the systemic obstacles the majority confronted or their economically desperate circumstances.

It must be emphasized that most Southern whites, as well as the freed people, had to learn how to operate in a system of wage labor, in contrast to a system where black workers were a form of property and performed unpaid labor on demand. Many freed persons, however, had gained some experience bargaining for wages during the war. Some, particularly in Louisiana and in the South Carolina Sea Islands, refused to work unless they were paid. Beginning in February 1864, the Union army recognized the right of blacks in Louisiana to negotiate the terms of their labor with prospective employers. General Nathaniel P. Banks, who commanded the First and Third Louisiana Native Guards, conceded that black workers "will be permitted to choose their employers, but when the engagement is made, they will be held to their engagements for the year, under the protection of the government."[34] General Banks and the officials who succeeded him adhered to the belief that black workers would renege on their agreements and that they would have to be coerced to honor them. This paternalistic and overtly negative view of blacks was shared by whites with varying degrees of intensity, regardless of their positions on the slavery question and the meaning of freedom.

Black workers, under the circumstances, had to negotiate in an environment where their capacity to work without the whip was questioned. Most importantly, they had to ensure that slavery did not return under a new guise, and the choices they made were dictated largely by their own desires. In fact, as one indication that times had changed, black women and children withdrew largely from plantation labor. Women exercised their right to attend to the needs of their own households and redefine the nature of their labor. White observers were unable to understand or accept black women's control over their labor. "They will merely take care of their own households and do but little or no work outdoors," one newspaper huffed.[35] Many black women also broke with the past, declining domestic work in white households. Women whose economic circumstances did not allow them to reject work outside of their own homes sought to control its timing and the conditions of their labor. Over the long haul, however, many women were forced by economic circumstances to accept whatever work was available. They also worked alongside their men on the land they rented and sharecropped.

Black workers, male or female, faced the ubiquitous and essentially exploitative labor contracts. These contracts established the terms of the labor arrangement, including such conditions as the wage or the nature of the crop share, the period of time, and the mutual obligations of planters and workers. In general, these contracts contained features that were similar to slavery. Speaking of them, one Louisiana newspaper concluded, "All of the important prohibitions imposed upon the slave, are also enforced against the freedman. . . . It is true that the law calls him a freeman, but any white man, subjected to such restrictive and humiliating prohibitions, will certainly call himself a slave."[36] For the most part, the contracts served the needs of the planters, guaranteeing them a controlled and dependable labor supply for a fixed period of time. Planters, acting with the tolerance of the Freedmen's Bureau, the power of the state authorities, and the prejudices of a prowhite judiciary behind them, frequently violated the terms of the contracts. They cheated freed persons out of their earnings or crop share and abused them in the process.

Freed persons responded in a variety of ways. Some adamantly refused to sign the contracts altogether, while others insisted on terms that they deemed to be advantageous. The most effective strategy, however, was to control the pace of their work routine, decline to do work not included in the contract, or engage in collective actions such as strikes. Such behavior was risky because the planters enjoyed more economic and political power than their workers and had the capacity to strike back by evicting them or calling the local authorities to bolster their control. Planters could also intimidate protesting blacks by organizing vigilante groups. When a freedman in Guilford County, North Carolina, left his employer's service, the angry planter boasted, "I gathered up some o' our boys and we went down to this place whar I thought he was at, and told him he'd make tracks before night, and if he was found in this neighborhood arter next day we'd shoot wherever we found him. . . . We a'n't agoin' to let niggers walk over us."[37]

By the late 1860s, the majority of rural black families had become either share tenants or sharecroppers. Share tenants rented land and paid what they owed with a share of the crop. They made the basic decision about what to produce and remained owners of what they grew. Sharecropping, a close relative of share tenantry, eventually became more widespread. Under this arrangement, blacks signed contracts granting them the right to cultivate a designated portion of the planter's land. The planter normally provided the tools, fertilizer, seeds, and so on that the cropper needed. As his "wage," the cropper received between one-fourth and one-half of what he produced, depending on the contractual agreement. Unlike the share tenant, the cropper did not own his crop. Still, the cropper enjoyed a precarious security. As long as he continued to work and if he were not evicted, the arrangement could take on an aura of permanence. Sharecroppers, although they made basic decisions about their own domestic lives, remained in a dependent economic relationship with the planters, often becoming chronically indebted to them. Unscrupulous planters cheated both renters and sharecroppers, usually by altering the books in their favor.

In time, probably by the 1880s, most sharecroppers in the South were black and most share tenants were white. Black women, and children too, worked along with the men in the fields. For many, such labor was a family enterprise, as the well-being of its members depended on the income that the crop produced. Farm labor increased the burdens that women bore, since they were largely responsible for the domestic chores. But it may be conjectured, in the absence of hard evidence, that such families negotiated the work patterns of its members, its timing, and nature.

Sharecropping eventually became synonymous with black rural poverty, trapping generations of blacks and becoming the seedbed of a pernicious system of debt peonage. It was one measure of freedom's failures and another confirmation of the illusory nature of its promise. As long as most freed persons and their children remained landless and dependent on former slaveowners and other whites for their livelihood, theirs would be a future of crushing poverty cushioned only by the dreams of escape, the balm of a strong religious faith, and the support of kin and brethren.

The Civil War had politicized many freed persons, and the requirements of freedom accelerated the process. They recognized that they needed to acquire political power to promote and protect their interests. Strength and power resided in collective behavior, and the freed people were quick to form their own organizations or participate in existing ones. Many joined the Union League, a racially integrated organization that had been founded in the North during the war. Although the league became increasingly divided along racial lines in the South, it was a strong advocate for the rights of the newly freed. The league raised the political consciousness of its members through meetings, discussions, parades, and so on. Most blacks, however, received their political education in less formal ways. The black churches provided opportunities for political meetings and discussions. Friends and family members also discussed information with one another, enhancing their political awareness.

With the passage of the Reconstruction Act in 1867, blacks became actively involved in electing representatives to the constitutional conventions. This was the first occasion on which the freed persons exercised the franchise, their first real involvement in the formal political arena. Many Southern whites referred derisively to these racially mixed legislative assemblies as "black-and-tan" conventions, using the term "tan" to question the racial loyalty of the white legislators. The black delegates, generally speaking, represented districts with black majorities, inaugurating an electoral pattern that survives. Although most blacks lived in rural areas, most of their delegates were elected by urban constituencies, probably a function of more effective organization and a higher degree of political sophistication among city residents.

A close study of the backgrounds of the delegates reveals that slightly more than 50 percent had been free before the war. Of this group, most had been born free and a small minority had been manumitted. Prior free status was clearly an advantage in a variety of ways after 1865; these persons had not been limited by slavery, many had acquired an education and property and nurtured a strong belief in their possibilities. Some of these persons were born free in the North and came to the South during or after the war. A disproportionate share of the delegates consisted of mulattoes, despite the fact that most of the voters were not racially mixed but were phenotypically "black." It can be surmised that a mulatto ancestry created a privileged status for those individuals in a society where "whiteness" carried a superior aesthetic or social value. Mulattoes, particularly those in Louisiana and South Carolina, were generally better off economically than blacks, or other mulattoes elsewhere. Not surprisingly, mulatto delegates outnumbered blacks in those two states, but they formed a minority in Texas, Mississippi, and Georgia. The two groups were roughly equal in the other states, and, overall, an estimated 85 percent of the delegates were literate.

The occupational backgrounds of these black elected officials varied. Most were farmers and clergymen. Others were businessmen, artisans, and laborers. Some owned land; others were propertyless. Taken together, they represented a cross-section of the freed people. Most demonstrated a remarkable magnanimity to whites by opposing measures to disenfranchise the rebel leaders. They supported provisions designed to make land available to the poor, although few favored outright confiscation. Black delegates endorsed the creation of statewide educational systems and restricted attempts to establish racial segregation in public facilities. Not all blacks spoke with one voice, to be sure. Class divisions often surfaced particularly when economic issues were being addressed. Blacks who possessed real estate, for example, supported provisions that protected their property from seizure if they became insolvent, but poorer blacks who wanted land opposed such provisions.[38] For many delegates, service in the conventions paved the way for other kinds of political careers, including membership in Congress and the state legislatures.

Understandably, blacks became strong supporters of the Republican party. It was, in their view, the party of Lincoln, of emancipation, and of civil equality. Black support for the Republicans was never without its difficult times as some white Republican leaders, particularly in the early years of Reconstruction, courted the support of white Democrats at the expense of their black constituency. In dispensing patronage, white Republican governors were not above filling important posts with Democrats who were opposed to black interests. Nor were blacks treated as equals within the party except possibly in Mississippi and Louisiana, where their influence was greater than elsewhere. One black Louisianan, however, complained in 1874, "We share, neither . . . in the control of the government which we have created, nor participate in the patronage resulting from political victories we have won."[39] Recognizing that the balance of power rested with whites, some blacks even declined to run for office if that would alienate their white allies or harm the party. Black legislators confronted other problems as well. In 1869, in a desperate attempt to keep political power in their hands, white legislators in Georgia refused to seat two black senators and twenty-six black representatives. Henry McNeal Turner, then a thirty-five-year-old man, contested his exclusion in bold language, but to no avail:

I hold that I am a member of this body. Therefore, sir, I shall never fawn or cringe before any party, nor stoop to beg for my rights. Some of my colored fellow members, in the course of their remarks, took occasion to appeal to the sympathies of members on the opposite side, and to eulogize their character for magnanimity. It reminds me very much, sir, of slaves begging under the lash. I am here to demand my rights, and to hurl thunderbolts at the men who would dare to cross the threshold of my manhood. . . . The great question, sir, is this: Am I a man? If I am such, I claim the rights of a man.[40]

The election of blacks to office at local, state, or national levels and their seating did not necessarily mean that they shared power equally with whites or that they exercised power in their own right. The evidence is elusive, and it is difficult to measure political power and influence anyway. At the state level, only one black person, P. B .S. Pinchback (1857-1921), served as governor. He did so briefly in Louisiana, between December 1872 and January 1873. Six blacks served as lieutenant governors, a position of doubtful power. Louisiana and South Carolina elected a black state treasurer, and others filled positions of superintendent of education and secretary of state. In terms of their numbers in the population as a whole, blacks were generally underrepresented in the legislatures. South Carolina was an exception, as blacks formed a majority in the lower House. Few blacks received important committee chairmanships anywhere, an indication of their limited influence in the legislatures and the unwillingness of white Republicans to share power with them.

Blacks were elected to a range of positions at the local levels, particularly in Louisiana, South Carolina, and Mississippi. They served as mayor, aldermen, sheriffs, tax collector, county supervisor, justice of the peace, school board members, and so on. Some of them exercised tremendous influence at the grassroots level, constituting the basis of black electoral successes during Reconstruction. Many of these officials were relatively young, and some were illiterate. Some had been human property; others were born free men. Responding to the call to serve their brethren, these men were not deterred by educational deficiencies or political inexperience. Their desire to transform their own condition and that of other blacks was the motivational force, their limitations notwithstanding.

The South sent sixteen blacks to Congress during Reconstruction. Several were already accomplished persons in their chosen careers and developed into legislators of distinction. Hiram Revels (1822-1901), for example, was an ordained minister of the African Methodist Episcopal Church before he was elected to the Senate in 1870, representing Mississippi. Prior to his entry into politics, Revels served as a chaplain in the Union army, worked for the Freedmen's Bureau, and assumed the presidency of Alcorn College in Mississippi. Robert Smalls (1839-1915) represented South Carolina in the Congress, winning election in 1874. Unlike Revels, he was born a slave. Smalls worked as a seaman during the war and was elected to South Carolina's Constitutional Convention in 1868. He later served as a state legislator. Blanche K. Bruce (1841–1898) was born a slave in Virginia. Escaping from bondage, Bruce fled to Kansas, where he became a teacher. In 1869, he became a resident of Mississippi and held a number of political offices before being elected to the Senate in 1874. Francis Cardozo (1837–1903) had a different lifecourse. Born free, he attended the University of Glasgow in Scotland for four years. Ordained a Presbyterian clergyman, he worked as a missionary and a teacher. In 1868, Cardozo was a delegate to the South Carolina constitutional convention. He was elected secretary of state for South Carolina in 1868 and 1870 and state treasurer in 1872 and 1874.

Whether serving at the local, state, or national levels, black officials were consistent in their support of progressive legislation. Ever vigilant to the specter of racial prejudice and injustice, they opposed, sometimes unsuccessfully, legislation that promoted segregation or unequal treatment of blacks. Black legislators voted in favor of state-supported public education, civil rights laws, prison reform, and programs for land distribution. At the national level, they supported social welfare legislation and opposed terrorist violence. In 1875, when Congress approved the landmark Civil Rights Act, Congressman John Roy Lynch of Mississippi reflected the sentiments of his black constituents and brethren:

> I appeal to all members of the House—republicans and democrats, conservatives and liberals—to join with us in the passage of this bill, which has for its object the protection of human rights. And when every man, woman, and child can feel and know that his, her, and their rights are fully protected by the strong arm of a generous and grateful Republic, then can all truthfully say that this beautiful land of ours, over which the Star Spangled Banner so triumphantly waves, is, in truth and in fact, the "land of the free and the home of the brave."[41]

Black legislators bore heavy burdens not only because they were pioneers. The problems that their constituents expected them to solve were wide-ranging and difficult. But these were not challenges that could have been solved by black legislators alone, no matter how united, dedicated, or skilled. Black politicians, particularly at the state levels, were not always in agreement on policy issues. As we have noted, there were divisions born of class, and there were personal incompatibilities as well. None of this was unusual or confined to blacks, but it compromised their effectiveness. Their Republican allies never quite accepted them as equals, and their support was not always reliable or consistent. Black legislators achieved some successes, and they were often the voices of decency, compassion, and magnanimity in the halls of government. But a fundamental and enduring transformation of Southern society and the

The first colored Senator and Representatives, 41st and 42nd Congress of the United States. Standing (left to right), Robert C. DeLarge, M.C. of South Carolina; and Jefferson H. Long, M.C. of Georgia. Seated, U.S. Senator H. R. Revels of Mississippi; Benjamin S. Turner, M.C. of Alabama; Josiah T. Walls, M.C. of Florida; Joseph H. Rainy, M.C. of South Carolina; and R. Brown Elliot, M.C. of South Carolina. All were Republicans.

life-chances of black citizens required a combination of national will, courage, commitment, and tenacity. The failure to accomplish this transformation cannot be laid solely at the feet of the white South; it was a national responsibility.

Despite the storms that buffeted the freed persons, they had to make the best of their situation. Some organized conventions to politicize their brethren and promote the acquisition of their civil rights. Others established fraternal and benevolent societies, built schools, formed debating clubs and other organizations to meet their diverse needs. The Christian denominations stood at the core of this organizational energy. Not only did they allow their buildings to house these activities, but clergymen frequently provided leadership for them as well.

Once slavery began to crumble during the Civil War, Northern churches dispatched missionaries to the South to proselytize the slaves. The majority of the white missionaries were Baptists and Methodists, although there were Congregationalists and Presbyterians as well. There were also representatives from the African Methodist Episcopal and the African Methodist Episcopal Zion denominations. Black and white denominations competed for converts among the freed persons, starting new congregations and sometimes building schools for their members. These Northern missionaries also sought to change the former slaves culturally. In the missionaries' opinion, the freed persons had to acquire certain desirable habits–thrift, sexual control, temperance, industry, and so on–if they were to improve their condition. They also had to be less expressive and more vocally restrained in their religious practices. Christianity was the means by which the newly freed would cleanse themselves of the old ways deemed retrogressive, incompatible with Christian practice, or middle-class behavior.

Northern missionaries did not operate in a vacuum. Many former slaves and others had already embraced Christianity, and there were proselytizers among them as well. The receptivity to Christian ministrations after emancipation was widespread, and the increase in the number of converts was nothing if not phenomenal. For the first time, Christianity touched the lives of almost all blacks, winning its greatest successes since Africans came to America. The Christian message of sacrifice, redemption, and hope provided the freed persons with spiritual and emotional comfort in the difficult and turbulent times that characterized their postemancipation experiences. Christianity helped its black believers to maintain a belief in the possibility of white redemption and the promise of better days. Church gatherings fostered social intercourse among the faithful, even as they enhanced spiritual growth, provided an explanation for the uncertain present, and promised a secure afterlife.

The Baptists had the greatest appeal for the newly freed. Baptist congregations were autonomous, allowing members to control their religious affairs. Some of the faithful were undoubtedly attracted by the practice of baptism by immersion, reminiscent of some African religions. By 1890, Baptists constituted 54 percent of those who attended all black churches in the South.[42] The various Methodist denominations also achieved notable successes. The African Methodist Episcopal Church and the African Methodist Episcopal Zion expanded appreciably, both attracting members away from the white-controlled Methodist Episcopal Church, South (ME). When the Colored Methodist Episcopal Church (CME) was organized in 1870, it inherited those blacks who had remained members of the ME, as well as gaining new ones.

Throughout the South, blacks withdrew from white-dominated denominations and congregations. This was in part an indication of their desire to control their own institutions. It was a healthy expression of independence and a recognition of the differences between black and white Christians. Whites still manifested a paternalistic attitude toward their black brethren, generally confining them to subordinate roles in the churches. In some congregations, blacks still occupied separate pews and had little or no say in church governance. Some whites were pleased that blacks withdrew from their congregations, although most wished to exercise some control over the churches the blacks organized. In order to avoid such interference, blacks embraced the denominations they controlled and joined the congregations where they were most comfortable.

The black churches nurtured a talented group of religious leaders, many of whom distinguished themselves in secular spheres as well. Alexander Payne (1811–1893) was one such person. An AME clergyman, Payne was elected bishop in 1852. Committed to the education of blacks, he established several schools for their instruction. Payne served as president of Wilberforce University in 1863, one of the first black institutions of higher learning in the nation. Richard Cain (1825–1887) served as a missionary to the freed persons in South Carolina and later as a congressman. Similarly, Henry McNeal Turner (1834–1915) became a leading clergyman and bishop, politician, and proponent of emigration to Africa.

While freed blacks were energized by matters spiritual, they did not ignore the means to their material improvement. They responded enthusiastically, for example, to the Freedman's Bank and its gospel of thrift and savings. In March 1865, Congress passed a law incorporating the Freedman's Saving and Trust Company. A mutual savings bank, it was created "to receive on deposit such sums of money . . . offered . . . by or on behalf of persons heretofore held in slavery in the United States, or their descendants."[43] The bank established branches throughout the South and launched an aggressive campaign to attract black investors. It experienced an astounding success as many freed persons entrusted their paltry resources to its care. The bank may have attracted as many as 100,000 investors before it folded in 1874. Plagued by corruption and mismanagement, the bank represented a worthy idea undermined by human weaknesses. Frederick Douglass, the distinguished former slave who was appointed president of the bank in its last months, was unable to save the enterprise. The bank's collapse killed the hopes of its investors for economic uplift under its aegis and robbed them of their hard-earned resources.

Although the Freedman's Bank represented a disaster for its investors, blacks continued to create economic passageways. Over time, a small group of successful businessmen and entrepreneurs emerged. Joined by a steadily expanding group of professionals and large landholders, a black elite could be discerned among the recently freed. Blacks began to divide along class lines in residential patterns, church affiliations, and organizational memberships. These boundaries were elastic, and the interests of the race as a whole often blurred distinctions generated by class. At another level, some black women chafed under their exclusion from the franchise and promoted the cause of civic equality with men. Others expressed unhappiness with male domination. "Now is the time," recommended Frances Watkins Harper in 1870, "for our women to lift up their heads and plant the roots of progress under the hearth-stone."[44]

The dynamism that characterized the interior lives of blacks never waned in the face of the difficulties they confronted in the larger society and the largely unrealized promise of Reconstruction. Understandably, many freed people became disenchanted with either the pace or the possibility of change in the South, and some left for Africa, the Pacific Northwest, or the North. George Horton, a former slave and accomplished poet, abandoned the United States for Liberia in December 1867, but not before composing the poem "Song for the Emigrant":

>Almost as soon I'd be a slave,
>As struggling with a treacherous wave,
>A friend is but a foe;
>Then fearless let us spread our sail,
>To meet the unmolesting gale,
>Come, *Brother*, let us go!
>
>Let us desert this friendless place,
>To stay is nothing but disgrace;
>Few are our friends we know;
>LIBERIA! breathe from every mouth,
>To Leave the North and travel South,
>Come, *Sister*, let us go!
>
>Suffer no tear to wet the eye,
>Nor heave a melancholy sigh
>For leaving vales of snow;
>There vegetation ever thrives,
>There corn in winter still revives,
>Come, *Father*, let us go!
>
>LIBERIA, flow from every tongue,
>For there the old are waxing young,
>No lasting pain they know;
>Where milk and honey flow along,
>And murmurs kindle into song,
>Come, *Mother*, let us go!
>
>This place is nothing but a strife,
>Distressing all the peace of life,
>We nothing have to show;
>Let others scorn me or degrade,
>I'll take my hatchet and my spade,
>Come, *all*, and let us go![45]

The end of Reconstruction precipitated more intense fears about the future of the black condition and fed the desire to emigrate. In the spring of 1879, about 25,000 blacks migrated to Kansas in a frenzied escape from an oppressive southern environment. One black Texan observed in mid-1879:

> There are no words which can fully express or explain the real condition of my people throughout the south, nor how deeply and keenly they feel the necessity of fleeing from the wrath and long pent-up hatred of their old masters which they feel assured will ere long burst loose like the pent-up fires of a volcano and crush them if they remain here many years longer.[46]

There had been a trickle of black migrants to Kansas before 1879. Lured by the promise of land and stimulated by the efforts of former slave Benjamin ("Pap") Singleton, several hundred Tennessee blacks migrated to that state. But Singleton was not directly responsible for the "Kansas Fever Exodus" of 1879. It was not orchestrated by any one person. Driven by the promise of a better life in Kansas, the Exodusters came from everywhere in the South but primarily from the border states. Many of them could ill afford to pay for their transportation to Kansas. Thousands had come to believe that the federal government would pay their way once they reached the banks of the Mississippi or St. Louis. This was a cruel illusion. When the steamships failed to transport those who were unable to pay, thousands were stranded on the banks of the Mississippi. Prodded by anxious whites who feared that the Exodus would produce a labor shortage, some ships even refused to accept passengers who could afford the fare. Confronted by such obstacles and lacking funds, many potential Exodusters stayed home and the movement sputtered to its end. But this did not result in an abatement of the urge to abandon the South. Ten years later, in 1889, about 7,000 black Southerners left for Oklahoma in a frantic quest for land, and perhaps as many as 100,000 persons sought new lives in the North and the West over the next two decades.[47]

The "Kansas Fever Exodus" must be seen as a defining moment in black history. The majority of those who left for Kansas or tried to do so had been slaves, a dispossessed class of people who aspired to become landowners and to be free from the racially sanctioned impediments of their region. The black educator and politician John Mercer Langston thought the Exodus represented "an exigent demand" by the newly freed "for independence without which no individual and no people can rise to the level of dignified and honorable manhood."[48] One contemporary journal, the *New West*, captured the driving spirit behind the movement. "Whatever befalls them in Kansas," it suggested, "they at least have a chance to rise and fall on their own merits."[49]

The Exodus brought the postemancipation experiences of blacks to an end and inaugurated a new period in their history. To many, liberty's promise remained unfulfilled in the South and they concluded that a secure future resided elsewhere. That blacks were willing to uproot themselves and chart new directions in their lives represented a dramatic exercise of their rights as free citizens. The brevity of the Exodus and its extent belie its deeper significance. It bore all of the signs of a new beginning and all of the uncertainties too. The road ahead would get worse before it would slowly improve.

Notes

1. Dorothy Sterling, ed., *The Trouble They Seen: The Story of Reconstruction in the Words of African Americans* (New York: Da Capo Press, 1994), 1.
2. Leon Litwack, *Been in the Storm So Long: The Aftermath of Slavery* (New York: Random House, 1979), 192.
3. James M. McPherson, *Ordeal by Fire: The Civil War and Reconstruction* (New York: Knopf, 1982), 391.
4. Ibid., 397.
5. William S. McFeely, "Unfinished Business: The Freedmen's Bureau and Federal Action in Race Relations," in Nathan I. Huggins, Martin Kilson and Daniel M. Fox, eds., *Key Issues in the Afro-American Experience*, vol. ii (New York: Harcourt Brace Jovanovich, 1979), 9.
6. Eric Foner, *Reconstruction: America's Unfinished Revolution 1863–1877* (New York: Harper & Row, 1988), 180.
7. McPherson, *Ordeal by Fire*, 501.
8. Gerald David Jaynes, *Branches Without Roots: Genesis of the Black Working Class in the American South, 1862–1882* (New York: Oxford, 1986), 59.
9. Ibid.
10. Foner, *Reconstruction*, 195–225.
11. McPherson, *Ordeal by Fire*, 515–516.
12. Ibid., 542.
13. Ibid., 571.
14. Ibid., 593.
15. Foner, *Reconstruction*, 529–534.
16. Clarence E. Walker, *A Rock in a Weary Land: The African Methodist Episcopal Church during Civil War and Reconstruction* (Baton Rouge: Louisiana State University Press, 1982), 138.
17. Henry Louis Gates, Jr. and Nellie Y. McKay, eds., *African American Literature: The Norton Anthology* (New York: W. W. Norton, 1997), 462.
18. Booker T. Washington, *Up From Slavery* (New York: Airmont Publishing, 1967), 27.
19. The two quotations are from Litwack, *Been in the Storm*, 297–299.
20. Mel Watkins, *On the Real Side: Laughter, Lying, and Signifying–The Underground Tradition of African-American Humor . . .* (New York: Simon and Schuster, 1994), 79.
21. Litwack, *Been in the Storm*, 329.
22. Ibid., 328–329.
23. William Cohen, *At Freedom's Edge: Black Mobility and the Southern White Quest for Racial Control 1861–1915* (Baton Rouge: Louisiana State University Press, 1991), 148.
24. Litwack, *Been in the Storm*, 251.
25. Ira Berlin and Leslie S. Rowland, eds., *Families and Freedom: A Documentary History of African-American Kinship in the Civil War Era* (New York: The New Press, 1997), 17–19.

26. Jaynes, *Branches Without Roots*, 19.
27. Loren Schweninger, *Black Property Owners in the South, 1790–1915* (Urbana: University of Illinois Press, 1990), 145.
28. See Litwack, *Been in the Storm*, 399; Julie Saville, *The Work of Reconstruction: From Slave to Wage Labor in South Carolina, 1860–1870* (New York: Cambridge University Press, 1994), 40.
29. Claude F. Oubre, *Forty Acres and a Mule: The Freedmen's Bureau and Black Landownership* (Baton Rouge: Louisiana State University Press, 1973), 182–184.
30. Foner, *Reconstruction*, 105.
31. Jay R. Mandle, "Black Economic Entrapment after Emancipation in the United States," in Frank McGlynn and Seymour Drescher, eds., *The Meaning of Freedom: Economics, Politics and Culture after Slavery* (Pittsburgh: University of Pittsburgh Press, 1992), 77.
32. Schweninger, *Black Property Owners*, 146–153.
33. Loren Schweninger, "Property Owning Free African-American Women in the South, 1800–1870," in Darlene Clark Hine, Wilma King, Linda Reed, eds., *We Specialize in the Wholly Impossible: A Reader in Black Women's History* (Brooklyn: Carlson Publishing Inc., 1995), 266.
34. Cohen, *At Freedom's Edge*, 10.
35. Foner, *Reconstruction*, 85.
36. Litwack, *Been in the Storm*, 413–414.
37. Ibid., 443.
38. See Richard L. Hume, "Negro Delegates to the State Constitutional Conventions of 1867–69," in Howard N. Rabinowitz, ed., *Southern Black Leaders of the Reconstruction Era* (Urbana: University of Illinois Press, 1982), 129–153.
39. Eric Foner, "Black Reconstruction Leaders at the Grassroots," in Leon Litwack and August Meier, eds., *Black Leaders of the Nineteenth Century* (Urbana: University of Illinois Press, 1988), 229.
40. Charles Christian, *Black Saga: The African-American Experience* (Boston: Houghton Mifflin, 1995), 228.
41. John Hope Franklin, "John Roy Lynch: Republican Stalwart from Mississippi," in Rabinowitz, *Southern Black Leaders*, 46.
42. William E. Montgomery, *Under Their Own Vine and Fig Tree: The African-American Church in the South, 1865–1900* (Baton Rouge: Louisiana State University Press, 1993), 107.
43. Carl Osthaus, *Freedmen, Philanthropy, and Fraud: A History of the Freedman's Savings Bank* (Urbana: University of Illinois Press, 1976), 5.
44. Paula Giddings, *When and Where I Enter: The Impact of Black Women on Race and Sex in America* (New York: William Morrow, 1984), 71.
45. Cited in Charles Melvin Christian, *Black Saga* (Boston: Houghton Mifflin, 1995), 222–223.
46. Nell Irvin Painter, *Exodusters: Black Migration to Kansas after Reconstruction* (New York: Knopf, 1977), 184.
47. James R. Grossman, *Land of Hope: Chicago, Black Southerners, and the Great Migration* (Chicago: University of Chicago Press, 1989), 22.
48. Thomas C. Cox, *Blacks in Topeka, Kansas, 1865–1915: A Social History* (Baton Rouge: Louisiana State University Press, 1987), 39.
49. Ibid., 42.

Maintaining White Supremacy: From the Compromise to 1917

The Compromise of 1877 that ended the experiment in reconstructing the Union did not represent a watershed in the history of black America. It was designed to effect a rapprochement in a divided white majority, a conscious attempt to heal the national wounds occasioned by the Civil War and Reconstruction. As such, the compromise was a significant development in the history of white America and the nation state, although it was not without its impact on black America as well. Seen through the black American optic, however, the compromise initiated no immediate and dramatic breaks in a people's internal history, no new direction was charted, no new ground claimed. For white Americans, at least for many Northerners, the compromise reflected a retreat from the battle to make freedom meaningful for the former slaves and to protect their constitutional rights. Northern industrial capitalists who depended on raw materials in the South for their ventures and the Southern planters who supplied them also recognized that it was in their interest to join forces to keep blacks a subordinate, exploited, and politically powerless labor force.

We are concerned in this chapter with the battery of controls that whites, particularly in the South, imposed upon blacks after Reconstruction ended. Consequently, most of the principal actors in this chapter are whites and not blacks, who are the primary subjects of this volume. We cannot, however, fully understand the struggle that blacks waged after 1877 without some knowledge of the obstacles they faced.

Blacks were challenged by racist violence, hostile courts, discriminatory legislation, and a wholesale assault on their rights as citizens.

Most white Southerners never accepted the changes in the societal order presided over by the Reconstruction governments. Once Reconstruction ended, the forces of reaction in some states moved to reestablish the control over blacks that had been reduced by the Civil War and subsequent developments. The pace of this reaction varied; the triumphant Democrats began to restrict the voting rights of blacks in the Deep South, but in states like Arkansas and Texas, where they formed a very small minority, these assaults did not begin in earnest until the 1890s. Blacks faced intimidation at the polls, and the white authorities employed fraudulent means to guarantee the results they wanted. Electoral boundaries were also redrawn to dilute the influence of black voters. In spite of such chicanery, however, a few blacks won elections until the restrictive laws of the 1890s made that impossible.

The initial attempts to regain political power by manipulating the electoral system were soon followed by an array of laws designed to formally separate the races and ensure the maintenance of white supremacy. Historians still debate why the white South felt compelled to establish a rigid form of segregation with such deliberation and often with ingenuity. But as we suggested in Volume I of this work, whites and blacks occupied separate spaces since the eighteenth century and, in effect, constituted two nations, one free and white, the other black and primarily composed of human property. The lives of these people crossed at many points, but they never really met.

Black slaves and white masters, of necessity, came into contact with one another, but this should not be taken to mean that integration existed in the sense that that word is normally understood. Slaves were pieces of property with no independent agency in the eyes of the law and presumably in those of their owners as well. The slaves knew their place even if they did not always accept it, and whites, regardless of their social status, were aware of their superior positions also. Whatever whites were before 1865, they were never defined as property. Nor was their humanity ever questioned. Seen in this context, any claim that America was an integrated society prior to 1865 is untenable. Interaction between masters and slaves did not integration make. The divides of race, power, and culture proved to be unassailable, if not unbridgeable.

Similarly, it is fallacious to point to any period in the nation's history up to, and including the period under discussion, as constituting a time when relationships between the races were not characterized by harshness. The majority of blacks were human property from 1619 to 1863, so the question of any halcyon period in American race relations could hardly have arisen as long as racial slavery existed. Seen through a black optic, the period of slavery was unquestionably the long nadir of race relations in North America, a period of time when whites legally owned blacks. The texture of race relations changed, to be sure, after 1863 when freedom came to most blacks, but there was never a prior time in the nation's history when harmonious race relations existed. History stood in the way of that reality, and the power differentials between whites and blacks had not been substantially altered with emancipation, least of all in economic terms.

The segregation that came in the wake of Reconstruction was new only in the sense that it was supported by a wide-ranging set of laws. The ideology that gave it life was not new. Nor was the notion that blacks should occupy an inferior station in society of recent vintage. The times were new, however. The enslaved were now legally free, potentially able to exercise control over their lives, and they and their children could even compete with whites for jobs, and if they were men they could exercise the franchise and occupy the halls of the legislature. The Thirteenth, Fourteenth, and Fifteenth amendments were reminders of how much things had changed or could change.

Complicating the picture was the fact that the post–Civil War generation of whites had come of age by the 1880s. More distanced than their slaveholding parents had been from blacks, the racism that they embraced was generally not tempered by day-to-day intimacies with the human objects of their fear, distrust, and even hate. This generation of whites never knew blacks in the way in which their forebears had done; their attitude toward them lacked the understanding that came with intimacy and the tolerance that is often the product of dependence and interdependence. *De jure* segregation was the response of an insecure generation that felt threatened by the unknown black "Other." In 1889, the *Fisk Herald* attributed violent assaults on blacks to "the younger whites who are even more hostile and bitter than the older ones."[1] But the people's representatives in the legislatures did not have to resort to overt physical assaults. They used their monopoly of the machinery of political, legislative, and economic power to perpetuate their superior places in society and to staunch their fears. The Jim Crow laws that sanctioned segregation were, therefore, the political expression of more systemic cancers.

But blacks had changed after 1865 as well. Like whites, a new generation of people who were children when freedom came had now reached maturity. Others had been born after 1865 and were adults in the 1880s. More literate and aware of their possibilities than their parents, becoming aggressive in the defense of their rights, they heightened white fears and invited resentment. In 1889, the *Fisk Herald* also recognized this changing black mood. It charged: "The younger Negroes are ignorant of the so-called instinctive fear of their fathers . . . prone to brood in bitterness and suppressed rage over their wrongs, are more sensitive to injustice and quick to resent."[2]

Similar sentiments came from a Louisiana newspaper in 1890. It bemoaned the fact that:

> The younger generation of negro bucks and wenches have lost their wholesome respect for the white man, without which two races, the one inferior, cannot live in peace and harmony together. . . . Is it not everyday manifest when your house-girl informs you that Miss Johnson (your cook) says dinner is ready; that Mr. Jones (your butler) will hitch up the buggy in a minute as he is busy talking to a lady (your washerwoman) at the gate. If you address one of the younger generation with the "uncle" or "auntie" the older ones delighted in the chances you will hear "I ain't yah uncle, doggone you. . . ."[3]

And to cite a final example, in 1896 *the Greensboro Herald and Journal* was displeased that "the colored people of to-day" lacked:

> the genuine conservative feeling of respect and humble obedience to patriotism as we are apt to portray in the old slave time darkey. Just a few of them survive, and I very often wonder what will become of this new-born race when the old ones are gone. Only a few of the scions that sucker up from the old stumps can afford to raise their hats to a white lady, and very seldom does a white man even get a handle to the first end of his name.[4]

Walter Hines Page, a white man, said more than he realized in 1893. "Most of the men who were masters and most who were slaves are dead," he ventured.[5]

Although whites as a group agreed that they were superior to blacks, they did not all speak with one voice on this matter. Some whites harbored more extreme views than others about the place of blacks in postemancipation society, their rights, and roles. The views of these whites can be fit into three broad categories, but there was some overlapping among them. First, there were the conservatives, who firmly believed in the inferiority of blacks but still wanted to accord them a place–albeit a subordinate one–in society. Progressives, the second category, shared many of the racial perceptions of the conservatives but wanted to remove most barriers to the participation of blacks in the body politic. The extremists, the third group, embraced a rabid racism, asserted a vigorous, inflexible, and uncompromising ideology of white supremacy and advocated the control of the black population.

Racial extremists were never absent from the national landscape. But they rose to particular prominence after the late 1880s and continued a murderous intellectual and physical assault on blacks well into the twentieth century. The extremists began to dominate the political life of the South after about 1890, and the rest of the nation looked in the other direction as blacks saw their rights diminish and *de jure* segregation reigned.

The causes of this development are not particularly difficult to fathom, and we have already mentioned some of them. The economic recession of the late 1880s and the depression of the early 1890s exacerbated white fears of competition with blacks for diminishing jobs and resources. Blacks had never been perceived as competitors with whites under slavery, but freedom altered the situation. To maintain their control over the available resources, whites used the machinery of the state to consolidate their power, in addition resorting to terrorist violence. In the early 1890s, for example, white farmers known as Whitecaps used violence to force black tenants off the fertile lands of southwestern Mississippi.[6]

Economically hard times by themselves cannot fully explain the venom and accompanying violence directed at blacks. The white action was shaped by a racist ideology that had become deeply embedded in the fabric of the culture. Not fully understanding the reasons for their economic difficulties and feeling threatened by a rising group of people whom they had been socialized into thinking were inferior to them, whites found psychic release in waging a sort of retributive warfare against blacks. But the black person was not the enemy of Southern whites or the reason for the economic hardships that many endured. Blacks became the scapegoats for capitalism's weaknesses and the difficulty of some whites to survive well, if at all, in a changing society. It was an easy explanation for a complex problem, but it is one that has had a surprising longevity in the nation.

CONSTRUCTING JIM CROW

The legislative assault on the rights that blacks had won during Reconstruction began gradually after the Compromise of 1877. Now left to their own devices, Southern whites began to re-create a racially hierarchical society that placed themselves unquestionably at the top with blacks at the bottom. As the old order in new dress took shape, whites established legally defined boundaries to formally separate the two races, emphasizing the privileges of the "superior" group and the disabilities of the "inferior" one. In rebuking a white advocate of integration in 1885, the *New Mississippian* newspaper affirmed that "sensible, refined" whites would "see to it that the separation of the two races in our theatres, concert halls, public schools, churches, and so forth, shall be enforced in the interest of both blacks and whites." They would never allow the races to be "mixed together promiscuously."[7] The *New Mississippian* was really trying to uphold contemporary and, undoubtedly, past practices. Blacks, in many places, ate in the same restaurants with whites but sat at different tables, often in specially designated parts of the building. They occupied "nigger cars" in the trains and separate sections in the saloons, theatres, cafes, and so on. There were exceptions, of course, but racial distinctions had always been a factor in social relationships and in the public sphere.

The first deliberate step toward a legally sanctioned separation of the races that had statewide applicability was taken in Tennessee in 1881. A pioneering law created segregated facilities in the railroad cars. Passed over the opposition of black members of the two legislative branches, the law stated, "All railroad companies shall furnish separate cars, or portions of cars cut off by partition walls, which all colored passengers who pay first-class rates of fare may have the privilege to enter and occupy."[8] Florida (1887), Mississippi (1888), Texas (1889), and Louisiana (1890) followed. Only the Carolinas and Virginia resisted this early tide, but they too would soon succumb to it. Saddened by the prospect of *de jure* segregation in the railroad cars, a group of black South Carolinians enquired, "Are you not content with separate places of public entertainment, separate places of public amusement, separate places of public instruction, and even separate places of worship? Why in the name of common sense, of common humanity, of the common high-bred sensitiveness of every decent person of color, should you wish to force further unnatural separation even upon the thoroughfares of daily travel?"[9]

The timing and the occasion for these first segregation or Jim Crow laws, so named after a song made popular in minstrel shows, are not without interest. The close physical association of blacks and whites in railroad cars, frequently for long periods of time, offended many whites and especially those who did not want white women to be in such close quarters with black men. Consequently, the laws were designed to address this specific problem and not necessarily set a precedent for other forms of interaction between blacks and whites. They were nevertheless undergirded by a heavy dose of racism, so it is hardly surprising that they would provide the impetus for a broader range of laws. Historians have now generally agreed that formal segregation found its earliest expressions in the inland cities. Cities, by their nature, were conducive to a sharing of public spaces, erasing social and racial differences. Looking askance at this, whites sought to establish boundaries between black and white, using the force of the law to accomplish these ends.

With the segregation of the railroads accomplished, white Southerners began the process of removing blacks from the electoral rolls, or at least making it more difficult for them to vote. The stakes were particularly high, since the disfranchisement of blacks would result in their political powerlessness. Whites had exhibited much creativity in the methods they devised to thwart the will of black voters. Such a constant preoccupation with dishonest and covert methods to maintain white superiority placed a burden on the perpetrators. As one Mississippi newspaper noted in 1889, "There must be devised some legal defensible substitute for the abhorrent and evil methods on which white supremacy lies."[10]

Mississippi led the way in developing the legally defensible substitutes. In 1890, the legislature adopted a constitution that included a series of measures designed to remove vast numbers of blacks from the voters' lists. These clauses ostensibly applied to whites as well, but the numerous loopholes they included ensured that their principal targets were blacks. The constitution, for example, excluded from the exercise of the franchise men who had been found guilty of such crimes as fraud, arson, and theft, presumably the offenses most frequently committed by blacks. On the other hand, the crimes that white men were allegedly more likely to commit–rape, murder, and grand larceny–did not constitute a disqualification. The constitution also included provisions for a two-year residency, a requirement that affected blacks more than whites, given the mobility that had come to characterize blacks' lives. Voters also had to demonstrate an understanding of certain constitutional provisions to the satisfaction of the registrar. A white registrar bent on denying the franchise to blacks could resist being persuaded that they understood the constitution or gave appropriate answers to the questions asked. Some Mississippians doubted that even educated blacks possessed the capacity to exercise the franchise intelligently, even if they understood the constitution. In 1890, one newspaper stated: "If every negro in Mississippi was a graduate of Harvard and had been elected class orator . . . he would not be as well fitted to exercise the rights of suffrage as the Anglo-Saxon farm laborer."[11]

The Mississippi Constitution also contained a requirement that all registered voters pay a poll tax of $2 and that the receipt be presented at the time of voting. This device was intended to prevent black voters from registering, since the monetary requirement was felt most keenly by those who were poor. In addition, it was expected–and experience supported it–that most poor and illiterate voters would not keep their poll tax receipts. These and other measures accomplished the intent of those who framed the 1890 constitution. As James K. Vardaman, one of the framers, acknowledged: "There is no use to equivocate or lie about the matter . . . Mississippi's constitutional convention of 1890 was held for no other purpose than to eliminate the nigger from politics. . . . Let the world know it just as it is."[12]

Given the growing harshness of the racial climate in the South during the 1890s, it is little wonder that white supremacists elsewhere adopted constitutions broadly similar in their content to the one in Mississippi. South Carolina did so in 1895, and Louisiana followed suit in 1898. Louisiana's constitution was noteworthy for its infamous "grandfather clause," a measure that restricted the franchise to those men whose fathers and grandfathers had enjoyed the franchise on January 1, 1867. Since only whites could claim such an ancestry, the measure

A black man and a white man drink from separate water fountains. Jim Crow laws adopted in the South during the nineteenth and early twentieth centuries established strict segregation of the races.

made it impossible for blacks to qualify. Booker T. Washington, who was becoming the best-known black American of the time, pleaded with the Louisiana Constitutional Convention to "enact a fundamental law which will be absolutely just and fair to white and black alike." He assured the convention:

> The negro agrees with you that it is necessary to the salvation of the South that restriction be put upon the ballot. I know that you have two serious problems before you; ignorant and corrupt government on the one hand, and on the other, a way to restrict the ballot so that control will be in the hands of the intelligent, without regard to race. With the sincerest sympathy with your efforts to find a way out of the difficulty, I want to suggest that no State in the South can make a law that will provide an opportunity or temptation for an ignorant white man to vote and withhold the same opportunity from an ignorant colored man, without injuring both men. No State can make a law that can thus be executed, without dwarfing for all time the morals of the white man in the South. Any law controlling the ballot, that is not absolutely just and fair to both races, will work more permanent injury to the whites than to the blacks.[13]

Louisiana's legislators were not persuaded by Washington's abstract arguments and his astute claim that it was in their best interest to have a racially neutral electoral system. They were moved by the simple imperative to maintain white supremacy, and constitutionally sanctioned chicanery represented a giant step in that direction. The implementation of the grandfather clause achieved the desired results immediately. In 1896 there were 130,344 blacks on the electoral rolls in Louisiana, but this number fell to 5,320 in 1900. Alabama limited the franchise for blacks in 1901; Virginia acted similarly in 1902, Georgia in 1908, and Oklahoma in 1910. These disfranchisement measures were followed after 1900 with the passage of a spate of Jim Crow laws establishing separate public facilities for blacks and whites. These laws segregated hospitals, schools, bathrooms, cemeteries, hotels, theatres, restaurants, parks, residential areas, and a host of other public places.

The new state constitutions and the Jim Crow laws, it must be stressed, did not create the racism that manifested itself in such an acute form in the twentieth-century South. They reflected, in large measure, what was already at the core of white society. These constitutional provisions and laws codified white fears, racial beliefs, and attitudes and gave state approval to the supremacy of one race over the other. In time, these legal sanctions both reflected and shaped behavior and attitudes. The two races had their interaction in the public sphere carefully circumscribed.

The U.S. Supreme Court gave its approval to the segregationist maneuvers in the South. In 1883 the Court declared the Civil Rights Act of 1875 unconstitutional. In essence, the decision upheld the segregation of the races in public places and paved the way for the proliferation of Jim Crow statutes. Thirteen years later, in 1896, the Court, in *Plessy* v. *Ferguson,* espoused the "separate but equal" doctrine. The occasion was a challenge to a Louisiana law that had sanctioned separate accommodations for blacks in the railroad cars. The black plaintiffs argued that they could not be properly excluded from a first-class car if they paid the appropriate fare. Such an act violated their rights under the Fourteenth Amendment and other constitutional protections as well. Their skin color was not a legitimate ground for discriminatory treatment, they maintained. But the Court, voting seven to one, was not convinced. The majority maintained that separate accommodations were legitimate provided that both were of a similar quality or "equal."

Writing for the Court's majority, Justice Henry Billings Brown maintained that Louisiana could pass laws that reflected "the established usages, customs and traditions of the people." The "people," presumably, consisted only of whites. Justice Brown's opinion also questioned the efficacy of laws in transforming racial attitudes. His words, which bear quoting, would be echoed by the opponents of equality for blacks in later years:

> We consider the underlying fallacy of the plaintiffs' argument to consist in the assumption that the enforced separation of the two races stamps

the colored race with a badge of inferiority. If this be so, it is not by reason of anything found in the act, but solely because the colored race chooses to put that construction upon it. . . . The argument also assumes that social prejudices may be overcome by legislation, and that equal rights cannot be secured to the Negro except by an enforced commingling of the two races. We cannot accept this proposition. . . . Legislation is powerless to eradicate racial instincts or to abolish distinctions based upon physical differences, and the attempt to do so can only result in accentuating the difficulties of the present situation. If the civil and political rights of both races be equal, one cannot be inferior to the other civilly or politically. If one race be inferior to the other socially, the Constitution of the United States cannot put them upon the same plane.[14]

The lone dissenter was Justice John M. Harlan. His words were to no avail in 1896, but in the long run, they claimed the constitutional high ground. Harlan wrote:

Our constitution is color-blind, and neither knows nor tolerates classes among citizens. In respect of civil rights, all citizens are equal before the law. The humblest is the peer of the most powerful. The law regards man as man, and takes no account of his surroundings or of his color when his civil rights as guaranteed by the supreme law of the land are involved.[15]

Plessy v. *Ferguson* took its place with the Dred Scott decision of 1857 as two racially inspired verdicts that made nonsense of the ideals of the Declaration of Independence and the constitutional principles upon which the nation rested. Unlike the Dred Scott decision, which was eventually superseded by the Fourteenth Amendment, *Plessy* v. *Ferguson* provided the legal precedent and rationale for the separate and unequal treatment of blacks well into the twentieth century. The Supreme Court had placed its imprimatur on segregation and removed itself as a protector of the rights of black citizens.

Understandably, blacks were outraged by the Court's decision. It came at a time when a new and assertive generation had begun to succeed in a variety of professional and business spheres, threatening the place and power of whites. Charles Pettey, a bishop of the AME Zion church, did not believe that the decision could halt the pace of change within black America. He haughtily dismissed the "frowns in the highest courts of the land," noting, "we as a race are enjoying the brightest rays of Christian civilization. . . . The evils we are enduring are more than compensated for through God's providence by placing us within the touch of the greatest intellectual battery the world has ever witnessed."[16]

Although segregation attained its most refined and odious expression in the South, it was a fact of life wherever the lives of blacks and whites intersected. Local ordinances and custom provided the requisite legitimacy, and white public sentiment was hardly opposed. Even the institutions of the federal government, the collective voice of the citizenry, practiced invidious forms of racial segregation. In 1913, the National Association for the Advancement of Colored People (NAACP) lamented the fact that blacks thought that "living [in Washington] under the shadow of the National Government itself they were safe from the persecution and discrimination which follow them elsewhere because of their dark skin."[17] Another critic noted, this time in 1923, that "while . . . segregation exists in the departments of Washington, the United States sets an example which justifies the Ku Klux Klan and every other effort to keep the colored people down."[18]

The Woodrow Wilson administration enjoyed the dubious reputation for intensifying the process of segregation in the federal government's departments and agencies. Protesting the practice, William Monroe Trotter, an outspoken black journalist, told President Wilson in 1913 that government policies constituted "inequality of citizenship." To Trotter, segregation meant "the segregated are considered unclean, diseased or indecent as to their persons, or inferior beings of a lower order, or that other employees have a class prejudice which is to be catered to, or indulged."[19] The NAACP also complained to the president but received no redress. In defending his administration's behavior, Wilson claimed that segregation was actually "in the interest of the colored people, as exempting them from friction and criticism in the departments, and I want to add that a number of colored men with whom we have consulted have agreed with us in this judgment."[20] The president did not name these persons.

Segregation remained entrenched in federal offices and agencies despite the strenuous objections of black citizens. The administration of justice was not color-blind either, as blacks seldom served on juries, invariably faced biased judges, and lacked appropriate legal defense. The judicial system operated essentially the way it did under slavery. Many local ordinances and state laws, particularly in the South, were designed to ensure the subordination of blacks to whites and to establish distinctions based on race. Judges, by and large, were the interested and prejudiced upholders of an unjust order. Consequently, it was not difficult to understand why blacks lacked confidence in the judicial system and why it has remained tarnished in the eyes of many.

De jure segregation occurred at a time when the nation began to assume imperial obligations and established itself as a world power. Much of this suzerainty was exercised over black and brown peoples, and its impetus was not without racial overtones. In 1898, the United States annexed the Hawaiian islands ostensibly for strategic and economic reasons. Their acquisition strengthened the American presence in the Pacific Ocean and allowed for an ever-expanding investment in the islands.

The prolonged Cuban struggle for independence from Spain during the 1890s also provided America with another opportunity to solidify its place in the ranks of the white, imperial nations. After one of the nation's battleships, the Maine, exploded and sank in Havana's waters in January 1898, killing about 250 Americans, President William McKinley used the incident as a pretext to demand war against Spain. At the end of the ensuing Spanish-Cuban-American War, the United States gained possession of Puerto Rico and the Philippines and became a virtual protectorate of Cuba. Nineteen years after the war with Spain ended, the United States purchased St. Croix, St. Thomas, and St. John from Denmark, adding the Virgin Islands to the nation's list of colonial possessions. Taken together, these territories brought a substantial number of people who were not white under America's supervision. To many white Americans, this was a providential unfolding of things. A superior white "race" had assumed the white man's burden to "civilize" and elevate these peoples. The Anglo-Saxons were achieving their destiny by expanding all over the globe, vanquishing the "weaker" and "inferior" races in their path. This, of course, was arrant nonsense, but it helps to explain the racial status quo and sheds further light on white American attitudes toward blacks at home.

Writing in 1875, a southern newspaper predicted that whites would nullify the constitutional rights of blacks. The Fourteenth and Fifteenth amendments, the paper threatened, "may stand forever; but we intend . . . to make them dead letters on the statute-book."[21] By 1910, the threat had become a reality as *de jure* segregation was fully established in the South, setting it apart from the rest of the nation. This did not mean the absence of racial discrimination elsewhere, however. The South was distinctive in the sense that it codified racial animus and unabashedly declared blacks to be second-class citizens. Support for racial segregation was not confined to poor, uneducated whites. Its appeal transcended class, and the educated and privileged embraced its tenets as fully as did the illiterate and the economically marginal. The federal government also betrayed the interests of its black citizens by its practice of segregation. President Wilson thought it benefited blacks, and in 1921, President Warren G. Harding expressed his opposition to "every suggestion of social equality."[22] A. Philip Randolph, a black labor leader, reflected the sentiments of many when he charged in 1943 that blacks shared:

> a position different from that of any other section of the population of this country. . . . The Negroes are in the position of having to fight their own Government . . . because the Government today is the primary factor, the major factor, in this country in propagating discrimination against Negroes. It is perpetuating and freezing an inferior status of second-class citizenship for Negroes in America.[23]

The existence of Jim Crow laws did not mean the absence of cordiality, intimacy, and respect between some whites and some blacks. There were always those who created their own social and private spaces even if the law, custom, and their neighbors disapproved. Blacks and white transgressors of the legal and social codes traversed their own passageways but always with a backward glance. Still, such interracial interactions should not lead us to underestimate the rigidity, pervasiveness, and harshness of the system of racial control and the misery it created. Pauli Murray, a lawyer, crusader for social justice, and priest, later recalled:

> learning about race did not for the most part come in terrifying shocks although there were those too—especially news of lynchings, which, frequently unreported in the newspapers, traveled by word of mouth. More often race was the atmosphere one breathed from day to day, the pervasive irritant, the chronic allergy, the vague apprehension which made one uncomfortable and jumpy. We knew the race problem was like a deadly snake coiled and ready to strike, and that one avoided its dangers only by never-ending watchfulness.[24]

For blacks, the emerging New South, as it has been characterized, was really not new at all. It was, in many respects, the old racial order *sans* slavery.

In sum, segregation and the dubious "separate but equal" doctrine confined blacks to a subordinate place in society. Jim Crow legislation and its animating ideology defined blacks as inferior peoples, circumscribed their opportunities, and assaulted their personhood. Blacks shielded themselves as best they could, developing strategies to deal with their oppression and to affirm their dignity and belief in their human capacities. None of this came easily, and not all of it was successful. Whites paid a price, too, and the nation's institutions and its ideals were corroded and compromised. Whether they realized it or not, whites were diminished morally and maimed psychologically by their complicity in the wounding of their fellow human beings. No one escaped from the collective tragedy; all were trapped and debased by it.

Notes

1. Edward L. Ayers, *Vengeance and Justice: Crime and Punishment in the 19th-Century American South* (New York: Oxford, 1984), 236.
2. Howard Rabinowitz, *Race Relations in the Urban South, 1865–1890* (New York: Oxford, 1978), 335.
3. Edward L. Ayers, *The Promise of the New South: Life after Reconstruction* (New York: Oxford, 1992), 134.
4. Ayers, *Vengeance and Justice*, 236.
5. Ibid., 237.

6. Joel Williamson, *The Crucible of Race: Black-White Relations in the American South Since Emancipation* (New York: Oxford, 1984), 114.
7. Neil R. McMillen, *Dark Journey: Black Mississippians in the age of Jim Crow* (Urbana: University of Illinois Press, 1990), 3–4.
8. Ayers, *The Promise of the New South*, 143.
9. Ibid., 141.
10. Ibid., 147.
11. McMillen, *Dark Journey*, 44.
12. Ibid., 43.
13. Cary Wintz, ed., *African American Political Thought, 1890–1930* (Armonk, N.Y.: M.E. Sharpe, 1996), 31.
14. James W. Ely, Jr., "The South, the Supreme Court, and Race Relations, 1890–1915," in Larry J. Griffin and Don H. Doyle, eds., *The South as an American Problem* (Athens: University of Georgia Press, 1995), 128.
15. Ibid., 129.
16. Glenda Gilmore, *Gender and Jim Crow: Women and the Politics of White Supremacy in North Carolina, 1896–1920* (Chapel Hill: University of North Carolina Press, 1996), 20.
17. Desmond King, *Separate and Unequal: Black Americans and the US Federal Government* (New York: Oxford, 1995), 5.
18. Ibid.
19. Ibid., 12.
20. Ibid.
21. Foner, *Reconstruction*, 590.
22. Lawrence W. Levine, "Marcus Garvey and the Politics of Revitalization," in John Hope Franklin and August Meier, eds., *Black Leaders of the Twentieth Century* (Urbana: University of Illinois Press, 1982), 132.
23. King, *Separate and Unequal*, 4.
24. Pauli Murray, *Song in a Weary Throat* (New York: Harper & Row, 1987), 36.

Struggling for Direction after 1879

Freedom unleashed a plethora of intellectual energies in black society. With seemingly insuperable barriers placed in their path by elements in the larger society, the newly freed struggled to remove these impediments and shape their future. There were, understandably, differences of opinion on the appropriate path to pursue and much debate among the leaders, intellectuals, and average citizens alike on such issues as whether the acquisition of civil rights should be the primary focus of the struggle or whether economic uplift should take precedence. Others urged blacks to embrace socialism, some recommended that their brethren unite with white workers and farmers to advance their common interests, and there was sentiment in favor of emigration.

In debating the direction of the future, blacks had no models that suited their circumstances. They could not draw upon the experiences of blacks in the British Caribbean who had been freed in 1838 but who continued to live under colonial rule and for the most part in abject poverty. Nor could they draw much inspiration from the experiences of the Haitians, who had liberated themselves from slavery in 1803, only to fall into the grip of a series of rapacious dictators. Brazil remained a slave society until 1888, and Cuba would liberate its slaves only in 1886. If blacks hardly benefited from the experiences of others after emancipation, their own struggles and achievements would in time help shape developments elsewhere in the diaspora.

The strivings for direction after 1879 are reflected in the ideas of several personages. They included Booker T. Washington, W. E. B. Du Bois, Henry McNeal Turner, T. Thomas Fortune, and Asa Philip Randolph, among others. These are some of the names preserved in the historical record, but we cannot fully understand a people by viewing them solely through the lens of those who operated in the public sphere and whose views have survived. The ideas of these men have been used to define an age, but as yet we have no firm handle on the perspectives that came from below, the ideas of that majority who constituted a people's bedrock and its soul.

Washington and Du Bois were the best-known of the persons who operated in the public sphere after the death of Frederick Douglass in 1895. The older of the two, Booker Talliaferro Washington was born in Franklin County, Virginia, in 1856. He spent his first nine years as a slave, and after freedom came in 1865, he attended the Hampton Normal and Agricultural Institute. Under the influence of the white principal, Samuel Chapman Armstrong, he acquired an educational philosophy that emphasized the virtues of vocational training and self-help for blacks. In 1881, Washington became the principal of Tuskegee Institute in Alabama, a school that reflected this educational orientation.

William Edward Burghardt Du Bois was born in Great Barrington, Massachusetts, in 1868, three years after the Thirteenth Amendment was ratified and almost a hundred years after Massachusetts had legislated the end of slavery. After graduating from high school, the intellectually gifted young man entered Fisk University in 1885. Founded in 1866, Fisk soon became the nation's premier institution of higher education for young black men and women. Its curriculum offered instruction in chemistry, philosophy, history, Latin, Greek, and French among other disciplines and fields. A serious student, Du Bois worked hard and excelled at his studies. His exposure to a wide range of courses in the humanities made him recognize the importance of these disciplines and nurtured in him a lifelong commitment to their study. After graduating from Fisk in 1888, Du Bois was admitted to Harvard University, where he earned the Ph.D. in history in 1895.

Du Bois and Washington possessed contrasting political styles born of their regional backgrounds, education, and individual temperaments. The two men, while they came to represent somewhat different approaches to the strategies that blacks should embrace to improve their condition, also shared much. Their thinking evolved as they confronted new issues and also as a consequence of their own growth and maturation.

A child of the South, Washington saw national problems in Southern terms. Possessed of a personality that seemed to be wary of extremes, he was intimately familiar with the ways of the white Southerner and with the texture of the racism that waged unchecked after the Compromise of 1877. He had witnessed the enthusiasm and high expectations that blacks harbored after 1867 and had seen the promise and ultimate disappointment of the experiment with Reconstruction. Washington recognized that whites still exercised power in the South and that they defined the boundaries within which black citizens had to operate. He also embraced the view that blacks had to work hard to convince whites that they were deserving of the full rights of citizenship. Unlike Du Bois, he was suspicious of the practical value of the humanities as fields of study for blacks and urged the acquisition of vocational and agrarian skills.

In advocating essentially vocational education for blacks, Washington was drawing upon his own experiences as a Southerner, since only farming, service, and artisanal jobs had been generally open to blacks. Many Southern whites and their Northern brethren continued to share the view that blacks were better suited for manual labor because of their presumed mental incapacities. Washington did not endorse this pernicious reasoning, but he saw much to be recommended in a life of toil with one's hands and in the acquisition of saleable and practical skills. He lacked the vision that would have enabled him to see that if blacks were to secure an equal place in society and for each individual to reach his potential, there could be no restrictions placed on the content of their education or on their occupational dreams.

Washington's positions were rooted partly in his belief that blacks and whites had to carve out a *modus vivendi* in the South. While blacks would chip away at the power that whites exercised and obtain their civil rights, they needed to conform to the social etiquette of the South and avoid a frontal challenge to racism. In effect, this meant a temporary acceptance of white supremacy and the accommodation of blacks to its ideology and practice. Washington saw this accommodation as a practical, if not a pragmatic, matter. Washington's seemingly visionless stance on the issue of civil rights earned him the approval of a white population that still wanted to confine blacks to a subordinate place in society. It was comforting to them to have an articulate black man espouse ideas that seemed to endorse white supremacy and tutelage.

Although Booker T. Washington's ideas were becoming known in the 1880s and 1890s, it was not until 1895 that they received national attention. In that year he was invited to deliver an address at the opening of the Cotton States and International Exposition held in Atlanta. Speaking to thousands of blacks and whites at the trade fair, Washington urged blacks to remain in the South and to "cast down your buckets where you are." Similarly, whites were enjoined to establish a working relationship with blacks, since they had "without strikes and labor wars, tilled your fields, cleared your forests, built your railroads and cities, and brought forth treasures from the bowels of the earth, and helped make possible this magnificent representation of the progress of the South." His meaning was inescapable. Black labor had built the South, and whites could expect more of the same. In fact, Washington sought to assure white Southerners that blacks would not be aggressive in their assault on racial segregation. "The wisest among my race understand that the agitation of questions of social equality is the extremest folly," he noted, "and that progress in the enjoyment of all the privileges that will come to us must be the result of severe and constant struggle rather than of artificial forcing."

Washington's endorsement of segregation gained him strong approval among whites but a more diverse reaction from blacks. The Tuskegee educator told his white listeners: "In all things that are purely social we can be as separate as the fingers, yet one as the hand in all things essential to mutual progress." Such a concession was soothing to the soul of Southern whites, and they greeted it with thunderous applause. Washington had accepted the terms on which white Southerners had defined the future of the races for the foreseeable future. His speech established him, in some people's minds, as the successor to Frederick Douglass and the most highly respected and authentic voice of black America.

If whites breathed a sigh of relief when they heard or read Washington's speech, blacks were far from unanimous in their praise of its content and implications. The editor of the *New York Age*, T. Thomas Fortune, Bishop Abram Grant of the African Methodist Episcopal Church, and W. E. B. Du Bois offered their gratitude for it. Du Bois, whose philosophy was still taking shape, congratulated Washington on his "phenomenal success at Atlanta—it was words fitly spoken." Fortune told Washington that it appeared "as if you are our Douglass, the best equipped of the lot of us to be the single figure ahead of the procession."

Other blacks were not so certain. Henry McNeal Turner, now a bishop of the AME Church, was certain that Washington "will have to live a long time to undo the harm he has done our race." The editor of the *Washington Bee,* a prominent black newspaper, lamented that Washington had "said something that was death to the Afro-American and elevating to the white people." Similar criticisms appeared in other sections of the black press, underscoring the fact that Washington's accommodation to the nation's racists would be contested by other blacks.

Washington's Atlanta Compromise, as his speech came to be known, occurred at a time when Jim Crow laws were being passed across the South with a malevolent urgency. It was a plea for good relationships between the races, but the understanding and "mutual progress" that it envisaged would occur only on the terms established by the white population. This was unacceptable to many blacks in all regions of the country. Washington had proposed a compromise that whites liked but one that could ultimately delay the achievement of full citizenship for the peoples of African descent.

Still, Washington drew support from blacks, principally in the South, who shared his views, and he quickly became the most visible black spokesperson in the nation. Usually eloquent in his delivery, peppering his speech with telling anecdotes and homespun humor, Washington

Booker T. Washington (1856–1915) in his office at Tuskegee Institute with Emmett J. Scott, 1906.

spoke to black and white audiences, frequently captivating both. He repeated his recipe for black progress with predictable regularity. "Each day convinces me that the salvation of the negro in this country will be in the cultivation of habits of thrift, economy, honesty, the acquiring of education, Christian character, property and industrial skill," he confessed.[1] In 1901, Washington published his autobiography, *Up From*

Slavery, detailing his ideas on the black condition and the challenges he successfully confronted in the first four decades of his remarkable life.

Washington espoused his core ideas unwaveringly until his death in 1915. But his actions were not always in conformity with his words. He cleverly supported a number of civil rights causes privately, while staunchly refusing to endorse them publicly for fear of alienating his white supporters and admirers. It was a steep price to pay; a racist society forced him to make the choice of being true to himself and his oppressed race or to smilingly and obligingly contain his beliefs because that was what a larger white society required of him if he were to be taken seriously. The inner storms that he must have experienced would have vanquished lesser men, but Washington possessed an uncommon strength.

In time, Booker T. Washington acquired the title Wizard of Tuskegee, which was bestowed upon him by his admiring private secretary, Emmett J. Scott. As Washington's national stature grew, he sought to influence the activities of other black individuals and organizations. Wary of competing ideas and strategies and suspicious of other black spokespersons, Washington endeavored to undermine their effectiveness. Relying upon his Tuskegee Machine, a group of spies and *agent provocateurs* in his employ, Washington infiltrated black organizations, created internal divisions and ill will among them, and ultimately limited their appeal and success. Such underhanded behavior reflected Washington's own insecurities and would later tarnish his reputation. Yet this deviousness could have worked only in the absence of strong institutions that depended more upon their programs, policies, and structure for their legitimacy and approval and less on the personalities of their leaders.

Washington's covert behavior, in matters small and large, was not always designed to destroy competitors. In a societal environment where political, institutional, and economic power wore hostile white faces, Washington undoubtedly felt that he had to create secret passageways to advance the interest of the people in whose name he spoke. He eschewed a frontal assault on the bastions of white supremacy, but his abiding commitment to his race's eventual achievement of full equality was never in doubt. His obsequiousness to whites, particularly to those who supported Tuskegee Institute with their funds, tell us as much about the man as it does about the times and the accommodation that some would have to make to a social system that tried to deny to blacks a sense of self.

In trying to construct passageways within the system, Washington discretely and sometimes openly supported challenges to the disenfranchisement of blacks in Georgia, Louisiana, and Alabama. In 1899 and 1900, for example, he not only contributed his own funds to a case contesting the constitutionality of Louisiana's grandfather clause, but also undertook to raise money for the suit. The black newspaper *Indianapolis Freeman* contained a modicum of truth when it observed in 1895 that "humble as Mr. Washington seems, he rings out in the right place."[2]

During almost four decades of active public life, Washington held steadfastly to his core beliefs, but he seemed to become less conservative on some issues in his final years and somewhat more critical of the racial status quo. When Woodrow Wilson was elected president in 1912, the new administration embraced a decidedly unsympathetic stance to the claims of black America for equality and social justice. Wilson's administration reduced the number of blacks appointed to federal offices, sanctioned segregation in the civil service, and generally retreated from the promise made in the campaign "for absolute fair dealing" insofar as the "interests" of blacks were concerned.[3] Symptomatic of the president's insensitivity to black America was his endorsement in 1915 of the overtly racist film, *The Birth of a Nation*. After viewing the film, which depicted blacks as savages, rapists, and degenerates, Wilson proclaimed it as "all so terribly true."[4] In spite of its condemnation by Washington, journalist Monroe Trotter, and many others, the film played to enthusiastic white audiences throughout the nation. It struck a deep resonance among whites who believed or wanted to believe the worst about blacks. That President Wilson approved of this calumny on an entire people reflected the temper of the times as much as it did his own racial biases and a profound failure of presidential leadership.

Woodrow Wilson was not an aberration in terms of his racial attitudes. But his administration's indifference to blacks, along with the lack of any measurable improvement in the black condition nationally, must have influenced Washington to modify his accommodationist stance in the last years of his life. He came to oppose segregation in housing in stronger terms than he had previously done, spoke out against *The Birth of a Nation*, and condemned the inferior and separate facilities for blacks on the railroad cars that traversed the South.

If Booker T. Washington represented the last black leader of national stature who was both shaped and limited by his experiences as a slave, W. E. B. Du Bois represented the kind of leadership style that would come to characterize the more esteemed spokespersons of black America in the twentieth century. Educated, assertive, uncompromising in their assault on racism and vigorous in their demand for equality, these leaders were attuned to the urgent needs of their constituency and of the virtue of their quest for justice. Invariably rejecting the temporizing approach of Washington, these men and women did not always agree on their definition of the problem, the strategies that should be embraced, or the priorities to be established.

Blessed with a powerful intellect, Du Bois developed into the most farsighted and progressive black spokesperson of the times. While Frederick Douglass was acknowledged as the foremost leader that black

America produced in the nineteenth century, Du Bois would, arguably, inherit that mantle for much of the first half of the twentieth century. His differences with Booker T. Washington were sometimes born of dissimilar leadership styles and personalities, but they were regional, ideological, and generational as well. A Southerner and a former slave, Washington saw the nation as the South writ large, and his prescriptions for change reflected the experiences of a black person who lived his life within the boundaries set by whites and who was unable by temperament, personality, and habit to penetrate those boundaries or to assault them aggressively. On the other hand, the younger Du Bois was a child of the North, whose liberal and advanced education and aggressive personality prepared him to beat down barriers and to be uncompromising in the face of racial injustice. While Washington accepted the view that blacks had to show they were deserving of equal rights, Du Bois was certain that all citizens enjoyed the same privileges as a matter of birthright.

When Du Bois graduated from Harvard, he accepted a teaching position at Wilberforce University in Ohio. His chosen career was teaching and the life of the mind, and the radicalism that would later define his work was not yet then evident. His endorsement of Washington's Atlanta Compromise suggested that his position on the black condition had not yet taken shape, and his admiration of the Wizard of Tuskegee was clear. In 1896, he accepted an appointment at the University of Pennsylvania, undertaking the research that would lead to his landmark study, *The Philadelphia Negro*.

The product of extensive fieldwork, *The Philadelphia Negro* was a close study of the lives of blacks in an urban environment. Detailing the horrible conditions of life in the city's Seventh Ward, the book was a forerunner of similar studies that became staples of scholarship on blacks in the twentieth century. This classic book, together with Du Bois's earlier study of the suppression of the slave trade, established him as the premier scholar of black America. In fact, throughout his long career, Du Bois was able to publish books of distinction while simultaneously working in the trenches to advance the cause of his people. This combination of scholarship with activism would earn Du Bois the reputation as one of the preeminent personalities of twentieth-century America.

Unlike Washington, Du Bois strongly supported an education deeply rooted in the humanities. Although he recognized the value of an industrial education, he believed firmly that blacks should not be denied access to the wider worlds of knowledge. His vision was one of the infinite possibilities of a black person if provided with the opportunities that others in society enjoyed.

The most extended statement of Du Bois' emerging positions on the black condition appeared in his 1903 book, *The Souls of Black Folk*.

Chapter 3 *Struggling for Direction after 1879* 55

William Edward Burghardt Du Bois (1868–1963)

Composed of fourteen essays, the book acknowledged the psychological struggle to define oneself simultaneously as black and as American, given the treatment of the African-American in the land of his birth. The black person, he wrote, "ever feels his two-ness–an American, a Negro; two souls, two thoughts, two unreconciled strivings, two warring ideals in one dark body, whose dogged strength alone keeps it from being torn asunder. The history of the American Negro is the history of this strife– this longing to attain self-conscious manhood, to merge his double self into a better and truer self."[5]

But this inner tension, in Du Bois's view, was not so debilitating that it left the black person without any agency. Rather, the tension invited struggle and out of this "strife" would emerge a more complete person. Taking issue with Washington and his philosophy of a quiet accommodation to racism, Du Bois asserted, "In the history of nearly all other races and peoples the doctrine preached has been that manly self-respect is worth more than lands and houses . . . , that a people who surrender voluntarily such respect, or cease striving for it, are not worth civilizing."[6]

Led by Du Bois, thirty blacks met at Niagara Falls, Canada, in July 1905 to formulate demands for their rights as Americans and to chart a new direction in the long black struggle for justice. The gathering included representatives from all of the regions of the country, with at least six coming from the South. Their ranks included Monroe Trotter, William Hart, a Howard University law professor, and Harry Clay Smith, the editor of the *Cleveland Gazette*. Still, it was Du Bois's show, and the "Declaration of Principles" that the meeting issued bore his stamp. It was a passionate denunciation of America's mistreatment of its black citizens and a notice to the country that a different kind of civil rights organization had been created.

When the second meeting of what became known as the Niagara Movement was held in August 1906, the delegates were ready to endorse a set of specific proposals. Du Bois's electrifying presentation galvanized support for a stronger assault on the nation's racist institutions even as it heralded a new era of black defiance and struggle. Signaling a change in the mood of blacks, Du Bois warned:

> We claim for ourselves every single right that belongs to a freeborn American, political, civil and social; and until we get these rights we will never cease to protest and to assail the ears of America. The battle we wage is not for ourselves alone but for all true Americans. It is a fight for ideals, lest this, our common fatherland, false to its founding, become in truth the land of the thief and the home of the slave–a by-word and a hissing among the nations for its sounding pretensions and pitiful accomplishments.[7]

By the time the convention dispersed, the delegates had demanded the franchise, equal opportunities for jobs, and an end to segregation. The Niagara Movement was a public and dramatic break with the ideals and pace of change espoused by Booker T. Washington. For Du Bois, the movement meant that he had embarked on a life of activism and a more overtly public career. There would be no repairing of the breach with Washington. Yet we should not be overly concerned with the personal differences, if not animus, that would continue to characterize the relationship between the two men. Their conflicts should not be confused with the history and struggles of the people in whose name they both attempted to speak.

The Niagara Movement, in spite of its high ideals and the spirit that gave it birth, failed to achieve its promise. The ambitious task that it defined required the support of those who walked in the halls of power for its success, as well as a radical change in the larger society's stance on the question of race. None of this occurred. Lacking any broad-based support, confronting the opposition of the Tuskegee Machine, and operating in an atmosphere of heightening racial tension, the movement was unequal to the challenges it confronted.

The desire to give organizational structure to the cause of equal rights received a boost in 1909. Outraged by a bloody attack by whites on blacks in Springfield, Illinois, in 1908, a number of prominent blacks and progressive whites gathered in New York in May 1909 to discuss racial questions. Those in attendance included Du Bois, Mary Church Terrell, Monroe Trotter, Ida Wells-Barnett, and Oswald Villard, who was a descendant of the abolitionist William Lloyd Garrison. The speeches of these luminaries were filled with calls to action; their analyses of the black condition and the national crises trenchant, and their rhetoric passionate. At the end of the two-day conference, the conferees established a working group that was the foundation stone of the National Association for the Advancement of Colored People (NAACP). The organization, dedicated to achieving equal rights for the peoples of African descent, was officially created in 1910, at the second meeting of this group. Du Bois was named the director of publicity and research. He was soon to become the editor of the NAACP's influential magazine, the *Crisis*, which appeared monthly.

The creation of the NAACP marked an important stage in the black struggle to make the Constitution applicable to all peoples. It was an exercise in black and white cooperation, a coalition of elites of the two races. Under Du Bois's editorial direction, the *Crisis* became the principal instrument for the dissemination of ideas about the black struggle and the public assault on racism. Blacks and whites alike used the magazine to debate issues and to express their point of view on questions relevant to its editorial mission. Barely two years after its appearance, the *Crisis* boasted a circulation of 22,500, a resounding success by any measure. Its appeal resided in its bold editorial stance on issues of race and its uncompromising position on the injustice of the nation's treatment of its black citizens.

While many blacks placed their faith in transforming the nation and calling it to its promise, some promoted emigration overseas. These persons, like their predecessors Martin Delany, Samuel Coker, and John Russwurm, had lost faith in the ability of the United States to create a just society for its black citizens. Foremost among those who articulated a rejection of black America after emancipation was Henry McNeal Turner, who had been born free in South Carolina in 1834. In his long and distinguished career, Turner served as a chaplain in the army, as a

Bishop Henry McNeal Turner

member of the Georgia Constitutional Convention in 1867, as bishop of the AME Church, and as president of Morris Brown College in Atlanta. Turner, unlike many of his contemporaries, visited Africa on four occasions, sometimes painting a romantic picture of his ancestral home.

In spite of his admiration for Africa, however, Turner was a product of the West and shared many of the negative assumptions about Africa and her peoples. He believed that black Americans had a special obligation to "redeem" Africans by taking Christianity to them. He was certain that "Africa will be the thermometer that will determine the status of the Negro the world over. . . . The Negro will never be anything here while Africa is shrouded in heathen darkness."[8] Thus, Africa had to be redeemed before the black person in America could experience an elevation in his status.

But Turner grew increasingly pessimistic about the future of blacks in America. He had witnessed the failure of Reconstruction, the violence against blacks, and the efforts to confine them to a subordinate place in society. Despairing of blacks' being able to achieve equality in America and calling his country a "bloody lynching nation," he urged black repatriation to Africa and the payment of reparations to them for being enslaved and forced to provide free labor for whites. "A man who loves a country that hates him is a human dog and not a man," he asserted in 1892.[9]

It is difficult to gauge how many people shared Turner's position on emigration. But most would have experienced, in varying degrees of intensity, the alienation from American society that he felt so sharply. Writing at the end of Reconstruction, AME clergyman Richard A. Cain concluded that there was a "deep and growing interest taken by the Colored people . . . in the subject of Emigration." He knew that "the Colored people of the South are tired of the constant struggle for life and liberty . . . and prefer going where no such obstacles are in their way of enjoying their liberty."[10]

Few blacks, even if they had the inclination, could afford the cost of emigrating to Africa. To facilitate this effort, two South Carolina pastors, Benjamin F. Porter and Harrison N. Boney, organized the Liberian Exodus Joint Stock Company in 1876. Under its auspices, 206 persons sailed for Liberia in 1878. But the experiment was hardly a success. Twenty-three persons died en route, and many survivors were unprepared for the hazards of life in their adopted country. The company went bankrupt and the venture ended.

The truth, of course, was that black Americans, despite their circumstances, were Americans. Few were willing to take the ultimate step of severing their ties to their homeland. Benjamin T. Tanner, editor of the AME's newspaper and virulent critic of Turner's emigrationism, rejected the claim that black Americans had any ties with Africans. "To speak plainly," he asserted, ". . . we are simply black white men." To him, the African was "savage, or at most, semi-civilized. . . . We know we are not, and yet by destructive sentiment, not a few of us insist upon linking our destiny with him, when the fates have marked out for a destiny far different . . . an American destiny."[11] This was probably an extremist position, but Tanner spoke for many. Frederick Douglass, for one, was a firm believer in the notion that blacks should remain in the United States and strive to be assimilated into the larger society. But Booker T. Washington had another reason for voicing opposition to emigration schemes. In 1900, he noted that "for every negro that is sent to Liberia, a negro baby is born in the cotton belt, so that scheme is a failure. As we came to this country at the urgent solicitation and expense of the white man, we would be ungrateful to run away and leave him now."[12] Some blacks did not need slavery's chains to bind them to an unjust status quo; for them the habits of subservience acquired during years of subordination proved difficult, if not impossible, to exorcise.

Bishop Turner was also uncompromising in his assault on the racism that infected his nation. He maintained that "to the negro in this country the American flag is a dirty and contemptible rag."[13] He saw no reason why blacks should have to fight for their rights. "We were born here," Turner reminded his countrymen, "raised here, fought, bled, and died here, and have a thousand times more right here than hundreds of thousands of those who help to snub, proscribe and persecute us, and that is one of the reasons I almost despise the land of my birth."[14] But Turner also felt conflicting pulls between his Americanness and his Africanity. During his trip to Africa in 1891, for example, he admitted to being pleased when he saw the American flag flying on an adjacent ship. "I was glad to see our flag," he said, "while there was not a star in the galaxy that recognized the manhood of her black inhabitants."[15]

Bishop Turner's inner tensions were also revealed in his frank admission: "The native African, from the kings down, cannot realize that the black man in America is at home across the sea."[16] This ambiguity was not lost on his detractors. As one of Turner's contemporaries noted rather uncharitably in 1893, he "speaks of the United States as Hades and of Africa as Eden; yet even he still holds his residence in Hades, only paying Eden a brief visit once a year."[17] The matter was not so simple; Turner was a black American, a descendant of Africans, and a person, like so many others, struggling to develop an identity as American, African, and black.

There would, of course, be no mass emigration of blacks to Africa. Several emigration schemes emerged, but they were short-lived. Measured in statistical terms, emigration was clearly a failure. But the emotional appeal of Africa to some blacks as a continent where they might attain their human possibilities never died. To critics, the notion of relocating to an African country was an easy escape from the struggle to transform America. But to view Turner and those who shared his view so narrowly is to miss the fundamental reasons that led them to advocate a rejection of their homeland. Made to feel like strangers, unable to participate fully in the nation's institutions, these persons experienced a profound alienation and marginalization as Americans.

The fact that only a small number of blacks left for their ancestral continent did not mean that the majority accepted their condition in America. A few even sought to effect their independence from whites by founding all-black communities. The idea was not a new one, since escaped slaves began to create free settlements during the eighteenth century. The process accelerated after the disappointments of freedom, as blacks despaired of living together on the basis of equality with whites. About sixty black communities were established between 1865 and 1915. They were located principally in the South and the West. Oklahoma boasted the most, probably as many as twenty-five by 1910. The best-known settlement was Mound Bayou, Mississippi, founded by former slave Isaiah T. Montgomery in 1887. George H. White, a former North Carolina congressman who fled that state after the 1898 Wilmington riots, created the settlement of Whitesboro, New Jersey, at the turn of the century. Other noteworthy settlements included Nicodemus, Kansas (1877), and Oklahoma's Langston (1891), Clearview (1903), and Boley (1904).

These black-run communities were exercises in autonomy, economic nationalism, racial uplift, and pride. In an attempt to inspire the settlers at Mound Bayou to greater effort, Montgomery asked:

> Have you not for centuries braved the miasma and hewed the forests like these at the behest of a Master? Can you not do it now for yourselves and your children into successive generations?[18]

Boley's founder, Thomas Haynes, thought that the settlement represented "an imperishable attestation of the power, might and intellectual genius of a race."[19] Although these settlements were important and admirable experiments in self-rule, there was hardly much chance that they would survive. Lacking resources and frequently facing white hostility, they fought losing battles. These fledgling enclaves could not flourish apart from the larger society. Blacks and whites who shared the nation-state were more structurally interdependent than many realized.

Not wanting to emigrate or to establish all-black settlements, a growing black working class and its leaders had their own views on ways to enhance their interests and improve the overall black condition. Some persons such as the editor T. Thomas Fortune and the politician John R. Lynch thought that black workers should combine forces with white workers and small farmers in their struggles with management and capital because their interests were similar. The formation of the Colored Farmers' National Alliance and Cooperative Union in 1888 represented one such attempt to foster interracial cooperation. Led by a white man, Richard Manning Humphrey, the alliance claimed a membership of 1.2 million in 1891. The alliance was short-lived, however. Its demise came in late 1891 when a cotton pickers strike that it sponsored failed in the face of strong opposition from white farmers. Black farmers and workers also supported the Populist party in the 1890s. Having its greatest appeal in the South, the party promoted political unity among the poor regardless of race, eschewed racial prejudice, and opposed lynching as well as the intimidation of black voters and the movement to disfranchise them. Black and white farmers cooperated uneasily, and along with the Republicans enjoyed electoral victories in states such as Georgia and North Carolina. This experiment in racial and class collaboration eventually died by 1896, as white Populists retreated from the alliance in the face of stiff opposition from other whites, particularly the Democrats.

Chapter 3 Struggling for Direction after 1879

The white-dominated labor unions varied in their attitudes to black workers. Founded in 1881 as the voice of skilled workers, the American Federation of Labor made little or no attempt in its early years to include blacks in its ranks. Although the various railroad unions ignored black workers, the United Mine Workers of America claimed 20,000 black members in 1900. White workers, in the main, were actively hostile to their black peers. They frequently opposed the hiring of blacks, refused to work with them, and accused them of incompetence. White workers were themselves the creations of a racist social order that blinded them to the possibilities of interracial cooperation to advance their common class interests. Consequently, the vision of black and white workers–and farmers–uniting to improve their condition collapsed on the altar of American racism.

While one section of black opinion wanted black and white workers to forge an alliance, another embraced a revolutionary transformation of the social order as a prerequisite for an elevation of the black economic condition. These persons found socialist principles attractive. Their numbers were not impressive, at least before 1917, when a socialist candidate for office in New York garnered 25 percent of the votes cast in Harlem. T. Thomas Fortune was one of the earliest black voices to embrace some socialist ideas. In 1884, for example, he endorsed "restrictions on the power and extent of monopoly and corporate extortion."[20] W. E. B. Du Bois was more emphatic in his support, declaring in 1907 that socialism was "the one great hope of the Negro American. We have been thrown by strange historic reasons into the hands of the capitalists hitherto. We have been objects of dole and charity, and despised accordingly. We have been made tools of oppression against the working man's cause–the puppets and playthings of the idle rich. Fools! We must awake!"[21]

Asa Philip Randolph and Chandler Owen worked most aggressively in the trenches to promote socialism among blacks. Born in Jacksonville, Florida, Randolph arrived in New York City in 1911 and soon embraced socialism. In 1917, he became editor of the *Messenger*, a publication that characterized itself as the "only Radical Negro Magazine in America." Randolph spoke a gospel of self-help for blacks, urging the employed to join trade unions and to work together to improve their condition. His ideology was not based on a narrow "race-first" philosophy, although he was unquestionably committed to the advancement of his people and the achievement of an equitable society. As a socialist, his politics recognized the class interests of all workers, irrespective of racial identification. Chandler Owen was a North Carolinian who became a member of the Socialist party in 1916. Thereafter, he became associated with the better-known Randolph in the publication of the *Messenger*.

Believing that capitalism was inherently racist and exploited black and white workers alike, Randolph promoted cooperation between the races in the creation of a new socialist order. He maintained: "When no profits are to be made from race friction, no one will longer be interested in stirring up race prejudice."[22] As editor of the *Messenger*, Randolph endorsed socialist candidates for political office, promoted the interests of the working class and rhetorically assaulted capitalism whenever he could. He railed against the "greed, selfishness, oppression, [and] murder" of capitalists.[23] Although Randolph supported socialist candidates for office in New York, regardless of race, an editorial in the *Messenger* maintained: "No white man is good enough to rule black men without their consent. And it is pretty well ascertained that it is unsafe for one class to leave its fortunes, political and economic, to another class."[24] Socialist candidates obtained little electoral success. A dismayed Randolph wrote in 1918: "Future historians will marvel at the political contradiction of a race of tenants and workers accepting political leaders selected by landlords, bankers, and capitalists."[25] Randolph's aggressive espousal of socialism and his criticism of American society led to his being harassed by the federal authorities. The government denied the *Messenger* mailing privileges from time to time, and the Department of Justice denounced the paper in 1919 as "the most able and the most dangerous of all the Negro publications."[26]

It should not be assumed that those who embraced interracial cooperation and socialism inhabited mutually exclusive camps. The period was characterized by considerable ideological fluidity, and individuals modified their positions over time. T. Thomas Fortune, who urged interracial cooperation in the 1880s, abandoned that position by 1900. W. E. B. Du Bois embraced socialism as well as interracial cooperation, recognizing that black and white workers possessed similar class interests. By the 1930s, however, Du Bois despaired of the possibility of black and white workers acting cooperatively. In 1933 he concluded:

> . . . while Negro labor in America suffers because of the fundamental inequities of the whole capitalistic system, the lowest and most fatal degree of its suffering comes not from the capitalists but from fellow white laborers. It is white labor that deprives the Negro of his right to vote, denies him education, denies him affiliation with trade unions, expels him from decent houses and neighborhoods, and heaps upon him the public insults of open color discrimination.[27]

A. Philip Randolph espoused radical structural change as a socialist, but he was also an effective trades unionist who operated within the boundaries of the system, even as he attempted to transform it.

The broad currents that characterized black America's response to second-class citizenship–accommodation, protest, emigration, interracial cooperation, and socialism–do not capture the fluidity in most people's positions and the changes that some embraced over time. These were not rigid distinctions, nor did the individuals remain frozen in their positions. It may be recalled, for example, that Du Bois congratulated Washington on his Atlanta Compromise speech. On the other hand, the Wizard of Tuskegee supported court challenges to the disfranchisement laws and became more critical of the racial status quo toward the end of his life. This healthy receptivity to change in accordance with new understandings and experiences remained an important characteristic of the thought of many black spokespersons throughout the twentieth century.

The different ideas that emerged as solutions to the problems of black America reflected the diversity within the black population as a whole. Booker T. Washington, Henry McNeal Turner, W. E. B. Du Bois, and the others spoke for different constituencies. The solutions to the complex problems that blacks confronted were never obvious, and the various ideas that were advanced reflected the struggle for direction. In retrospect, some of these ideas were lacking in vision; others came to define the black struggle for several generations and provided its intellectual rationale. But none of these ideas were destined to bear substantial fruit until the larger society modified its racial ideas and blacks acquired the strength to beat down some of the overt barriers that confined them as a people.

Notes

1. The quotations we cite come from Louis Harlan, *Booker T. Washington, The Making of A Leader, 1856–1901* (New York: Oxford, 1972), 218–237.
2. Ibid., 290.
3. Louis Harlan, *Booker T. Washington, The Wizard of Tuskegee, 1901–1915* (New York: Oxford, 1983), 357.
4. Williamson, *The Crucible of Race,* 176.
5. W. E. B. Du Bois, *The Souls of Black Folk* (repr. New York: Penguin, 1989), 5.
6. Ibid., 43.
7. David Levering Lewis, *W. E. B. Du Bois, Biography of a Race 1868–1919* (New York: Henry Holt, 1993), 330.
8. Wilson Jerimiah Moses, *The Golden Age of Black Nationalism, 1850–1925* (New York: Oxford, 1988), 201.
9. Rayford Logan and Michael Winston, eds., *Dictionary of American Negro Biography* (New York: W.W. Norton, 1982), 609.
10. Montgomery, *Under Their Own Vine and Fig Tree,* 197.
11. Ibid., 205.
12. Edwin S. Redkey, *Black Exodus: Black Nationalists and Back to Africa Movements, 1890–1940* (New Haven: Yale University Press, 1969), 252–253.
13. Montgomery, *Under Their Own Vine and Fig Tree,* 215.
14. Edwin S. Redkey, "Bishop Turner's African Dream," in Okon Edet Uya, *Black Brotherhood: Afro-Americans and Africa* (Lexington, MA: Heath, 1970), 100.
15. Montgomery, *Under Their Own Vine and Fig Tree,* 209.
16. Ibid.
17. Logan and Winston, *Dictionary,* 609.

18. Norman L. Crockett, *The Black Towns* (Lawrence: University of Kansas Press, 1979), 45–46.
19. Ibid., 46.
20. Mary Frances Berry and John Blassingame, *Long Memory: The Black Experience in America* (New York: Oxford, 1982), 221.
21. Ibid., 222.
22. Paula F. Pfeffer, *A. Philip Randolph, Pioneer of the Civil Rights Movement* (Baton Rouge: Louisiana State University Press, 1990), 10.
23. Berry and Blassingame, *Long Memory,* 222.
24. Jervis Anderson, *A. Philip Randolph: A Biographical Portrait* (New York: Harcourt Brace Jovanovich, 1972), 95.
25. Ibid., 96.
26. Pfeffer, *A. Philip Randolph,* 18.
27. Wintz, *African American Political Thought,* 149.

Uplifting the Race: 1879–1917

Prior to the end of slavery, free blacks founded their own institutions wherever they could. Undaunted by the obstacles they confronted, these persons established mutual aid societies, schools, religious bodies, and literary societies. They opposed slavery, fought for the suffrage, and demanded their equal rights as citizens. Theirs was an honorable and vigorous tradition of self-help that would contradict later and palpably erroneous claims that blacks had done nothing for themselves. For a people who could not rely on the benevolence of the state in which they lived, blacks had to create their own space and build their institutions, all the while seeking their rightful place in the society where most of them had been born. Such struggles took their inevitable toll even among the most strong-willed, but the spirit of a people had never been vanquished, and the belief in the possibility of progressive change was never stilled.

Freedom brought new options and released new energies. The failure of the larger society to cleanse its institutions, social fabric, and people of a cancerous racism was a rude setback to the hopes of black America. The attempt at reconstructing the South had failed, and an aggressive white racism was unleashed after the federal troops departed in 1877. The succeeding decades have been characterized by historians as the nadir in race relations and black life, a metaphor for hopes dashed, rights destroyed, and lives crushed.

Such a reading, however, sees the black experience of the times primarily through the lens of the larger society. The horrible mistreatment of blacks, particularly after 1890, scarred the soul of the nation as a whole, constituted a repudiation of its values, compromised its moral fiber, and created an embarrassing legacy that it has proved impossible to eradicate. Seen from the perspective of blacks, however, the years after 1877, as difficult as the times were for them, bustled with activity as they sought to create the passageways that would allow them to survive as a people. In spite of the external difficulties and probably because of them as well, blacks established a vast number of organizations to meet their needs, started businesses, entered the professions, and migrated. These were stressful years for blacks everywhere, but it was also a time when the generation born in freedom matured and demonstrated much energy, restlessness, and impatience.

This is not to suggest that there was a common vision among all blacks and that divisions based on class, region, skin color, and other variables did not exist. These distinctions emerged among the free people and the slaves before 1863, although they manifested themselves to a far greater degree as people tried to create their own spaces when freedom came. These divisions, inevitably, created tensions in black life, but they were a product of a complex history, changing opportunities, and material circumstances.

The black elite that emerged after emancipation was composed disproportionately of individuals whose families had enjoyed years of freedom. In some cases, these individuals had been born as slaves but acquired their freedom before the Civil War. A high proportion of the elite boasted a mixed racial ancestry and were well off, if not rich. They were found in all regions of the country, but the largest number resided in Washington. The capital city was home to the grand names of black history and society, such as the Pinchbacks, Terrells, Bruces, Grimkés, Purvises, Shadds, and Cardosos.

Proud of their free heritage and oftentimes of their mixed racial ancestry, these elites sought acceptance by white society. To advance that process, they constituted themselves as a relatively closed group and distanced themselves from the masses of their black brethren. They formed exclusive social clubs, embraced a white aesthetic, and worshipped primarily in the elite Episcopal, Presbyterian, and Congregational churches. They placed great emphasis on education, sending their children to exclusive white schools and universities. The curriculum in these schools reflected the needs and priorities of white Americans, neglecting black history and culture.

Keenly aware of their privileged status, many members of the elite assumed the burden of fostering racial uplift. Several embraced Booker T. Washington's philosophy of racial accommodation and self-help. Others had been influenced by W. E. B. Du Bois's vigorous assertion that blacks should be led by the best male members of the race or "The Talented Tenth." A confirmed elitist by training and temperament, Du Bois said: "The Negro race, like all races, is going to be saved by its exceptional men." In answering his own question as to whether there was a nation that was "civilized from the bottom upward," Du Bois affirmed that "it is, ever was, and ever will be from the top downward that culture flows."[1]

The desire to elevate other members of the race was not entirely altruistic. Frequently embarrassed by what they deemed the "uncivilized behavior" of less-privileged blacks, members of the elite sought to correct these "moral" deficiencies so that the entire race would not be disparaged by their actions. As the Reverend Elam White of Kentucky expressed it in 1902: "It is the ignorant, lazy, dishonest and dangerous Negro that impedes our progress."[2] The antisocial behavior that the black elite condemned and the habits they denounced were the inevitable consequences of the marginalization of blacks in society, the absence of equal opportunities, and the impact of unrelenting racial assaults. Du Bois, who was certainly more enlightened than most of his black or white contemporaries, noted in *The Philadelphia Negro* that his data "revealed the Negro as a symptom, not a cause; as a striving, palpitating group, and not an inert, sick body of crime."[3]

Elite women were particularly active in the cause of racial uplift. Mary Church Terrell, a wealthy resident of Washington was one of those outstanding leaders. Born in Tennessee in 1863, she obtained a degree from Oberlin College and eventually worked as a teacher and activist for the cause of racial justice. Mary Terrell was certain that "Self-preservation demands that [black women] go among the lowly, illiterate and even the vicious, to whom they are bound by ties of race and sex . . . to reclaim them."[4] Women, in keeping with the wisdom of the times, were deemed to possess the kinds of inner qualities–caring, nurturing, and sensitivity–that made them ideally suited to "reclaim" the less fortunate. In many respects, the cause that the women embraced was akin to a missionary effort but one that had a secular garb. "Lifting as we climb," the motto of the National Association of Colored Women, aptly characterized the force behind their activities. Not covered by the societal restrictions placed upon white women, these black women defined their own spheres and carved their own spaces. In time, white women would follow the trail of public service that they blazed and embrace the traditions of activism that they did so much to create and shape. These black women redefined the societal roles appropriate for all women and in so doing enlarged the horizons and possibilities of their gender.

Some women, like the writer and lecturer Frances Watkins Harper and the essayist Anna Julia Cooper hoped to transform the prevailing understandings of race, identity, and gender. Harper's novel, *Iola Leroy*, published in 1892, challenged the bases of racism and segregation and espoused a nascent feminism. Cooper eloquently denounced racism in her collection of essays *A Voice from the South*, but her articulation of women's rights emerged as the defining characteristic of her work.

Anna Julia Cooper

Declaring that inasmuch as whites could not represent the voice of blacks, "neither should the dark man be wholly expected fully and adequately to reproduce the exact Voice of the Black Woman."[5] Cooper believed that women held the keys to the transformation of the black condition. As she expressed it, "Only the Black Woman can say 'when and where I enter, in the quiet, undisputed dignity of my womanhood, without violence and without suing or special patronage, then and there the whole *Negro race enters with me.*'"[6]

Born in North Carolina in 1858 as Anna Julia Haywood, she married George Cooper in 1877 only to become a widow two years later. Cooper was highly educated; she obtained a master of arts degree, and the University of Paris awarded her a Ph.D. in 1925. *A Voice from the South* captures the obstacles that Cooper and other women confronted in their quest for gender equality. As she noted, "while our men seem thoroughly abreast of the times on almost every subject, when they strike the woman question they drop back into sixteenth century logic. . . . I fear the majority of colored men do not yet think it worth while that women aspire to higher education."[7]

As was the case with other black spokespersons of the time, Cooper belonged to a small elite group, but her commitment to transforming the role of her gender and that of her race as a whole was unquestioned. In 1902, she became principal of Washington's famous M Street High School, where she maintained the tradition of preparing students for entrance to some of the finest universities. Her creative stewardship there was short-lived, but her dismissal in 1906, allegedly for insubordination, did not silence her voice or crush her spirit. In looking back at the course of her career in 1932, Cooper underscored "the education of the underprivileged" as the core of her life.[8]

Drawing upon a long tradition of black women's involvement in voluntary associations, a handful of elite women founded the Colored Women's League in Washington in 1892. Its ranks included such notables as Mary Church Terrell, Anna Cooper, Charlotte Grimké, and Helen A. Cook. The new association aimed to promote, among other goals, "educational and improvement of Colored Women and the promotion of their interests."[9] Three years later, forty women meeting in Boston established the National Federation of Afro-American Women. The following year, the two organizations merged to create the National Association of Colored Women's Clubs of America (NACW). This was a momentous development because it meant that black women had formed a potentially powerful national organization to enhance the interests of their race and gender. The NACW declared its intention: "To secure and enforce civil and political rights for ourselves and our group. To obtain for our colored women the opportunity of reaching the highest standard in all fields of human endeavor. To promote interracial understanding so that justice and goodwill may prevail among all people."[10]

In time, the NACW included both elite and nonelite women in its ranks. It could hardly have become a significant national voice if it remained the preserve of upper-class women. In the early years, elite women dominated the organization, but they were replaced by representatives of the middle class by around 1910. This change reflected the deeper transformations in the social structure of black America. A darker-skinned generation born in freedom had begun to come into its own, outnumbering and pushing aside those who had characterized themselves as the "civic mothers of the race."[11]

In order to effect its goals, the NACW's members spearheaded a number of social activities. They established kindergartens, nurseries, and schools that emphasized home economics. By 1914, the NACW was said to have a membership of 40,000, distributed in all regions of the nation. But the organization was not free from criticism. Ida Wells-Barnett, a journalist and antilynching crusader, for example, chastised it in 1922 for being elitist and neglecting its mission. Despite the paternalism that permeated the NACW's attitude toward and work among the poor, it served a useful function for those whom it reached. On another level, the NACW provided its members with a socially positive outlet for their energies, fostered a solidarity among women that often transcended class differences, and allowed them to acquire a deeper sense of the possibilities of their gender and race.

The NACW was not the only organizational voice of black women. In fact, it stood on the shoulders of countless numbers of women's church societies scattered across the nation. These societies—and the secular ones as well—had provided women with crucial leadership skills, and many of them had pioneered the social service programs that the NACW would adopt. A significant number of these women were Baptists, but others belonged to various Christian denominations. Educated at such schools as Spelman College in Georgia, most of these women joined the teaching profession or entered other service-related occupations. By 1900, 86.7 percent of all professionally trained black women were teachers.[12]

Such women, in a fundamental sense, were really teachers and missionaries. Not only did they seek to improve the literacy levels of the black population, but they also were committed to achieving cultural transformations as well. They preached the gospel of Victorian morality and sought to make their people culturally refined and respectable. The women who formed a separate convention within the National Baptist Convention were particularly active in helping to improve the overall black condition.

The National Baptist Convention, USA, was founded in 1895. By 1916, it counted almost 3 million members in its ranks, making it the largest black-controlled Christian denomination in the nation. Although the NBC was firmly controlled by men, about two-thirds of the membership consisted of women. Chafing under their exclusion from the leadership ranks and inspired by the imperative to advance the interest of their gender and race, they formed the Woman's Convention in 1900. Meeting annually, they espoused an ideology of self-help for blacks, promoted the ideals of a Victorian respectability, and fostered a unity among the sisters that seemed to transcend class distinctions. Questioning the authority of men in the denomination, such women as Lucy Wilmot Smith and Mary Cook of Kentucky, as well as Virginia Broughton of Tennessee, urged an expansion of women's roles in the denomination and in the larger society, frequently using examples from the Bible to buttress their case. Smith was troubled by the notion that women should be dependent on men. She believed that "one of the evils of the day" was "that from babyhood girls are taught to look forward to the time when they will be supported by a father, a brother, or someone else's brother."[13] Cook prodded her church to "Emancipate woman from the chains that now restrain her and who can estimate the part she will play in the work of the denomination."[14] While some men responded sympathetically to such urgings, it was the women themselves who created their own public spaces, invited their own challenges, and built their own passageways. These Baptist women did not change the power arrangements within their church, but they affirmed their own voice within its institutional structures, paralleling that of the men.

The remarkable energy that characterized black life during these years was not the exclusive function of any one gender or class. While the acknowledged leaders such as Booker T. Washington, W. E. B. Du Bois, and Mary Church Terrell garnered the limelight, countless others provided leadership in other ways. These men and women built from the bottom up, brick by brick, layer by layer, post by post, until black America's diverse institutional structure emerged. Blacks had internalized the gospel of self-help, recognizing that they had to shape their own destinies. But a philosophy of self-help would be most efficacious in a societal milieu that placed no structural barriers in the path of its citizens' upward climb. Success also required access to capital, resources of all kinds, and a social environment encouraging of equal opportunities, irrespective of race and ethnicity. None of these prerequisites existed in American society; in fact, much of the black accomplishments during these times were realized in spite of the unfriendliness of the nation. As a people confined to the margins of society, blacks had to struggle to enter into the societal mainstream, chipping away at the edges as they did so.

MATTERS ECONOMIC

In spite of their best efforts, blacks had considerable difficulty in improving their economic condition. They remained largely Southern; 90 percent of them lived in the South at the turn of the century. Of this number, 80 percent were residents of the rural areas. In 1910, 90 percent of rural blacks were either sharecroppers, tenants, or contract laborers.[15] Wracked by poverty and disease, men and women had a life expectancy of thirty-three years. Infant mortality rates remained high; probably one child in three died before its tenth birthday.[16] Black men and women worked in the white-owned cotton fields, fostering a wretched dependence on a way of life that served them ill.

Life in the urban areas held greater promise for some, but was still depressingly harsh for the majority. In 1890, one in ten black Southerners lived in urban areas, but the proportion doubled by 1910. Escaping from the oppressive circumstances of rural life, some men found jobs as artisans and craftsmen, although such opportunities declined drastically by the end of the nineteenth century as they were successfully displaced, by immigrant whites in particular. As a rule, black men worked in construction, factories, and odd jobs. These jobs were frequently seasonal or irregular, so a high proportion of men was often unemployed.

Women were in similar straits. Most worked as domestics in white households or as washerwomen. Domestic workers labored long hours and received little more than subsistence wages. Those who lived in the residence of their employers lost their independence, while those who did not usually had little time for their own families. In general, washerwomen picked up the laundry at their employer's residence and did the work in their own homes. Consequently, they worked at their own pace and enjoyed their autonomy.

Washerwomen and household workers frequently contested the nature of their work situations, demanding higher wages, quitting, or temporarily withholding their services. Washerwomen went on strike in Jackson, Mississippi, in 1877, Galveston, Texas, in 1877, and in Atlanta in 1881. The women in Atlanta demanded a wage of $1 for every twelve pounds of wash. Their organization, the Washing Society, led the struggle, and as many as 3,000 women refused to work. Landlords intimidated the strikers by threatening to raise rents, and the municipal authorities began considering the imposition of a $25 licensing fee on the "washing amazons," as they were characterized. Undaunted, the women issued a statement affirming their determination "to stand our pledge . . . we mean business this week or no washing."[17] Faced with such class and gender solidarity, the authorities relented, but it is uncertain whether the women as a group obtained the wage increase they sought.

Not all blacks occupied domestic or unskilled jobs. Some entered the professions as teachers, nurses, physicians, and clergymen. A few made their fortunes in business. Together these people formed the nucleus of a slowly expanding middle class in the South and in the North. Understandably, this development accentuated class differences among blacks. Black professionals, entrepreneurs, undertakers, contractors, and prosperous farmers could become distanced from the plight of their brethren who were trapped at the bottom of society. These class distinctions were more readily observed in the Upper South and in the North, and they were present in urban areas to a greater degree. By the first decades of the twentieth century, this economic elite had begun to be comprised of the children of the people who had been freed in 1863.

Recognizing their minority status, their economic marginality, and the racial barriers in their path, some blacks tried to maximize their chances for economic advancement through collective action. Southern farmers, for example, were among the first to unite to promote their economic interest. In 1890, Booker T. Washington organized the Tuskegee Negro Farmers Conference, a group that met annually to promote self-help and a cooperative spirit. This was probably the best known of such conferences, but there were many others throughout the South. In general, these conferences encouraged their members to purchase their own property, avoid credit, and to buy and sell cooperatively.

Success in agrarian matters represented only one avenue to economic advancement. In a rapidly urbanizing and industrializing America, opportunities abounded in business and related fields for those with capital and entrepreneurial skills. The vast majority of blacks lacked the requisite capital and possessed little or no experience in managing an industrial economy. In 1900, Booker T. Washington formed the National Negro Business League to promote the participation of blacks in business enterprises. Washington controlled the organization from Tuskegee, but its philosophy of economic cooperation among blacks and a strong belief in the virtues of American capitalism attracted adherents nationwide. Successful businessmen shared the secrets of their triumph at the annual meetings of the league, inspiring the audience to emulate their examples and strategies. The league and the similar organizations that it spawned celebrated a belief in the capacity of the economic system to be elastic enough to welcome black entrepreneurs and businesses. Theirs was a profound faith in a system that could become color-blind in its acceptance of competition and its sharing of the market.

This construction was overly optimistic. There can be no doubt, however, that the number of black-owned businesses increased markedly after 1880. By 1920, about 70,000 blacks were employed by or were involved in their own enterprises. Table 4.1 provides a breakdown of these businesses.

The overwhelming majority of these businesses had limited capital and existed on the margins of the nation's economy. There were notable exceptions, however. One was the beauty-culture and hair-care business established by Madame C. J. Walker. Born in Louisiana in 1867 as Sarah Breedlove, Madame Walker developed a formula for hair care that sold well and made her the first black female millionaire in the country. In 1910, she employed as many as 5,000 workers, and owned numerous beauty parlors and her own laboratory. The size of her enterprise paled in comparison, however, to the North Carolina Mutual Life Insurance Company. Founded in Durham in 1898 by John Merrick, A. M. Moore, James E. Shephard, and W. G. Pearson, the company expanded rapidly. Merrick was the inspiration behind the business and served as its president.

The insurance company filled a need in black society, and its success reflected this reality. By 1915, the company was operating in twelve other states and in Washington, D.C. Its insurance-in-force grew to $16 million in 1918. Seen from another perspective, the company had assets of $350 in 1899, $93,000 in 1908, and $43 million in 1952.

The presence of the North Carolina Mutual Life Insurance Company helped to give Durham the reputation as the business capital of black

TABLE 4.1
Number of Black-Owned Business Enterprises, 1920

Business	Number
Restaurants and luncheon keepers	7,511
Grocers	6,339
Truck farmers	6,242
Hucksters and peddlers	3,194
Butchers and meat dealers	3,009
Miscellaneous retail dealers	1,754
Pool-room keepers	1,582
Undertakers	1,558
Contractors and builders	1,454
Real-estate dealers	1,369
Junk dealers	1,132
Hotel keepers and managers	1,020

SOURCE: Charles M. Christian, *Black Saga*. (Boston: Houghton Mifflin, 1995), 320.

America. "You haven't seen anything yet. Wait 'til you get to Durham" became the refrain of those who admired the city's economic vitality. Booker T. Washington, who visited the city in 1910, noted the profusion of black-owned "farms, truck farms, grocery stores, thriving drugstores, insurance houses, and beautiful though modest homes."[18] W. E. B. Du Bois was equally impressed. "There is in this city," he commented, "a group of five thousand or more colored people, whose social and economic development is perhaps more striking than that of any similar group in the nation."[19]

These black business entrepreneurs, large or small, represented a minute share of the nation's gross domestic product. Catering to a predominantly black clientele, they met the needs of a people ill-served by the larger society, but who were pushing their way into the economic mainstream. These gains, however, were never impressive enough nor sufficiently broad-based to give most blacks a feeling that they had a secure stake in the economy. Simply put, the economy did not work as well for blacks as it had for whites.

While the National Negro Business League promoted the interests of black entrepreneurs, the Urban League (later the National Urban League) saw urban workers as its special constituency. Founded in New York City in 1911, the Urban League (UL) was an interracial organization. Members of its board included such notables as the Howard University professor Kelly Miller, Mary Church Terrell, and Adam Clayton Powell Sr., of the Abyssinian Baptist Church in Manhattan. The UL, in many respects, saw itself as a social welfare agency. It assisted blacks in procuring jobs, eased the transition of migrants to the cities by providing assistance, offered vocational guidance, and mediated disputes between employers and employees. Its affiliates in such industrial cities as Chicago, Detroit, and Cleveland worked effectively to ease the unfavorable conditions in the factories under which blacks worked. By the early 1960s, the organization would become one of the major advocates of civil rights for blacks.

MATTERS PROFESSIONAL AND EDUCATIONAL

Although the economic health of blacks as a whole was far from being good, there were clear signs of growth in the professional class. Its members included lawyers, physicians, professors, journalists, clergymen, and other university-trained and salaried individuals. Excluded from membership in white professional organizations, they formed their own. Between 1880 and 1920, physicians, journalists, teachers, bankers, and morticians had all created separate organizations. These organizations not only reflected and advanced the interests of the growing number of professionals, but they also showed that even though blacks and whites had similar occupations, race remained an insurmountable barrier to their cooperation until well into the twentieth century.

The years after Reconstruction saw an expansion in the literacy level of blacks. This improvement occurred within the context of the national debate over the nature of the education to which they should be exposed. This debate focused more on black Southerners, although its ramifications were national in scope. Arrayed on one side of the debate were the industrial philanthropists who urged and promoted vocation-based education. These philanthropic organizations included the Peabody Educational Fund, the John F. Slater Fund, the Phelps-Stokes Fund, and the Carnegie Foundation. They were committed to the position that blacks should be trained to perform manual labor, as befitting their status. A white Northern philanthropist, William H. Baldwin, expressed this philosophy quite well in 1899:

> The potential economic value of the Negro population properly educated is infinite and incalculable. In the Negro is the opportunity of the South. Time has proven that he is best fitted to perform the heavy labor in the Southern States. 'The Negro and the mule is the only combination, so far, to grow cotton.' The South needs him; but the South needs him educated to be a suitable citizen. Properly directed he is the best possible laborer to meet the climatic conditions of the South. He will willingly fill the more menial positions, and do the heavy work, at less wages, than the American white man or any foreign race which has yet

come to our shores. This will permit the southern white laborer to perform the more expert labor, and to leave the fields, the mines, and the simpler trades for the Negro.[20]

This was more than an educational philosophy. It was a profound expression of white supremacy at work. Blacks were to be trained to serve the needs of whites and to play subordinate roles in society, their individual talents notwithstanding.

Arrayed against the industrial philanthropists were the black philanthropic organizations. These were essentially religious bodies, most notably the African Methodist Episcopal Church. Rejecting the arguments associated with the industrial philanthropists, the AME Church established a number of institutions of higher education, including Allen University, Wilberforce University, and Morris Brown College. The African Methodist Episcopal Zion Church founded Livingstone College. The Baptists and the Colored Methodist Episcopal Church also started colleges in a number of states. White missionaries from the North supported higher education for blacks with a view to preparing them to take their place in society and, in the words of one, "to regenerate their own people." The American Missionary Association also sponsored colleges, high schools, and normal schools throughout the South. These included Fisk University, Straight University (later Dillard), Tougaloo College, and Talladega College. The Presbyterians, Baptists, and the Methodist Episcopal Church supported black colleges such as Bennett College, Morehouse College, Shaw University, and Meharry Medical College.[21]

Short of funds and frequently lacking qualified instructors, most of the institutions of higher education functioned as such in name only. The industrial philanthropists poured funds into Hampton Institute and Tuskegee, the two most prominent institutions that reflected their philosophy. Not until the second decade of the twentieth century did they begin to support a humanistic education for blacks. A new generation of blacks had surfaced, and most were critical of the Tuskegee-Hampton educational philosophy. The social disturbances of 1917 and 1919 showed that blacks would retaliate against white-inspired violence and reflected an acute dissatisfaction with their condition. The accommodationist stance associated with Booker T. Washington had died with him or had become enfeebled. If the white industrial philanthropists could no longer define black education and control the evolution of a people, they would move with the times and not risk becoming irrelevant. Such pragmatism led some philanthropists to pledge their grudging support for liberal arts education, particularly if they could determine its content and ensure that the graduates would not challenge the social order.

A small but increasing proportion of blacks enjoyed the advantages of higher education. Between 1870 and 1900, for example, 2,177 blacks received college degrees, in contrast to the 66 who did so between 1820 and 1870. By 1910 about 70 percent of the 10 million blacks in the nation were at least functionally literate. This was an achievement against terrible odds, particularly in the South. Northern blacks, after prolonged struggles in the antebellum years, had been allowed to attend public schools. Southern whites resisted public education for blacks until the new, Reconstruction-era constitutions established public schools supported by state funds. The impetus for this development came largely from black politicians and leaders.

Blacks placed a great premium on literacy, and as we have seen, on economic strength as well. These were perceived as constituting two of the principal means to full participation in society. Once slavery ended, Southern blacks pooled their resources everywhere to construct schools and hire teachers. They also received the assistance of Northern missionaries as well as that of the Freedmen's Bureau. Churches created "Sabbath" schools where students were taught on weekends and in the evenings. In 1869, it was estimated that there were 1,512 Sabbath schools in the South and 107,109 students.[22]

Although Southern whites eventually accepted the view that public education for blacks was necessary, black schools everywhere were woefully underfunded. Spartanly equipped, staffed inadequately, and often possessing poorly trained teachers, these schools reflected the low priority that was placed on black education. As A. A. Kincannon, the Mississippi superintendent of education, confessed in 1899: "It will be readily admitted by every white man in Mississippi that our public school system is designed primarily for the welfare of the white children of the state and incidentally for the negro children."[23] Kincannon could well have spoken for the rest of the South and for much of the nation.

The curriculum of the black schools, for the most part, followed that of their white counterparts. Students were taught reading, writing, history, geography, algebra, geometry, and so on. Northern whites who went to the South to teach tried to remake their students in the image of the dominant white group. They were paternalistic to a fault, believing it their obligation to change the culture of their students. The educational gospel was often one of black passivity and subordination to whites. Much to the chagrin of some of these teachers and missionaries, students sometimes abandoned these free schools in favor of those run by blacks even when they had to pay tuition fees.

Impressed by the intense desire of Southern blacks for literacy after emancipation, Booker T. Washington observed, "It was a whole race trying to go to school. Few were too young, and none too old, to make the attempt to learn."[24] In 1865, barely 5 percent of the black population was literate. Fifty years later, probably only 30 percent could not read or write at a basic level. An increasingly literate people with institutions of their own could not be contained, as the larger society would ultimately

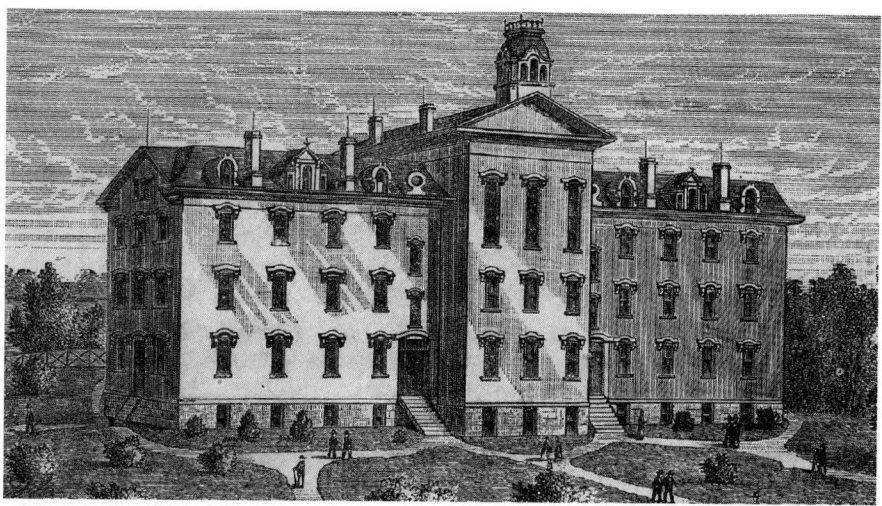
Wilberforce University in Ohio was chartered in 1856 as an all-black college.

discover. James K. Vardamann, the virulently racist politician from Mississippi, saw the implications all too well. "In educating the negro we implant in him all manner of aspirations and ambitions which we then refuse to allow him to gratify," Vardamann cautioned in 1899.[25]

Building upon the tradition established by free blacks before 1865, blacks also continued to create a wide range of fraternal and social welfare organizations. The Odd Fellows, a secret male lodge formed in 1843, boasted a membership of 285,000 in 1904. In 1864, the Colored Knights of Pythias of North America, South America, Europe, Asia, Africa, and Australia was established, followed by others such as the Mosaic Templars of America in 1882, and the Improved Benevolent and Protective Order of Elks of the World in 1899. Black women formed the Order of the Eastern Star and the Sisters of Calanthe. In addition to these fraternal organizations, blacks established scores of benevolent societies to meet the social needs of their membership. These were supplemented by black-controlled and black-operated hospitals, orphanages, and nursing homes.

In spite of these clear manifestations of internal energy, we should not exaggerate the degree to which blacks were able to improve their overall condition during the period. There were obvious limitations to what they could and did accomplish. Despite their creativity, determination, and aggressive spirit, blacks could not transform their condition measurably without the sustained assistance of the larger society and the organized state. The political economy would have had to undergo structural changes and a redistribution of power in order to create an equal place for black citizens. These changes were never contemplated

Freedmen's school

by those who exercised power in society. In fact, the federal, state, and local governments, as well as the judiciary, frequently stood in the way of black progress. Important sections of the white majority remained indifferent to the needs of blacks or actively collaborated in their oppression.

Notes

1. Lewis, *W. E. B. Du Bois*, 288.
2. Cited in Kevin Gaines, *Uplifting the Race: Black Leadership, Politics and Culture in the Twentieth Century* (Chapel Hill: University of North Carolina Press, 1996).
3. W. E. B. Du Bois, *The Philadelphia Negro: A Social Study* (reprint, Millwood, NY: Kraus-Thomson, 1973), 198–199.
4. Giddings, *When and Where I Enter*, 97.
5. Anna Julia Cooper, *A Voice from the South: Edited with an Introduction by Mary Helen Washington* (New York: Oxford, 1990), i–iii; Hazel Carby, *Reconstructing Womanhood: The Emergence of the Afro-American Woman Novelist* (New York: Oxford, 1987), 97.
6. Cooper, *A Voice from the South*, 31.
7. Ibid., 75.
8. See Mary Helen Washington's introduction to the above edition of *A Voice from the South*, li.
9. Cynthia Neverdon-Morton, *Afro-American Women of the South and the Advancement of the Race, 1895–1925* (Knoxville: University of Tennessee Press, 1989), 191.

10. Ann Firor Scott, "'Most Invisible of All': Black Women's Voluntary Organizations," *Journal of Southern History*, LVI:1 (February 1990), 12.
11. Willard B. Gatewood, *Aristocrats of Color: The Black Elite, 1880-1920* (Bloomington: University of Indiana Press, 1990), 246.
12. Evelyn Brooks Higginbotham, *Righteous Discontent: The Women's Movement in the Black Baptist Church, 1880–1920* (Cambridge: Harvard University Press, 1993), 41.
13. Ibid., 135.
14. Ibid., 144.
15. Jacqueline Jones, *Labor of Love, Labor of Sorrow: Black Women, Work and the Family, From Slavery to the Present* (New York: Vintage, 1986), 80.
16. Ibid., 92.
17. Tera W. Hunter, "Domination and Resistance: The Politics of Wage Household Labor in New South Atlanta," in Darlene Clark Hine, Wilma King, Linda Reed, eds., *We Specialize in the Wholly Impossible: A Reader in Black Women's History* (Brooklyn: Carlson Publishing Inc., 1995), 343.
18. John Sibley Butler, *Entrepreneurship and Self-Help Among Black Americans: A Reconsideration of Race and Economics* (Albany: State University of New York Press, 1991), 166.
19. Ibid.
20. James D. Anderson, *The Education of Blacks in the South, 1860–1935* (Chapel Hill: University of North Carolina Press, 1988), 82.
21. Ibid., 239–278.
22. Ibid., 13.
23. McMillen, *Dark Journey*, 72.
24. Anderson, *The Education of Blacks in the South*, 5.
25. McMillen, *Dark Journey*, 72.

Constructing an Identity: From Turner to Garvey

The search for and articulation of a black identity was one of the principal themes in the writings of black intellectuals during the nineteenth century. Recognizing the differences in history, culture, and ethnicity between themselves and whites, David Walker, Robert Young, Martin Delany, and others attempted to define a black sensibility and identity. The search for an appropriate nomenclature was one part of this process, and the ambivalent embrace of an African homeland represented another. These writers denounced slavery, racism, and the mistreatment of blacks and urged the peoples of African descent everywhere to unite, espouse a confident belief in their human possibilities, and assume control of their future.

These early black nationalists did not necessarily agree on the ingredients of a black identity. But all of them were conscious of their marginality in the United States and convinced that blacks needed to create and control their own institutions. There was also a growing and deepening sense of racial identification that transcended class differences and legal status, particularly in the years prior to the end of slavery. The years after 1863 were more complex, as an increasing number of fissures surfaced among blacks. Freedom, understandably, unleashed the energies of the people, improved their life chances to some extent, and generated all kinds of internal tensions. While Booker T. Washington, W. E. B. Du Bois, and others debated the strategies to be pursued to advance the black condition, some like Henry McNeal Turner concentrated on constructing and establishing the contours of a black identity in a society where whites exercised power and other peoples were socially marginalized.

The urge to define a black identity in a hostile white environment was not only understandable but compelling as well. But there was never any one black identity to be delineated, since the peoples of African descent were increasingly divided along class lines, generational cohorts, political perspectives, and phenotype, among other differences. Not everyone possessed the same level of political consciousness or embraced with the same intensity the pulls of a shared black history. While some individuals such as Bishop Turner espoused a strong emotional identification with Africa, others stressed their commonalties with white America.

An identity, to be sure, is self-constructed, although in some situations it can be imposed upon a people. Identities usually emerge as the inevitable consequence of common historical experiences and cultural moorings. The strands that comprise any identity are myriad, and a people's conception of who they are is never frozen. Identities are constructed and reconstructed as a people's needs, the sense of their history, and their vision of the future change. The construction of a black identity saw its first literate expression in the late eighteenth and the early nineteenth centuries. But the elaboration of the boundaries of this identity was a complex and ongoing process, judging by the competing ideas that were generated throughout the nineteenth century and later. The ideas that bear on the construction and shaping of a black identity espoused by Henry McNeal Turner, Marcus Garvey, and others provide some understanding of its complex ideological streams. These individuals, it should be stressed, did not create a collective black identity; they were the public articulators of ideas that had deep roots among many blacks of all social classes.

The struggle to construct a black identity included attempts to change the negative meanings that white society had imposed upon the color black, in contrast to the color white and its pantheon of positive attributes. The secular and religious symbols of the larger society privileged the "whiteness" of the Caucasian majority and devalued those of another hue. Even the Christian God was constructed in the image of whites, and the devil wore a black face. Acutely aware of the negative effects such religious representations had on blacks, Bishop Turner claimed that his God was "a Negro." This led a white publication, the *Observer,* to accuse the bishop in 1898 of "becoming demented."[1] Turner's response revealed why, in his judgment, it was necessary for blacks to envision a deity in their own image:

> We have as much right biblically and otherwise to believe that God is a Negro, as you buckra or white people have to believe that God is a fine looking, symmetrical and ornamented white man. For the bulk of you

and all the fool Negroes of the country believe that God is a white-skinned, blue-eyed, straight-haired, projecting-nosed, compressed-lipped and finely-robed white gentleman, sitting upon a throne somewhere in the heavens. Every race of people since time began who have attempted to describe their God by words, or by paintings, or by carvings, or by any other form or figure, have conveyed the idea that the God who made them and shaped their destinies was symbolized in themselves, and why should not the Negro believe that he resembles God as much as other people? We do not believe that there is any hope for a race of people who do not believe they look like God.[2]

Turner emphasized, "We certainly protest against God being a white man or against God being white at all. . . ." Blacks should emigrate to Africa, he suggested, because "as long as we remain among the whites, the Negro will believe that the devil is black and that he (the Negro) favors the devil, and that God is white and that he (the Negro) bears no resemblance to Him, and the effects of such a sentiment is contemptuous and degrading. . . ."[3]

Bishop Turner's position on the need for a people to envision their God in their own image had enormous political and religious ramifications. Blacks had Africanized the practice of Christianity in their own churches and meeting places, but its theology and symbols had remained largely untouched. Turner knew that blacks had to embrace a deity who looked like them if they were to construct a healthy identity independent of whites and embrace a form of Christianity that met their psychic and spiritual needs. Christian symbols had to be shorn of a white bias because of their deleterious effects on blacks.

The degree to which the views of this eminent bishop informed and shaped the practice of black Christianity at the turn of the century has not been established. The major black denominations such as the African Methodist Episcopal, the African Methodist Episcopal Zion, the Christian Methodist Episcopal, and the National Baptist Convention did not embrace the notion that God was black. But it is clear that some of the black Pentecostal groups did and incorporated this view into their catechisms. The Church of the Living God, which was founded in Arkansas in 1889, was one such body. Its catechism included the following:

> Was Jesus a member of the black race?
>   Yes. Matthew 1.
>   How do you know?
>   Because he was in the line of Abraham and David the king.
>   Is this assertion sufficient proof that Christ came of the black generation?
>   Yes.

Why?
Because David said he became like a bottle in the smoke. Psalm 119:83.[4]

During the early years of the twentieth century, members of a group commonly known as the Black Jews also believed that Jesus was black. They saw themselves as the authentic believers; others were fraudulent. Their leader, Prophet F. S. Cherry, was fond of offering a $1500 reward to any one of his followers who could prove otherwise. Members of the Moorish Science Temple of America (MST), which was founded in Newark, New Jersey, in 1913 by Timothy Drew (later Noble Drew Ali), shared this belief in a black deity. Ali, a North Carolinian, told his followers that he was both a prophet and an emissary from Allah. By 1925 there were temples in such cities as Detroit, Chicago, and Pittsburgh.

The MST's theology maintained that blacks "are not Negroes, Colored Folks, Black People or Ethiopians, because these names were given to slaves by slave holders."[5] Accordingly, blacks should embrace their identity as Moorish Americans. In effect, Ali developed a creolized version of Islam with black symbols and an eclectic theology. Although they were primarily Muslims, the faithful also saw themselves as disciples of Buddha, Jesus, and Confucius. Overall, the MST and its theology met the psychoreligious needs of those who found Christianity and its association with whites unacceptable.

Marcus Garvey, the nationalist and founder of the secular Universal Negro Improvement Association (UNIA), argued in the 1920s that blacks needed to see the deity in their own image. Since human beings were made in the image of their God, Garvey reasoned, then the God of the black people must share their color. Garvey railed against whites who used Christianity to serve their own needs, violating its principles. As he expressed it in 1923:

> The Negro is now accepting the religion of the real Christ, not the property-robbing, gold-stealing, diamond-exploiting Christ, but the Christ of Love, Justice and Mercy. The Negro wants no more of the white man's religion as it applies to his race, for it is a lie and a farce; it is a propaganda pure and simple to make fools of a race and rob the precious world, the gift of God to man, and to make it the exclusive home of pleasure, prosperity and happiness for those who have enough intelligence to realize that God made them masters of their fate and architects of their own destinies.[6]

In 1924, the Garveyites gathered in convention and proclaimed Christ the "Black Man of Sorrows" and the Blessed Virgin Mary the "Black Madonna." Those in attendance endorsed "The Idealization of God as a Holy Spirit, without physical form, but a Creature of imaginary semblance of the black race, being of like image and likeness."[7]

These positions did not mean that the Garveyites wanted to establish a new religion with its own dogma. Rather, they sought to redefine Christian imagery to meet their symbolic needs. Garvey thought that blacks needed "to see God through our own spectacles . . . we shall worship him through the spectacles of Ethiopia." He felt that if whites "say that God is white, this organization says that God is black; if they are going to make the angels beautiful white peaches from Georgia, we are going to make them beautiful black peaches from Africa."[8] The incongruity of a savior depicted as possessing the same phenotypical characteristics of the whites they blamed for their condition was evidently not lost on Garvey and the UNIA.

There were others, not necessarily Garveyites, who claimed that Christianity had had psychologically negative effects on blacks. The poet Countée Cullen, for example, lamented the fact that Christianity made him "quench my pride and cool my blood." Speaking for himself and presumably for other blacks, he complained:

> My conversion came high-priced,
> I belong to Jesus Christ . . .
> Lamb of God although I speak
> With my mouth thus, in my heart
> Do I play a double part . . .
> Wishing he I served were black . . . ?
> Not yet has my heart or head
> In the least way realized
> They and I are civilized.[9]

Although there was no organized "God is Black" movement in black America, the practice of Christianity in many black congregations reflected the culture of the faithful. Such features as spirit possession, shouts, and the call and response interaction between the preacher and the congregation were derived from African religious traditions. These practices sometimes frustrated ministers like Daniel Alexander Payne, a bishop of the African Methodist Episcopal Church, who wanted to cleanse Christian worship from such "fanaticism."[10] Some of this opposition was class based. A growing middle class saw such practices as afflictions of the ignorant masses, from whom they sought to distance themselves. But this was a misreading of the roots of such religious expression. As Zora Neale Hurston, the novelist and anthropologist, observed in the 1930s:

> . . . the Negro has not been Christianized as extensively as is generally believed. The great masses are still standing before their pagan altars and calling old gods by a new name . . . so the congregation is restored to its primitive altars under the new name of Christ. Then there is the expression known as "shouting" which is nothing more than a contin-

uation of the African "Possession" by the gods. The gods possess the body of a worshipper and he or she is supposed to know nothing of their actions until the god decamps. This is still prevalent in most Negro Protestant churches and is universal in Sanctified churches.[11]

Such beliefs and practices could not be easily exorcised. They were at the heart of a people's religious ethos and helped define an Africanity that set them apart from others in society.

The claim that the Christian God was black constituted a significant part of black cultural and religious nationalism. Although the proponents of such a view remained relatively small, they fit squarely within a black religious optic that maintained that Christianity should be refashioned to meet the needs of the peoples of African descent. Black Christians, regardless of their denominational identification, would have been quite familiar also with the important role that Africa played in their religious imagination.

Western Christians had at least two competing and contradictory visions of Africa and her peoples. In the first place, Africa was seen as a land populated largely by heathens and as such, it presented a challenge to Christians to fulfill their proselytizing mission. But not all Africans were seen as heathens historically. Westerners of the Middle Ages believed in the existence of Prester John, a fabulously wealthy ruler of Ethiopia. Not only was Prester John a Christian, but it was also thought that he would soon join his Western brothers in their struggles with the forces of Islam. The commonly used nomenclature "Ethiopia" referred to all of Africa, probably from the late Middle Ages or earlier. Africans were known in English literature and folklore as "Ethiops."

The second vision of Africa in Western Christendom was rooted in the expectation that Africans would cleanse Christianity of its practical imperfections and produce a purer faith. Many were grounded in this belief by a passage in Psalms 68: "Princes shall come out of Egypt; Ethiopia shall soon stretch forth her hands unto God." God's kingdom on Earth, it was expected, would be redeemed through the efforts of these princes. This Ethiopianism, as the belief in the prophecy was characterized, would help inform much black and white Christian eschatology, particularly during the nineteenth century and much later.

Black Christians, in particular, interpreted the prophecy to mean that Africa and Africans had a sacred destiny. But the nature of this destiny was not entirely clear. For one thing, nineteenth-century black Christians sought some understanding of why God had allowed their enslavement. The Episcopal priest Absalom Jones raised this question and speculated on its answer in a sermon he preached in 1808:

> It has always been a mystery why the impartial Father of the human race should have permitted the transportation of so many of our fellow

creatures to this country to endure all the miseries of slavery. . . . Perhaps his design was, that a knowledge of the gospel might be acquired by some of their descendants, in order that they might become qualified to be the messengers of it, to the land of their fathers.[12]

In this rendering, God may have permitted the suffering of blacks temporarily in order to promote a greater and more lasting good. Although the Reverend Jones did not claim emphatically that he knew God's design, others were not given to such doubt or temporizing. A deeply Christianized David Walker concluded in 1829, "a grovelling servile and abject submission to the lash of tyrants . . . are not the natural elements of the blacks, as the Americans try to make us believe; but these are misfortunes which God has suffered our fathers to be enveloped in for many ages, no doubt in consequence of their disobedience to their maker."[13] Writing in 1882, the historian George Washington Williams opined:

God often permits evil on the ground of man's free agency but he does not commit evil. The Negro of this country can turn to his Saxon brothers and say, as Joseph said to his brethren who wickedly sold him, 'As for you, you meant it unto evil but God meant it unto good'; after learning your arts and sciences, I might return to Egypt and deliver the rest of our brethren who are yet in the house of bondage.[14]

Henry McNeal Turner came to a similar conclusion. "I believe that God permitted the black man to be brought here and to serve a term of bondage to the white man for the black man's good," he ventured. Slavery, in God's design, allowed Africans "direct contact with the mightiest race that ever trod the face of the globe." But blacks would only remain in America "until God in His wisdom shall see it is time for us to move, and then I think the American nation will aid us in getting to Africa."[15]

Arguments such as these acknowledged a providential design for blacks. But they also provided an explanation for slavery, seeing it as an expression of God's will. This formulation could be interpreted as absolving whites of any responsibility for the enslavement of blacks since the institution was divinely ordained. For such black believers, this explanation helped them understand and accept the burdens that slavery imposed. But the providential design for blacks not only required the sacrifice of slavery, but it also compelled them to assume the task of "redeeming" and Christianizing Africa.

As in other instances, black Christians did not all subscribe to this explanation for slavery. The editor of the *New York Age*, T. Thomas Fortune, dismissed it contemptuously. "The talk about black people being brought to this country to prepare themselves to evangelize Africa is so much religious nonsense boiled down to a sycophantic platitude," he wrote in 1884. "The Lord who is eminently just, had no hand in their forcibly coming here, it was preeminently the work of the devil. Africa will have to be evangelized from *within, not from without.*[16] Marcus Garvey also denounced the view that the Christian God ordained slavery for blacks, preferring to blame blacks themselves for the institution. "That the Negro race became a race of slaves," he suggested, "was not the fault of God Almighty . . . it was the fault of the race." He thought that "sloth, neglect, indifference caused us to be slaves." But the race could rise again, because "confidence, conviction, action will cause us to be free men to-day."[17] The rejection of a religious explanation for slavery did not mean that an individual distanced himself from Africa or Africans or declined, in the parlance of the times, a responsibility for the "redemption" of that continent's peoples.

Although the principal thrust of Ethiopianism was religious, its claims rested on very negative assumptions about the African peoples. Westerners had long viewed African societies through an Eurocentric lens, finding their cultures "uncivilized." Black Americans were not immune to these cultural influences and saw it as their special obligation to "uplift" their ancestral brethren. This meant that Africans had to be Christianized and Westernized, or, more narrowly, Americanized. In the black imagination, Africans even desired and pleaded for this transformation of their condition. The Baptist missionary Thomas Johnson depicted Africans as imploring American blacks to:

"Come over and help us" is their cry,
"Come now, oh, do not pass us by,
We are seeking truth, we are seeking light,
We seek deliverance from dark night,
Can you who have the Gospel fail
To hear our Cry, our doleful wail?"[18]

The Christianization and "redemption" of Africa were not all inspired by the impulse of Ethiopianism. Some black Americans believed that a transformation of Africa's image would lead to a lessening of their own disabilities. In 1883, for example, the *AME Church Review* predicted: "Never will Africa's sons [in America] be honored until Africa herself sits among the civilized powers."[19] Not only was this an expression of enlightened self-interest, but it was also a charitable and misleading analysis of the reasons for the survival of American racism.

Regardless of the motivation, black American Christians shared the ancestral pulls of Africa. In acknowledging this, C. S. Brown, a North Carolina clergyman, proclaimed: "Africa is our land, our mission field by the natural right of heredity."[20] Similar sentiments were echoed by the AME in 1896. At its general conference that year, those in attendance agreed that "Africa is the largest and most important of the fields that lie before us . . . on account of the relationship that exists between our race and the inhabitants of the Dark Continent."[21] White denominations had sent black missionaries to Liberia from the 1820s. But it was not until 1878 that the AME became the first black denomination to establish African missions. The AME-Zion followed suit in 1880 and the Baptists three years later. By 1900, at least 110 blacks had served as missionaries in Africa, primarily under the auspices of these denominations. Women comprised almost one-third of these evangelists.

Support for these African missions strained the budgets of the denominations and congregations involved. The black denominations were never wealthy, and the missions competed with domestic needs for scarce resources. Still, many congregations made heroic sacrifices to support these ventures. They did so because of the genuine belief that African souls would not be saved otherwise. The president of the Louisiana Baptist Convention, for example, exhorted the faithful in 1885 to "consecrate" themselves "more fully to the work of saving the perishing millions of Africa."[22] Black women were central to the fund-raising efforts of their congregations, sponsoring bake sales and bazaars to help the cause.

In the process of helping Africa and Africans, many black Americans discovered themselves. In 1893, for example, the poet James T. Franklin wrote:

>Oh, send me home to Africa,
>Back across the sea,
>From America's cruel shores
>To my own country.[23]

Writing in 1914, another poet, Maurice N. Corbett, celebrated Africa's ancient kingdoms and predicted the political resurgence of the continent:

>Kingdoms and empires will they form
>In Afric's fertile bosom warm;
>Liberia will important grow;
>An empire great will be Congo;
>Ashantee's greatness will return;
>The Zulu's great distinction earn;
>Proud Abyssinia's lurid skies;
>To leading kingdom will arise.[24]

The increasing presence of Africa in the black imagination in the late nineteenth and early twentieth centuries raised anew the issue of the ingredients of a black identity. This issue was contested quite intensely on the terrain of nomenclature. Were blacks to be called Afro-

Americans, Colored, African, or just simply American? Should black organizations such as the AME retain "African" in their name or substitute the word "American"? This struggle over names had varied in intensity at different times during the nineteenth century. At bottom, it was a search for identity and an affirmation of difference from the larger white society.

The question of names was bitterly contested in the ranks of the AME church. In 1888, the Reverend C. C. Astwood suggested the elimination of the word "African" from the denomination's name because its efficacy ended "when the race became citizens of the United States, and accepted that citizenship." Astwood believed that by using the word "African" blacks ran the risk of accentuating their difference, helping to perpetuate "the odious discrimination which we have battled so long and so faithfully to destroy."[25]

The Reverend J. T. Jenifer did not agree. He accused Astwood and those who supported his position of being ashamed of their African heritage. Noting that white ethnic groups acknowledged their ancestral ties, Jenifer thundered:

> Why, then should the Negro of this country, with African blood and of African parentage, be ashamed of Africa? . . . Ashamed of Africa! The seat of the earliest civilization, the cradle of arts and sciences; the earliest nursery of the Church of God. Ashamed of the place where Abraham and Jesus went for refuge! Ashamed of the land of the Pyramids and the Ptolemies. . . . Ashamed of Africa![26]

The AME name survived, but the larger names controversy never died. The National Association of Colored Women's Clubs, for example, also divided over whether "Colored" or "Afro-American" should be a part of its nomenclature. The conflict would remain a recurrent part of black life as long as the struggle to affirm a positive identity continued in a society that did not always concede black people that right.

The writers associated with the Harlem Renaissance were not overly preoccupied with the names controversy. But individuals such as Claude McKay, Langston Hughes, and Countée Cullen focused on the historical experience of blacks, sometimes celebrating the emotional and spiritual ties with Africa. Hughes' poem, "Afro-American Fragment," was a nostalgic embrace of Africa:

> So long,
> So far away
> Is Africa.
> Not even memories alive
> Save those that history books create.
> Save those that songs

Beat back into the blood–
Beat out of blood with words sad-sung
In strange un-Negro tongue–
So long,
So far away is Africa.

Subdued and time-lost are the drums–
And yet, through some vast mist of race
There comes this song
I do not understand,
This song of atavistic land,
Of bitter yearnings lost, without a place–
So long,
So far away
Is Africa's
Dark face.

Countée Cullen also probed the meaning of Africa for the peoples of African descent in the timeless poem "Heritage":

What is Africa to me?
Copper sun or scarlet sea,
Jungle star or jungle track,
Strong bronzed men, or regal black
Women from whose loins I sprang
When the birds of Eden sang?
One three centuries removed
From the scenes his fathers loved,
Spicy grove, cinnamon tree,
What is Africa to me?

Hughes, in the poem "Negro," evoked the travails of the black past to affirm an identity that was both black and African:

I am a Negro:
Black as the night is black,
Black like the depths of my Africa.

I've been a slave:
Caesar told me to keep his door-steps clean.
I brushed the boots of Washington.

I've been a worker
Under my hand the pyramids arose
I made mortar for the Woolworth Building.

I've been a singer:
All the way from Africa to Georgia
I carried my sorrow songs.
I made ragtime.

I've been a victim:
The Belgians cut off my hands in the Congo.
They lynch me still in Mississippi.

I am a Negro:
Black as the night is black,
Black like the depths of my Africa.

Hughes also claimed his place as an American in "I, Too, Sing America":

I am the darker brother.
They send me to eat in the kitchen
When company comes,
But I laugh,
And eat well,
And grow strong.

Tomorrow,
I'll be at the table
When company comes.
Nobody'll dare
Say to me,
"Eat in the kitchen,"
Then.

Besides,
They'll see how beautiful I am
And be ashamed,–
I, too, am America.[27]

GARVEYISM

The contest over names, and the affirmation of Africa in the written word, represented the quest for an identity among the middle class and the educated. But the masses of the people did not remain untouched by similar pulls. Those who embraced Marcus Garvey's brand of black nationalism responded to the same pulls. Garvey was born in rural Jamaica in 1887, when the island was still under British colonial domination. The product of peasant stock, young Garvey was socialized into the colonial ethos that privileged whites and devalued the peoples of African descent. Attracted to the world of books, he read the ones available and "gathered inspiration" from them, as he expressed it.[28] Garvey embraced Booker T. Washington's philosophy for black uplift and created the Universal Negro Improvement Association (UNIA) in 1914. According to Garvey, the association was nonpolitical. Among its objectives, the UNIA sought "to promote the spirit of race pride and love; reclaim the fallen of the race, administer to and assist the needy, assist in civilizing the backward tribes of Africa and establish universities, colleges and secondary schools for the further education and culture of the boys and girls of the race."[29]

These goals reflected a desire to raise the racial consciousness of the peoples of African descent and a commitment to improve the condition of the dispossessed. On the other hand, they reflected the prevailing Western condescension toward Africa and Africans and the degree to which Garvey, like many of his contemporaries, accepted the negative depictions of his ancestors constructed by Europeans and others. Garvey was the child of British colonialism, and he was never able to exorcise his belief in the superiority of European cultures when contrasted with those of the African societies from which blacks in the Americas descended.

Garvey's attempt to gain support for his organization and the cause it represented realized only a modest success in Jamaica. The fledgling organization devoted its energies primarily to humanitarian concerns as well as to educational uplift. The UNIA sponsored adult-education classes, debates, and lectures. Short of funds, Garvey visited the United States in 1916 to seek donations and to learn firsthand about Booker T. Washington's Tuskegee experiment. This visit was destined to have a transforming effect on Garvey's philosophy and the nature and future of the UNIA.

Garvey never met the Wizard of Tuskegee, since Washington died in 1915. Garvey, however, soon learned that the Washingtonian philosophy of vocational education and political accommodation that he admired from a distance was seriously deficient in its ability to meet the needs of a changing black America. The America of the First World War seemed to require individuals with the skills necessary to survive in an industrial economy, and an increasingly hostile racial climate compelled a new generation of blacks to participate actively in the political process and to demand their rights as citizens.

Establishing his base in Harlem, Garvey visited Pittsburgh, Baltimore, Philadelphia, Washington, and Chicago, giving speeches and soliciting funds for his work in Jamaica. The fund-raising effort met with only scant success, but Garvey learned a great deal about the conditions prevailing in urban black America and realized that he could become a leader of the dispossessed and the powerless. In late 1917, he started a branch of the UNIA in Harlem and began his advocacy of an aggressive stance against white racism. The race riots that occurred in East St. Louis, Illinois, in July 1917 and an increasing disillusionment with the status quo had a radicalizing effect on Garvey and an emerging number of new black American leaders.

Although black spokespersons recognized the centrality of race in the divisions that plagued the nation, they were not always in agreement on the nature of a black response to injustice and separate treatment. Hubert Harrison, for example, advocated a broad-based assault on segregation, lynching, disfranchisement, Jim Crow laws, and other evils. A native of St. Croix, Harrison came to New York in 1900 and embraced socialism as one means of transforming America. By 1917, he had come to espouse a nationalist or "race-first" philosophy, maintaining: "Any man today who aspires to lead the Negro race must set squarely before his face the idea of 'Race First.'"[30] Harrison founded the Liberty League to give organizational expression to his ideas, but it met with little success and soon disappeared. On the other hand, the socialists A. Philip Randolph and Chandler Owen represented an alternative vision, one rooted in the destruction of capitalism and the creation of a nonracial and just social order.

While the National Association for the Advancement of Colored People (NAACP) appealed to the more privileged blacks, Garvey's UNIA and those who shared the views of Hamilton, Randolph, and such emerging spokespersons as Cyril Briggs and W. A. Domingo drew their primary support from urban residents. In general, however, these leaders were also concerned with the fate of blacks in the diaspora, particularly those under European colonial domination in Africa. Inspired by emerging pan-Africanist ideals, these men supported the cause of self-determination of blacks everywhere, sometimes founding organizations to promote their cause. W. E. B. Du Bois supported these initiatives although he doubted in 1918 whether the "principle of self-determination" could be "wholly applied to semi-civilized peoples." In his opinion, the African colonies that Germany lost at the end of the war "should be guided by the chiefs and western educated elite of Africa, educated Afro-Americans and the independent Negro governments of Abyssinia, Liberia and Hayti."[31]

The pan-Africanist pull, although largely confined to the Northern black elite, was a positive development. It suggested that blacks either continued to embrace a healthy emotional connection with Africa or were developing one, in spite of their own domestic travails. On the other hand, some of them, such as Du Bois, had doubts about the capacity of African peoples to govern themselves, betraying a paternalism toward Africa that was not qualitatively different from the view held by whites.

But while black elites shared some emotional identification with Africa, most of their energies were consumed by their own domestic struggles. Before Garvey's advent, no one had attempted to organize the people to determine and shape the kinds of changes they desired. His was primarily a movement of urban residents in the North and the South, with a high representation of workers, as well as marginal entrepreneurs, the poor, and the unemployed. Its energy came from these people, the style of the organization and the goals it articulated bore their imprint and encapsulated their dreams. The coal-black and charismatic Marcus Garvey spoke their language, voiced their passions, convinced them of their potential organized strength, and created visions of a great and powerful race. Given the problems that black America confronted, Garvey's timing was impeccable.

Short in stature but of a robust build, Marcus Garvey's persona exuded a pugnacious confidence. Calling himself a self-made man, Garvey later attributed his "success in life to 'grit,' determination and refusal to bow to anyone but God."[32] An eloquent and spell-binding speaker, Garvey electrified his audiences in the manner of an inspirational preacher. In time, his followers proclaimed him "a black Moses." Not everyone, to be sure, reacted positively to the Jamaican. Du Bois dismissed him as possessing "very serious defects of temperament and training." He found Garvey to be "dictatorial, domineering, inordinately vain and very suspicious."[33]

Du Bois lacked Garvey's rapport with the mass of black people. While Garvey's personal qualities were enormously important in advancing his appeal, the nature of his message was more significant. To a people buffeted by a vicious racism and whose human worth was constantly assaulted, Garvey promoted the doctrine of race pride and the appreciation of self. "No man can convince me contrary to my belief," he asserted, "because my belief is founded upon a hard and horrible experience, not a personal experience, but a racial experience. The world has made being black a crime, and I have felt it in common with men who suffer like me, and instead of making it a crime I hope to make it a virtue."[34]

Garvey doubted whether black Americans could ever become autonomous in a nation where they constituted a minority. Their destiny was linked to the liberation of Africans on the African continent. As he put it in 1919:

> Negroes have got to win their freedom just as the Russians and the Japanese have done—by revolution and bloody fighting. Negroes in the United States cannot do this. They would be hopelessly outnumbered and it would be foolish to attempt it. But in Africa, where there are over four hundred million Negroes, we can make the white man eat his salt.[35]

Garveyism 97

Marcus Garvey (1887–1940) during the 1922 UNIA convention parade.

Africa was the place where blacks could best realize their human possibilities. Garvey predicted that if "the Negro were to live in this Western Hemisphere for another five hundred years he would still be outnumbered by other races who are prejudiced against him." Consequently, "the future of the Negro . . . outside of Africa, . . . spells ruin and disaster."[36]

Garvey wanted to construct a "nation" for blacks that transcended geographic boundaries. He emphasized that the UNIA "speaks in the language of building government: of building political power and all that goes with it."[37] Assuming the trappings of a nation without borders, the UNIA adopted a red, black, and green flag and a national anthem, and promulgated the Declaration of Rights of the Negro Peoples of the World. The declaration urged "the various governments of the World to accept and acknowledge the Negro Representatives who shall be sent to the said governments to represent the general welfare of the Negro peoples of the world."[38] The UNIA's ambassadors met with mixed receptions in the countries to which they were assigned, partly because the UNIA did not represent a nation in the traditional sense and partly for other political and racial reasons. One British official who opposed recognition of the UNIA believed that recognition would create a loss of confidence by West Indian colonies in the mother country since the UNIA "has a record of fraud, sedition and incitement to violence."[39]

By couching his appeal in racial terms, Garvey also linked the struggles of blacks in the United States to those of their brothers and sisters in other parts of the world. The UNIA, with its branches in Africa, the Caribbean, North America, and Latin America, was the first international organization, as opposed to a movement, of the peoples of African descent. Not only was it organized and led by blacks, but its inspiration derived from a race consciousness that transcended national boundaries and that had threatening implications for American whites and the European powers in Africa and the Caribbean. Marcus Garvey inspired his black followers to believe in themselves and to reject the white man's negative definition of them. To many, Garveyism had all the ingredients of a new religion. In fact, Garvey in 1920 expressed the view: "The masses of the race absorb the doctrines of the UNIA with the same eagerness with which the masses in the days of the supremacy of imperial Rome accepted Christianity. The people seem to regard the movement in the light of a new religion."[40]

The religious-like fervor of Garvey's race-based ideology does not fully explain the success of the UNIA in becoming a mass movement. In 1925, Garvey claimed with some exaggeration that the UNIA had 6 million members worldwide. There were probably about 1 million members in the United States at the time. In addition to the racial appeal of the organization, many embraced the UNIA's commitment to improve the material conditions of Africa's children everywhere. Garvey urged blacks, as members of a "Mighty Race," to transform their condition through their own efforts and to construct "a tradition of success." The vision of an oppressed group rising and controlling its own economic destiny and altering the power relationships in society had a compelling appeal. As Garvey expressed it: "If we are . . . to become a great national force, we must start business enterprises of our own; we must build ships and start trading with ourselves between America, the West Indies, and Africa."[41] This was a classic expression of black economic nationalism, although never before was it promoted so aggressively.

The UNIA opened its first restaurant in 1919, and Garvey announced its plans to found a shipping line, the Black Star Line. This black-owned enterprise was intended to promote trade among the constituent parts of the black world. In order to raise the necessary funds, the UNIA invited the black public to purchase shares in the shipping line. Emphasizing that the venture would allow its participants to "climb the great ladder of industrial and commercial progress," Garvey and the shipping line's business managers traveled across the United States urging blacks to purchase $5 shares in the company. On September 17, the UNIA announced the purchase of its first ship, the *Yarmouth*.

The purchase of the *Yarmouth* was an exercise in misjudgment. The ship was old and needed expensive refurbishing. It made three trips to the Caribbean before it was taken out of service for unpaid debts and ordered sold by a United States marshal in 1921. The two other ships in the Black Star Line-the *Shadyside* and the *Kanawha*–also proved to be bad investments. Burdened by debts and the victim of mismanagement and corruption, the Black Star Line was a failure. Its demise in 1922 did not represent the death of the ideas and dreams that inspired it; rather, its problems reflected the inexperience, venality, and poor judgment of those associated with the venture. The concept of black economic nationalism, although shaken, did not die. In later years, organizations such as the Nation of Islam would achieve the realization of those dreams.

Still, any success that the Black Star Line achieved would not have altered the economic condition of most black Americans. Substantial improvements in the economic realities of blacks required structural changes in the economic arrangements of the nation and, with the exception of the socialists, few persons were willing to contemplate that prospect. Black economic nationalism promoted the economic interests of a minority that was economically marginalized, but it did not address the larger structures that threatened to keep blacks permanently dispossessed.

In addition to its economic initiatives, the UNIA embraced other programs for the improvement of the black condition, nationally and internationally. Drawing upon a long tradition of black nationalist sentiment to "redeem" Africa, Garvey wanted some pioneering blacks to go to Africa to assist in the development of the continent. Although some members of the UNIA were willing to respond to this appeal, no one actually went to Africa under its sponsorship. The financial problems that befell the organization and its other internal difficulties prevented the accomplishment of that dream, even in a limited way. Since most black African countries were under colonial rule, their local leaders were hardly in a position to welcome black Americans as "redeemers." Even the quasi-independent nation of Liberia vacillated on the question before firmly opposing it in 1924.

The UNIA reached its organizational apogee in the United States in 1921, boasting a total of 859 branches.[42] The organization's first international conference, held the previous year, attracted 25,000 persons. But with success came difficulties as well. The United States government launched a campaign to destroy the largest black organization that the nation had yet seen. Competing organizations such as the NAACP saw Garveyites as separatists, a stance that conflicted with the politics of integration. W. E. B. Du Bois, for example, was of the opinion that "Marcus Garvey is, without a doubt, the most dangerous enemy of the Negro race in America and in the world. He is either a lunatic or a traitor."[43]

There were other criticisms of the movement, albeit less vitriolic. Some of it came from women. The UNIA, unlike some other contemporary organizations, accorded women, in theory, a place in its structure. They directed women's auxiliaries and the Universal African Black Cross Nurses consisted of women. Women held administrative positions in the organization and its constitution gave them equal rights with men. Still, there was no question that women, in practice, were subordinated to men. One woman, Madame M. L. T. De Mena, expressed her concern that "women were given to understand that they were to remain in their places, which meant nothing more than Black Cross Nurse or a general secretary of a division."[44] Amy Jacques Garvey, the second wife of Marcus Garvey and an influential figure in the organization, was not at all pleased with the status of women in the organization. She argued:

> If the United States Senate and Congress can open their doors to white women, we serve notice on our men that Negro women will demand equal opportunity to fill any position in the Universal Negro Improvement Association or anywhere else without discrimination because of sex. We are very sorry if it hurts your old-fashioned tyrannical feelings, and we not only make the demand but we intend to enforce it.[45]

Amy Jacques Garvey seems to have been the most articulate and outspoken voice in behalf of women in the UNIA. She was the editor of the Women's Page of the association's journal, the *Negro World*. As a feminist voice, however, she confronted the cult of masculinity that had long been a feature of black nationalist organizations and the male-centered ideology upon which they invariably stood. In 1925, Amy Jacques Garvey fired a salvo at the men who ran her embattled organization and presumably at black men in general:

> We are tired of hearing Negro men say, "There is a better day coming" while they do nothing to usher in the day. We are becoming so impatient that we are getting in the front ranks and serve notice that we will brush aside the halting, cowardly Negro leaders, and with prayer on our lips and arms prepared for any fray, we will press on and on until victory is ours.[46]

This was a critique of the failures of black leadership, and it probably reflected Amy Garvey's frustration at the declining fortunes of the UNIA. If the men proved inadequate to meet the challenges facing the peoples of African descent, then the women would push them aside. She threatened:

> Africa must be for Africans, and Negroes everywhere must be independent, God being our helper and guide. Mr. Black Man watch your step! Ethiopia's queens will reign again and her Amazons protect her shores and people. Strengthen your shaking knees and move forward, or we will displace you and lead on to victory and glory.[47]

The UNIA and Marcus Garvey also sowed the seeds of their problems. In a classic misjudgment, Garvey held a meeting with the acting imperial wizard of the Ku Klux Klan in Atlanta in June 1922. The two men spoke for two hours, each man discussing the philosophy of his organization. Garvey's opponents denounced Garvey for meeting with a white supremacist, and his popularity suffered a major decline. In defending his actions, Garvey declared:

> I regard the Klan, Anglo-Saxon clubs and White American societies, as far as the Negro is concerned, as better friends of the race than all other groups of hypocritical whites put together. I like honesty and fair play. You may call me a Klansman if you will, but, potentially, every white man is a Klansman . . . and there is no use lying about it.[48]

Garvey's meeting with the Klan member and his defense of the Klan helped to ignite a "Garvey Must Go" campaign among some blacks. The NAACP and the editors of the *Messenger* were vitriolic in their assaults on the Jamaican. In ugly outbursts, Chandler Owen, a journalist and socialist, described Garvey as an "ignoramus," and an editorial in the *Messenger* called him "A Supreme Negro Jamaican Jackass." Writing in the *Messenger*, Robert Bagnall, an NAACP official, denounced Garvey as:

> a Jamaican Negro of unmixed stock, squat, stocky, fat and sleek, with protruding jaws, and heavy jowls, small bright pig-like eyes and rather bull-dog-like face. Boastful, egotistic, tyrannical, intolerant, cunning, shifty, smooth and suave, avaricious; . . . as adept as a cuttle-fish in

beclouding an issue he cannot meet, prolix in the n'th degree in devising new schemes to gain the money of poor ignorant Negroes; gifted at self-advertisement, without shame in self-laudation, promising ever, but never fulfilling, without regard for veracity, a lover of pomp and tawdry finery and garish display, a bully with his own folk but servile in the presence of the Klan, a sheer opportunist and demagogic charlatan.[49]

These venomous attacks on Garvey revealed deep fissures between some blacks of West Indian descent and some black American elites. A. Philip Randolph believed, "We are justified in asking the question, that if Garvey is seriously interested in establishing a Negro nation why he doesn't begin with Jamaica, West Indies?"[50] Randolph was also certain that the Garvey movement

> will not only not liberate Africa, but it will set back the clock of Negro progress by cutting the Negro workers away from the proletarian liberation movement expressed in the worker's efforts, political and economic, to effect solidarity, class consciousness, by setting them against, instead of joining them with, the white worker's struggle for freedom.

Although he opposed Garvey, the Jamaican socialist and *Messenger* editorial board member W. A. Domingo chastised the *Messenger* for its anti-West Indian stance. "I certainly maintain," he wrote, "that to oppose Garvey on the score of his birthplace is to confess inability to oppose him formidably on any other ground."[51] Domingo later resigned from the *Messenger's* board.

Garvey did not fully appreciate the passion that his meeting with the acting imperial wizard of the Klan engendered. The meeting united his opponents and provided the occasion for the open expression of anti-Garvey sentiment of many stripes. His Jamaican ancestry was one issue, but so were his ideological positions and his threatening popularity among the urban masses. With the UNIA's financial affairs grossly mismanaged, the U.S. government capitalized on this anti-Garvey fervor and arrested him on dubious charges of mail fraud. Several prominent middle-class blacks including Chandler Owen, as well as Robert Bagnall and William Pickens of the NAACP's leadership, wrote to the U.S. attorney general, urging him to "vigorously and speedily push the government's case against Marcus Garvey." They wanted him to "disband and extirpate" Garvey's "vicious movement." Garvey was incensed by the letter, describing it as "the greatest bit of treachery and wickedness that any group of Negroes could be capable of."[52] He was convicted in 1923, imprisoned, and deported to Jamaica in 1927. "I am here because I dared to tell the Negro that the time has come for him to lift up his head and be a man," Garvey complained in 1923 as he languished in jail.

Garvey's legal problems and his eventual deportation constituted major blows for the Universal Negro Improvement Association and what it represented. Many of the branches survived for a time. But the ideas that gave the movement life could not be destroyed and would help animate other leaders and movements worldwide. Garveyism failed to achieve its practical goals, but its importance in the history of blacks resided elsewhere. The UNIA gave to its members an abiding belief in their possibilities, made them proud of their race and ancestry, and promised them a future that they could create, shape, and control. Garveyism gave to the black downtrodden everywhere a sense of their own power and a faith in the possibility of improvements in their material and political circumstances.

Garvey, to be sure, was anathema to an insecure middle class that was embarrassed by his bombast, rhetoric, undisguised appeals to race pride, and flirtation with racial separation. That thousands of black workers and the poor responded to the UNIA's message, rejecting the appeals of integrationist black organizations, frightened the middle class. By denouncing Garvey and by cooperating with a government openly hostile to Garvey in order to silence him, some members of the black middle class failed to realize that they shared more with their working-class brethren than they did with their common oppressors. But this was merely a stage in a people's evolution; these wounds healed in time, and Garvey's ideas were repackaged to suit the needs of a later generation.

Many blacks who never doubted the righteousness of their claim to be American also opposed Garvey's back-to-Africa schemes, as they had done the others before him. James Weldon Johnson, a literary scholar and activist, thought "the overwhelming majority of thoughtful American Negroes" rejected such appeals because it reminded them of earlier attempts by whites to remove them from the nation. The NAACP and other blacks, Johnson asserted, saw America as their home and rejected Garvey's "central idea" that "this is a white man's country, a country in which the Negro has no place, no right, no chance, no future."[53]

The search for a black self was, in many respects, masculinist in its thrust and rhetoric. By asserting a pugnacious confidence in themselves and their ancestry, black men sought to recover a "manhood" that some thought had been wounded by American racism. Black men manifested a tendency to conflate their identity and struggles as men with those of blacks as a people. But black women's voices were never muted as the writings of Anna Cooper, Frances Harper, and others clearly attested.

Still, the process of constructing an identity, whatever its texture, was incomplete during these years. The process continued as new generations redefined its nature and contours. There were contradictions along the way as well. Madame C. J. Walker amassed a fortune selling hair straighteners at a time when some spoke about a black God, claimed their blackness, and responded to Garveyism. Many of the proponents of a liberating blackness ignored the sexism in their ranks. But struggles for self-definition, as is true of other battles, are never easy. Nor are they immune to contradictory expressions. For black Americans, the struggle for blackness was a struggle for a people's soul.

Notes

1. John H. Bracey Jr., August Meier, and Elliott Rudwick, eds., *Black Nationalism in America* (New York: Bobbs-Merrill Co., 1970), 154.
2. Ibid.
3. Ibid., 155.
4. Gayraud S. Wilmore, *Black Religion and Black Radicalism: An Interpretation of the Religious History of Afro-American People* (2nd edition, New York: ORBIS Books, 1983), 153–154.
5. Mattias Gardell, *In the Name of Elijah Muhammad: Louis Farrakhan and the Nation of Islam* (Durham: Duke University Press, 1996), 37.
6. Tony Martin, *Race First: The Ideological and Organizational Struggles of Marcus Garvey and the Universal Negro Improvement Association* (Dover, MA: Majority Press, 1986), 71.
7. Ibid., 70.
8. Levine, "Marcus Garvey and the Politics of Revitalization," in Franklin and Meier, *Black Leaders,* 124.
9. St. Clair Drake, "Hide My Face? The Literary Renaissance," in Uya, *Black Brotherhood,* 196.
10. Sterling Stuckey, *Slave Culture: Nationalist Theory and the Foundations of Black Culture* (New York: Oxford, 1987), 95.
11. Ibid., 97.
12. Albert Raboteau, *A Fire in the Bones: Reflections on African-American Religious History* (Boston: Beacon Press, 1995), 45.
13. David Walker, *David Walker's Appeal to the Colored Citizens of the World,* introduction by James Turner (Baltimore: Black Classics Press, 1993), 41.
14. George Washington Williams, *History of the Negro Race in America 1619–1880,* 2 vols. (repr. New York: Bergman Publishers, 1988), I: 113–114.
15. John W. Cell, *The Highest Stage of White Supremacy: The Origins of Segregation in South Africa and the American South* (Cambridge: Cambridge University Press, 1982), 35–36.
16. Ibid., 50.
17. Levine, "Marcus Garvey and the Politics of Revitalization," in Franklin and Meier, *Black Leaders,* 17.
18. Montgomery, *Under Their Own Vine and Fig Tree,* 219.
19. George M. Fredrickson, *Black Liberation: A Comparative History of Black Ideologies in the United States and South Africa* (New York: Oxford, 1995), 75.
20. Montgomery, *Under Their Own Vine and Fig Tree,* 218.
21. Ibid., 217.
22. Ibid., 222.
23. Berry and Blassingame, *Long Memory,* 412–413.
24. Ibid., 413.
25. Stuckey, *Slave Culture,* 237.
26. Ibid., 238.
27. For poems by Hughes, see Langston Hughes, *Selected Poems of Langston Hughes* (New York: Vintage Books, 1974).

28. Robert Hill, ed., *The Marcus Garvey and Universal Negro Improvement Association Papers,* vol. 1 (Berkeley: University of California Press, 1981), XL.
29. Judith Stein, *The World of Marcus Garvey* (Baton Rouge: Louisiana State University Press, 1986), 30.
30. Ibid., 45.
31. Ibid., 51.
32. Hill, *The Marcus Garvey . . . Papers,* XL.
33. Ibid., XXIII.
34. Martin, *Race First,* 23.
35. Fredrickson, *Black Liberation,* 155.
36. Ibid., 155.
37. Martin, *Race First,* 42.
38. Ibid., 45.
39. Ibid., 49.
40. Hill, *The Marcus Garvey . . . Papers,* XXXVI.
41. Stein, *The World of Marcus Garvey,* 64.
42. Martin, *Race First,* 13.
43. .Ibid., 273.
44. Giddings, *When and Where I Enter,* 194.
45. Ibid., 195.
46. Ibid.
47. Ibid.
48. Anderson, *A. Philip Randolph,* 130.
49. Ibid., 132.
50. Ibid., 133.
51. Ibid., 134.
52. Ibid., 136–137.
53. James Weldon Johnson, *Black Manhattan* (New York: Knopf, 1930), 258.

The Generation of 1917

On July 28, 1917, some 10,000 blacks participated in a protest demonstration in New York City. Marching down Fifth Avenue, the protesters carried banners proclaiming their grievances and enjoining the nation to live up to its promise of liberty and justice for all of its citizens. "Your hands are full of blood" read one long banner, and "Give me a chance to live" pleaded another. This impressive demonstration, silent except for the beat of drums, represented a watershed in the nature of black protest after emancipation. Blacks had taken to the streets in unprecedented numbers to claim their birthright, helping to chart a new era in the long tradition of resistance.

The Silent Protest Parade, as it came to be called, dramatized a people's unhappiness with their condition in society and their recognition that changes had to be implemented. A leaflet circulated at the march expressed this sentiment clearly:

> We march because the growing consciousness and solidarity of race, coupled with sorrow and discrimination, have made us one, a union that may never be dissolved. . . . We march because we are thoroughly opposed to Jim Crow cars, Segregation, Discrimination, Lynching, and the host of evils that are forced upon us. . . . We march because we want our children to live in a better land and enjoy fairer conditions than have been our lot.[1]

The dignified and peaceful march for "fairer conditions" contrasted rather vividly with the violence that some whites had routinely employed against blacks since emancipation. The brutal attacks on free blacks after 1863 did not represent a fundamental departure from past practice. Slaveowners had enjoyed enormous private powers of discipline over their slaves, although only a few murdered their human property. The preemancipation social system had an arsenal of private and public mechanisms to keep slaves in thrall, so mob violence was not necessary to bolster white domination. Still, violence and coercion were the foundations upon which slavery rested. Seen in this light, the postemancipation mobs were merely exercising the kind of power over blacks that many whites had always claimed to be their right.

In order to establish the context in which the Silent Protest Parade occurred and the degree of change in black temper that it represented, this chapter details the nature of white violence against blacks since emancipation and describes the nature of their responses. The chapter argues that around 1917, a new generation of blacks emerged who were more insistent in their demand for justice and that from then on, the style of protest in black America was more vigorous, sustained, and multifaceted.

WHITE VIOLENCE

White assaults on blacks, particularly violence associated with lynch mobs, became more widespread after the 1880s, paralleling the passage of the Jim Crow segregation laws. By 1893, its incidence led one white Methodist bishop to observe that the murder of blacks "is not so extraordinary an occurrence to need explanation; it has become so common that it no longer surprises."[2] The victims of these outrages could be anyone who aroused the wrath of the white populace. Blacks who violated the etiquette of deference to whites or were accused of rape or thievery were singled out for special attention. In an address to the State Agricultural Society of Georgia in 1897, a white woman proclaimed, "If it takes a lynching to protect women's dearest possession from drunken, ravening human beasts, then I say lynch a thousand a week if it becomes necessary."[3] The allegation that a black man raped a white woman was guaranteed to inflame emotions.

There was probably a higher incidence of sexual assaults by white men on black women than those alleged by black men on white women. But this did not arouse the passions of the white guardians of morality and social order. Ida Wells-Barnett, the staunch defender of black womanhood and an indefatigable crusader against lynching, noted in her autobiography that the "rape of helpless Negro girls and women, which began in slavery days, still continued without hindrance, check or reproof from church, state, or press" in the South during the heyday of lynching.[4] Fannie Barrier Williams, a New Yorker and a member of the Chicago Women's Club, reminded the women gathered at the World

Silent protest parade on Fifth Avenue in New York City, in response to the East Saint Louis race riots.

Columbian Expedition in 1893 that white men sexually abused black women with impunity. She pleaded for the protection of these women. "I do not want to disturb the serenity of this conference by suggesting why this protection is needed and the kind of man against whom it is needed," she declared. Anna Julia Cooper agreed. She knew "the painful, patient, and silent toil of mothers to gain title to the bodies of their daughters."[5]

The increased incidence of lynching in the 1880s and continuing with ebbs and flows for the next five decades represented the desperate attempts by some whites to maintain control over an increasingly aggressive and mobile black population. Why these attempts to preserve white supremacy and a racial hierarchy assumed such horrific forms is still imperfectly understood and remains a matter for debate among historians and others. Lynch mobs manifested a bloodthirstiness and a passion for a frenzied and highly ritualized infliction of pain on its victims suggestive of a psychological disorder among the participants. The *Chicago Defender*, a black newspaper, described a lynching that occurred at Dyersburg, Tennessee, in 1917 as follows:

> Bound to an iron post by the most savage fiends in existence on the face of the globe or even in the depths of hell below, Scott stood one-half hour, while men heated pokers and s[m]oothing irons until they were

Ida B. Wells

white with heat and were as fiery as the flames as they heated them. Scott lay flat on his face beneath the yoke of the iron post. Children on the outskirts of the mob played merrily on and their voices could be heard above the hubbub of the mob. Then a red streak shot out and the holder began to bore out the prisoner's eyes. Scott moaned. The pokers were worked like an auger, that is, they were twisted round and round.

The smell of burning flesh permeated the atmosphere, a pungent, sickening odor telling those who failed to get good vantage points what their eyes could not see. Smoothing irons were searing the flesh. Swish. Once, twice, three times a red hot iron dug gaping places in Lation Scott's back and sides.[6]

Lynching was not confined to the South, nor were blacks the sole victims. Between 1880 and 1930, 3,220 blacks and 723 whites were lynched in the Southern states, with the greatest incidence occurring in the Deep South and Texas.[7] In the West, where few blacks resided, there were 447 white casualties and 38 black ones during the same period. W. Fitzhugh Brundage, an astute student of lynching, notes that 85 percent of all lynch victims in the South were black, while 83 percent of those killed outside the South and the border states were white. He finds that "the proportion of lynching victims in the South who were white decreased from 32 percent to 9 percent" between 1880 and 1930. Lynching, according to Brundage, "had become primarily a southern and racial phenomena" by the end of the nineteenth century.[8]

Lynching and other forms of white violence help to explain black migration from the South in the late nineteenth century and the first decades of the twentieth. But there were other reactions. Black newspapers frequently led the way in denouncing mob violence and served as a vehicle for the expression of the anger of the black citizenry. John L. Mitchell Jr., editor of the *Richmond Planet*, was one of the most outspoken opponents of lynching. His newspaper described incidents of lynching in Virginia and published angry letters from his readers. In 1891, Mitchell said it was the duty of blacks to "howl, yes, howl loudly, until the American people hear our cries."[9] Later that year, his pen dripped with a bitter humor: "Southern white folks have gone to roasting Negroes, we presume the next step will be to eat them."[10]

Crusading black newspapers ran the risk of having their presses and buildings destroyed by enraged whites. When the *Free Speech and Headlight*, a Memphis newspaper, published Ida B. Wells's (Ida Wells-Barnett after 1895) investigative report on lynching in 1892, a mob wrecked the building in which the newspaper was housed. But this act did not silence Wells's voice. The *New York Age* reprinted her article, and she went on to become one of the best-known critics of lynching and an advocate for a federal statute making it illegal.

While the press sought to raise the nation's consciousness against such atrocities, black churches and civic organizations were not silent. Preachers denounced the atrocities and, in some cases, organized demonstrations against the perpetrators. Such actions ran the risk of arousing greater white animus and could be employed only sparingly and after careful deliberation. On occasion, black clergymen, their white counterparts, and civic leaders met to condemn the murders. There were also times when blacks confronted lynch mobs to defend their turf, life, and limb.

There were also voices of protest outside of the South. In 1886, Frederick Douglass denounced mob violence, noting, "This mob takes the place of 'due process of law,' of judge, jury, witness, and counsel. It does not come to ascertain the guilt or innocence of the accused, but to hang, shoot, stab, burn or whip him to death."[11] Shortly before his death in 1895, Douglass railed against the "perfect epidemic of mob law and persecution" in the South.[12] He enjoined white America to allow "the organic law of the land to be honestly sustained and obeyed."[13]

Unlike Douglass and his forceful condemnation of lynching, Booker T. Washington at first embraced a more compromising stance. In 1899, he issued a statement affirming his attachment to the South and appealing to "our citizens of our Southern States, to assist in creating a public sentiment such as will make human life here just as safe and sacred as it is anywhere else in the world." [14] Washington disassociated himself from any organized protest against lynching and condemned any behavior by blacks that might precipitate white violence against them. But mob violence also harmed Southern whites, he hinted. "Lynching injures, hardens and blunts the moral sensibilities of the young and tender manhood of the South," Washington maintained. In his opinion, the problem could be solved if "the best white people and best black people" united "in favor of law and order and justice."[15]

When the incidence of lynchings did not abate, Washington became more strident in his denunciation of it. By 1908 he came to see lynching as a "danger that threatens our civilization." "How long can our Christian civilization stand this?" he inquired. Washington was now certain that "lynching is not only wrong, but a mistake–an awful mistake." Still, the principal of Tuskegee continued to hold blacks partly responsible for white violence. He hoped:

> . . . the betters of the black race could use their influence, especially in the cities, to see that the idle element that lives by its wits without permanent or reliable occupation or place of abode is either reformed or gotten rid of in some manner. In most cases, it is this element that furnishes the powder for these explosions.[16]

Not surprisingly, W. E. B. Du Bois denounced mob violence in much harsher terms. When Sam Hose, a black man, was lynched in Georgia in 1899, Du Bois was particularly outraged by the carnival atmosphere that surrounded the victim's torture and burning. The professor felt that "one could not be a calm, cool, and detached scientist while Negroes were lynched, murdered, and starved."[17] Hose had been accused of murdering his boss and raping his boss's wife. When apprehended, he admitted the murder but denied the second charge even though he was tortured. The *New York Tribune* described Hose's treatment by a white mob:

> In the presence of nearly 2,000 people, who sent aloft yells of defiance and shouts of joy, Sam Hose (a Negro who committed two of the basest acts known to crime) was burned at the stake in a public road, one and a half miles from here. Before the torch was applied to the pyre, the Negro was deprived of his ears, fingers and other portions of his body with surprising fortitude. Before the body was cool, it was cut to pieces, the bones were crushed into small bits and even the tree upon which the wretch met his fate was torn up and disposed of as souvenirs. The Negro's heart was cut in several pieces, as was also his liver. Those unable to obtain the ghastly relics directly, paid more

fortunate possessors extravagant sums for them. Small pieces of bone went for 25 cents and a bit of the liver, crisply cooked, for 10 cents.[18]

Du Bois would later urge blacks to resist such atrocities by meeting violence with violence. He wrote a stinging indictment of blacks in Gainesville, Florida, who had failed to protect victims from lynch mobs in 1916. "In the last analysis," Du Bois concluded, "the lynching of Negroes is going to stop in the South when the cowardly mob is faced by effective guns in the hands of people determined to sell their souls dearly."[19]

Men did not constitute the only articulate opponents of lynching. Ida Wells-Barnett, as we have seen, and Mary Church Terrell were two of the most effective and passionate voices in the struggle. Wells popularized the cause through her speeches and writings. In 1909, she concluded that lynching was "a national crime and requires a national remedy."[20] She denounced white politicians for their inaction in the face of "color-line murder," as she characterized lynching. To her, the remedy for this national crime resided in the passage of federal legislation prohibiting it. Like Wells-Barnett, Terrell saw mob violence as a national problem and urged federal action. As she expressed it in 1904, "It is just as impossible for the negroes of this country to prevent mob violence by any attitude of mind which they may assume, or any course of conduct which they may pursue, as it is for a straw dam to stop Niagara's flow."[21]

Although blacks had a few white allies in this struggle, they lacked an effective organizational voice to advance their cause, at least in the years before the formation of the National Association for the Advancement of Colored People (NAACP). Blacks were politically powerless in the South, so white elected officials, with the exception of those who were opposed to mob violence or were embarrassed by it, could ignore their concerns. After its creation in 1910, the NAACP gradually adopted an oppositional stance to lynching. But this was a fledgling organization, and it lacked the resources and the staff to sustain a campaign against racial violence. There were few NAACP branches in the Deep South because potential members feared white reprisals. Not until a decade after its formation did the NAACP begin to increase its membership in the Southern states, thanks to the energies of its new field secretary, James Weldon Johnson.

Still, much of the effectiveness of the NAACP depended on the strength of the local branches, and this varied from state to state and within them as well. Working in tandem with the local leadership, the national leadership in New York supported federal antilynching legislation, denounced mob terror, publicized atrocities when they occurred, and urged the arrest and conviction of the offenders. Possibly by around 1917 and certainly by 1920, the NAACP had become an important voice for the protection of blacks in some states such as Georgia. Rural blacks who had borne the brunt of the lynchings now had an organization acting on their behalf and committed to ending extralegal violence.

RIOTS

Lynching was the most horrible form of violence that whites unleashed against blacks after emancipation. But there were numerous occasions on which mobs of rioting whites invaded black neighborhoods, killing, wounding, burning, and destroying the objects of their rage. The mob's fury could be precipitated at any time by an incident, real or imagined, or by a perceived threat to white privilege. More often than not, blacks resisted these invasions, but they were seldom any match for the better armed and more numerous whites, who were usually aided by law enforcement officials.

One of the earliest incidents of mob violence directed at blacks occurred at Memphis in May 1866. When Memphis fell to the Union in 1862, the city attracted thousands of blacks searching for a sanctuary. Whites were openly hostile to these new residents and harassed them. Tensions intensified at the end of the war, when black soldiers were given the task of patrolling the city. Rumors abounded that when the black soldiers ended their assignment on April 30, there would be a riot. On May 1, blacks attempted to prevent a black soldier who had been arrested from being transported to jail. This became the occasion for a white mob to invade the black residential district, killing, destroying, and raping. By the time the violence was spent, forty-six blacks had lost their lives. None of the perpetrators were arrested. Commenting on the riot, the *Cleveland Leader* observed that "if anything could reveal, in light as clear as day, the demoniac spirit of the southern white toward the freedmen, . . . it is such an event as this."[22]

There were also racial clashes in New Orleans in July 1866 and October 1868. The first incident occurred when the police and a group of former citizens of the Confederacy plotted to prevent blacks from obtaining the franchise. They attacked a number of unarmed black supporters of such a proposal, killing thirty-four of them. In addition, three white allies of blacks lost their lives. In the October 1868 riot, whites assaulted a group of black Republicans but this time they encountered strong resistance. By the time the fighting ceased, fourteen black men, as well as either six or seven white men, had lost their lives.[23] One scholar has suggested that there were thirty-three race riots during Reconstruction that resulted in at least one death. There were also similar incidents in the North. In 1871, for example, whites attacked black voters in Philadelphia, killing four of them.

THE SHAME OF AMERICA

Do you know that the United States is the Only Land on Earth where human beings are BURNED AT THE STAKE?

In Four Years, 1918-1921, Twenty-Eight People Were Publicly BURNED BY AMERICAN MOBS

3436 People Lynched 1889 to 1922

For What Crimes Have Mobs Nullified Government and Inflicted the Death Penalty?

The Alleged Crimes	The Victims	Why Some Mob Victims Died:
Murder	1288	Not turning out of road for white boy in auto
Rape	571	Being a relative of a person who was lynched
Crimes against the Person	615	Jumping a labor contract
Crimes against Property	333	Being a member of the Non-Partisan League
Miscellaneous Crimes	453	"Talking back" to a white man
Absence of Crime	176	"Insulting" white man.
	3436	

Is Rape the "Cause" of Lynching?

Of 3,436 people murdered by mobs in our country, only 571, or less than 17 per cent., were even accused of the crime of rape.

83 WOMEN HAVE BEEN LYNCHED IN THE UNITED STATES

Do lynchers maintain that they were lynched for "the usual crime"?

AND THE LYNCHERS GO UNPUNISHED

THE REMEDY

The Dyer Anti-Lynching Bill Is Now Before the United States Senate

The Dyer Anti-Lynching Bill was passed on January 26, 1922, by a vote of 230 to 119 in the House of Representatives

The Dyer Anti-Lynching Bill Provides:
That culpable State officers and mobbists shall be tried in Federal Courts on failure of State courts to act, and that a county in which a lynching occurs shall be fined $10,000, recoverable in a Federal Court.

The Principal Question Raised Against the Bill is upon the Ground of Constitutionality.

The *Constitutionality* of the Dyer Bill Has Been Affirmed by —
The Judiciary Committee of the House of Representatives
The Judiciary Committee of the Senate
The United States Attorney General, legal adviser of Congress
Judge Guy D. Goff, of the Department of Justice

The Senate has been petitioned to pass the Dyer Bill by—
29 Lawyers and Jurists, including two former Attorneys General of the United States
19 State Supreme Court Justices
24 State Governors
3 Archbishops, 85 bishops and prominent churchmen
39 Mayors of large cities, north and south.

The American Bar Association at its meeting in San Francisco, August 9, 1922, adopted a resolution asking for further legislation by Congress to punish and prevent lynching and mob violence.

Fifteen State Conventions of 1922 (3 of them Democratic) have inserted in their party platforms a demand for national action to stamp out lynchings.

The Dyer Anti-Lynching Bill is not intended to protect the guilty, but to assure to every person accused of crime trial by due process of law.

THE DYER ANTI-LYNCHING BILL IS NOW BEFORE THE SENATE
TELEGRAPH YOUR SENATORS TODAY YOU WANT IT ENACTED

If you want to help the organization which has brought to light the facts about lynching, the organization which is fighting for 100 per cent. Americanism, not for some of the people some of the time, but for all of the people, white or black, all of the time

Send your check to J. E. SPINGARN, Treasurer of the

NATIONAL ASSOCIATION FOR THE ADVANCEMENT OF COLORED PEOPLE
70 FIFTH AVENUE, NEW YORK CITY

THIS ADVERTISEMENT IS PAID FOR IN PART BY THE ANTI-LYNCHING CRUSADERS.

NAACP advertisement, New York Times, November 23, 1922.

Blacks were not the passive targets of white violence and offered some resistance in the overwhelming majority of cases. In 1876, black Republicans in Cainhoy, South Carolina, were the apparent aggressors, attacking Democrats and killing five white persons while losing one of their own. Henry McNeal Turner, ever the indefatigable defender of black interests, enjoined blacks to resist the violence directed at them in a poem he wrote in 1874:

> The Freedman is dying 'mid carnage and gore
> God of our Fathers!–hast thou given us o'er
> In this bloody embrace, to these tigers a prey?
> Let Vengeance be thine! Thou wilt repay.
> Away with the thought!–for this is no dream;
> They war against civil rights! that is their theme.
> But soon will they cringe, as we know full well
> The crisis has come and the tolling bells tell
> We will not yield, not in fear of the grave,
> The rights that belong to the free and the brave.[24]

The violence unleashed by white mobs against blacks continued with regularity as long a whites feared any challenges to the racial order. Wilmington, North Carolina, was the scene of one of the major white riots of the nineteenth century. Fearing competition by blacks for jobs, opposed to their holding political office, and bent on preserving white supremacy, the disgruntled resorted to violence. The emotional issue of miscegenation became the rallying cry for the mob, giving a kind of perverse legitimacy to the assault on black North Carolinians.

Racial extremists had, during the election campaign of 1898, fanned white fears by raising the specter of miscegenation and black male sexuality run amok. In order to inflame emotions and get fearful white men to defend their allegedly beleaguered women, the extremists sang:

> Rise, ye sons of Carolina!
> Proud Caucasians, one and all;
> Be not deaf to Love's appealing–
> Hear your wives and daughters call,
> See their blanched and anxious faces,
> Not their frail, but lovely forms
> Rise, defend their spotless virtue
> With your strong and manly arms.[25]

The purveyors of hate also unleashed a barrage of rumors about black male assaults on white women and made "safety of the home" their battle cry.[26] White fears intensified when a black newspaper editor, Alex Manly, ran a piece in the *Daily Record* suggesting that white women had sexual relationships with black men because they were sexually attracted to them. Such women, if their liaisons were discovered, accused the men of rape in order to protect their reputations,

Manly charged. Incensed by such an assault on the character of their women, white newspapers reprinted Manly's article daily, whipping up emotions.

The elections were held as scheduled on November 8, and the major offices were won by the Democratic party, the citadel of officially organized racism. Manly was run out of town, and a white mob destroyed the building that housed his newspaper. Tensions rose, and whites menaced blacks with their guns. A number of blacks congregated on one of the streets and, as a white attorney reported, "there were several white men over there with guns, but not a great many; that there had been some talk, but a half grown negro boy fired the first shot, when there was a fusillade of shots from the white people, which dropped four or five negroes."[27] The violence served its purpose; black officeholders resigned and "were replaced by the white people," the attorney recounted.[28]

Black citizens abandoned the city when the violence ceased. Some fled to sanctuaries in the North; others simply retreated to wooded areas. The national leadership was largely silent on the atrocities, although President William McKinley asked the U.S. attorney to investigate. In an emotional letter to the president, one black woman queried: "Is this the land of the free and the home of the brave? How can the Negro sing my country tis of thee?"[29] Shocked by the brutality of the white citizens, some blacks endeavored to find explanations for the violence. Inevitably, a few blamed themselves, thinking that they had committed some terrible wrong for which God had divined their punishment. Others thought that if they had avoided any participation in politics, whites would not have been so exercised. There was even one man, John Dancy, an AME clergyman, who intimated that whites had behaved justifiably since they acted to defend their women from Alex Manly's charges.[30] This was a classic case of victims blaming themselves in the absence of any other credible explanations, or it may have been an expression of Christian magnanimity.

Some blacks, of course, knew all too well the reasons for the riot. Congressman George White was convinced that his future resided elsewhere. "I can no longer live in North Carolina and be a man," he concluded before leaving to found the settlement of Whitesboro in New Jersey.[31] But things were hardly better elsewhere for black citizens. In fact, the riot by Wilmington's whites was duplicated by their New Orleans brethren two years later. The immediate cause of the violence was different, but the larger issues were similar: racial fears, competition with blacks for jobs, and a profound uncertainty about the place of whites in a changing society. New Orleans erupted into violence on July 23, 1900, when Robert Charles, a black man, shot and killed a white policeman, who had come to arrest him, and seriously wounded a second. Soon, mobs of whites joined in the pursuit of Charles, who had escaped arrest.

Groups of young men patrolled the streets, assaulting blacks. The situation worsened by the third day, and three blacks lost their lives at the hands of the mob. The death toll rose to six on the fourth day, and by then about sixty-five blacks had been seriously wounded.

When the police finally discovered Charles's whereabouts, he shot and killed one of the men in the arresting party. By the time reinforcements arrived and a mob gathered, Charles had shot another white man. In spite of a hail of bullets directed at his sanctuary, Charles was able to avoid being shot, at least for a while. Holding off the mob of 10,000 to 20,000 persons, Charles killed two more men and wounded nineteen. Eventually, he was killed by a student, and his body mutilated by the police officers and others. Not satisfied with Charles' death, the mob continued to assault blacks, killing three more. By the time the passions were spent, as many as twelve blacks had been murdered. On his part, Charles had murdered seven whites, including three policemen.[32]

Although Charles must bear responsibility for his actions, his was an individual assault. Whites responded as a group to his behavior and took out their anger on all blacks they encountered. Such a collective reaction underscored the seriousness of the nation's racial problems even as it demonstrated the inability of whites to see a black person as an individual and not as the representative of his or her race. This conflation of an individual black identity with a larger racial identity would remain a feature of American society. The events in Wilmington and New Orleans were precursors to the more barbarous Atlanta riot of September 1906.

For several months preceding the riot, white Atlantans had listened to politicians blame blacks for the social ills of the city, whipping up racist fears in the process. As was the case in Wilmington eight years earlier, white politicians depicted black men as rapists, dissolute, and given to uncontrollable passions. There were 80,000 whites and 50,000 blacks in the city in 1905, a ratio that had begun to alarm segments of the white population.

White hostilities found release against blacks when it was reported on September 22 that four black men, in separate incidents, had attempted to rape four white women. In spite of the fact that two of these reports had no substance, white mobs went on a rampage. To cries of "Kill the Niggers," the mob destroyed black-owned buildings and attacked black citizens. By the time the rage was spent several days later, between twenty-five and forty blacks had been killed. One white man lost his life. Writing after the event, W. E. B. Du Bois composed a prayer of pain, bewilderment, and despair:

> Bewildered we are and passion-tossed, mad with the madness of a mobbed and mocked and murdered people; straining at the armposts of Thy throne, we raise our shackled hands and charge Thee, God, by the

bones of our stolen fathers, by the tears of our dead mothers, by the very blood of Thy crucified Christ: What meaneth this? Tell us the plan; give us the sign!

Keep not Thou silent, O God! Sit not longer blind, Lord God, deaf to our prayer and dumb to our suffering. Surely thou, too art not white, O Lord, a pale, bloodless, heartless thing?[33]

Blacks were also disturbed in 1906 by the nation's handling of a racial incident at Fort Brown on the outskirts of Brownsville, Texas. The relocation of the First Battalion of the 25th Infantry from Nebraska to Fort Brown enraged the local white residents because the infantrymen were black. Subjected to a variety of racial insults and assaults, the men found the environment most inhospitable. On August 13, whites invoked fears of the "black beast" rapist and spread a rumor that a soldier had tried to rape a white woman. Later that night, a white mob went on a shooting frenzy. One white bartender was killed, and a police officer was wounded.

Although there was no conclusive evidence that black soldiers were involved in the incident, twelve men were indicted for murder and conspiracy to murder. When all members of the regiment denied any involvement in or knowledge of the incident, they were threatened with dishonorable discharges and loss of any opportunity for reenlistment. President Theodore Roosevelt supported this action after a flawed investigation upheld the charges against the men. In November, 167 black men were summarily discharged from the army. Not until 1972 were the men exonerated, but by then all of them save one had died.

The Brownsville incident underscored once again how racism had corrupted the institutions of society as well as the powerlessness of the black citizenry. President Roosevelt ignored the protests of their leaders and the populace as a whole. When Booker T. Washington sought to intervene on the men's behalf, the president coolly reminded him of his place. "You cannot have any information to give me privately, to which I could pay heed, my dear Mr. Washington," the president informed Washington.[34]

White mob violence against blacks was not confined to the Southern states. Such attacks occurred in New York City in 1900 and 1905; Evansville, Indiana, in 1905; Springfield, Ohio, in 1904 and again in 1906; and Greensburg, Indiana, in 1906.[35] The most serious outburst in the first decade of the twentieth century, however, occurred in Springfield, Illinois, in 1908. Springfield, the hometown of Abraham Lincoln, had a population of 47,000, of whom 2,500 were black. The details of the mob violence were all too familiar; the underlying causes of the outburst were also similar. The immediate cause of the violence was the charge that a white woman had been raped by George Richardson, a black man. Hurling insults at blacks, a white mob invaded black neighborhoods, beating their victims and destroying their property. "Lincoln freed you, we'll show you where you belong," whites threatened. At least ten blacks died as a result of the melee, and scores were injured. The violence in Springfield showed that a cancerous racism knew no state borders; blacks were at risk everywhere.

The racial fault lines in American society were starkly revealed in a riot in East St. Louis, Illinois, in July 1917. Blacks from the South arrived in East St. Louis, particularly after about 1910, in search of jobs in industrial plants and stockyards. Known as "the Pittsburgh of the West," the city was home to the Aluminum Ore Company, the Missouri Malleable Iron Company, and the Swift and Armour packing companies. The black population numbered about 13,000 in 1917.

There were ominous signs in 1916 that whites resented the increasing presence of blacks, and unscrupulous leaders exploited racial fears. During the election campaign that fall, white Democrats accused the Republicans of importing blacks from the South to swell their ranks. This charge was untrue. When white workers at the Aluminum Ore Company struck in early 1917, the management hired black and white strikebreakers. The hiring of blacks enraged whites, who blamed them for the demise of their union. White labor leaders began a campaign to restrict black migration to the city and even to expel those already there. This exacerbated racial tensions and, as one white labor leader recalled, "It was a terrible feeling in the air. Everyone felt something terrible was going to happen. On the street corners, wherever you went, you heard expressions against the negro. You heard the negro was driving the white man out of the locality."[36] The newspapers fanned racial fears; whites armed themselves, and the authorities ignored the harassment of blacks. At a union meeting held on May 28, white workers shouted, "East St. Louis must remain a white man's town." Alexander Flannigan, an attorney, told the gathering that "there is no law against mob violence."[37]

Leaving the meeting in a frenzy, the men assaulted blacks and destroyed black-owned businesses as the police looked on. The white mob met little black resistance, and the police arrested and disarmed blacks whom they found with weapons. The rampage continued for about three days, with sporadic resistance by blacks. Some blacks abandoned the city but returned when an uneasy calm was restored. Blacks continued to be assaulted with impunity through June by roving gangs of whites. On July 1, a group of blacks fired on a police car, killing two officers. It is not entirely clear whether this was a spontaneous or premeditated act.

The response of the white mobs was immediate, violent, and bloody. They invaded black neighborhoods, beating and murdering their victims, and burning their homes and businesses. "Get a nigger . . . get another" became the crazed chant.[38] The atrocities inflicted on blacks were cheered by white bystanders. A newspaper reporter revealed that "everyone that I saw killed had both hands above his head begging for mercy." He had heard one victim plead: "My God, don't kill me, white man."[39] Many blacks fled in fear, but others refused to budge, defending their lives and homes. By the time order was restored, thirty-nine blacks and nine whites had lost their lives.

When the riot ended, blacks drew strength from the fact that many had defended themselves. W. E. B Du Bois reported, "The Negroes fought. They grappled with the mobs like beasts at bay. They drove them back from the thickest cluster of their homes and piled the white dead on the street."[40]

This was probably an exaggeration, but the fact that blacks resisted in the face of overwhelming white might and terror was of enormous psychological importance. The *Chicago Defender* told its readers, "The younger members of the Race were not afraid to die . . . the firing of the whites was promptly returned by hot lead from the Race quarters."[41] Some blacks, predicting more race-based riots, urged increased vigilance. The *California Eagle* thought, "It's up to the Negro to strike the first blow . . . be not afraid to die."[42] Not surprisingly, there were also voices that cautioned restraint as well. Writing in the NAACP's *Crisis,* Du Bois thought that racial harmony would be restored if the nation decided:

> To stop lynching and mob violence.
> To stop disfranchisement for race and sex.
> To abolish Jim Crow cars.
> To resist the attempt to establish an American ghetto.
> To stop race discrimination in Trade Unions, in Civil Service, in places of public accommodation, and in the Public School.
> To secure Justice for all men in the courts.
> To insist that individual desert and ability shall be the test of real American manhood and not adventitious differences of race or color or descent.[43]

The racial violence that once more engulfed the nation in 1919 attested to the continued seriousness of the racial divide and the depth of the society's wounds. Between May and October 1919, race riots erupted in twenty-five towns and cities, constituting what the NAACP's James Weldon Johnson characterized as "the Red Summer." There were no regional boundaries as Americans fought one another in the East, the West, the North, and the South. No region could claim that it was free from the racial virus. There were riots in Elaine, Arkansas; Longview, Texas; Washington, D.C.; Chicago; Knoxville, Tennessee; and Omaha, Nebraska, among other places.

The Chicago riot was the most costly in terms of lives lost. Thirty-eight persons were killed; twenty-three blacks and fifteen whites. Two years later, in 1921, about 10,000 whites in Tulsa, Oklahoma, invaded Little Africa, a black enclave in the city, seeking revenge for a black man's alleged assault of a white woman. The charge was erroneous, but the passions would not be contained. Blacks defended themselves, but Walter White of the NAACP felt that "the odds were too great." By the time the violence was over, as many as 200 blacks had died, as well as about 50 whites.[44]

RESISTING MISTREATMENT

Blacks could do little to stop white violence at its source, but they defended themselves as best they could, sometimes meeting violence with violence. They also employed a number of nonviolent strategies. Angered and humiliated by segregation in public transportation, blacks sued, protested, and staged boycotts. When Ida B. Wells was ejected from a whites-only rail coach in Memphis in 1883, she sued the Chesapeake and Ohio Railroad seeking redress. The lower court found in her favor, but the Supreme Court of Tennessee reversed the decision and questioned her motives for bringing the suit. "We think it is evident that the purpose of the defendant in error was to harass with a view to this suit," the court charged, "and that her persistence was not in good faith to obtain a comfortable seat for the short ride."[45]

When segregation was enforced on horsecars during Reconstruction, blacks mounted protests in New Orleans, Charleston, Louisville, Richmond, and elsewhere. They also boycotted segregated streetcars with increasing regularity in the 1890s and the early decades of the twentieth century. Boycotts lasting anywhere from a few weeks up to several years took place in Atlanta, Montgomery, Mobile, Memphis, New Orleans, Augusta, Charleston, and other cities. Mobile's boycott was maintained for two months, Atlanta held out for ten months, and Augusta folded after three years.

The boycott strategy was also used to oppose segregation in public schools. Such was the case in Chicago in 1863, and in 1867 in Buffalo and Lockport, New York; New Orleans, Richmond, and Charleston. Blacks in Alton, Illinois, boycotted segregated schools from 1897 to 1908, as did those in East Orange, New Jersey, in 1905-06, and in Oxford, Pennsylvania, in 1909. Such protests knew no regional boundaries, and in some cases the courts ruled in favor of protesting black citizens and ordered the desegregation of the schools. There were boycotts of other kinds of segregated public spaces as well. In 1913, blacks boycotted a segregated theatre in Louisville, forcing the financially beleaguered owners to acquiesce to their demands.[46]

Black citizens also used the judicial system to contest the rampaging forces of segregation and the unequal distribution of public resources based upon racial considerations. In 1885, the Arkansas Supreme Court ruled in favor of some blacks who petitioned for equal schools for their children. Black plaintiffs were not always successful. The U.S. Supreme Court consistently upheld segregation and unequal treatment of blacks in several of the decisions it handed down after the landmark decision in *Plessy* v. *Ferguson* in 1896. In 1899, the Court in *Cumming* v. *School Board of Richmond County* allowed a Georgia school board to pay the tuition of white students to attend a private school while simultaneously closing the lone black high school, claiming lack of funds. The Court did not agree with the plaintiffs that the actions of the school board violated the equal protection clause of the Fourteenth Amendment. Five years later, the Court upheld a Kentucky statute that prevented white and black students from attending integrated schools. In 1898 and again in 1903, the Court rejected challenges to laws in Mississippi and Alabama, respectively, that restricted the access of blacks to the franchise.

In 1915 and in 1917, however, the NAACP wrung two landmark decisions from the Supreme Court. Ruling in *Guinn* v. *United States* in 1915, the Court invalidated Oklahoma's "grandfather clause," which restricted the rights of blacks to the franchise. The justices maintained that the grandfather clause constituted "an unconstitutional evasion of the Fifteenth Amendment guarantee that states would not deny citizens the right to vote because of their race." Many states found ingenious ways to thwart the ruling. For example, Oklahoma passed a law requiring potential black voters to register within twelve days or forever lose their right to vote.

Two years after the Oklahoma decision, the NAACP won *Buchanan* v. *Warley*, a case that struck down a Louisville statute that sanctioned segregated housing. The Court held that "all citizens of the United States shall have the same right in every state and territory, as is enjoyed by white citizens thereof, to inherit, purchase, lease, sell, hold and convey real estate and personal property." This was not an unqualified victory for racial justice, however; the Court was more concerned with the fact that the law violated the right to "acquire, use, and dispose" of property.[47] As was the case with the earlier decision on disfranchisement, local authorities passed measures that nullified its intent. Homeowners, with the connivance of the courts and elected officials, adopted covenants that prevented the construction of houses by blacks or the rental or sale of property to them in specific neighborhoods.

AN EMERGING NEW GENERATION

Judicial and legislative defeats, continuing violent assaults, and the awful racial climate stimulated black resolve to force societal change. Writing in 1919, the Jamaican-born poet Claude McKay reflected the defiant spirit that had begun to characterize black America:

If we must die, let it not be like hogs
Hunted and penned in an inglorious spot,
While round us bark the mad and hungry dogs,
Making their mock at our accursed lot.
If we must die, O let us nobly die,
So that our precious blood may not be shed
In vain; then even the monsters we defy
Shall be constrained to honor us though dead!

Oh, kinsmen! We must meet the common foe!
Though far outnumbered let us show us brave,
And for their thousand blows deal one death blow!
What though before us lies the open grave?
Like men we'll face the murderous, cowardly pack,
Pressed to the wall, dying, but fighting back!

Blacks who fought back aggressively in the St. Louis riot in 1917 epitomized the spirit of this new age in formation. They did so again in the riots of 1919 and after. This refusal to be the cowed victims of white rage, coupled with a vigorous demand for their rights, became the staples of black challenges to societal mistreatment after 1917. Blacks' tactics included violence and nonviolent means: suing to end discriminatory legislation and segregation, protest demonstrations, and boycotts. While these strategies were not particularly new, they would be pursued more aggressively and simultaneously.

Members of the Generation of 1917 were born free; many were the grandchildren of those who had been enslaved and had been nurtured in a societal atmosphere where the promise of freedom had been dishonored. More urbanized, literate, and politicized than their parents and grandparents, they wanted to claim a better life for themselves. By 1915, a new generation of black leaders had begun to emerge. More impatient of change than their predecessors, they were also less preoccupied with the "stock" and "ancestry" concerns that had characterized the older black elite. This new generation of elites and their leaders included more persons of a darker hue as well as a growing number from the secular professions, as opposed to the church.

The First World War played a significant role in heightening the political consciousness of the Generation of 1917. When the Europeans began fighting among themselves in 1914, President Woodrow Wilson declined to take sides. All of this changed in April 1917, and black men enthusiastically responded to the nation's call to register and serve. Many were driven by a patriotic fervor, and some hoped that service in the war would establish their credentials as good citizens deserving of societal equality.

Black intellectuals and others had held diverse positions on the European conflict and America's role in it. In 1917, James Weldon Johnson, then the field secretary for the NAACP, argued that "even if there is no sense of patriotism . . . the bald truth is that the negro cannot afford to be rated as a disloyal element in this nation." Even as he urged participation in the war, Johnson felt that the black soldier should do so "with his eyes wide open . . . repeating his demand that this nation do its duty."[48] Roscoe Conkling Simmons, Booker T. Washington's nephew, was more optimistic about the consequences of black participation. "When the war is over and the smoke is cleared," he predicted, "we shall see a new nation baptized with the fire of suffering; one people with their faces set toward the future; one law for all and all for the law. . . ."[49]

In recommending support for entering the war, W. E. B. Du Bois struck patriotic chords. Writing in the NAACP's *Crisis,* he urged blacks to suspend their struggle for social justice "while the war lasts." He advised them to "forget our special grievances and close our ranks shoulder to shoulder with our white fellow citizens and the allied nations that are fighting for democracy."[50] Du Bois's call for a temporary halt to the struggle for civil rights in the name of national unity elicited some opposition. The Reverend Francis Grimke, who resided in Washington, spoke for many. In his opinion:

> It is astounding, almost incredible, that any colored man, even to the stupidest of them, should be led into such utter folly as to counsel the cessation of the struggle for our rights, even for a moment, when nothing is ever accomplished except by struggle, by earnest, persistent effort. The colored man, if he has an ounce of brains in his head, will have but one policy in regard to his rights, and that is the policy of being always on the job. Eternal vigilance is the price of liberty, and unless we are willing to pay the price, unless we are eternally vigilant, we will never get it. Let us hear no more of this nonsense, never mind from whom it comes, about letting up for a season.[51]

Du Bois's support for the war was unwavering, but some have questioned whether he supported it in exchange for a commission in the army. Years later, in reflecting on the transforming effect that the war had on him, Du Bois confessed, "I became during the World War nearer to feeling myself a real and full American than ever before or since."[52]

There were, of course, voices raised against black participation. The Boston editor William Monroe Trotter felt that the United States should concentrate on "making the South safe for the Negroes," instead of protecting democracy in Europe.[53] Although they would mute their criticism of the war once blacks enlisted, such prominent newspapers as the *Baltimore Afro-American,* the *Chicago Defender,* and the *Cleveland Gazette* believed that blacks had no role in it. There was, it appears, also an unorganized opposition to black participation among other black citizens. In an unsigned circular that surfaced at Friars Point, Mississippi, in 1917, the writer asked:

> Young Negro men and boys what have we to fight for in this country? Nothing! Some of our well educated negroes are touring the country urging our young men to be killed up like sheep, for nothing. If we fight in this war time we fight for nothing. Rather than fight I would rather commit self death.[54]

Such voices did not prevail, however, and 367,000 blacks enlisted. In an address to a group of black ministers on March 14, 1918, President Woodrow Wilson assured them that a grateful nation would confer "full citizenship rights" upon blacks as a consequence of their wartime service:

> I have always known that the Negro has been unjustly and unfairly dealt with; your people have exhibited a degree of loyalty and patriotism that should commend the admiration of the whole nation. In the present conflict your Race has rallied to the nation's call, and if there has been any evidence of slackerism manifested by Negroes the same has not reached Washington. . . . With thousands of your sons in the camps of France, out of this conflict you must expect nothing less than the enjoyment of full citizenship rights—the same as are enjoyed by every other citizen.[55]

Such encouraging sentiments notwithstanding, America exported its racial virus by confining black soldiers to separate units and subjecting them to demeaning treatment. Members of the Ninety-Second Division in France, for example, were checked hourly in their camp so that they would not become "a menace to women." The U.S. army warned the French "not to commend too highly the [black] Americans."[56] Black soldiers were excluded from the victory parade in Paris, and the U.S. government opposed any attempts by the French to honor them. But black Americans would honor their own. On February 17, 1919, thousands of black New Yorkers greeted the Fifteenth Regiment of New York's National Guard as its men paraded along Fifth Avenue. Another celebration for the veterans occurred in Chicago.

The war transformed those who fought in it and many who stayed behind. Service in the army was largely a response to patriotic pulls, but it also raised the consciousness of the participants to the pervasiveness of injustice in their country and produced in them a feeling that they could force societal change back home. "The Negroes will come back feeling like men, and not disposed to accept the treatment to which they have been subjected," predicted Moorfield Storey, an NAACP stalwart in Boston.[57] W. E. B. Du Bois was even more insistent that the war should be a catalyst for deeper changes in America. While reaffirming black patriotism, he opined in May 1919:

... we are cowards and jackasses if now that the war is over we do not marshal every ounce of our brain and brawn to fight a sterner, longer, more unbending battle against the forces of hell in our own land.
We return.
We return from fighting.
We return fighting.[58]

The *Houston Informer* voiced a similar position in October:

When called upon to defend this country's honor and integrity and to save civilization from the clutches of the cruel and heartless Huns of Europe, the black American went forth to battle the mighty Goliath of autocracy, militarism and kultur.

Having performed a "brown skin" job "over there," he now expects Uncle Sam to clean up his own premises and since the BLACK MAN FOUGHT TO MAKE THE WORLD SAFE FOR DEMOCRACY, he now demands that AMERICA BE MADE AND MAINTAINED SAFE FOR BLACK AMERICANS.[59]

Statements such as these had appeal because of the persistence of white mistreatment of blacks. Increasingly, some blacks had come to question the capacity of the nation to tranform itself into a racially just society. Mordecai Johnson, a clergyman who later became the president of Howard University, observed that "the Negro's faith in the righteous purpose of the Federal Government has sagged. . . . All the colored people, in every section of the United States, believe that there is something wrong, and not accidentally wrong, at the very heart of government." Johnson thought that blacks were "no longer able to believe with Dr. Booker T. Washington, or with any other man, that their own efforts after intelligence, wealth, and self-respect can in any wise avail to deliver them." He was certain that blacks would "no longer feed on the bread of repression and violence."[60]

Although President Wilson had promised that wartime service would result in the amelioration of the black condition, it is clear that such patriotism alone, no matter how fervent or courageously expressed, would not have been enough. Amelioration would have required a softening or abandonment of the racial ideology that so many whites had embraced for so long and with such intensity. The national leaders and the white public were not yet ready to confront the race question and its attendant political and economic implications, and that would only come when blacks were able to force the issue in a substantial way.

The inviting promise of the war, the transforming experiences of fighting in it, and its eventual failure to change the racial situation at home helped to shape and create the mood of the Generation of 1917. Black soldiers who fought in Europe's war were not disposed to avoiding confrontations at home. As one former soldier declared in Chicago:

I went to war, served eight months in France. I wanted to go, but I might as well have stayed for all the good it has done me. . . . I done my part and I'm going to fight right here till Uncle Sam does his. I can shoot as good as the next one. . . . I ain't looking for trouble, but if it comes my way I ain't dodging.[61]

Marcus Garvey had also captured this spirit at war's end. "The first dying that is to be done by the black man in the future will be done to make himself free," the leader of the Universal Negro Improvement Association declared.[62]

Above all, however, a new generation of people was emerging, unencumbered by the memories and habits of slavery, unwilling to be intimidated by whites, protective of themselves, and demanding of their rights. When James Weldon Johnson of the NAACP visited Washington during the 1919 riot, he described the black people as "calm and determined, unterrified and unafraid. . . . They had reached the determination that they would defend and protect themselves and their homes at the cost of their lives, if necessary and that determination rendered them calm."[63]

Writing to the *Crisis* after the riot in Washington, one woman confessed:

The Washington riot gave me the thrill that comes once in a lifetime. . . . At last our men had stood like men, struck back, were no longer dumb, driven cattle. When I could no longer read for my streaming tears, I stood up, alone in my room, held both hands high over my head and exclaimed aloud: "Oh, I thank God, thank God!" When I remember anything after this, I was prone on my bed, beating the pillow with both fists, laughing and crying, whimpering like a whipped child, for sheer gladness and madness. The pent-up humiliation, grief and horror of a lifetime–half century–was being stripped from me.[64]

These defining moments occurred all across the land, in myriad ways and circumstances. Collectively, they constituted the continuing and complex processes of a people realizing themselves. As the succeeding chapters demonstrate, the Generation of 1917 and its children would radically transform black America and the nation-state in which they lived.

Notes

1. Douglass, *Terrible Honesty*, 326.
2. W. Fitzhugh Brundage, *Lynching in the New South: Georgia and Virginia, 1880–1930* (Urbana: University of Illinois Press, 1993), 8.
3. Ibid., 198.
4. Ida B. Wells, *Crusade for Justice: The Autobiography of Ida B. Wells* (Chicago, 1970), 70.
5. Giddings, *When and Where I Enter*, 87.

6. James R. Grossman, "Blowing the Trumpet: The Chicago Defender and Black Migration During World War I," *Illinois Historical Journal*, 78:2 (1985), 85.
7. Brundage, *Lynching in the New South*, 8.
8. Ibid.
9. Ibid., 164.
10. Ibid.
11. Herbert Shapiro, *White Violence and Black Response: From Reconstruction to Montgomery* (Amherst: University of Massachusetts Press, 1988), 35.
12. Ibid.
13. Ibid., 38.
14. Ibid., 133.
15. Ibid., 134–135.
16. Wintz, *African-American Political Thought*, 67–68.
17. Shapiro, *White Violence*, 63.
18. Michael J. Cassity, *Chains of Fear: American Race Relations Since Reconstruction* (Westport: Greenwood, 1984), 57.
19. Shapiro, *White Violence*, 91.
20. Ibid., 120.
21. Ibid., 122.
22. Foner, *Reconstruction*, 262; Altina L. Waller, "Community, Class and Race in the Memphis Riot of 1866," *Journal of Social History*, 18 (Winter 1984), 233–246.
23. Melinda M. Hennessey, "Race and Violence in Reconstruction New Orleans: The 1868 Riot," *Louisiana History*, 20:1 (1979), 77–91.
24. Edwin Redkey, ed., *Respect Black: The Writings and Speeches of Henry McNeal Turner* (New York: Arno Press, 1971), 38.
25. Gilmore, *Gender and Jim Crow*, 91.
26. Ibid., 93.
27. Williamson, *The Crucible of Race*, 201.
28. Ibid.
29. Gilmore, *Gender and Jim Crow*, 113.
30. Ibid., 115–117.
31. Ibid., 117.
32. Williamson, *The Crucible of Race*, 201–209.
33. W. E. B. Du Bois, *Dark Water* (New York: Harcourt Brace, 1920), 27.
34. Williamson, *The Crucible of Race*, 355.
35. Roberta Senechal, *The Sociogenesis of a Race Riot: Springfield, Illinois, in 1908* (Urbana: University of Illinois Press, 1990), 2.
36. Elliott Rudwick, *Race Riot at East St. Louis, July 2, 1917* (Carbondale: Southern Illinois University Press, 1964), 24.
37. Ibid., 28.
38. Ibid., 46.
39. Ibid.
40. Ibid., 40.
41. Ibid., 55.
42. Ibid., 66.
43. Ibid.
44. Shapiro, *White Violence*, 113.
45. Darlene Clark Hine, *Speak Truth to Power* (Brooklyn: Carlson Publishing Co., 1996), 139–140.
46. August Meier and Elliott Rudwick, "The Origins of Non Violent Direct Action in Afro-American Protest: A Note on Historical Discontinuities," in their *Along the Color Line: Explorations in the Black Experience* (Urbana: University of Illinois Press, 1976), 308–312.

47. Ely, "The South, The Supreme Court, and Race Relations, 1890–1965," in Griffin and Doyle, eds., *The South As An American Problem*, 131–132.
48. Mark Ellis, "W.E.B. Du Bois and the Formation of Black Opinion in World War I: A Commentary on 'The Damnable Dilemma,'" *Journal of American History*, 81:4 (March 1995), 1587.
49. Ibid.
50. William Jordan, "'The Damnable Dilemma': African American Accommodation and Protest during World War I," *Journal of American History*, 81:4 (March 1995), 1562.
51. Wilson Jeremiah Moses, *Black Messiahs and Uncle Toms: Social and Literary Manipulations of a Religious Myth* (University Park: Penn State University Press, 1982), 117.
52. Jordan, "'The Damnable Dilemma,'" 1574.
53. Ibid.
54. Ellis, "W.E.B. Du Bois and the Formation of Black Opinion," 1584.
55. Henry A. Bullock, *A History of Negro Education in the South: From 1619 to the Present* (New York: Praeger, 1967), 198.
56. David Levering Lewis, *When Harlem Was in Vogue* (New York: Oxford, 1981), 14.
57. Ibid., 15.
58. Ibid.
59. Bullock, *A History of Negro Education*, 198.
60. Moses, *Black Messiahs*, 110–111.
61. William M. Tuttle, *Race Riot: Chicago in the Red Summer of 1919* (New York: Atheneum, 1970), 209.
62. Levine, "Marcus Garvey and the Politics of Revitalization," in Franklin and Meier, *Black Leaders*, 117.
63. Lawrence Levine, *Black Culture and Black Consciousness: Afro-American Folk Thought from Slavery to Freedom* (New York: Oxford, 1977), 439.
64. Cassity, *Chains of Fear*, 91.

Intellectual and Cultural Life: From Emancipation to the Harlem Renaissance

Black America has never had a dearth of talent in literature, political thought, music, and the expressive arts. The enslaved created a rich and vibrant culture, drawing upon their African heritages and the cultures of the Americas. Prior to 1865, a number of slaves and free blacks wrote and published literary works, political treatises, and autobiographies. Jupiter Hammon, a slave, succeeded in getting a broadside that he wrote in 1760 published in 1761, becoming the first of his peers to appear in print. Twelve years later, the African-born Phillis Wheatley published her book of poems. George Moses Horton repeated this feat in 1829. Not until 1853 did the first novel written by a black person appear. In that year, William Wells Brown published *Clotel*. Six years later Harriet E. Wilson published her novel, *The Nig*.

In spite of the difficulties they confronted, the intellectual energies of literate free blacks were never stayed during the antebellum years. Individuals such as David Walker, Martin Delany, Richard Allen, Ann Plato, and a host of others published treatises on the black condition. Former slaves such as Frederick Douglass, William Craft, Henry Bibb, Lunsford Lane, and many others published autobiographies. The development of the black press and the proliferation of periodicals provided free blacks with an opportunity to get their voices heard. During these formative years, and after 1865, writers focused on the place of Africa in the black imagination, the nature and construction of racism in the United States, the politics of protest and resistance, the search for a racial identity, and the history of a people, among other themes.

An analysis of the historiography of black America should begin, arguably, with the publication in 1836 of Robert Benjamin Lewis's *Light and Truth: Containing the Universal History of the Colored and Indian Race, from the Creation of the World to the Present Time.* Lewis, of African and Indian ancestry, was born in Boston. His book, which was reprinted and expanded in 1844, focused more on biblical references and blacks in Antiquity and less on the history of blacks in America. But however flawed it was, the book constituted a necessary beginning. In 1841, James W. C. Pennington, a former slave, published his *Textbook of Negro History,* geared to a younger readership. It was admirable in intent, since it aimed to foster racial pride in black children. Although the work was strikingly elementary and focused almost exclusively on heroic personages, it was well received.

The best historical study of blacks to appear before 1865 was written by William Cooper Nell, a free-born Bostonian. Nell published his *Colored Patriots of the American Revolution, with Sketches of Several Distinguished Colored Persons, to which is Added a Brief Survey of the Condition and Prospects of Colored Americans* in 1855. This work sketched the lives of many black individuals and represented a valiant attempt to provide appropriate documentation for its conclusions. Still, it was uncritical in its use of sources and was hagiographic in its tone. Seventeen years later, the well-known abolitionist William Still published *The Underground Railroad,* a study that was essentially a collection of documents on the roles of heroic individuals and sympathetic institutions in the struggle against slavery.

The years after 1880 saw a greater sophistication in writings about the black past. Not only did history books appear with greater frequency than in previous years, but at least two of them represented major and enduring contributions to the historiography of black America. George Washington Williams's *History of the Negro Race from 1619 to 1880: Negroes as Slaves, Soldiers, and as Citizens* appeared in 1882. Williams was born to free parents in Pennsylvania in 1849. As a young man he entered the army in 1864 and saw service in the waning months of the Civil War. At war's end he became a preacher, and in 1879 he was elected to the legislature in Ohio and served in that capacity until 1881. In the preface to his *History,* Williams noted, "My whole aim has been to write a thoroughly trustworthy history; and what I have written, if it have [sic] no other merit is reliable."[1]

Published in two volumes, the book discussed the African heritage of black Americans, paying proper attention to the societies of West Africa. He traced the history of blacks in America from their enslavement in Virginia, concluding with a brief examination of Reconstruction.

Extensively researched, informed, and often balanced in its conclusions, the book was a remarkable achievement for its times.

The publication of W. E. B. Du Bois's *The Suppression of the African Slave Trade to the United States of America, 1638–1870* in 1896 constituted another landmark in the development of black historiography. This was a specialized study, unlike Williams's more general contribution. But it was an outstanding work of scholarship that emphasized the dimensions of the slave trade and the roles of blacks and others in ending the human traffic. This was destined to be the first of many important contributions that Du Bois would make to black intellectual life over the next six decades.

The first decades of the twentieth century, as has been noted, brought a new generation of blacks to the forefront, ushering in profound changes in black life. Among other things, several black intellectuals urged the study of black history and its teaching in the schools as one of the ways to promote racial consciousness. Kelly Miller, a Howard University professor, noted, "All great people glorify their history, and look back upon their early attainments with a spiritualized vision."[2] Arthur A. Schomburg, an indefatigable, self-taught, Puerto Rican-born bibliophile, urged the teaching of black history, since "it is the season for us to devote our time to kindling the torches that will inspire us to racial integrity."[3]

Black Americans published several works of history between 1900 and 1915. They included Pauline Hopkins's *Primer of Facts Pertaining to the Early Greatness of the African Race* (1905), Booker T. Washington's *Story of the Negro* (1909), and James Morris Webb's *The Black Man, The Father of Civilization* (1910). The two most outstanding books were Benjamin Brawley's *Short History of the American Negro* (1913) and Du Bois's *The Negro*, which appeared in 1915. Taken together, these books served the needs of a literate black public hungry for historical information as well as those of the colleges that had begun to teach black history. In 1911, for example, Fisk University inaugurated a course in black history, and similar courses were soon introduced at Atlanta Baptist College (later Morehouse) and at Teacher's College, Howard University.

With the possible exception of Du Bois's *The Negro*, these works have not endured. But survival is hardly the measure of their importance. These books attempted to fill a lacunae in black intellectual life, to celebrate a past thought to be lost to history, and simultaneously meeting contemporary social, educational, and psychic needs. They focused primarily on the deeds of men, were elitist in their choice of heroes, and sometimes even inaccurate. Contemporary works by white authors shared similar weaknesses. But for blacks buffeted by unfriendly forces and whose voices were silent in the history texts of the nation, the need to claim their history was not only necessary but immediate.

Carter G. Woodson, early 1900s.

Given the developing interest in black history, it is hardly surprising that organizations more narrowly devoted to its study and dissemination would also be formed. In 1897, for example, the American Negro Historical Society of Pennsylvania was founded. Fifteen years later, the Negro Society for Historical Research came into being. These were forerunners to the organization of the larger, more significant, and more enduring Association for the Study of Negro Life and History (ASNLH) in 1915. The inspiration behind its formation was Carter G. Woodson, a Harvard-trained historian. Born in 1875 to former slaves, the brilliant young man received his Ph.D. in history in 1912, becoming the second black person in the country to do so. Woodson taught at the M Street High School in Washington from 1911 to 1917, publishing his first book, *The Education of the Negro Prior to 1865* in 1915.

The founding of the ASNLH represented one of the most important developments in black intellectual life in the twentieth century. It emphasized the importance of the black past to black people themselves and provided the institutional framework within which research, discussion, and the cross-fertilization of ideas could occur. In order to disseminate research on black history, the ASNLH published the *Journal of Negro History*, which Woodson edited from 1916 to 1950. In 1926, Woodson inaugurated Negro History Week in order to focus attention on the black past as well as to underscore its importance in the evolution of the national experience. Negro History Week popularized black history and black personages, and according to Woodson, it was designed "to demonstrate what Negroes have actually achieved in spite of their handicaps."[4]

Paralleling the developments in history were significant achievements in black literature. Black writers had produced four novels before the Civil War. Between 1865 and 1880, at least three additional works appeared. James Roberts Gilmore published *Among the Pines* in 1862, and in 1867 Lorenzo D. Blackson wrote what was essentially a work of prose, *Rise and Progress of the Kingdoms of Light and Darkness; or, The Reigns of Kings Alpha and Abadon*. Gilmore's novel was really about the Civil War, while Blackson's book was suffused with Christian symbolisms and seemed to offer to blacks the promise of a better life. The third novel, published by Thomas Detter in 1871, was titled *Nellie Brown or The Jealous Wife*. The work, set in San Francisco, does not appear to have survived and remains largely unknown.[5]

Although a few literary works appeared in the 1880s, the years roughly from 1892 to 1910 represented a veritable oasis of black creativity. In fact, it can be maintained that what has been characterized as the Harlem Renaissance of the 1920s and 1930s was essentially a continuation of a literary outpouring that began in the 1890s. These writers were not concentrated primarily in one location as would occur in Harlem, but some of the themes they addressed—black cultural roots, protest, the struggle against racism, the search for a black identity—were very much present in the works of their successors.

These men and women writers came to maturity at a time when literacy was expanding for blacks, guaranteeing them at least a modest readership. But they also wrote for whites as well, since they addressed the horrors of racism and articulated the need for larger societal and moral transformations. There was, of course, a pressing need to address the issues of racial prejudice, given the worsening relationship between the races after 1890. The poet and writer Paul Laurence Dunbar, for example, questioned the vision of a just and integrated society. In 1903, he gave a Fourth of July address in which he sought to capture the mood of black disillusionment with the promise of the nation. "Aye, there be some on this festal day kneel in their private closets and with hands upraised and bleeding hearts cry out to God, if there still lives a God, 'How long, O God, How long?'"[6]

Disillusion, to be sure, was not the primary motive force behind black creativity, although historians would be foolhardy to deny it a role. The essayists, poets, and novelists reflected their people's spirit, gave voice to their struggles and hopes, even as they celebrated the past and sought meaning in the present. In general, the writers after 1890 were bolder in their assertion of black difference, less optimistic about the promise of integration, more aggressive in their espousal of a black identity, and more strident in their assault on racism than were their predecessors. Not everyone followed the same drummer, but after 1900 and particularly after about 1906, most black writers spoke to the traditions of their people, demonstrating a marked race consciousness and a rejection of racial injustice. These themes would become the hallmarks of their writing throughout the twentieth century. As in other aspects of life, black writing experienced a watershed during the early years of the twentieth century.

The change in black writing in the 1890s and during the first decades of the twentieth century was not necessarily one of literary form, versification, and style. Rather, it resided primarily in the vigor of the ideas presented, the willingness on the part of some to root their work in black culture, and a readiness to affirm their place on America's soil. This did not happen all at once, and some writers were ambivalent in their assertion of a black identity and the implied rejection of one that was more broadly American and deracinated.

Many of the political essays written after 1890 had much in common with the ideas of earlier writers, such as David Walker, in their condemnation of a racist social order. But these works also reflected the changing temper of the times. Anna Julia Cooper, for example, condemned racism and rejected a subordinate place for women in *A Voice from the South*. Writing in 1899, seventy years after Walker wrote his *Appeal*, Paul Laurence Dunbar railed against the assaults on the franchise that blacks had won as a free people. While Walker had urged an end to slavery, Dunbar did not have that battle to fight. At a time of diminishing rights, he urged resistance. "Let these suffering people relinquish one single right that has been given them," he predicted, "and the rapacity of the other race, encouraged by yielding, will ravage from them every privilege that they possess."[7]

W. E. B. Du Bois was certainly the best-known essayist of the period. His *The Souls of Black Folk* broke new ground in capturing the inner tension between being black and being American. Du Bois demanded the right of blacks to define themselves in a society where they had not been allowed to do so. This did not mean a rejection of America, however. In fact, the black person "could not Africanize America, for America has too much to teach the world and Africa." On the other hand, "He would not bleach his Negro soul in a flood of white Americanism, for he knows that Negro blood has a message for the world."[8] Du Bois rejected

Booker T. Washington's accommodationism and called attention to his country's shortcomings. "The nation has not yet found peace from its sins," he wrote. "The freedman has not yet found in freedom his promised land."[9]

Du Bois became the preeminent intellectual of his time, but the ideas he expressed were also present in the poetry and fiction of others. Paul Laurence Dunbar's first novel, *The Uncalled*, published in 1898, celebrated individual freedom and pointed to the systemic roots of oppression. In *The Sport of the Gods*, Dunbar drew attention to the crippling effects of racism on its victims. Breaking with the literary techniques of his predecessors, Dunbar used the dialect form in much of his poetry, a practice that other black writers would copy. In fact, he became the most popular poet of his time.

Pauline Hopkins, the publisher of four novels, was also a major writer during the early years of the twentieth century. She served as literary editor of the *Colored American Magazine* from 1900 to 1904. Her best-known work was *Contending Forces*, which was published in 1900. Hopkins, a native of Portland, Maine, hoped her writing would "raise the stigma of degradation from my race."[10] *Contending Forces* raised questions relating to the terror of lynching, rape, miscegenation, the politics of white male power, and the construction of black womanhood.

Sutton Griggs, a native of Texas and the author of five novels, was the angriest of the writers in his criticism of the racist social order. His *Imperium in Imperio*, published in 1899, painted an exceedingly dismal and pessimistic picture of race relations in the nation. Charles Chesnutt was more restrained, and in the words of one contemporary, "thinks and writes more as an American, from the broad standpoint of country rather than of race."[11] He wrote three novels focusing principally on the theme of race mixture and the debilitating effects of racism on the personhood of its victims. His novel, *The Marrow of Tradition* (1901), was inspired by the 1898 race riot in Wilmington, North Carolina. Chesnutt, himself of mixed ancestry, hoped the book would "create sympathy for the colored people of the South in the very difficult position which they occupy."[12]

The multitalented James Weldon Johnson was probably the best-known writer, poet, and lyricist after 1910. His novel, *The Autobiography of an Ex-Colored Man* (1912), addressed the phenomenon of "passing" and its tragic human cost. Toward the end of the novel, the successful protagonist laments: "I cannot repress the thought that, after all, I have chosen the lesser part, that I have sold my birthright for a mess of pottage." In his poem "Fifty Years," which he published in 1913 on the golden anniversary of the signing of the Emancipation Proclamation, Johnson voiced his continuing faith in integration but strongly affirmed that:

> This land is ours by right of birth,
> This land is ours by right of toil;
> We helped to turn its virgin earth.
> Our sweat is in its fruitful soil.[13]

As a lyricist, Johnson became best-known for his writing of what became the "Negro National Anthem." Composed in 1900, the song "Lift Ev'ry Voice and Sing" captured the hope, promise, and travails of black life:

> Lift ev'ry voice and sing
> Till earth and heaven ring;
> Ring with the harmonies of Liberty;
> Let our rejoicing rise
> High as the list'ning skies
> Let it resound loud as the rolling sea.
> Sing a song full of the faith that the dark past has taught us,
> Sing a song full of the hope that the present has brought us;
> Facing the rising sun of our new day begun,
> Let us march on till victory is won.

These intellectual developments were taking place at a time when the debates over the merits of vocational education in contrast to a more humanistic one raged. In 1897, a group of intellectuals gathered in Washington, D.C., for the first organizational meeting of the American Negro Academy (ANA). Those in attendance included its principal initiator, Alexander Crummell, a lecturer, writer, Episcopal priest, and nationalist. Crummell was ordained in 1845, and in 1853 he received a degree from Cambridge University. He served for the next two decades as a missionary in Liberia, returning to Washington in 1872. He became rector of St. Mary's Chapel, a congregation that expanded rapidly and moved to a new building in 1879, renamed St. Luke's. Crummell presided over that congregation until his retirement in 1894.

Crummell was a profound admirer of Western civilization. An elitist to the core, he was an ardent proponent of the racial uplift philosophy then in vogue. Crummell was also the earliest proponent of the notion of black leadership being confined to the Talented Tenth. Like Booker T. Washington, he recognized the value of vocational training for blacks, but he was also a strong supporter of humanistic education. It was partly because of the latter that the ANA came into existence. Crummell believed that "trained and scholarly men" should shape "the opinions and habits of the crude masses."[14] At the inaugural meeting of the Academy and in the presence of such men as Du Bois and the writer and lecturer William Ferris, Crummell declared that the challenge that blacks confronted was to make recognizable contributions to world civilization and to American life. He saw this as the responsibility of the group and not solely that of individuals, since "mere individuality cannot be recognized as the aggregation of a family, a nation, or a race." Failure to "attain the role of civilization" meant that blacks could not claim a place "in the world of culture and enlightenment."[15] In its constitution, the ANA committed itself to "a. To promote the publication of scholarly work; b. To aid youths of genius in the attainment of the higher culture, at home and abroad; . . . d. To aid, by publications, the dissemination of the truth and the vindication of the Negro race from vicious assaults."[16]

The ANA survived for three decades, holding annual conferences, publishing occasional papers, and serving as a voice for black intellectuals. At its formation it was an exclusively male organization, but it came to include women. Its membership remained small, however, and its influence limited. But the academy was not without significance. It was the most prestigious interdisciplinary black intellectual organization of the time, and it defined the importance of a black thought that transcended disciplinary and professional boundaries.

The disillusionment that followed the First World War, remarkably, did not paralyze black America. In fact, if the 1920s and 1930s are measured by the range and vitality of black cultural creativity, a crisis of spirit hardly existed. The times were harsh for many, but the writers, poets, musicians, and other creative people spoke to their spirit, combining protest with praise, disillusionment with hope, the promise of the future with a rediscovery of the past. Mostly young, born in freedom, often the grandchildren of slaves, they were the product of their people's changed circumstances, but they, too, would invite change. Harlem would be the stage for many.

The movement of blacks from the South produced significant demographic changes in several Northern cities. New York, for example, had a black population of 91,709 in 1910, but by 1930 it had increased to 327,706. Harlem, an area extending from 130th Street to 145th Street and from Fifth Avenue to Eighth Avenue, had a black population of 73,000 in 1920. Black Harlem had an expanding frontier, and by 1930 it had reached 155th Street, boasting a population of 164,000. The area attracted an amorphous group of black people, including workers, sharecroppers, farmers, intellectuals, and especially the young. This part of Manhattan quickly acquired a reputation for intellectual vitality, cultural creativity, and a vibrant and bohemian nightlife. It had an intoxicating mystique for blacks. As James Weldon Johnson romanticized Harlem in 1930:

So here we have Harlem—not merely a colony or a community or a settlement—not at all a "quarter" or a slum or a fringe—but a black city located in the heart of Manhattan, and containing more Negroes to the square mile than any other spot on earth. It strikes the uninformed observer as a phenomenon, a miracle straight out of the skies.[17]

Years earlier, the young poet Langston Hughes declined his father's invitation to go to Europe "because I wanted to see Harlem. . . . More than Paris or the Shakespeare country, or Berlin, or the Alps, I wanted to see Harlem, the greatest Negro city in the world."[18] There was another side to Harlem. Its teeming black masses remained at the bottom of the economic ladder. This black enclave, in spite of the glitter, was a ghetto in the making. Most of the business enterprises in Harlem in the 1920s were owned by whites; blacks filled the most menial jobs, and many occupied tenements and suffered from disease and high mortality rates. Harlem embodied the contradictions of American society in the 1920s and later. Its tinsel masked the sheer poverty of the masses of the residents; many of those who came to Harlem in search of exotica never saw or wanted to see its musty underside. The cultural creativity that its people unleashed and that came to define Harlem in the 1920s and the 1930s celebrated a people's life and history, but it, too, masked the pain and contradiction of the present.

As a mecca for blacks in the 1920s, Harlem facilitated a cross-fertilization of ideas and cultures. There was a critical mass of black people there, energized by the urban environment, challenged by the vicissitudes of the black condition, and eager to claim their cultural spaces. But although the Harlem of the 1920s and early 1930s experienced a flood of literary productivity and much activity in music, art, and the theatre, it was only the scale of these creative energies that was new.

Black writers in Harlem published twenty-six novels, ten volumes of poetry, and many short stories between 1925 and 1935. Women wrote one-third of the novels in spite of the difficulties they experienced in finding publishers. These writers, for the most part, were young and were born after 1890, reflecting generational differences between themselves and those who had published in the 1890s and the early years of the twentieth century. James Weldon Johnson, alone among the major literary figures of the 1920s, had published at an earlier time.

The first years of the 1920s saw the appearance of three writers whose work helped to define black writing during that decade. The Jamaican novelist and poet Claude McKay, Kansas-born poet Langston Hughes, and Jean Toomer, a novelist born in Washington, D.C., set the stage for the literary effervescence. Born in 1890, McKay migrated to the United States in 1912. His most incendiary poem, "If we must die," appeared in 1919, and some have said that this marked the start of the Harlem Renaissance. His collection of poetry, *Harlem Shadows*, was published in 1922. James Weldon Johnson described McKay in 1924 as showing "the greatest range of imagination, the richest resources of material and the highest perfection of technique. He possesses both power and delicacy. He is both an Afro-American poet and a cosmic poet."[19]

Twelve years McKay's junior, Langston Hughes came to Harlem in 1921. His literary talents were quickly recognized, and his poems appeared with regularity in *Crisis*. Hughes drew his inspiration from the black masses, celebrating their lives, their strength, and their travails. Hughes admitted that the masses "furnish a wealth of colorful, distinctive material for any artist because they hold their own individuality in the face of American standardizations.[20] In one of his arresting early poems, "Mother to Son," Hughes used the dialect form to honor the struggles and resilience of black women:

> Well, son, I'll tell you
> Life, for me ain't been no crystal stair.
> It's had tacks in it,
> And splinters,
> And boards torn up,
> And places with no carpet on the floor–
> Bare;
> But all the time
> I'se been a climbing on,
> And reachin' landin's,
> And turnin' corners,
> And sometimes goin' in the dark
> Where there ain't been no light.
> So boy, don't you turn back;
> Don't you set down on the steps,
> 'Cause you find it's kinder hard;
> Don't you fall now–
> For I'se still goin' honey,
> I'se still climbin',
> And life for me ain't been no crystal stair.

Jean Toomer's novel, *Cane*, was published in 1923. Lyrical in style and elegant in its use of language, the novel established the author as a major writer. Its treatment of black life in the South and in the North was richly textured. William Stanley Braithwaite, a writer and critic, praised the novel as "a book of gold and bronze, of dusk and flame, of ecstasy and pain, and Jean Toomer is a bright morning star of a new day

Langston Hughes (1902–1967)

of the race in literature."[21] *Cane* was Toomer's primary contribution to black literature, as he wrote little thereafter.

The work of McKay, Hughes, and Toomer drew attention to themselves and to Harlem. Other young writers who would later become deservedly famous came seeking their literary voice, including the poet Countée Cullen and the novelists Zora Neale Hurston, Jessie Fauset, and Wallace Thurman. When Jessie Fauset's first novel appeared in 1924, a group of the Harlem literati, numbering about one hundred, gathered to celebrate the occasion in November of that year. W. E. B. Du Bois was present, and so were the philosophy professor Alain Locke and Charles Johnson, a sociologist and editor of the National Urban League's journal, *Opportunity*. Impressed by the attendance, Paul Underwood Kellogg, editor of *The Survey Graphic*, a monthly magazine, decided to highlight black literature and art in the March 1925 issue. Alain Locke was the guest editor. Locke eventually published the articles the special issue contained as well as some new ones in a book titled *The New Negro*. Appearing in the fall of 1925, the book was dedicated to the "younger generation." *The New Negro* would come to epitomize the spirit of the Harlem Renaissance.

The term "New Negro" was not coined by Locke. In fact, its earliest recorded usage was in 1895. In an editorial written in June of that year, the *Cleveland Gazette* noticed "a class of colored people, the 'New Negro,' who have arisen since the war." These persons, the paper noted, were not contented with their subordinate place in society. They were a group of people "with education, refinement and money." The accommodationist Booker T. Washington employed the term in a more restricted sense. To him, it described those blacks who were in the process of improving their economic condition by applying his concept of self-help. Writing in 1908, white journalist Ray Stannard Baker saw the "New Negro" as an economic nationalist. He was the person who "urges his friends to patronize Negro doctors and dentists and to trade with Negro shopkeepers." He was different from "the old fashioned Negro [who] preferred to go to the white man for everything." In 1916, educator and activist William Pickens published a book titled *The New Negro*. The work espoused a philosophy of protest, race pride, and cultural achievement.[22]

Locke was probably aware of the term and its various meanings and representations. In any event, he used it to define the literary movement that was being born. Locke assembled a distinguished group of black contributors including Jessie Fauset, Langston Hughes, W. E. B. Du Bois, Arthur Schomburg, and James Weldon Johnson. Among the white authors was Melville J. Herskovits, an anthropologist who would later write the landmark study *The Myth of the Negro Past*. *The New Negro* emphasized literature and the arts, probably in keeping with the editor's questionable assumption that the most "immediate hope" for blacks "rests in the revaluation by white and black alike of the Negro in terms of his artistic endowments and cultural contributions. . . ."[23]

Alain Locke was 39 years old when he edited the anthology. A brilliant student, he had won a Rhodes Scholarship and received degrees from Oxford and Harvard. Locke had not published much before 1925, but his editorial work on the *New Negro* and his own contributions to it established him as a significant intellectual. In his foreword to the book, he noted that many of the earlier studies of blacks had seen them through "external" eyes. According to him, nine-tenths of such works had been "*about* the Negro rather than of him so that it is the Negro problem rather than the Negro that is known and mooted in the general mind." Breaking with this genre of studies, Locke's book "concentrated upon self-expression and the forces and motives of self-determination." He wanted to "let the Negro speak for himself."[24] This was a significant change in perspective, an important methodological advance, since blacks were to have their own voices. Locke recognized that "Negro life . . . is finding a new soul" and that "there is a fresh spiritual and cultural focusing." Asserting that the "Old Negro had long become more of a myth than a man," Locke hailed the "vibrant . . . new psychology" of the younger generation.[25]

Recognizing the emergence of a new generation of blacks and understanding the aggressive temper of the times, Locke maintained that "the day of 'aunties,' 'uncles' and 'mammies'" was over, and that "'Uncle Tom' and 'Sambo' have passed on." The New Negro should, accordingly, reject the badge of subservience, and aggressively command the future. "By shedding the old chrysalis of the Negro problem," Locke wrote, "we are achieving something like a spiritual emancipation."[26]

Locke rejected "radical" solutions to the black condition. While the black person was "a radical on race matters," Locke opined, he was "conservative" on other issues, more of "a social protestant" than "a genuine radical."[27] Probably as a consequence of this stance, the *New Negro* did not include contributions from the prominent socialists A. Philip Randolph and Chandler Owen. Nor were the ideas of Marcus Garvey and other black nationalists represented in the book. On the other hand, eight of the contributors were women. With the exception of the one by Elise Johnson McDougald, their essays avoided any reference to issues of gender. A teacher, social worker, and trade unionist, McDougald highlighted the existing unflattering representations of black women:

> She is conscious that what is left of chivalry is not directed toward her. She realizes that the ideals of beauty, built up in the fine arts, have excluded her almost entirely. Instead, the grotesque Aunt Jemimas of the street-car advertisements proclaim only an ability to serve, without grace of loveliness. Nor does the drama catch her finest spirit. She is most often used to provoke the mirthless laugh of ridicule; or to portray feminine viciousness or vulgarity not peculiar to Negroes. This is the shadow over her.[28]

Locke, as his later statements underscored, wished to separate art from politics and seemed not to understand the need for systemic changes if black Americans were to have their condition transformed. Literature and the arts, cultural politics as it were, could help transform some of white society's assumptions about blacks, but the locus of power would remain resistant to change unless its institutional apparatus and economic arrangements were assaulted frontally and aggressively.

Locke's belief in the capacity of the arts to inaugurate deeper societal change was embraced by James Weldon Johnson. "It is through the arts," he maintained in 1924, "that we may find the easiest approach to the solution of some of the most vital phases of our problem as a particular group in this country. It is the path of least friction. It is the plane on which all men are more willing to meet and stand with us."[29] As a leading activist, Johnson, unlike Locke, also believed in the efficacy of political struggles. W. E. B. Du Bois, however, linked art and literature to the movement for civil rights and social change. As editor of the *Crisis*, he did not refrain from taking political positions. In 1926 Du Bois maintained:

> . . . all Art is propaganda and ever must be, despite the wailing of the purists. I stand in utter shamelessness and say that whatever art I have for writing has been used always for propaganda. . . . I do not care a damn for any art that is not used for propaganda.[30]

Marcus Garvey agreed. Rejecting the notion that "the solution to the race problem depends on our development in music, in art, in literature," Garvey maintained that a "nation was not founded first of all on literature or on writing books, it is founded first upon the effort of real workers."[31]

Most writers associated with the Harlem Renaissance eschewed the linking of literature with politics. Claude McKay and Langston Hughes were the two most notable exceptions, although McKay retreated from his political stance in his later years. The most overtly political enterprise to be launched in Harlem in the 1920s was the short-lived magazine *Fire!!: A Quarterly Devoted to the Younger Negro Artists*. According to Langston Hughes, the magazine was created to "burn up a lot of the old, dead, conventional Negro-white ideas of the past."[32] Its inspiration came from the younger writers, including Hughes, Zora Neale Hurston, and Aaron Bennett. Wallace Thurman served as the editor. Sometimes mocking blacks and the intelligentsia, *Fire!!* suggested a politically radical tone. In its foreword, the magazine proclaimed:

> Fy-ah,
> Fy-ah, Lawd
> Fy-ah gonna burn ma soul!

Coincidentally, the building that housed the magazine was destroyed by a fire shortly after the first issue. But the magazine had done its job, shocking many critics and not a few members of the black middle class. But *Fire!!*, in spite of its quick disappearance, had manifested the emerging faces and spirit of the Renaissance. It was politically radical but also conciliatory, simultaneously bohemian and respectable, independent in spirit but also traditional in some of its literary forms and styles.

Always short of funds, several writers found white patrons. Langston Hughes, Claude McKay, Zora Neale Hurston, and others benefited from this support. The arrangement worked well enough in some instances, but the writers were sensitive to the charge that white philanthropy compromised their work. Hughes, who eventually received and rejected the assistance of a white benefactor, saw a danger in such support since "the Negro artist works against the undertow of sharp criticism and misunderstanding from his own group and unintentional bribes from the whites."[33] In justifying the parting of ways with his white patron, Charlotte Osgood Mason, Hughes noted that she wanted him to write a kind of poetry that would have muted his voice. "I was not what she wanted me to be," Hughes insisted.[34] Du Bois also believed that some whites harbored ulterior motives when they supported black writers. In 1926 he complained:

> there are today a surprising number of white people who are getting a great satisfaction out of these younger Negro writers, because they think it is going to stop agitation of the Negro question.... And many colored people are all too eager to follow this advice; especially those who are weary of the eternal struggle along the color line, who are afraid to fight and to whom the money of philanthropists and the alluring publicity are subtle and deadly bribes.[35]

Whites were also important in another sense to the black writers since it was whites who owned the publishing houses and could determine whether or not a writer's work appeared. Such interest on the part of the publishers was not entirely altruistic. With a developing interest in black literature in the larger society, some of these works actually sold well. Although the black writers wrote about their own people, the mercenary ears of many were attuned to the sounds emanating from white society. Attracted to urban black life in voyeuristic fashion, whites purchased books that satisfied their inner needs. When Claude McKay published his novel, *Home to Harlem*, in 1928, for example, his graphic depiction of Harlem's underside guaranteed its success. W. E. B. Du Bois denounced McKay for pandering to the "Purient demand on the part of white folk for a portrayal in Negroes of that utter licentiousness which conventional civilization holds white folk back from enjoying . . . and after the dirtier parts of its filth, I felt distinctly like taking a bath."[36]

Du Bois overreacted. The slice of life that McKay depicted was very much a part of Harlem's realities, probably parts that were invisible to the middle class and to the outsiders who came to sample black exotica. Harlem, like black America as a whole, possessed many faces, all of them reflecting a people's strengths, weaknesses, failures, and successes. None of these faces merited a self-conscious apology from black spokespersons, then or now.

While McKay exposed Harlem's underbelly, Jessie Fauset focused on the life and travails of the middle class. She published four novels dealing with such themes as male/female interactions, gender politics, and the quest for a black identity, as well as class, miscegenation, and interracial relationships. One of the central premises that informed her writing was that "the colored American . . . was not so very different

Nella Larsen (November 23, 1934) after her divorce. She is known for her novels and short stories that examined the lives of the middle class.

from any other American, just distinctive."[37] Like Fauset, Nella Larsen also examined the lives of the middle class in her novels and short stories. *Quicksand* (1928), her first novel, focused on the alienation among the Northern middle class as well as on issues of class and mixed-race identity. Her second and arguably more successful novel, *Passing* (1929), also addressed the painful and complex questions of racial identity and the search for place, respectability, and autonomy. The women in her novel could be seen as victims, frequently burdened by societal demands they were unable to defeat.

Although Zora Neale Hurston published her most famous novel, *Their Eyes Were Watching God*, during the waning moments of the Harlem Renaissance, she must rank as one of the outstanding literary figures of the time. A prolific writer, Hurston published short stories, poetry, two books of folklore, and four novels. Hurston's works were grounded in a deep understanding of the life of black Southerners, par-

Chapter 7   *Intellectual and Cultural Life*   147

Zora Neale Hurston with Langston Hughes and Jessie Fauset in front of Booker T. Washington statue.

ticularly those who lived in rural areas. Her fictional characters are strong women dealing with the barriers imposed upon them because of their gender. *Their Eyes Were Watching God,* a work that received a lukewarm reception when it appeared in 1937, is now rightly celebrated as a classic feminist novel.

One of the lesser-known poets of the Renaissance, Georgia Douglas Johnson (1880-1966), wrote the poem "Wishes" in 1927. It could be read as reflecting a desire for women's autonomy and liberation:

> I'm tired of pacing the petty round of the ring of the thing I know—
> I want to stand on the daylight's edge and see where the sunsets go.
> I want to sail on a swallow's tail and peep through the sky's blue glass.
> I want to see if the dreams in me shall perish or come to pass.
> I want to look through the moon's pale crook and gaze on the moonman's face.
> I want to keep all the tears I weep and sail to some unknown place.[38]

The founding of a number of periodicals and magazines in the 1880s and later facilitated intellectual exchange among the writers and the cross-fertilization of ideas. They catered to a wide variety of interests, although those devoted to educational and religious matters constituted the majority. These publications were often short-lived, but a few survived long enough to play significant roles in the dissemination of ideas and works by black Americans. The AME Church *Review* was one of the most long lasting and influential. Founded in 1884 by the General Conference of the African Methodist Episcopal Church, the *Review's* objective was to publish the work of black scholars "of the A.M.E. Church . . . of the country, of the West Indies, of Africa and of the world."[39] Similarly, the *Colored American Magazine*, founded in Boston in 1900, played an important role in publishing the literary works of blacks. After it ran into financial difficulties shortly after its founding, Booker T. Washington subsidized its publication from 1904 to 1909. Pauline Hopkins became literary editor in 1900, a position she held for about four years. Before its demise in 1909, such writers as Paul Laurence Dunbar, Pauline Hopkins, William Braithwaite, T. Thomas Fortune, and Ralph W. Taylor appeared in its pages.

Several writers associated with the Harlem Renaissance had their poems and shorter works published in a number of magazines founded in 1910 or later. Jessie Fauset, as the literary editor of *Crisis* in the mid-1920s, published the work of many young writers. *Opportunity*, the organ of the National Urban League, however, developed a much better reputation among the writers for being sympathetic to their literary efforts. Charles Johnson, the editor from 1923 to 1928, advanced the careers of these writers, even sponsoring literary contests for them. The *Negro World*, the newspaper published by Marcus Garvey's Universal Negro Improvement Association, also supported, albeit for a short time, the literary efforts of the young writers. Garvey's desire to blur the distinction between art and politics led those not so inclined to seek other publication outlets.

The Harlem Renaissance was, of course, more than just a literary movement. There was much creative activity in music, the theatre, and art as well, in Harlem and elsewhere in the nation. Harlem boasted the largest concentration of writers, but black America as a whole was aglow with cultural icons of every sort. As in the case of the literary productivity, these developments built upon a rich tradition of black culture, drawing their strength, vitality, and inspiration from them. The black music of the 1920s, for example, reflected the styles honed by a people throughout their history; the new creations were rooted in the old. Unlike literary works, a people's musical life does not lend itself to quantification. Most of their creations, particularly those that are the work of people at the margins, are often not written down or recognized, much less celebrated.

Some of the mostly middle-class literary icons of the Renaissance saw little to admire in the earlier forms of black music. Alain Locke characterized them as "broken, musically illiterate dialect."[40] Such music had to be refined and transformed into high art if it were to be palatable to the elite of the Renaissance. At one level, some of the guardians of the Harlem Renaissance had their feet planted in their own cultural soil, but on another level, they sought the approval and sustenance of white society. Langston Hughes did not share this tension. As he put it:

> We younger Negro artists who create now intend to express our dark-skinned selves without fear or shame. If white people are pleased we are glad. If they are not, it doesn't matter. We know we are beautiful. And ugly too. The tom-tom cries and the tom-tom laughs. If colored people are pleased, we are glad. If they are not, their displeasure doesn't matter either. We build our temples for tomorrow, strong as we know how, and we stop on top of the mountain, free within ourselves.[41]

In New York, Harlem's bustling nightlife provided outlets for the musicians. But other cities such as New Orleans and Chicago were alive as well. During the latter part of the nineteenth century, ragtime piano players became popular in these cities and in other parts of the country. In piano-rag music, "the left hand took over the task of stomping and patting while the right hand performed syncopated melodies using motives reminiscent of fiddle and banjo tunes."[42] Lyricists composed ragtime songs, and pianists adapted European classics to the new musical form. Scott Joplin, who wrote "Maple Leaf Rag," "Steptime Rag," "Binks' Waltz," "The Entertainer," and others, was probably the best known rag pianist and composer. James Sylvester Scott, composer of such pieces as "Kansas City Rag" and "Frog Legs Rag," was also quite renowned, as was James Hubert "Eubie" Blake. Blake composed several hundred pieces, among them the well-known "Sounds of Africa," or "Charleston Rag."

Rag music was not the only precursor to jazz, which was to become the rage of the 1920s. The blues, an aural music, appeared at the turn of the century. Unlike spirituals, the blues are markedly secular songs. Drawing upon the cultural traditions of the rural people, the blues employed a call-and-response style. The songs, however, captured the pain and disappointment of an individual's life experiences as opposed to the more collective voice of the spirituals. William Christopher Handy (1873-1958), a band leader, is usually acknowledged as the father of the blues. His first composition, the "Memphis Blues," appeared in 1912. This was soon followed by the "St. Louis Blues" in 1914, a composition that did much to popularize this musical idiom.

The late nineteenth century also saw a proliferation of orchestras and brass bands in black America. These groups played in dance halls, at a variety of social occasions, and at funerals. New Orleans, New York, and Chicago were the principal centers for these forms of entertainment. Together with ragtime and the blues, the bands and orchestras reflected the creative energies of a people and their success in claiming their cultural space. The appearance of jazz on the scene after 1915 and its flourishing in the 1920s was a continuation of this internal vitality. Students of jazz note that its style was heavily influenced by both ragtime and the blues in its use of the piano, call-and-response technique, and syncopation.

The jazz sound, ragtime, and the blues were decidedly black American creations, fertilized and incubated in the crucible of the black experience. The blues became one of the crazes in the 1920s, particularly after Mamie Smith recorded her hit, "Crazy Blues," selling 75,000 copies in a month. Most of the stars of this idiom were women, and the distinguished list included Ethel Waters, Ida Cox, Clara Smith, Jane Martin, Mae Barnes, and Gertrude "Ma" Rainey. Bessie Smith, who reigned between 1923 and 1929, was the most popular of them all, recording some 180 songs on the Columbia label.[43] The list of celebrated bluesmen included Charlie Jackson, Gus Cannon, Sylvester Weaver, and Alger Alexander.

While the blues remained important during the 1920s, the period has also been described as the "Jazz Age." Jazz bands appeared almost everywhere. New Orleans, Chicago, Los Angeles, and New York became centers of the jazz world. The legendary jazz soloist Louis "Satchmo" Armstrong became an immediate sensation when he arrived in Chicago in 1922 to play in the band led by the famous Joseph Oliver. Edward "Duke" Ellington, one of the greatest jazz composers, wrote his first song at fourteen and took his band to Harlem in 1927. Over the course of his life he composed more than 2,000 pieces, establishing a place for himself as one of the greatest figures in American music. The Jazz Age was distinguished not only for its great bands and composers, but for outstanding singers and instrumentalists as well.

In addition to the rise of the blues and jazz, there were other significant cultural developments such as the growth in the musical theatre. The black theatre, of course, predated the Harlem Renaissance. The enslaved population laid the foundations of this theatre by the performances they staged for their entertainment, and that of others, on special occasions. At Christmastime, for example, slaves in an African-derived ceremony called John Kunering donned their costumes, paraded, played musical instruments, and acted. After emancipation, some black artists performed in minstrel troupes before blacks as well as whites, "blackening" their faces and playing the stereotypical "darky."

The two most popular performers in blackface at the turn of the century were the West Indian Egbert Austin Williams and the Kansan George Walker. Williams was a gifted comic, and Walker was renowned for his skill in dancing the cakewalk. The two men worked as a team on stage in minstrel shows and in musicals until Walker retired in 1909. Walker frequently took advantage of Williams' presumed gullibility in their performances:

Walker: I tells you I'm lettin' you in on this 'cause you're a friend of mine. I could do this alone . . . but I wants you to share in it 'cause we's friends. Now after you gets into the bank you fill the satchel with money.
Williams: Whose money?
Walker: That ain't the point. We don't know who put the money in there, and we don't know why they got it. And they won't know why we got it. All you have to do is put the money in the satchel. I'll get you the satchel–ain't nothin' to bother 'bout–that's 'cause you're a friend of mine, see.
Williams: And what do I with dis satchel?
Walker: All you got to do is bring it to me at the place where I tells you.
Williams: When they come to count up the cash and finds it short, then what?
Walker: By that time, we'll be far, far away–where the birds is singin' and the flowers is in bloom.
Williams: And if they catch us they'll put us so far, far away we never will hear no birds singin'. Everybody knows you can't smell no flowers through a stone wall.[44]

Williams and Walker sang "coon" songs as well, entertaining both blacks and whites. These songs depicted blacks in negative terms, albeit humorously. "All Coons Look Alike to Me" became one of the most popular of these creations. Others included "I'm the Luckiest Coon in

Town" and "Those Chicken Stealing Coons."[45] Blacks such as Williams and Walker who sang songs and "blackened" up to play "darkies" or to mock whites playing blacks were earning a living. Walker maintained that he and other performers had no real choice because whites were not receptive to:

> . . . natural black performers . . . on account of racial and color prejudice. . . . [The problem was] how to get before the public and prove that ability we might possess. . . . As there seemed to be a great demand for black face on stage . . . we finally decided that as white men with black faces were billing themselves as "coons," Williams [and] Walker would do well to bill themselves as The Two Real Coons, and so we did. Our bills attracted the attention of managers and gradually we made our way in.[46]

In addition to Williams and Walker, several black stars of the twentieth century started their careers in minstrelsy. They included Bessie Smith, Ma Rainey, and Charles Gilpin.[47] Modern historians have generally avoided the difficult question of the psychic price that black performers paid for debasing themselves in order to entertain whites or even fellow blacks. But they surely paid a painful price, even if, as some scholars have suggested, the performers consciously subverted the traditional stereotypes of black behavior. "Nothing seemed more absurd than to see a colored man making himself ridiculous (imitating the blackface white comedian) in order to portray himself," declared George Walker.[48] The passageways that blacks constructed for themselves almost always came with a price.

Black musical theatre of the 1920s, therefore, drew upon a long and varied tradition of performance. There were at least six black musicals on the Broadway stage between 1895 and 1911. These included *In Dahomey* (1902), *Abyssinia* (1906), and *The Red Moon* (1908). Almost all of these shows addressed such questions as black-white relations, the place of Africa in the black imagination, and common human foibles. In 1921, the musical *Shuffle Along* made its debut on Broadway to much critical acclaim and inaugurated an active decade of black theater. A partial list includes *Running Wild* (1923), *Lucky Sambo* (1925), *Bottomland* (1927), *Keep Shuffling* (1928), and *Deep Harlem* (1929). The stars of the period included Josephine Baker, Jules Bledsoe, and Paul Robeson.

The 1920s also saw the emergence of a number of composers of classical, concert, and recital music. William Grant Still was one of the earliest and most distinguished of the group. His earliest composition, *Darker America*, was completed in 1924, and there followed a spate of works, including symphonies, ballets, chamber compositions, and works for orchestras. Henry T. Burleigh, Robert Nathaniel Dett, Florence Price, and Clarence Cameron White all composed notable works during the period. One historian of the music of black Americans notes that these composers "constantly turned to the folk music of their people as a source of inspiration for their compositions."[49]

In art, as in music, the most gifted figures of the 1920s built upon the traditions of their predecessors. Slaves, as recent works clearly demonstrate, used their art to celebrate their heritage and to serve their religious and other needs. This kind of living art, which serves particular functions both secular and religious, should be distinguished from that which is more aesthetic in appeal and purpose. Black Americans excelled in the two idioms. Edward Mitchell Bannister was a portrait painter of distinction, and Henry Ossawa Tanner won many prizes for his work.

The years following World War I witnessed the talents of the Kansas-born Aaron Douglas. Drawing upon African styles, his art graced the pages of many magazines of the time, including *Fire!!* Laura Wheeler Waring was essentially a portrait painter of the 1920s, although she produced landscapes as well. Archibald Motley Jr., depicted urban scenes, and Edward Harleston celebrated the masses. The productivity of these and other artists was so great and the quality so high that in 1931 a traveling exhibit comprising the work of about 150 artists visited fifty cities.

As the preceding discussion shows, women played crucial roles in the literary and cultural history of the times. The times, however, remained male dominated, and women had to confront obstacles that the men did not face, at least not to the same degree. Publishers frequently ignored their work, and women were less successful than the men in finding patrons. Nevertheless, novelists such as Zora Neale Hurston, Nella Larsen, and Jessie Fauset in varying degrees addressed the ways in which the lives of black women were circumscribed by their gender.

Notably, several of the leading and gifted writers of the time were homosexual. This was not an age that encouraged an open discussion of sexuality, although same-sex relationships were as much a part of Harlem's life as they were elsewhere. By the 1920s, however, Greenwich Village in Manhattan had become well known for its gay population, but Harlem was regarded "as the most exciting center of gay life."[50] The nightclubs and speakeasies attracted blacks as well as whites in search of a furtive and precarious sexual freedom.

The gay writers of the Renaissance did not discuss their sexual orientation openly; the social costs of such an admission would have been too great. Still, as recent historians have shown, Alain Locke, Countée Cullen, Wallace Thurman, Claude McKay, Bruce Nugent, Harold Jackman, and possibly Langston Hughes were gay. To be black and gay meant a double marginalization by the larger society. Whether this marginalization enhanced, restricted, or had no effect upon individual creative energies is a contentious but ultimately unanswerable question. It should be added that such outstanding blues artists as Bessie Smith, Ma Rainey, Ethel Waters, and Alberta Hunter also crossed the accepted sexual boundaries of the time.[51]

The Harlem Renaissance, if one defines it narrowly and solely as a literary movement, sputtered to a close by the mid- to late 1930s. The Great Depression had taken its toll on the resources of the writers and their patrons and may even have clogged the wellsprings of literary creativity. Harlem no longer captured the imagination of young, brilliant, and restless black writers and artists. In fact, this expanding enclave of Manhattan became less an exemplar of black creative achievement and more a signifier for creeping squalor and urban decay. But this did not mean a cessation of cultural creativity. Vibrant new idioms would emerge from the enclave's underside.

Seen at another level, the literary renaissance was merely another moment, albeit an exciting one, in a people's intellectual and cultural trajectory. Such moments are never sustainable indefinitely; their creative energies are often spent as soon as the circumstances that spawned them change or the social and other needs that gave them life diminish or no longer exist. The men and women of the literary Renaissance did not all disappear; Langston Hughes, Arna Bontemps, and Sterling Brown remained active for many years. Zora Neale Hurston produced her best work in 1937. The bright moment was dimmed, not extinguished. Black literary creativity would flourish again at different moments in later years.

Notes

1. George Washington Williams, *History of the Negro Race from 1619 to 1880: Negroes as Slaves, Soldiers and as Citizens*, 2 vols. (repr. New York: Bergman Publishers, 1988), I: 4.
2. August Meier, *Negro Thought in America, 1880-1915* (Ann Arbor: University of Michigan Press, 1971), 260.
3. August Meier and Elliott Rudwick, *Black History and the Historical Profession, 1915-1980* (Urbana: University of Illinois Press, 1986), 7.
4. Ibid., 11.
5. Blyden Jackson, *A History of Afro-American Literature, Vol. 1: The Long Beginning, 1746-1895* (Baton Rouge: Louisiana State University Press, 1989), 378-399.
6. Dickson Bruce, *Black American Writing from the Nadir: The Evolution of a Literary Tradition, 1877-1915* (Baton Rouge: Louisiana State University Press, 1989), 82.
7. Ibid.
8. Du Bois, *Souls of Black Folk*, 5.
9. Ibid., 7.
10. Carby, *Reconstructing Womanhood*, 128.
11. Bruce, *Black American Writing*, 164.
12. Ayers, *The Promise of the New South*, 390.
13. Quoted in Bruce, *Black American Writing*, 239.

14. Wilson Moses, "Alexander Crummell: Black Nationalist and Apostle of Western Civilization," in Leon Litwack and August Meier, eds., *Black Leaders of the Nineteenth Century* (Urbana: University of Illinois Press, 1982), 246.
15. Ibid., 262.
16. Alfred Moss, *The American Negro Academy: Voice of the Talented Tenth* (Baton Rouge: Louisiana State University Press, 1981), 1.
17. Johnson, *Black Manhattan*, 3-4.
18. Langston Hughes, *The Big Sea: An Autobiography* (repr. New York: Hillard Wang, 1964), 62-64.
19. Cary Wintz, *Black Culture and the Harlem Renaissance* (Houston: Rice University Press, 1988), 71.
20. Ibid., 201.
21. Ibid., 79.
22. Meier, *Negro Thought*, 258-259.
23. Alain Locke, ed., *The New Negro: Voices of the Harlem Renaissance* (repr. New York: Atheneum, 1992), 15.
24. Ibid., xxv.
25. Ibid., xxvii; 3.
26. Ibid., 4-5.
27. Ibid., 11.
28. Ibid., 369-370.
29. Wintz, *Black Culture and the Harlem Renaissance*, 104.
30. Ibid., 145.
31. Ibid., 149.
32. Hughes, *The Big Sea*, 385.
33. Thadious Davis, *Nella Larsen: Novelist of the Harlem Renaissance: A Woman's Life Unveiled* (Baton Rouge: Louisiana State University Press, 1994), 240.
34. Ibid., 240; Hughes, *The Big Sea*, 325.
35. Davis, *Nella Larsen*, 241.
36. Wintz, *Black Culture and the Harlem Renaissance*, 145.
37. Jessie Fauset, *The Chinaberry Tree* (New York: Frederick A. Stokes, 1931), Foreword.
38. Cheryl Wall, *Women of the Harlem Renaissance* (Bloomington: Indiana University Press, 1995), 14.
39. Bullock, *A History of Negro Education*, 93.
40. For discussions of the use of dialect in black writing and other criticisms, see Wintz, *Black Culture and the Harlem Renaissance*, 49-51; 68-70; 130-153.
41. Lewis, *When Harlem Was in Vogue*, 191.
42. Eileen Southern, *The Music of Black Americans* (2nd ed., New York: W. W. Norton, 1983), 309.
43. Douglas, *Terrible Honesty*, 391-392.
44. Watkins, *On the Real Side*, 175-176.
45. Ibid., 146.
46. Arnold Shaw, *Black Popular Music in America* (New York: MacMillan, 1986), 69.
47. Douglas, *Terrible Honesty*, 77.
48. Ibid., 69.
49. Southern, *Music of Black America*, 266.
50. George Chauncy, *Gay New York: Gender, Urban Culture, and the Making of the Gay Male World 1890-1940* (New York: Basic Books, 1994), 227.
51. Ibid., 227-267; Douglas, *Terrible Honesty*, 407-410.

A People in Motion, 1915–1955

The structure of black life experienced rapid and fundamental changes during the twentieth century. Black America, of course, had been transforming itself since 1619, but the pace of that structural change accelerated during this action-packed and achievement-filled century. We have maintained throughout this work that the changes in the interior lives of blacks emanated primarily from within, although the larger society was not without important influences. White Americans controlled the legislative and judicial institutions as well as the machinery of the state. The commanding heights of the economy also rested in white hands. But this did not mean that blacks were unable to develop their own organizations, make decisions about their interior lives, and create their own passageways within an oppressive system. This chapter and the one that follows focus on the enormous energy that characterized black life after about 1915, demonstrating the numerous ways in which a people made and remade themselves.

The interior changes in black life occurred in the context of profound transformations in the larger society. As a nation, America became a world power after its participation in the Spanish-Cuban-American War and its intervention in World War I. Its wartime economy expanded job opportunities, a development that helped to spur black migration northward. An increasingly industrial economy produced internal demographic shifts, accelerated the growth of cities, and fed numerous changes in lifestyles and social organization. The Great Depression of the 1930s expanded the role of the federal government and laid the foundations of the modern welfare state. These years also saw the women's struggle for the franchise, the strengthening of the labor movement, and the efforts to make Americans of vast numbers of immigrants from Europe and elsewhere.

MIGRATION

The trajectory of black life after about 1915 cannot be understood without an appreciation of the transforming influences of the migration to the cities of the Northeast, the Midwest, and to some extent the West. Rejecting Booker T. Washington's admonition to cast their bucket down in the South, blacks migrated for the next half a century. There were ebbs and flows in the intensity of the movement, but it was an extended process that would not abate until certain larger societal changes had occurred. This internal demographic change was the consequence of a complex set of variables that were both individual and societal in their underpinnings. The decision to migrate is never made in the abstract; it is usually the product of a desire to escape intolerable realities and embrace better opportunities elsewhere. Migrants also wish to join relatives, seek more hospitable climates, and begin anew. Although the timing of their departure is sometimes not of their making, we should not view migrants as passive persons, always reacting to circumstances they cannot control and unable to command their lives.

Black migrants from the South made quiet if anguished decisions to realize their human possibilities in other parts of their nation. These life-transforming decisions, in their contemplation and execution, were exercises in positive behavior and not the nihilistic writhings of the beaten and the defeated. In fact, the movement by black citizens or any other group of citizens in their own country should never be seen as surprising. This is a phenomenon that knows no ethnic, geographic, or temporal boundaries. The most noteworthy aspect of the movement of blacks in the twentieth century is not that it occurred, but rather its scope. Between 1916 and 1920, for example, about one million blacks left the South; between 800,000 and one million did so during the 1920s, and 398,000 in the 1930s. About 1.5 million migrated in the 1940s, and a similar number moved during the 1950s. By 1960, five million African-Americans had abandoned the South. (See Table 8.1.)

The rate of black migration from the South began to decline in the 1970s, probably as prospects for the improvement of the black condition in that region improved as a consequence of the civil rights movement and its legislative successes. In fact, during the 1970s many blacks began to return to the South, reversing the out-migration trend. Once again, they had come to a mature assessment of their best interests and acted accordingly. The dramatic migration from the South reduced the proportion of blacks who lived in that region from 90 percent in 1910 to

TABLE 8.1
Black Out-Migration from the South, 1870-1970 (in thousands)

Decade	Black Population in the South at the Start of the Decade	Estimated Net Out-Migration of Blacks	Out-Migrants as Percentage of Mid-Decade Population
1870–1880	4,421	71	-1.4%
1880–1890	5,594	80	-1.3
1890–1900	6,761	174	-2.4
1900–1910	7,923	197	-2.4
1910–1920	8,749	525	-5.9
1920–1930	8,912	877	-9.6
1930–1940	9,362	398	-4.1
1940–1950	9,905	1,468	-14.6
1950–1960	10,225	1,473	-13.7
1960–1970	11,312	1,380	-11.9

SOURCE: Reynolds Farley and Walter R. Allen, *The Color Line and the Quality of Life in America* (Russell Sage Foundation, New York, 1987), p. 113.

50 percent in 1970. Concomitantly, by 1970, 20 percent of blacks lived in the Midwestern states, about the same percentage in the Northeast, and 10 percent in the West. Although the South had lost so many of its black residents, an increase in the birthrate coupled with a decline in mortality rates ensured that it would remain home to half of the African-Americans in the nation.

The withdrawal by so many from the South accelerated the pace at which blacks became urbanized. Between 1910 and 1930, the black population of Philadelphia increased by 59 percent, New York City by 66 percent, Los Angeles by 100 percent, Chicago by 148 percent, Cleveland by 308 percent, and Detroit by 611 percent.[1] Overall, 40 percent of blacks lived in urban areas by 1940, and in 1970 seven out of ten did so. In 1940 one out of every four blacks in the South was a city dweller; thirty years later, the proportion had climbed to 70 percent.

While the decision to move was largely theirs, the societal context in which blacks made it deserves to be examined. For many, the decision to abandon the South was not taken easily since their kin had fertilized the soil with their flesh, helped build its economy, stamped their culture upon its landscape, and registered claims to the region that were just as compelling as those of their white counterparts. There were also existing ties of kith and kin that had to be considered, and many thought they were too old to uproot themselves and begin a new and uncertain life elsewhere.

Under the circumstances, many blacks decided to remain in the South. As one newspaper, the *Atlanta Independent*, observed in 1917, "This is our home and . . . we are not going to leave, unless we are driven by want or lack of freedom."[2] The two situations, ironically, existed at the time. Most black citizens remained poor because racial and structural barriers impeded their quest for equal opportunity and full citizenship. To exacerbate their economic plight, the boll weevil invaded the United States from Mexico in 1892 and began its ferocious assault on cotton bolls a few years later with disastrous consequences. Many black and white farmers experienced financial ruin. Forced off the land, black farmers and tenants were eager to seek their fortunes elsewhere.

Those who left the land for urban areas did not do so without considerable misgiving. For rural peoples, the land was, paradoxically, the source and symbol of their oppression, but also the wellspring of their hope for a better life. Generations of blacks had worked on the land as slaves or had been tied to it as exploited tenants, sharecroppers, and peons. On the other hand, some had become farmers, and cultivated it in their own right. Almost everyone had seen land ownership as being synonymous with success; many had left for Kansas, Oklahoma, and other places to acquire real estate. Leaving the soil for the pavement of the city was more than just a change in residence; it represented the close of a chapter, the abandonment of a particular kind of dream, and the imagination of a different future.

The decision to leave was also the product of white violence against blacks. Lynch mobs made the South an insecure place for blacks, and Jim Crow laws institutionalized white supremacy. Outside of the South, the outbreak of war in Europe in 1914 slowed the immigration of Europeans to the United States. In 1914 the country welcomed 1.2 million Europeans, but the number fell to 376,000 in 1915, 298,000 in 1916, and 110,000 in 1918. Northern industrialists had long depended on white immigrants to meet their labor needs, largely ignoring native-born black workers. With the decline in the number of European immigrants, employers had no choice but to hire black workers. The industrial and support sectors expanded to meet the requirements of a wartime economy, creating new jobs for the skilled and the unskilled alike. Aware of these developing opportunities, many blacks in the South began the fateful journey to the North.

Some white employers in the South were alarmed at the prospect of losing their black workers. "If the Negroes go," lamented the *Montgomery Advertiser* in 1916, "where shall we get labor to take their places?" A newspaper, *The Columbia State* of South Carolina, echoed the position of many whites: "Black labor is the best labor the South can get," it proclaimed. "No other would work long under the same conditions."[3] Accordingly, some whites urged a ban on Northern recruiters of black migrants and on newspapers such as the *Chicago Defender* that encouraged blacks to leave. A number of states and cities adopted anti-enticement laws and required recruiters to possess licenses. Railroads found ingenious ways to deny transportation to the migrants.

Such harassment failed their purpose, because neither the *Chicago Defender* nor the recruiters were the root causes or the motivating factors behind the exodus. Moderate whites recognized that some of the impetus for the migration resided in structural barriers that blacks confronted and in the high incidence of racial violence. Acting from a position of enlightened self-interest, some whites urged reforms such as the payment of higher wages, the reduction of rents, and the provision of better educational opportunities for blacks. In addition, they condemned the violent assaults on black citizens that had become a feature of the Southern racial culture. Some employers responded positively to these suggestions by offering higher wages and improving the conditions under which blacks worked. But these were mere palliatives; the migration tide could not be slowed until the racial environment in the South had been transformed, blacks were protected from abuse by whites, and their rights as equal citizens were accepted in theory if not altogether in practice.

There were whites, on the other hand, who actively welcomed the departure of blacks from the region. These persons wanted to create a white South, blaming blacks for the "race problem." The *Vicksburg Herald* concluded in 1916: "A more equitable distribution of the sons of Ham will teach the Caucasians of the Northern states that wherever there is a negro infusion, there will be a race problem." The *New Orleans Times-Picayune* welcomed the prospect that "as the North grows blacker the South grows whiter."[4]

Blacks who left the South liberated themselves physically and psychologically from an oppressive environment. By doing so, they helped to undermine the control that whites had exercised over them. The migrants withdrew their labor, altering the nature of social and economic relations in the region. Migration was an expression of independence from whites as well as a rejection of the lowly societal place that they had been assigned. By leaving, blacks called into question white society's definition of them as dependent, docile, and incapable of living without the "benevolent" exploitation of their white neighbors. Blacks who abandoned sharecropping and tenant farming broke their economic dependence on the white landowners, affecting the economic well-being of their exploiters in the process.

Many migrants made intermediate moves in the South before they ended up in the North or the distant West. Some moved short distances from one rural area to another, others moved from one city to another, and the vast majority made the trek from rural areas to urban areas. The states varied in the proportion of their black citizens who migrated. Much depended on the local context, the racial climate, and the nature of the economic relations between blacks and whites. Blacks, particularly members of the middle class, who had created a tolerable space for themselves in certain states or localities were also less likely to move. The rate of out-migration is an imperfect barometer of the texture of black life in the various states, but it does suggest something about how blacks viewed the prospects for an improvement in their condition. The states that produced the largest number of migrants included South Carolina, Georgia, Alabama, Louisiana, and Mississippi.

Migration, even under the best of circumstances, disrupts lives and is very stressful. Those who had kin in the cities or other areas in which they relocated may have had an easier time adjusting to their new environment. These kin networks provided the newcomers with temporary lodging, assisted them in procuring jobs, passed on survival strategies, and helped them when they fell on difficult times. Although their roles and effectiveness varied from city to city, a number of organizations emerged to help ease the migrants' transition. The National Urban League provided help in finding jobs; the Young Men's Christian Association and the Young Women's Christian Association provided similar services, established day nurseries, and organized social events. Churches everywhere served as more than spiritual homes for the migrants; they introduced them to potential friends, allowing them to draw psychic sustenance from others in similar circumstances. To the degree that their resources permitted, churches offered food, shelter, advice, and emotional support to the new residents. There was also a large number of community-based organizations of varying sizes, resources, and longevity that met their various needs.

Migration to the North, Midwest, and West represented more than the movement of human bodies and the quest for jobs. Southern blacks also brought their culture with them to their new destinations. One black newspaper, the *Chicago Whip*, complained, "It's no difficult task to get people out of the South, but you have a difficult job on your hands when you attempt to get the South out of them."[5] In general, migrants placed great emphasis on their religious lives by establishing storefront churches or by joining existing congregations. The number of black churches, particularly in the cities, increased dramatically, consistent with the population change. In 1865, there were 13 black churches in New York City, but their number jumped to about 200 in 1930. Chicago had 58 Baptist and Methodist churches in 1916, a figure that stood at 122 four years later. The Baptist and Holiness churches had a special appeal for these new residents. A high proportion of their congregations were small, a development that the migrants preferred because of the intimacy that this fostered. In the mid-1920s, for example, 75 percent of the black churches in Harlem were storefront structures. In 1930, 72 percent of Chicago's black churches were of the storefront variety, 48 percent in Philadelphia, and 45 percent in Detroit.[6] In time, the style of

Black workers and their families, like this one shown in 1910, began migrating to the North during World War I to fill the jobs that otherwise would have been filled by European immigrants.

worship in migrant-dominated congregations emphasized exuberant singing, congregational participation, shouting, and so on. Such practices were neither exclusively Southern nor exclusively black, but they seemed to have constituted a much more pervasive feature of the worship services of migrants.

The churches were sometimes unequal to the task of responding to the myriad needs of the newcomers. As the social problems that newcomers confronted multiplied, dashed hopes produced crippling moments of despair. Capturing the spirit of a people on the move who sometimes questioned the efficacy of their faith, the poet Gwendolyn Brooks wrote in "The Sundays of the Satin-Legs Smith":

> The pasts of his ancestors lean against
> Him. Crowd him. Fog out his identity.
> Hundreds of hungers mingle with his own,
> Hundreds of voices advise so dexterously
> He quite considers his reactions his,
> Judges he walks most powerfully alone,
> That everything is—simply what it is.[7]

While observing that the migrants had not lost their faith, W. E. B. Du Bois thought that their religion, "instead of worship, is a complaint, and a curse, a wail rather than a hope, a sneer rather than a faith." Still, many black Christians found their church and the networks of the faithful to be sources of comfort in troubled times. Some could even use their faith to poke fun at the racial status quo:

> Our Fadder, Which are in Heaben!–
> White men owe me leben and pay me seben
> D'y Kingdom come! D'y Will be done!–
> An' if I hadn't tuck dat, I wouldn't git none.[8]

Migrants everywhere also retained many of their culinary practices, styles of dress, speech patterns, and other habits. Not surprisingly, long-time residents of the North, particularly members of the middle classes who were overly concerned about white perceptions of blacks, attempted to establish codes of conduct for the new arrivals. The newcomers were also given advice on how to avoid getting into trouble and what habits to inculcate. The *Chicago Defender* frequently told the migrants:

> Don't use vile language in public places.
> Don't act discourteously to other people in public places.
> Don't allow yourself to be drawn into street brawls.
> Don't use liberty as license to do as you please.
> Don't take the part of lawbreakers, be they men, women, or children.
> Don't make yourself a public nuisance.
> Don't encourage gamblers, disreputable women or men to ply their business any time or place. . . .
> Don't live in unsanitary houses, or sleep in rooms without proper ventilation. . . .
> Don't allow children to beg on the streets.
> Don't allow boys to steal from or assault peddlers. . . .
> Don't leave your job when you have a few dollars in your pocket. . . .[9]

Most migrants made the appropriate adjustments to Northern and urban life. A disillusioned few returned to the South to confront the familiar problems they had left behind. Those who remained in the North experienced fundamental changes in the texture of their lives in the short run and over the long haul. For some, the adjustment to harsh Northern winters posed serious but not insurmountable challenges. Those who arrived directly from the rural South faced the problem of adjusting to the pace and nature of city life. Lacking the requisite skills necessary to procure employment in an industrializing economy, others floundered a while before they found jobs, even if the jobs did not meet their expectations. Most migrants, however, would eventually create their own passageways to survival and in some cases, even success.

Migration to the Northeast, Midwest, and the West helped to produce major shifts in the patterns of black employment and hastened the creation of a black industrial proletariat. Indeed, the face of industrial America, at least at the bottom rungs of the labor pool, was radically transformed after 1915. Black men found employment in the automobile, steel, meatpacking, and other industries. In western Pennsylvania, for example, the number of black steelworkers numbered about 7,000 in 1918, a far cry from the 800 who were employed in that industry in 1914.[10] By 1923, the Ford Motor Company could boast 5,000 blacks in its labor force; it was 10,000 in 1926. One employer in Cleveland captured this change in the nature of the industrial workforce when he reported that his company had black "molders, coremakers, chippers, fitters, locomotive crane operators, melting furnace operators, general foremen, foremen, assistant foremen, clerks, timekeepers . . . [and] there is no work in our shop they cannot do and do well." But they had to be "properly supervised," the employer added rather condescendingly.[11]

Black women fared less well than their men in finding suitable or even tolerable employment. Between 50 to 60 percent of adult women eventually joined the labor market, a proportion that far exceeded that of their white counterparts. Most black women could find employment only as domestics, a category of labor that became increasingly reserved for them. In 1900, only 3 percent of black women found employment in manufacturing, a proportion that rose to 5.5 percent in 1930. In contrast, 19 percent of native white women and 27.1 percent of foreign-born women (usually white) were similarly employed.[12] As more and more blacks left the South, there was a dramatic decline in the proportion of the population engaged in agriculture. In 1890, for example, 57.4 percent of blacks were employed in agriculture. By 1920, the percentage had declined to 42.8; it fell to 28.7 in 1940, and in 1960, it stood at a mere 7.5 percent.

The emergence of blacks as significant parts of an industrial proletariat dramatized the need to have trade unions to protect and enhance their interests. Facing the hostility of white workers and excluded from membership in most of the existing unions, black workers pursued several organizing strategies. Influenced by the National Association for the Advancement of Colored People and the National Urban League, some workers pushed for an integration of the white-controlled unions. Others supported the creation of their own unions, while a third sector preferred to rely on the benevolence of their employers to improve the conditions of their labor.

Acting on their own volition, black railway workers organized the Railway Men's International Industrial Benevolent Association in 1915. Five years later, the Brotherhood of Dining Car Employees came into existence. The short-lived American Labor Congress and the Trade Union Committee for Organizing Negro Workers were both founded in 1925. A. Philip Randolph also created the Brotherhood of Sleeping Car Porters (BSCP), the most successful and enduring union of all.

Porters employed by the Pullman Company had tried and failed to create a collective bargaining union on several occasions. When he assumed the leadership of the BSCP, Randolph promised to "bring the company to its knees."[13] The company was more intransigent than he expected and declined to recognize the union. The protracted struggle for recognition continued until 1937, when Pullman relented. It was a momentous victory that signaled the growing strength of black workers and their tenacity in the fight for fair treatment.

The Depression years, however, stymied the process of unionization by blacks. Propelled by the desire to protect white workers from black competition in a declining labor market, the white unions adhered even more strictly to their racially based exclusionary policies. When the Congress of Industrial Organizations (CIO) was founded in 1935, however, its leadership made special efforts to recruit black workers in such industries as textiles, steel, meatpacking, and automobile manufacturing. In 1955, the CIO merged with the American Federation of Labor (AFL), bringing much unity to organized labor. The creation of the AFL-CIO was not necessarily good news for black workers, since the AFL had not been aggressive in recruiting blacks into its fold, tolerated the existence of segregated locals, and even had unions in its ranks whose constitutions forbade the membership of blacks. Thereafter, such labor leaders as A. Philip Randolph carried out a dogged campaign to cleanse organized labor of overt manifestations of racism.

Regardless of whether they achieved their dreams or not, black migrants helped change the character and cultural flavor of those cities and states where their numbers were significant. Blacks went North at a time when the face, fiber, and structure of the receiving states were being transformed by the forces unleashed by industrial capitalism. Manufacturing districts not only provided jobs for many, but the presence of these workers led to increased urbanization and the concomitant need for housing, schools, hospitals, and a variety of social services. Congested housing patterns developed over time and neighborhoods became increasingly segregated. Refusing to live adjacent to blacks and often aided by discriminatory housing ordinances, whites confined them to specific areas of the cities. By 1930, most blacks in Chicago, for example, lived in areas that were at least two-thirds black. In that year, 72 percent of Manhattan's black population lived in Harlem. The experiences of the smaller black populations in the West in procuring adequate housing differed, at least for a time, from this pattern. In 1930, one-third of the black families in Los Angeles owned their own homes, while 35.6 percent did so in Oakland, and 13.6 percent in San Francisco.

In contrast, 10.5 percent of the families in Chicago were homeowners, 15 percent in Detroit, and 5.6 percent in New York City.[14]

There was, on the face of it, nothing pernicious about blacks living in their own neighborhoods if they chose to do so. But the element of choice was largely denied black citizens, while their white counterparts were not circumscribed in that manner. The residential restrictions imposed upon blacks were accompanied by a white societal message that indicated that they were inferior beings. As the number of blacks increased, they became cramped in too little space and confronted high rents and substandard housing. Thus, these ghettos-in-formation reflected the residential boundaries that whites placed on blacks. Viewed in this light, ghettos and the societal ills they came to represent were not a necessary nor an inevitable consequence of black migration and urbanization.

But ghettos were more than residential prisons. Denied access to many of the social services that whites enjoyed, blacks developed their own organizations and support networks to meet their needs as best they could. Women, in particular, functioned at the center of these networks of community survival, in addition to shouldering enormous burdens as workers, mothers, and wives. The ties of kith and kin took on new meanings and encountered new challenges in a swiftly transforming urban environment. Families became atomized in an urban and industrial milieu, absorbing all of the pressures that the society heaped upon them. Most families developed creative strategies to control, if not overwhelm, the storms they confronted. Others weathered them less well. Men at the bottom of the economic ladder seemed to have had greater difficulty than women in coping, although this statement can be made only cautiously. Unable to find jobs and the victims of other pressures, some men abandoned their families, enlarging the roles of women. By 1960, 53 percent of urban families with a household income of less than $3,000 had no man present. In contrast, 82 percent of the rural families with the same household income had a male presence.[15]

In contrast to how they have been depicted by outsiders, the vast majority of those who lived in the ghettos were law-abiding citizens who struggled to make a life for themselves in the face of structural and racial barriers. Many became trapped in a cycle of poverty that bore striking similarities to the one that had defined sharecroppers in the South. A few who by dint of determination, hard work, and fortune's smile inched their way into the middle class left the neighborhoods entirely or moved to the more upscale streets.

Such moves, while they reflected divisions and interests born of class, did not mean that more privileged blacks could psychologically distance themselves from their poorer brethren. Few black families, no matter how successful their members were, could claim that they had no poor relatives. Black families were nothing if not elastic in their class compositions. Those members who were able to put a physical distance between themselves and their less fortunate kin could hardly do so without a backward glance.

Responding to their situation, or probably because of it, the residents of ghetto communities created vibrant cultural signifiers that bore their distinctive imprint. Ghettos became seedbeds of a rich cultural production, reflecting the lived experiences of the people and their strivings. Their songs, music, dances, and speech patterns would influence the national culture. The existence of this remarkable cultural energy and exuberance, however, should not lead us to underestimate the ways in which many lives were circumscribed and blighted in the ghettos, hopes crushed, confidence in human possibilities shaken, and the vaunted American dream largely unrealized.

INTELLECTUAL AND CULTURAL LIFE

Migration ushered significant changes in the life of black America, but it is not synonymous with the entire history of a people. Nor was the increasing urbanization of blacks the signifier of a people's complete trajectory. There were other kinds of motions in black life, some spawned by the migration and others that were not directly connected to it.

We noted in an earlier chapter that almost three out of every four blacks had acquired some degree of literacy by 1910. This figure, to be sure, masks considerable differences in the levels of educational attainment. By 1940, about 30 percent of blacks and 60 percent of whites had completed eight or more years in school. Put another way, 11 percent of black men and 14 percent of black women possessed high school diplomas, in comparison to 40 percent of white men and women. The number of black college graduates was also expanding, albeit slowly. Operating under the aegis of the doctrine of separate but equal, all of the Southern states and a few others established colleges for the instruction of blacks. Many of them were denied appropriate funding and provided a level of instruction that was inferior to that enjoyed by white students at white schools. These colleges, regardless of their deficiencies, joined historically black institutions such as Howard University, Fisk University, and Meharry Medical College that had met the higher education needs of the citizenry. As one measure of change, there were 29,269 black students enrolled in public and private colleges in the Southern states and the District of Columbia in 1935.[16] By 1950, there were 113,735 black students in the nation's colleges and universities.

Enrollment statistics and other traditional indicators tell us something about educational attainment in black America. But they are an inadequate measure of the broad understandings of a people. Judged by the proportion who graduated from high school or institutions of higher learning, the results were becoming increasingly better by 1950, but they were still not very impressive. But viewed through a more elastic lens, many blacks were schooled in more informal and less structured ways. In this regard, black newspapers such as the *Chicago Defender*, the *New York Age*, and the *Baltimore Sun* played significant roles in educating and instructing blacks about a variety of subjects relevant to their history, condition, prospects, and challenges. Family members and friends who were literate and had access to these papers read them to willing listeners. The churches provided opportunities for their members to discuss and learn about subjects of interest to their members. Organizations such as Marcus Garvey's UNIA sponsored forums, lectures, and discussions, educating blacks and raising their political and racial consciousness. Consequently, although most blacks were not "book learned," they were far from being unfamiliar with the ideas that were animating black society. To lack book learning was not to be uninformed.

The rise in literacy levels was reflected in the growing number of newspapers and the increase in their circulation. In 1940 there were 155 black newspapers in the nation, with a total circulation of 1,276,000. Slightly more than half of them were published in the South, and those had a circulation of 474,500. Circulation statistics, however, are a misleading measure of the number of persons that newspapers reach and influence. In 1920, for example, Walter White of the NAACP guessed that the *Chicago Defender* had a circulation of 75,000 in the South. "This means," he added, that "approximately 300,000 readers" consulted it each week.[17]

On another level, black America produced its share of outstanding intellectuals and literary figures during the years after the Harlem Renaissance. Black historians, building upon earlier studies, interpreted the black past essentially from the inside. Carter G. Woodson continued as an enormously influential public presence as director of the Association for the Study of Negro Life and History. With the money he received from white foundations up to 1933, when such funding virtually ceased, Woodson helped support the research of younger historians. As editor of the *Journal of Negro History*, he published articles and documentary sources on the black past. His book, *The Mis-Education of the Negro*, published in 1933, remains a classic work in black scholarship.

Woodson's indefatigable promotion of the study of black history helped to ensure its flowering in later years. Sharply critical of some white scholars and their interpretation of the black past, Woodson wrote from a black-centered perspective and placed a significant emphasis on black sources. In his use of folk tales and oral interviews, for example, Woodson was methodologically innovative. In 1935, W. E. B. Du Bois published his brilliant reinterpretation of Reconstruction, a work that responded to an earlier observation from Woodson that there was an absence of "scientific studies of the nation-wide reconstruction in which the Negroes took a part."[18] Du Bois's *Black Reconstruction* broke with the racist historiography of that era and focused on the roles of blacks and on the interplay of class, race, and economics in shaping the South after slavery's demise.

Other notable works that came from the pens of blacks during the period reflected the changing intellectual temper. Charles Harris Wesley published his *Negro Labor in the United States, 1850–1925* in 1927 and *Richard Allen, Apostle of Freedom* in 1935. Lorenzo Greene, who studied at Harvard and served on the faculty of Lincoln University for several decades, published *The Negro in Colonial New England, 1620–1776* in 1942.

Arguably, the most controversial work written by blacks prior to 1945 was an anthology edited by Rayford Logan, a historian on the faculty of Howard University. Commissioned by W. T. Couch, the editor of the University of North Carolina Press, the book was designed to reflect different perspectives by blacks on the racial question in the nation. The anthology included fourteen essays from such persons as W. E. B. Du Bois, Sterling Brown, Langston Hughes, Charles Wesley, Mary McLeod Bethune, and Roy Wilkins of the NAACP. Titled *What the Negro Wants*, the manuscript shocked Couch when he received it. Regardless of their political differences, all of the essayists demanded equality and the destruction of segregation. Du Bois urged "full economic, political, and social equality . . . in thought, expression and action, with no discrimination based on race or color."[19]

Couch, the seemingly progressive editor, was outraged that "a work of this nature would be written and submitted to us for publication." His letter to Logan was an extraordinary exercise in white paternalism:

> The things Negroes are represented as wanting seem to me far removed from those that they ought to want. Most of the things they are represented as wanting can be summarized in the phrase: complete abolition of segregation. If this is what the Negro wants, nothing could be clearer than that what he needs, and needs urgently, is to revise his wants.[20]

Pressured, Logan wavered in the face of Couch's advice that the contributors revise their essays "so as to make them more publishable."[21] Outraged, Du Bois, Brown, and the others declined to do so. When Couch summarily canceled the contract for publication, Logan threatened to sue. Alarmed, Couch relented and indicated that he would publish an introduction to the book, absolving the press of any responsibility for its contents. Repeating his belief in the inferiority of blacks, Couch's introduction emphasized that the "Negro's interests requires that he show qualities of greatness; that he not be so much concerned over the label 'equal,' but that he concentrate all his energies on being not merely equal to, but better than the white man."[22]

The uniform demand for equality articulated in the book reflected the increasing unwillingness of blacks to accommodate themselves to segregation. Virginius Dabney, a white Southerner and a liberal on racial issues, was closer to the pulse of black America when he told Couch that the book should be published because it represented the views of a substantial number of blacks. He was troubled, however, by "the psychopathic condition the manuscript reveals among Negro intellectuals."[23] But this was not a "psychopathic condition" at all; the book voiced the claims of black Americans for justice. Reviewing the book in the *New Republic*, J. Saunders Redding, a literary scholar, observed that the contributors "speak with authority. Ask any expert and any expert would be any literate Negro. Indeed, the validity of this book is derived from the undisputable fact that the editor might have chosen fourteen other contributors and achieved the same general result."[24]

The most comprehensive history of black America ever published appeared three years later. In 1947, John Hope Franklin published *From Slavery to Freedom*, a book that survives to the present day. Dispassionate in tone, measured in its judgments, and the product of wide reading, the book would influence generations of students and scholars. Its publication represented a major landmark in black scholarship, inaugurating another epoch in the intellectual life of a people. In 1954, Rayford Logan published his most celebrated historical work, *The Negro in American Life and Thought: The Nadir, 1877–1901*. It was a trenchant analysis of the rise of Jim Crow and the assault on the rights of blacks after Reconstruction ended. Narrower in its reach than Franklin's study, the book would nevertheless shape the nature of scholarship on blacks and race relations in the period it discussed.

These and other works reflected the achievements and intellectual energy of historians who worked under tremendous disabilities. Working essentially at teaching institutions, burdened by heavy teaching schedules, and lacking access to research support, these historians defined the future direction of research on black history. There were equally stunning developments in the worlds of poetry and literature. Several poets of the 1930s and the 1940s used their creative talents to protest the treatment of blacks in ways which the luminaries of the Renaissance—with the notable exception of Langston Hughes—never did. Sterling Brown's poem "Old Lem," published in 1939 captured the new literary stance:

> I talked to old Lem
> And old Lem said:
> "They weigh the cotton

> They store the corn
> We only good enough
> To work the rows;
> They run the commissary
> They keep the books
> We gotta be grateful
> For being cheated;
> Whippersnapper clerks
> Call us out of our name
> We got to say mister
> To spindling boys
> They make our figgers
> Turn somersets
> We buck in the middle
> Say, Thankyuh, sah'.
> They don't come by ones
> They don't come by twos
> But they come by tens.

Protest, or defiance, was also reflected in the poems of Robert Hayden, Margaret Walker, and Melvin Tolson. The theme of protest coupled with an embrace of contemporary international struggles is expressed in Tolson's "Dark Symphony":

> Out of abysses of illiteracy
> Through Labyrinths of Lies,
> Across wastelands of Disease . . .
> We advance!
> Out of dead-ends of Poverty,
> Through wildernesses of Superstition,
> Across barricades of Jim Crowism . . .
> We advance!
> With the Peoples of the World . . .
> We advance!

Writing in the context of the Second World War, Owen Dodson situated the black struggle within its ambit:

> V stands for Victory
> Now what is this here Victory?
> It what we get when we fight for it.
> Ought to be Freedom, God do know that.

Langston Hughes used the war to call attention to America's race problem:

> . . . Jim Crow Army,
> And Navy, too-
> Is Jim Crow Freedom the best
> I can expect from you? . . .

But he was also certain the war would transform race relations:

> Pearl Harbor put Jim Crow on the run.
> That Crow can't fight for Democracy
> And be the same old Crow he used to be-
> Although right now, even yet today,
> He tries to act in the same old way,
> But India and China and Harlem, too,
> Have made up their minds Jim Crow is through. . . .

The poetic voices of the period were not all confined to the black struggle at home. Some spoke to issues beyond race, reflecting concerns that World War II raised and embraced a universal human condition. Gwendolyn Brooks, who won the Pulitzer Prize in 1950 for her book of poems, *Annie Allen*, epitomizes this expanding vision:

> We knew how to order. . . .
> But nothing ever taught us to be islands.[25]

While poetry reflected or shaped the changes in the pulse of a people, the works of fiction played similar roles and were frequently more controversial. Richard Wright was the most vigorous articulator of the position that literature written by blacks should be unabashedly political. Writing in 1937, Wright maintained: "Every short story, novel, poem, and play should carry within its lives, implied or explicit, a sense of the oppression of the Negro people, the danger of war, of fascism, of the threatened destruction of culture and civilization; and, too, the faith and necessity to build a new world." [26]

Wright's celebrated and controversial novel, *Native Son*, appeared in 1940. The angry protagonist, Bigger Thomas, was depicted as deeply wounded by the demons of racism and capitalism. It was a searing indictment of white America and an exploration of the human consequences of unfettered racism and poverty. The book sold 200,000 copies in three weeks. Langston Hughes called it a "really great book which sets a new standard for Negro writers from now on."[27] Some black writers, if not the reading public, chafed at the depiction of Bigger Thomas. The young novelist and essayist James Baldwin would later accuse Wright of presenting a unidimensional portrait of black life. Bigger Thomas, Baldwin maintained:

> is the monster created by the American republic, the present awful sum of generations of oppression; but to say he is a monster is to fall into the trap of making him subhuman and he must, therefore, be made representative of a way of life which is real and human in precise ratio to which it seems to us monstrous and strange. It seems to me that this idea carries, implicitly, a most remarkable confession: that is that Negro life is in fact as debased and impoverished as our theology claims.[28]

Ralph Ellison, another outstanding writer of the period, published his novel, *Invisible Man,* which won the National Book Award in 1952. Ellison's book was not of the protest genre, but it nevertheless contained a strong critique of American racism. The novel's hero lamented how the larger society had erroneously constructed images of him, and by extension his race:

> I am invisible, understand, simply because people refuse to see me. Like the bodiless heads you see sometimes in circus sideshows, it is as though I have been surrounded by mirrors of dark, distorted glass. When they approach me, they see only my surroundings, themselves, or figments of their imagination—indeed, everything and anything but me.[29]

The novel celebrated the inviolability of the human spirit and its ability to triumph over oppression. In a thinly veiled criticism of Richard Wright, Ellison confessed that he "was forced to conceive of a novel unburdened by the narrow naturalism which has led, after so many triumphs, to the final and unrelieved despair which marks so much of our current fiction." [30]

Gwendolyn Brooks's novel, *Maud Martha,* was published in 1953, but it did not receive the attention that *Native Son* and *Invisible Man* garnered. It was an important novel that underscored the ways in which black women had been subordinated and denied an independent voice. The protagonist was an economically marginal black woman trapped in a Chicago ghetto struggling for her own space, voice, and self-definition. In time, the book would be rediscovered, as have the works of so many other female authors before Brooks. *Maud Martha* would be seen as subversive of existing gender, racial, and social conventions and as affirming women's voices.

These literary voices were not all in accord in their representations of the black condition. There was, of course, no monolithic black condition to represent, given the enormous structural changes then in motion and the growing diversity in demographic distribution, class composition, and generational perceptions. Undeniable, however, was the growing sense that blacks were preparing to force a reluctant larger society to change its racial etiquette and policies. Intellectuals were also increasingly sensitive to the ways in which black history and culture were interpreted. In 1945, for example, the Swedish economist, Gunnar Myrdal, published *An American Dilemma*, a book that investigated the nature of American racism and its centrality to the construction of the black condition. As valuable as his insights were, Myrdal viewed blacks through the prism of whites and attributed little independent agency to them. In his opinion, "The Negro's entire life and, consequently, also his opinions on the Negro problem are, in the main, to be considered secondary reactions to more primary pressures from the side of the dominant white majority." Ralph Ellison, for one, found this interpretation unacceptable and eloquently stated the case for black agency. "But can a people (its faith in an idealized American Creed notwithstanding) live and develop for over three hundred years simply by reacting?" he asked. "Are American Negroes simply the creation of white men, or have they at least helped to create themselves out of what they found around them? Men have made a way of life in caves and upon cliffs, why cannot Negroes have made a life upon the horns of the white man's dilemma?" Ellison wrote.[31]

Intellectual motions were not confined to the literary and the historical. Men such as George Washington Carver, Ernest Everett Just, and Charles R. Drew, distinguished themselves in the scientific field. Born in Missouri, Carver received a degree from Iowa State Agricultural College. As a student of plant chemistry, he joined the Tuskegee faculty in 1896 as head of its department of agriculture. In time, he pioneered research on the peanut, discovering at least 300 uses for it. He achieved similar success with the sweet potato, developing 118 products from it. Ernest Just was born in South Carolina in 1883 and received his graduate training in biology at the Marine Biological Laboratory in Woods Hole, Massachusetts. As a member of the faculty at Howard University, he made significant contributions to the field of experimental embryology, particularly in the areas of fertility, mutation, and cell division. Charles Drew, who was born in Washington, D.C. in 1904, pursued a medical degree at McGill University in Montreal. Before his tragic death as a result of an automobile accident in 1950, Drew had become widely known for his role in the development of blood plasma and in blood bank research.[32]

Those expressions of intellectual and scientific vitality had their counterpart in the expressive arts. Many blacks such as the outstanding operatic star Marian Anderson, the soprano Dorothy Maynor, and singers Paul Robeson and Roland Hayes gained international acclaim on the concert stage. Jazz and its performers continued to thrill audiences, producing great composers, saxophonists, drummers, pianists, and bassists, and singers. Outstanding among them were the singers Ella Fitzgerald and Billie Holiday, the bassist Jimmy Blanton, the drummer Warren Dodds, the saxophonists Johnny Hodges and Benny Carter, and the pianist Mary Lou Williams. Similarly, blues remained vibrant, producing such great performers as Willie "Rice" Miller, McKinley Morganfield ("Muddy Waters"), and Riley "B. B." King.

Gospel songs appeared in the early years of the twentieth century but saw their most rapid development in the 1930s. Black gospel's popularity in the early years was confined to the urban churches of the working classes and the poor. Otherworldly in their emphasis, gospel songs affirmed a deeply held faith in the power of Jesus to provide succor, strength, and salvation to believers. The message of these songs had a special meaning for the marginalized, fostered a measure of hope and celebrated the existence of a compassionate Jesus who would help them to endure and would ultimately welcome them to the Promised Land.

Thomas A. Dorsey, a Georgian who migrated to Chicago, is generally recognized as one of the earliest and most creative authors of gospel songs. Some have called him the "Father of Gospel Music." Dorsey may have written as many as one thousand songs, but "Precious Lord" remains his most enduring creation. Its words capture the animating impulse of gospel songs, proclaiming a dependence on Jesus and His ability to provide sustenance in difficult times:

> Precious Lord take my hand,
> Lead me on, let me stand,
> I am tired, I am weak, I am worn;
> Thru the storm, thru the night,
> Lead me on to the light,
> Take my hand precious Lord,
> Lead me home.
>
> When my way grows drear, precious Lord, linger near,
> When my life almost gone,
> Hear my cry, hear my call,
> Hold my hand lest I fall;
> Take my hand, precious Lord,
> Lead me home.

More secular in its impetus, but building upon the foundations laid at the turn of the century, the black theatre continued to develop during the period. In 1915, a black company, the Lafayette Players, was founded in Harlem. Recalling the reasons for its formation, Clarence Muse, an actor, emphasized:

> Our aim was to give vent to our talent and to prove to everybody who was willing to look, to watch, to listen, that we were as good at drama as anybody else had been or could be. The door was opened a tiny bit to us and, as always, the Black man when faced with an open door, no matter how small the wedge might be, eased in.[33]

The company provided opportunities for black actors and actresses to display their talent until it became insolvent. Before its demise in 1932, it had staged about 250 plays.

As editor of the NAACP magazine *Crisis*, W. E. B. Du Bois inaugurated the Krigwa Playwriting Contest in 1925, a venture that provided inspiration to young playwrights. Many of them had their plays published, and the competition spawned the Krigwa Little Theatre, a short-lived national performance company. In announcing its formation, Du Bois noted:

> The plays of a real Negro theatre must be:
>
> 1. *About us.* That is, they must have plots which reveal Negro life as it is.
> 2. *By us.* That is, they must be written by Negro authors who understand from birth and continual association just what it means to be a Negro today.[34]

Du Bois also wanted the Negro Theatre to exist "For us" and to be located where blacks lived. The Krigwa Theatre died after only two productions, but its creation had emphasized the need for a black-oriented production company.

Between 1935 and 1939, the Federal Theatre Project, which was created under the aegis of President Franklin D. Roosevelt's New Deal, sponsored black theatre in at least twenty-two cities across the nation. Apart from providing employment for artistes, the project actively involved blacks in the cultural life of the nation and popularized dramatic works by and about them. In 1940, Abram Hill, a playwright, and Frederick O'Neal, an actor, founded the American Negro Theatre (ANT) in Harlem.

The ANT intended "to break down the barriers of Black participation in the theatre; to portray Negro life as they honestly saw fit; to fill in the gap of a black theatre which did not exist."[35] The company produced nineteen plays between 1940 and 1949, some of them written by whites. It also sponsored workshops for actors and technicians and hosted a radio series. By 1950, however, the company had become a victim of its own success. When it began to produce shows on Broadway, the company lost much of the ethnic élan that it possessed in Harlem. Its community-based roots were weakened as actors began to use the productions as a stepping stone into the white theatre. It is important to emphasize that the black theatre both reflected and shaped the evolution of a black consciousness. Most of the productions deliberately rejected stereotypes of blacks that white playwrights had propagated and perpetuated. Some plays were animated by African themes and celebrated the African past. But the destruction of deeply embedded stereotypes is never an easy task, and no one can claim that the black theatre was able to reeducate the public substantially, even the theatre-going elite. The artistes and playwrights were acutely conscious, however, of their continuing political mission. As one member of the ANT expressed it:

> There was a great social revolution underway, the plays of protest, the plays of social meaning, and this was the kind of theatre we were trying to develop. Not just for entertainment and our own professional growth and artistry, but we wanted to say something significant and meaningful to the people. . . . We were a people's theatre. . . . We were trying to say something. We were trying to say it within the black media, with the rhythm and the quality of excitement.[36]

Blacks who appeared on the cinematographic screen became more numerous in the 1920s and later, but they struggled to provide a multifaceted representation of themselves. Pandering to, as well as creating and recreating stereotypes about blacks, white filmmakers depicted them as the stupid and carefree coon, the faithful mammy, the lascivious and predatory buck, the fawning Uncle Tom, the self-effacing and submissive servant, among other characterizations. Seeking work and eager to practice their craft, some blacks accommodated themselves to such roles, sometimes interpreting the characters they portrayed in ways unintended by the producers and directors. Lincoln Perry, who adopted the name Stephin Fetchit, became the quintessential coon in the 1920s and the 1930s, but he brought an ambiguity to some of his performances. Donald Bogle, a student of blacks in the cinema, noted:

> Fetchit's great gift was in rendering his coons as such thoroughly illiterate figures that they did not have to respond when demeaned because they were always unaware of what was being done. . . . By removing his characters' intellects–indeed their psyches–from the real world, Stephin Fetchit's dim wits never had to acknowledge the inhumanity that surrounded them.[37]

On the other hand, Hattie McDaniel brought a marked fiestiness to her perennial roles as a maid, most notably as Mammy in *Gone With the Wind* (1939). Criticized for taking such roles, McDaniel retorted: "Why should I complain about making seven thousand dollars a week playing a maid? If I didn't, I'd be making seven dollars a week actually being one!"[38] McDaniel won an Oscar as best supporting actress for her role in *Gone With the Wind*, becoming the first black person to be so honored.

In spite of the racially stereotyped roles that blacks frequently played, the cinema attracted an extraordinary number of talented performers. Louise Beavers excelled as the magnanimous cook in *Imitation of Life* (1934), Paul Robeson was the confident black man in *The Emperor Jones* (1933), and Eddie "Rochester" Anderson appeared as the coon in several films in the 1930s and 1940s. Lena Horne made her debut in the 1940s as a singer and actress. Her role in *Stormy Weather* (1943) established her as a major figure in the entertainment industry. Hazel Scott, Butterfly McQueen, Josephine Baker, Ethel Waters, Louis Armstrong, Rex Ingram, Fredi Washington, and a host of others became noted performers of the time.

The roles that blacks were offered tended to expand in the 1940s and the 1950s as a consequence of organized protest by groups such as the NAACP, the erosion of pejorative racial stereotypes, and the changing configuration of race relations in the nation. White studios, however, did not become color-blind in their casting, nor did they eschew racial stereotyping, but they began to allow black artists greater flexibility in demonstrating their talents. Although the talented Dorothy Dandridge, for example, continued to be cast as the tragic mulatto in the 1950s in such films as *Carmen Jones* (1954), Sidney Poitier had a greater range in some of his roles as in *No Way Out* (1950), *Cry the Beloved Country* (1952), and *The Blackboard Jungle* (1955).

Black filmmakers, understandably, attempted a much more nuanced representation of their people on the screen, particularly in the 1920s and 1930s. Most of them were chronically short of capital and could hardly compete with the white studios, even for black audiences. Some of these directors were unable to transcend the stereotypical images of blacks, and their products were not necessarily technical triumphs. On the other hand, these films provided employment for blacks and brought the cinema to their neighborhoods. Nor should the creative energies they both reflected and unleashed be ignored. The most successful and durable of these black filmmakers was Oscar Micheaux. His first production was the allegedly autobiographical *The Homesteader* (1919). Thereafter, Micheaux struggled, at least financially, in producing thirty other films.

THE ATHLETIC REALM

As in the film industry, blacks created their own passageways in sports even as they attempted to participate in the amateur or commercial athletics of the larger society. Knowing no regional boundaries, Jim Crow practices excluded blacks from most nationally organized sports by the turn of the twentieth century. Middle-class white men in particular feared the competition of black men in sports, since athletic prowess and manliness were deemed to be intertwined. The question of what constituted manhood or manliness had become racialized; white men saw it as their right by virtue of their belonging to a "superior" race to exercise power over others, most notably "inferior" and allegedly more "feminine" black men. Accordingly, whiteness and manhood were synonymous in the popular white imagination, but this hardly squared with the other constructions of black men as threateningly virile and physically the brute or beast.[39]

Boxing was the athletic arena in which uncertain claims to a superior white manhood were guarded most fiercely. The heavyweight champion was the manifestation of the ideal man: tough, virile, and strong. Since 1882, white men had declined to fight black men in this division for fear that their notions of superiority would be undermined if they were defeated. In 1903, the reigning white champion, Jim Jeffries, refused to fight black challenger Jack Johnson, stating, "When there are no white men left to fight, I will quit the business. . . . I am determined not to take a chance of losing the championship to a negro."[40] Upon Jeffries' retirement, Tommy Jones, the new champion, reluctantly agreed to fight Johnson, only to be whipped by him.

Jack (John) Johnson was the epitome of the proverbial "bad nigger." Born in Galveston, Texas, in 1878, Johnson exhibited a pugnacity that many whites found unacceptable and threatening. He consorted openly with white women, eventually marrying two of them while he held the championship crown. Exploiting and exacerbating white stereotypes and fears of black male sexuality, Johnson wrapped his penis in gauze and strutted around the ring in his boxing shorts, displaying the enhanced outlines of his genitals. Distraught and humiliated by Johnson's defeat of Burns, whites persuaded Jeffries to come out of retirement to restore a fallen white manhood to its rightfully superior place. One white reporter urged Jeffries to "emerge from his alfalfa farm and remove that smile from Johnson's face."[41] Cognizant of his role as the white hope, Jeffries agreed to fight. "I realize full well what depends on me," he said, "and I am not going to disappoint the public. That portion of the white race that has been looking to me to defend its athletic superiority may feel assured that I am fit to do my very best."[42]

Jeffries' best was not good enough, and Johnson humiliated him on July 4, 1910. White men took the defeat personally and responded by rioting in every Southern state and assaulting blacks in several cities such as Omaha, New Orleans, Houston, Baltimore, and Macon, among others. Thirteen blacks lost their lives to the marauders. Thereafter, the forces of white supremacy launched a campaign of harassment of the champion. Invoking the Mann Act, which prohibited the transportation of women across the state lines for "immoral" purposes, the authorities arrested Johnson in November 1912. The Mann Act, otherwise known as the White Slave Law, was used because Johnson had been traveling with his white lover, and soon-to-be wife, Lucille Cameron. Johnson was convicted, fined, and sentenced to jail. Refusing to go to jail, the champion fled with his new wife to Canada and later to France. In 1915, in a highly controversial bout, Johnson lost his title to Jess Willard in Cuba. Many believed that Johnson "threw" the fight in the misguided belief that his prison sentence in the United States would be waived. He eventually returned to the United States and served ten months in jail in 1920.

To many, Jack Johnson became an icon, a symbol of the plucky black man who stared the white man down. He became larger than life, and stories about him abounded as many of the powerless lived vicariously through him. One story had Tommy Burns taunting Johnson in the ring:

Burns: Boy, I'm gonna whip you good. I was born with boxing gloves on.
Johnson (grinning): I have news for you, white man. You're about to die the same way.[43]

Not only was Johnson the rebel in the popular imagination, but he also challenged white authority with flair even in potentially dangerous situations. As the story went:

> It was a hot day in Georgia when Jack Johnson drove into town. He was really flying: zoooom! Behind his fine car was a cloud of red Georgia dust as far as the eye could see. The sheriff flagged him down and said, "Where do you think you're going, boy, speeding like that? That'll cost you $50.00!" Jack Johnson never looked up; he just reached in his pocket and handed the sheriff a $100.00 bill and started to gun the motor: ruuummm, ruuummm. Just before Jack pulled off, the sheriff shouted, "Don't you want your change?" And Jack replied, "Keep it, 'cause I'm coming back the same way I'm going!" Zooooom.[44]

Not until 1937 was another black man given a chance to compete for the heavyweight crown. In that year, Joe Louis, a son of Alabama, defeated the white James Braddock. Louis was not as menacing to whites as Johnson had been. There were no riots in the aftermath of his victory, and Louis was destined to be recognized as one of the greatest pugilists of all time. Other blacks achieved outstanding successes in the ring in the 1930s, 1940s, and thereafter. John Henry Lewis won the light heavyweight crown in 1935. During the 1940s, Sidney Walker, Bob Montgomery, and Ike Williams also boasted lightweight championships. The best of them all, however, was Walker Smith Jr. Known as "Sugar Ray" Robinson, he won six world titles, the first in the welterweight division in 1946 and five in the middleweight division between 1951 and 1958.

The racially inspired policies that prevented blacks from participating in the white organized teams and leagues did not mean that their role in such sports as baseball, football, and basketball was negligible. On the contrary, they formed their own teams and organizations. Excluded from Major League Baseball, blacks created the National Negro League in Kansas City in 1920. The Southern Negro League was formed shortly thereafter and was reorganized as the Negro Southern League in 1926. These and other leagues fostered the development of black talent, helped provide income for the players, and entertained their fans. Players such as the hitter Oscar Charleston, the pitcher Leroy "Satchel" Paige, and the catcher Raleigh "Biz" Mackey became masters of the game. In 1947 the racial barrier in the national sport fell when the Brooklyn Dodgers signed Jackie Robinson over the protests of some intransigent segregationists. The victim of racial taunts and slights on and off the field, Robinson was named Rookie of the Year (1947) and Most Valuable Player in the National League (1949). He was inducted into the Baseball Hall of Fame in 1962.

Much the same story can be told for basketball, and to some extent football. After World War I black men founded such teams as the New York Renaissance Big Five, the Harlem Globetrotters, the Chicago Hottentots, and others. Women also had their own teams; two of the most notable being the Chicago Romas and the Philadelphia Tribune. Not until 1946 did the major leagues in basketball admit black players. In professional football, thirteen blacks played between 1920 and 1933, but they were excluded between the 1934 and 1945 seasons from teams belonging to the National Football League. The color bar began to collapse earlier on the West coast, as teams belonging to the Pacific Coast Professional Football League admitted black players toward the end of the war. This development was partially the consequence of the public's need for diversion during wartime, the popularity of black players, and the competition among the growing number of teams for available talent.

The lowering of the color bar in the athletic arena in the late 1930s and the 1940s was in large measure the result of protests by blacks. The Second World War provided the occasion for some of these challenges, revealing in sports as in other areas of life the stark contradiction between blacks fighting for freedom overseas but being denied equal rights in their country. "If he's good enough for the Navy, he's good enough for the Majors [Leagues]" became the organizing battle cry. The complete desegregation of sports would not occur overnight, if at all. Professional teams such as those in basketball and baseball had quotas for blacks for many years, and some were extremely slow in signing black players. Golf and tennis remained essentially all white, and golf courses and tennis courts in many places were, and are, still closed to black players.[45]

The changes and motions in black life that we have discussed in this chapter paralleled those in the larger society. White Americans, and black Americans as well, were deeply affected by the forces unleashed by industrialization, urbanization, the two world wars, immigration, the New Deal, the technological innovations in agriculture, and so on. The country weathered a severe economic depression and experienced a greater degree of intrusion by the federal government in their daily lives than ever before. The advent of the radio and television facilitated the dissemination of information and generated cultural changes as well. Some even complained, with good reason, that white supremacy was being slowly undermined by these organs of mass communication. Still, few people would have predicted that the second half of the century would have seen such a remarkable acceleration in the pace of change and the multiplicity of challenges to the nation's social, political, cultural, and institutional arrangements.

Notes

1. Seth M. Scheiner, "The Negro Church and the Northern City, 1890–1930," in William G. Shade and Roy C. Herrenkohl, eds., *Seven on Black: Reflections on the Negro Experience in America* (Philadelphia: Lippincott, 1969), 286–287.
2. William Cohen, "The Great Migration as a Lever for Social Change," in Alferdteen Harrison, *Black Exodus: The Great Migration from the American South* (Jackson: University Press of Mississippi, 1991), 73.
3. James R. Grossman, "Black Labor is the Best Labor: Southern White Reactions to the Great Migration," in Harrison, *Black Exodus*, 53.
4. Ibid., 56.
5. Grossman, *Land of Hope*, 154.
6. Scheiner, *The Negro Church*, 291.
7. Gates and McKay, *African American Literature*, 1584.
8. Ibid., 37; Wilmore, *Black Religion*, 224–225.
9. Grossman, *Land of Hope*, 145–146.
10. Joe William Trotter Jr., "Blacks in the Urban North: The 'Underclass Question' in Historical Perspective," in Michael B. Katz, ed., *The "Underclass" Debate: Views from History* (Princeton: Princeton University Press, 1993), 70.
11. Ibid.
12. Jones, *Labor of Love*, 166.

13. William H. Harris, *The Harder We Run: Black Workers Since the Civil War* (New York: Oxford, 1982), 81.
14. Laurence B. De Graff, "The City of Black Angels: Emergence of the Los Angeles Ghetto, 1890-1930," *Pacific Historical Review*, 39:3 (1970), 323-352; Albert S. Broussard, "Organizing the Black Community in the San Francisco Bay Area, 1915-1930," *Arizona and the West*, 23:4 (1981), 1-16.
15. Herbert Gutman, *The Black Family in Slavery and Freedom, 1750-1925* (New York: Vintage, 1977), 463.
16. Anderson, *The Education of Blacks*, 275.
17. Grossman, *Blowing the Trumpet*, 88.
18. Jacqueline Goggin, *Carter G. Woodson: A Life in Black History* (Baton Rouge: Louisiana State University Press, 1993), 185.
19. Rayford W. Logan, ed., *What the Negro Wants* (Chapel Hill: University of North Carolina Press, 1944). For a fine treatment of the problems with the University of North Carolina Press, see Kenneth R. Janken, *Rayford W. Logan and the Dilemma of the African-American Intellectual* (Amherst: University of Massachusetts Press, 1993).
20. Janken, *Rayford W. Logan*, 155.
21. Ibid., 156.
22. Ibid., 161.
23. Ibid.
24. Ibid., 164.
25. See Angelyn Mitchell, ed., *Within the Circle: An Anthology of African American Literary Criticism from the Harlem Renaissance to the Present* (Durham: Duke University Press, 1994), 122-135.
26. Ibid., 6.
27. Arnold Rampersad, *The Life of Langston Hughes, vol. 1: 1902-1941, I Too Sing America* (New York: Oxford, 1986), 383.
28. James Baldwin, "Many Thousands Gone," reprinted in his *Notes of a Native Son* (New York: Bantam Books, 1972), 32-33.
29. Ralph Ellison, *Invisible Man* (New York: Random House, 1952), 7-8.
30. Ibid., 70.
31. Ibid., 58-59.
32. See Linda O. McMurry, *George Washington Carver: Scientist and Symbol* (New York: Oxford, 1981); Kenneth R. Manning, *Black Apollo of Science: The Life of Ernest Everett Just* (New York: Oxford, 1983); Spencie Love, One Blood: *The Death and Resurrection of Charles R. Drew* (Chapel Hill: University of North Carolina Press, 1996).
33. Sister M. Francesca Thompson, "The Lafayette Players, 1915-1932," in Errol Hill, ed., *The Theatre of Black Americans* (New York: Theatre Book Publishers, 1980), 216.
34. Gates and McKay, *African American Literature*, 935.
35. Ethel Pitts Walker, "The American Negro Theatre," in Hill, *Black Theatre*, 251.
36. Ibid., 259-260.
37. Donald Bogle, *Toms, Coons, Mulattoes, Mammies, and Bucks: An Interpretive History of Blacks in American Films* (New York: Continuum Publishing, 1989), 1-18, 41-42.
38. Ibid., 82.
39. Gail Bederman, *Manliness and Civilization: A Cultural History of Gender and Race in the United States, 1880-1917* (Chicago: University of Chicago Press, 1995), 1-44.
40. Ibid., 1.
41. Ibid., 2.
42. Arthur Ashe, *A Hard Road to Glory: A History of the African-American Athlete*, vol. 1 (New York: Amistad, 1988), 36.
43. Levine, *Black Culture and Black Consciousness*, 433.
44. Ibid.
45. For a more detailed discussion of discrimination in sports see Arthur Ashe, *A Hard Road to Glory*, 2 vols. (New York: Amistad, 1988). Volume 1 covers the years 1619-1918 and volume 2 treats 1918-1945. My account draws heavily on Ashe's pioneering study.

Building Organizations, Weathering Storms before and after Garvey

To recognize and salute the energies that blacks demonstrated in constructing their lives is not to deny the obstacles they confronted or the opposition they faced. Most blacks seized the opportunities that were open to them and built their own passageways, but still the fruits of full freedom eluded them. Building upon the themes addressed in Chapters 4 and 8, this chapter describes some of the organizations that blacks established and the self-help programs that they created to meet their needs, particularly those of the working classes. It examines the remarkable contributions that women made in easing the burdens of the dispossessed. The impact of the New Deal's programs on the black poor is also analyzed, as well as black people's overall responses to the Depression and the forces it helped to unleash.

Nationalist organizations were among the most active in developing and fostering programs for their constituencies. They appealed primarily to members of the working class, particularly in urban areas. Committed to securing their place in an integrated society, middle- and upper-class blacks for the most part avoided membership in separatist organizations. This did not mean, as we have seen, that these blacks failed to create their own organizations and businesses. But as a rule, integrationist organizations such as the National Association for the Advancement of Colored People (NAACP) saw racially based enterprises as succumbing to the segregation to which they were unalterably opposed. In 1934 W. E. B. Du Bois resigned as editor of the *Crisis* magazine in a dispute with the NAACP board over his newly expressed support for segregation. Du Bois made a distinction between racial discrimination and voluntary segregation. As he put it:

> The opposition to racial segregation is not or should not be any distaste or unwillingness of colored people to work with each other, to cooperate with each other, to live with each other. The opposition to segregation is an opposition to discrimination. . . . never in the world should our fight be against the association with ourselves because by that very token we give up the whole argument that we are worth associating with. . . . It is the race-conscious black man cooperating together in his own institutions and movements who will eventually emancipate the colored race, and the great step today is for the American Negro to accomplish his economic emancipation through voluntary determined cooperative effort.[1]

The NAACP did not agree, affirming its opposition "to the principle and the practice of enforced segregation of human beings on the basis of race and color."[2]

Most working-class blacks undoubtedly shared those sentiments. But many of them found appealing the prospect of establishing and controlling their own institutions or even a separate state. Du Bois thought that "the upper class Negro has almost never been nationalistic. He has never planned or thought of a Negro state. . . . This solution has always been a thought upsurging from the mass, because of pressure which they could not withstand and which compelled a racial institution or chaos."[3]

The 1930s saw the emergence of one of the most important, effective, and long-lived nationalist organizations. In 1930, Farrad Mohammed, a man of uncertain ancestry and various aliases, including W. D. Fard, began to organize blacks in Detroit around the beliefs enshrined in the Holy Qur'an. Proclaiming, "I come from the Holy City of Mecca," Mohammed (or Fard) denounced whites for their mistreatment of blacks, instructed his growing number of followers in African and Asian history, built a temple, and taught the faithful that their God's "right and proper name is Allah."[4] When Mohammed mysteriously disappeared in 1934, Elijah Muhammad, a migrant from Georgia, assumed the mantle of leadership. In time, Muhammad became known as "Prophet" or as the "Messenger of Allah." Gifted with extraordinary talents as a leader and the ability to inspire his followers, Muhammad built the Nation of Islam into an important force in black life and in the country as a whole.

Not surprisingly, the struggling migrants were initially the persons most receptive to the appeal of the Muslims. Elijah Muhammad, in particular, understood the deep Christian foundations of these Southerners, and he sought to build upon them. The result was an eclectic set of beliefs. Allah replaced the Christian God, and the Qu'ran became the voice of religious authority. Christianity was cast as the religion of the white oppressor, but Muhammad never systematically assaulted those aspects of its theology that could be shorn of a white bias. The Nation of Islam possessed a black face and a black theology, and that was one source of its transcendental appeal to a largely working-class membership trying to define itself racially and in other ways.

Muhammad, as Marcus Garvey and others had done before him, realized that blacks also needed to control their own institutions and resources. Garvey, in particular, had founded a number of businesses owned and operated by members of the Universal Negro Improvement Association. Muhammad's genius, however, resided in his ability to get his followers to imagine themselves as a nation, cemented by their religion and their "race," and then attempt to function as such. Acting cooperatively and drawing upon their initially paltry resources, the Nation of Islam created an impressive number of enterprises designed to promote economic self-sufficiency. They ran stores, restaurants, and drycleaning establishments, and purchased vast amounts of land. The Nation eventually published its own newspaper, *Muhammad Speaks,* and built schools for the instruction of children.

The Nation of Islam espoused an aggressive philosophy of race pride and separation from white America. Women occupied a subordinate status in the Nation, and men assumed the responsibility for the support of their families. Members avoided liquor, promiscuity, and drugs, and the men were characterized in their behavior and demeanor by a military discipline. The steady growth in the Nation's membership clearly indicated that its theology and mission had a resonance among its largely urban and working-class constituency.

The embrace of this American variant of Islam by so many should hardly be seen as a reactive phenomenon. All too frequently, historians and other social scientists have assessed these strivings of the "Other" in negative terms, seeing them as being primarily reactors to their condition and lacking their own agency, dynamism, and compass. In adopting and shaping their own religious, racial, and economic trajectories, the Muslims were driven more by the need to define their own destinies as a people and less by their mistreatment by white America. The motive force came primarily from the inside.

The Nation of Islam was the largest of the nationalist-inspired religious organization that emerged after the Garvey movement declined. There were others, however, that commanded varying degrees of support. Groups of Black Jews, for example, continued to exist. In general, these nationalist groups accepted the basic tenets of the developing Black Christian Nationalist Creed:

> I believe that Jesus, the Black Messiah, was a revolutionary leader, sent by God to rebuild the Black Nation, Israel and to liberate Black people from powerlessness and from the oppression, brutality, and exploitation of the white gentile world. I believe that the revolutionary spirit of God, embodied in the Black Messiah, is born anew in each generation and that Black Christian Nationalists constitute the living remnant of God's Chosen People in this day, and are charged by Him with the responsibility for the Liberation of the Black People.[5]

Most blacks distanced themselves from this theology, preferring to remain in the institutionally black denominations or in all-black or integrated congregations of white-controlled counterparts. There were at least six major black denominations in existence before 1965. They included the pioneering African Methodist Episcopal Church and the African Methodist Episcopal Zion Church. The others were the Christian Methodist Episcopal; the National Baptist Convention, USA; the National Baptist Convention of America; and the Progressive National Baptist Convention. Heterogeneous in their class appeal, and possessing variations in the size of their membership, these denominations faced the competition of the nationalist-inspired churches, as well as those that can be characterized as constituting the Black Holiness-Pentecostal Movement. Encouraging an exuberant and participatory worship style, these churches emphasized what they called "sanctification." The faithful experienced the "Baptism of the Holy Spirit," a process that enhanced religious fervor and the practice of a puritanical lifestyle.[6]

Other expressions of Christian faith and practice cannot be easily categorized. From time to time, charismatic individuals arose and packaged a religious-secular message that appealed to substantial numbers of people. These persons did not start new denominations as such, but they developed a mass following. The best known of these personages was Father Divine, who was born as George Baker in Georgia, probably in 1880. By the 1930s, Divine had become an important religious leader in Harlem, with considerable influence nationwide. His brand of Christianity was not confined to the redemption of souls and the preparation for an afterlife. Nor was it essentially otherworldly. As he expressed it:

> I would not give five cents for a God who could not help me here on earth, for such a God is not a God at hand. He is only an imagination. It is a false delusion, trying to make you think you had just as well go ahead and suffer and be enslaved and be lynched and everything else here, and after while you are going to heaven someplace. If God cannot prepare heaven here for you, you are not going anywhere.[7]

To give organizational expression to his views, Father Divine created the Peace Mission. Its membership was predominantly working class and black, but whites and members of the middle class were

Father Divine's Peace Mission grocery store was one of the many businesses of the Peace Mission, founded to create economic improvements for blacks.

attracted as well. In fact, when branches were established in the West, the membership was significantly white. Under the aegis of the Peace Mission, Divine created a vast number of businesses, a development that was particularly appealing to former Garveyites. The Peace Mission's economic empire included grocery stores, restaurants, rental properties, and barbershops.

Divine attracted as many as two million followers at the peak of his popularity. He rejected segregation and supported political movements that fought racism, although he never claimed to be a leader of his race. He believed in the capacity of the nation to transform itself, and he was committed to the integration of blacks in it. Divine rejected the politics of racial separation espoused by Garvey, Elijah Muhammad, and others. The Peace Mission did not long survive Divine's death in 1965. By then, however, much of the energy that drove the movement had been spent. For his black followers, the movement's importance resided not only in its religious, economic, and political emphases. "Father has freed us from within," Mary Love, a devoted follower, said in 1964.[8]

It should be readily apparent that, as in other aspects of black life, Christian practice was characterized by diversity. Consequently, the appellation "black church" is sometimes misleading, since it suggests a monolithic institutional structure and a homogeneity of beliefs and practices that did not exist. Blacks, as was the case with whites, switched their denominational allegiances in accordance with their changing needs, beliefs, class positions, and politico religious consciousness.

To the degree that they were able, the black denominations supported a vast array of secular and social welfare activities. They established day-care centers, schools, orphanages, colleges, burial societies, newspapers, and so on. Black clergymen did not all share the same political positions, but many were in the forefront of the struggle against lynching and the fight for equal rights and social justice. Most of all, the organized church in its various denominational manifestations was a symbol of black potential if only the societal encumberances were removed.

Women provided much of the energy that the churches and the secular organizations manifested. Most of the mainline churches and the Nation of Islam denied leadership roles to women, but the Holiness and Pentecostal churches were more flexible. In spite of the sexism, women created spaces for themselves in these institutions and played the central roles in the humanitarian, uplift, and outreach programs.

The emergence of a small but growing number of middle-class women with the requisite time and resources helped to facilitate these expressions of black self-help. Working-class women were not inactive, to be sure. Many worked alongside their middle-class sisters in such organizations as the National Council of Negro Women, and at the local level in a large number of religious and secular groups. In Atlanta, middle-class and working-class women worked together in the Neighborhood Union (NU). Founded in 1908 by Lugenia Burns Hope, a social worker and teacher, the NU provided medical advice and assistance to blacks, sponsored cultural events, introduced classes in a number of subjects, and lobbied the municipal authorities on behalf of the city's residents for better services, among other functions.

Prior to the 1930s and the New Deal, blacks had been excluded from most public welfare programs at the local and federal levels. Even when the authorities discharged their obligations to black citizens, they allocated less funding. In 1914, for example, the Southern states spent an average of $4.01 for the education of a black child and $10.82 for each white child. In 1930, the average expenditure on a black child was $15.86, while that for a white child was $42.39.[9] Generally, blacks faced the challenge of providing social services for themselves where none existed or of supplementing public funds in situations where the money allocated was inadequate.

In promoting their desire for education, they pursued two strategies. Pooling their resources, black citizens built their own schools and struggled to pay teachers and maintain facilities. In 1907, Du Bois reported that there were 151 church-sponsored and 161 nonsectarian black schools in the nation. A second strategy involved the purchase of land, the construction of a school, and deeding it over to the local authorities where that was possible. Some communities supplemented the paltry salaries that the teachers received from the boards of education.

Although the enhancement of education received most attention from black proponents of change, the provision of adequate health care appears to have been a close second. Blacks constructed about 200 hospitals and health-care facilities between 1890 and 1930. Again, women assumed many of the fund-raising burdens. The club women instructed mothers about homemaking, proper child care, nutrition, sexual issues, and hygiene. Some women visited the sick and helped raise funds to purchase the medicines required by the patients. Others imparted useful information about methods of contraception. Newspapers also disseminated information about contraception. Many communities established birth control clinics, particularly after the mid-1920s. Although there was opposition by some to the practice of birth control, others supported it on economic grounds and because it freed women to reach their human possibilities in other ways. Writing in 1925, for example, the historian and journalist J. A. Rogers stated, "I give the Negro woman credit if she endeavors to be something other than a mere breeding machine. Having children is by no means the sole reason for being." Dr. Charles Garvin, a physician, agreed. Writing in 1932, he thought it was the "inalienable right of every married woman to use any physiologically sound precaution against reproduction she deems justifiable."[10]

Black women were also in the forefront of efforts to establish old people's homes, orphanages, and homes for the protection of young women. Migration to the North, the growth in the urban populations, and the attendant social disruptions left some unfortunate young women at the mercy of male predators. A relic of slavery, particularly in the South, black women also continued to be the victims of sexual exploitation by white men. Troubled by the situation, club women were instrumental in sponsoring homes that, at least for a while, protected these women from further abuse. Women also organized neighborhood clubs for girls, collected clothes for the needy, and served as volunteers at hospitals.

These and other worthy social endeavors were not the only preoccupations of the women reformers. Some black women, particularly after 1910, joined white women in the struggle to obtain the right to vote. The major black women's organizations such as the National Association of Colored Women, the National Federation of Afro-American Women, and the Alpha Kappa Alpha and Delta Sigma Theta sororities endorsed the passage of the Nineteenth Amendment, which guaranteed suffrage to women. White suffragists were not necessarily welcoming of such support, since many of them shared the racist sentiments of the white men who conceived and enforced the Jim Crow laws and the concomitant disenfranchisement of blacks in the South. Throughout the protracted campaign for the adoption of the amendment, the white-dominated National American Woman Suffrage Association declined to endorse the suffrage for black women.

Although black women supported the amendment, some worried that its passage might actually enhance the political power of the white supremacists. They knew that white women shared in the advantages that whites as a whole enjoyed as a consequence of racially based privileges. Annie Blackwell, a teacher in Charlotte, North Carolina, thought it conceivable that a "grandmother clause," patterned after the pernicious "grandfather clause" that Southern states adopted to disenfranchise black men, might be introduced in her state. "We . . . realize the influence that [white] women exert without the ballot," she stated. "[W]hat would it be with the ballot?"[11]

The ratification of the Nineteenth Amendment in 1919 confirmed black women's worst fears. They confronted numerous obstacles when they attempted to register in the South, a situation that white suffragists often abetted. In North Carolina, Delia Dixon-Carroll, a physician and racial moderate, took to the road, telling white women that "White Supremacy rests in women's hands."[12] Increasingly, many black women devoted their energies in the 1930s and later to the fight for civil rights. "The Negro is oppressed not because he is a negro—but because he will take it," Nannie Burroughs charged in 1941.[13]

The roles that women of all social classes played in helping to improve the black condition in myriad ways can hardly be exaggerated. That some of these efforts were inspired by an uplift ideology that tended to blame the less fortunate for their condition should not make us dismissive of the value of the programs the women initiated and the causes they supported. The animating impulses of their activities were decidedly philanthropic, but they were also political. Since blacks, particularly those in the South, had been excluded from the white-centered civil society, they had to create their own passageways. Less threatening to the white defenders of the social order than black men, women assumed critical roles in representing the needs of their constituency to the larger white society. One black woman, Sallie Mial of North Carolina, recognized as early as 1899 that the political disabilities that blacks faced presented women with unique challenges and opportunities. "We have a peculiar work to do. We can go where you can not afford to go," she told the men.[14] Mial's comment would serve as a parable for women's work on behalf of their brethren in subsequent years. The noted educator Charlotte Hawkins Brown was one person who never accommodated herself to Jim Crow facilities in public transportation and brought suits challenging their existence. In explaining her persistence, she observed in 1921:

> As for me, a Negro woman, I feel so intently the insults that are heaped upon me by the Railroad Company that I am willing to become a

martyr for Negro womanhood in this instance and give up my chance of holding, as friends, people who would withdraw because of my attitude. . . . A few of us must be sacrificed perhaps in order to get a step further.[15]

Many women did lose their friends, and not a few were "sacrificed," to use Ms. Brown's phraseology. In summarizing black women's role in behalf of their brethren over time, Mary McLeod Bethune said it well:

By the very force of circumstances, the part she played in the progress of the race has been of necessity, to a certain extent, subtle and indirect. She has not always been permitted a place in the front ranks where she could show her face and make her voice heard with effect. . . . [But] she has been quick to seize every opportunity which presented itself to come more and more into the open and strive directly for the uplift of the race and nation.[16]

WEATHERING THE STORMS OF THE GREAT DEPRESSION

The internal motions in black life that we have discussed should not blind us to the tenacity of some of the barriers that remained. Nor should we equate minor adjustments in the relationships between blacks and whites, and racially symbolic actions in the 1930s and later, with deeper transformations. Although the generation of 1917 charted an aggressive direction for themselves, the larger society, in the main, retained its old racial ethos in spite of the appearance of challenges to the pseudoscientific claims to white superiority in the 1920s and the 1930s. In the popular culture, black citizens remained white America's laughing stocks. At amusement parks, whites were invited to "Hit the coon and get a cigar." The popular radio show *Amos and Andy*, which began its run in 1928, depicted blacks as shiftless buffoons, and movies made by whites showed a similar pattern. The racial climate remained the harshest in the South, but no region in the nation could boast a commitment to equality for all of its citizens. In 1932, in a nascent show of independence, a number of blacks who possessed the franchise contemplated diluting their traditional support for the Republican party because they perceived—albeit dimly and inaccurately—that Franklin D. Roosevelt, the Democratic candidate, was sensitive to their strivings.

Only a handful of black districts in such cities as New York, Pittsburgh, and Knoxville actually provided significant support for the victorious Democratic candidate. This result notwithstanding, Walter White of the NAACP concluded that the election reflected an end to "the blind allegiance of Negroes to the Republican party."[17] The fact that some blacks seriously considered voting for the Democratic party, even if they did not do so in the end, indicated an important psychological shift or break with past behavior. Four years later, White's observation about the changing political climate would be proven accurate.

White expressed guarded optimism after the 1932 election. "It is an open question as to whether or not the Democrats nationally will do very much for the Negro," he said. "I doubt that they will do very much against him, which will be a vast improvement over the last four years." As soon as the new president assumed his office, the NAACP requested a meeting with him, only to be rebuffed. Roosevelt could not meet with these representatives of black citizens "due to pressure of work."[18]

The new president, like his predecessors, was never preoccupied with addressing the claims of black Americans. Since the Compromise of 1877, the executive and legislative branches of the federal and state governments were frequently more prone to violating the rights of black citizens as opposed to protecting their interests and improving their condition. Blacks entered the legislative consciousness, if they did so at all, not as citizens with just claims but as orphans who enjoyed only those rights that were seemingly the products of white benevolence and not necessarily theirs by birthright. For the most part, blacks, despite their daily interaction with whites, remained invisible except in times of social unrest or when both groups competed for the same jobs.

The profound human misery that the Great Depression of the 1930s produced and the questions that it raised about the efficacy of the nation's institutions compelled a vigorous, creative, and immediate presidential response. By 1932, it was quite clear that the poor, and this included most blacks, bore the brunt of the economic disaster. As the crisis worsened, many blacks and whites lost their jobs, but the unemployment rate for blacks was roughly twice that for whites. In Harlem, for example, the unemployment rate for blacks was about 50 percent in 1932; in Philadelphia it stood at 56 percent. Fifty-five percent of black women in Chicago and Detroit were jobless. In the South, black farmers fell victim to the dramatic reduction in cotton prices and were forced off the land because of their insolvency. Sharecroppers and tenant farmers suffered a similar fate. Overall, the unemployment rate for blacks during the worst stages of the Depression hovered around 50 percent nationally.

The decline in the number of available jobs exacerbated white fears of competition with blacks. Asserting their claims to white privilege, some whites in Atlanta advocated "No Jobs for Niggers Until Every White Man Has a Job." Writing to President Roosevelt, one white woman protested: "Negroes being worked ever where instead of white men it don't look like that is rite."[19] Whites everywhere urged the dismissal of blacks and their replacement by whites. "Niggers back to the cotton fields–city jobs for white folks," some desperate whites recommended.[20] Even those workers who kept their jobs experienced drastic declines in their incomes.

Out of work and destitute, poor blacks and their white counterparts had to seek public assistance. But the various agencies that administered relief were never color-blind, and they provided less support for black clients, or none at all. As usual, the situation was more dismal for blacks in the South. One black woman who lived in Reidsville, Georgia, complained to the president that the "releaf officials here . . . give us black folks each one, nothing but a few cans of pickle meet and to the white folks they give blankets, bolts of cloth and things like that." A black resident of Hattiesburg, Mississippi, hoped that Roosevelt "could see the poor hungry an naket half clad's at the relief office an is turned away with tears in their eyes. Mississippi is made her own laws and don't treat her destituted as her Pres. has laid plans for us to live."[21]

Ignoring the Jim Crow laws and customs and the systemic disabilities that blacks confronted, the Roosevelt administration contended that their problems were similar to those of whites. The president's wife, Eleanor, who was closely identified with the cause of racial justice, believed that the black condition could be attributed to the fact that blacks "not only in the South, but in the North as well have been economically at a low level." Another administration official, Harold L. Ickes, the racially progressive secretary of the interior, was convinced that the "Negro problem merges into and becomes inseparable from the greater problem of American citizens generally, who are at or below the line in decency and comfort from those who are not."[22] This astonishing interpretation of the reasons for the condition of blacks has endured to contemporary times. Ickes could hardly have been unaware of the panoply of racially inspired laws that restricted opportunities for blacks in the South and the numerous ways in which the larger society retarded their progress and accorded them a subordinate status in national life, and even in access to and distribution of the country's resources. Some blacks, probably a minority, shared Ickes' view of the inseparability of the black condition from that of whites. In 1933, an editorial in the *Star of Zion*, a newspaper published by the AME Zion Church, maintained, "The Negro is part of this great American citizenship and what affects the one affects the other. . . . The sooner the Negro understands this and quits his whining the better it will be for him."[23] In explaining why Roosevelt could not meet with a delegation of blacks and whites in 1933, Louis Howes, the president's secretary, declared, "The Negro people have no special problems; they are American citizens."[24]

Given its race-neutral assessment of the problems that blacks faced, it is not surprising that the Roosevelt administration did not frame any programs with their needs solely in mind. The administration was also very sensitive to the positions of the Southern representatives in Congress and had no desire to alienate them by appearing to recognize the special claims of black citizens. Roosevelt did not want to endanger the adoption of his program of economic recovery and reconstruction. As he put it, "I can't alienate certain votes I need for measures that are more important at the moment by pushing any measures that would entail a fight."[25] This pragmatic approach made sense when seen from Roosevelt's perspective. But an oppressed black citizenry with real problems and real grievances that needed a national response could not draw comfort from the administration's stance. With the possible exception of such persons as Eleanor Roosevelt and Harold Ickes, the Roosevelt administration did not understand the pulse of black America in 1932. In 1928 blacks sent Oscar De Priest, a black Republican representing a district in Chicago, to Congress. This was the first time that a black person had formed a part of a congressional delegation since George White from North Carolina left office in 1901. With migration from the South expanding the size of the black electorate in the North and newspapers vigorously aiding in their politicization, blacks were becoming increasingly aware of their potential power at the ballot box in some states. The hardships resulting from the depression had forced the NAACP to expand its emphasis on litigation to include economic issues. The National Urban League also became more aggressive in its advocacy of employment for blacks and on its assault on discrimination in the trade unions.

Black newspapers and a growing number of individual blacks criticized the Roosevelt administration for its tolerance of racial discrimination in its relief programs. These and other signs of motion did not yet become an earthquake, but the tremors were strong enough to effect changes—albeit chiefly symbolic ones—in the administration's attitude toward black citizens. Whereas Roosevelt ignored blacks and their spokespersons in 1932 and 1933, by 1935, and certainly in 1936, the president and his administration actively welcomed their support. Eleanor Roosevelt and a handful of other racially progressive whites played significant roles in the administration's changing tone, but the push came primarily from below, from the insistent demand of blacks for justice and their harsh critiques of the racist underpinnings of the New Deal. In 1935 several black intellectuals created an umbrella organization, the National Negro Congress (NNC), to promote the economic interests of blacks. The idea for its formation came from John P. Davis, who lambasted the programs of the New Deal as reflecting a "well defined philosophy that Negroes must be left to develop in a ghetto of their own and quite apart from the white population."[26] Davis became the executive secretary of the organization and A. Philip Randolph the president until he resigned in 1940, charging that the NNC was controlled by communists. Prominent members of the NNC, at least for a while, included Ralph Bunche, Robert C. Weaver, Abram Harris, and E. Franklin Frazier.[27] During the 1930s, the NNC and its affiliates sponsored rent strikes, "Don't Buy Where You Can't Work" campaigns, and worked actively to procure jobs for blacks.

Students learning to read at a Louisiana adult literacy class sponsored by the WPA.

The NNC drew attention to the economic plight of blacks, but it had considerable less impact on the construction and administration of the New Deal. Several different but interrelated programs formed the core of the New Deal. The National Recovery Administration (NRA) was designed to make the nation's economic system more rational and coherent. It required each industry to develop codes of acceptable labor practices and a wage structure. The Agricultural Adjustment Administration (AAA) was intended to increase prices by encouraging planters to reduce their production and thereby eliminate any "surplus." In effect, farmers received federal subsidies if they grew fewer crops and decreased their livestock production. The Federal Emergency Relief Administration (FERA) helped people in distress, introduced literacy programs, and facilitated instruction in a number of skills. Among the other agencies, the Public Works Administration (PWA) supervised federally created projects aimed at increasing employment and speeding economic recovery. The Social Security Act provided support for the elderly, the disabled, and the unemployed. The Federal Housing Administration (FHA) assisted members of the middle class in obtaining mortgage and home improvement loans.

Alfred Murphy, a 105-year-old slave, learning to write his name.

Although the administration said it opposed discrimination in the execution of these programs, it lacked the political will and muscle, particularly in the South, to achieve its objectives. Relief agencies provided less assistance for blacks or excluded them altogether from the programs. The FHA declined to guarantee mortgages to blacks who sought to purchase homes in all-white neighborhoods. The NRA condoned the practice of companies paying lower wages to blacks. Farmers who should have shared their subsidy payments with their black tenants and sharecroppers seldom did so, forcing many of them off the land.

There were other problems as well. The Social Security Act excluded domestic and agricultural workers from its purview. Since a disproportionate number of blacks fell into these categories of workers, their exclusion had racial undertones. Southern whites, in particular, spewed the venom that inspired the exclusion of these workers quite openly. "The average Mississippian can't imagine himself chipping in to pay pensions for able-bodied Negroes to sit in idleness on front galleries supporting their kinfolks on pensions," declared the *Jackson Daily News*, "while cotton and corn crops are crying for workers to get them out of the grass."[28] The Wagner Act, which was passed in 1935 to protect unions and the right of workers to organize, lacked a provision to protect black workers from the existing, widespread discriminatory treatment by organized labor.

Despite the race-based inequities that the New Deal fostered, the black poor undeniably reaped some benefits. Thousands obtained jobs under the aegis of the various programs and received public assistance of one sort or another. But the longer-term implications of the New Deal for blacks were equally significant. Many blacks became literate as a result of their enrollment in adult literacy classes sponsored by the FERA. Others obtained the skills they needed to fill certain jobs, and musicians, artists, and actors found employment in projects developed by the Federal Music Project, the Federal Art Project, and the Federal Theatre Project, respectively.

The Federal Writers Project provided employment for black writers as researchers and workers on a number of scholarly projects. It also subsidized the publication of the literary efforts of promising young writers. The Federal Writers Project also hired writers to conduct interviews with surviving former slaves, with a view to preserving their memories of the institution. These slave narratives, as they are called, have since become an indispensable source for the study of slave life and culture.

The administration's sensitivity to black culture stemmed in part from the influence that black employees of the federal government exercised. Although none of these individuals occupied positions of real power in the administration, they helped to define its public face, starting around 1935. Highly educated, these officials served primarily to interpret the needs of blacks to whites in the various departments and agencies and to represent the administration to a growing black constituency. The members of this "Black Brain Trust" included the scholars Rayford Logan, Robert Weaver, and Ralph Bunche, as well as newspaper publisher and lawyer Eugene Jones, Robert Vann of the National Urban League, and William Pickens of the NAACP. As many as 100 blacks held positions in the New Deal by 1940. The best known was Mary McLeod Bethune. A native of South Carolina, Bethune founded the Daytona Normal and Industrial School in 1904 in Daytona Beach, Florida; it was subsequently renamed Bethune-Cookman College. Active in the cause of racial uplift, she served as president of the National Association of Colored Women (1924-28) and founded the National Council of Negro Women in 1935.

Bethune became a member of the Roosevelt administration in 1935 when she was appointed an adviser on racial issues and later promoted to director of the National Youth Administration (NYA) Division of Negro Affairs. Enjoying the respect of other black appointees, Mary Bethune functioned as head of an informal group that they established. Known as

Mary McLeod Bethune was highly educated and an instrumental spokeswoman for blacks in the New Deal.

the "Black Cabinet," the members debated the ways in which to advance issues of importance to blacks in the administration and how to help shape its programs. With their ears close to the ground, they also transmitted black opinion on a range of issues to the appropriate departments and agencies.

As head of the NYA's Division of Negro Affairs, Bethune advanced educational programs for black youth, although she was forced to accept the prevailing "separate but equal" doctrine. In order to promote a deeper understanding of their difficulties, she organized two national conferences, "Problems of the Negro and Negro Youth" in 1937 and again in 1938. Possessing a close friendship with Eleanor Rooosevelt and a polite relationship with the president, she solicited their help in endorsing and enhancing programs important to blacks, at every opportunity. Bethune recommended blacks for various appointive positions, opposed Jim Crow laws, and promoted interracial cooperation.

The presence of black men and women in the administration–regardless of their roles-enhanced President Roosevelt's appeal among blacks as a whole. Eleanor Roosevelt was also enormously popular as she became increasingly identified with racial decency. In a break with past administrations, this one eschewed overt appeals to white racism for political advantage. Coupled with the benefits that some blacks had obtained as a consequence of the New Deal's programs, it is not surprising that Roosevelt received 71 percent of their votes in 1936 and 67 percent in 1940.

The overall condition of blacks when most of the New Deal programs ended in 1940 was not fundamentally different from what it was in 1932. There were no dramatic alterations in the distribution of income, the share of economic resources, or access to political power. Blacks still functioned under the debilitating strictures of "separate but equal," and the urban residents of the North were increasingly trapped in ghettos. On the other hand, blacks were no longer invisible members of the body politic, and no subsequent federal administration could remain indifferent to their needs. With their growing electoral strength in the industrial states of the North, they forced the politicians to recognize their presence even if their concerns were often ignored after election day. In symbolic ways at least, the New Deal came to be identified with racial decency, although it never assaulted the foundations of segregation and discrimination or embraced an unambiguous and consistent commitment to civil rights. Still, the New Deal's positive gestures on matters of race represented a departure from the pattern established after Reconstruction, and it would be difficult for succeeding presidents to return to the old ways.

Similarly, the pace of change within black America could not be contained. Most of these changes were not unleashed by the New Deal, but they may have been accelerated by the pressures created by the depression on the one hand, and the challenges it produced on the other. For their part, the mechanization of agriculture and the policies pursued by the Agricultural Adjustment Administration resulted in a steep decline in the number of black rent tenants and sharecroppers. This drove displaced blacks to the urban areas of the South and the North, where many joined the mass struggle for racial justice. Thousands who became literate as a result of the New Deal programs were able to participate more fully in the life of black America and probably became less willing to accommodate themselves to racially inspired disabilities.

Writing in the early 1940s after a racial assault on a black man in Georgia, Langston Hughes warned:

Negroes,
Sweet and Docile,
Meek, humble, and kind:
Beware the day
They change their minds! . . . .

Blacks, of course, were changing their minds in ways subversive of the status quo and affirming of themselves. The tremors that produced the cosmetic changes associated with the New Deal became a massive earthquake in the 1950s.

Notes

1. Wintz, *African American Political Thought*, 155-156.
2. Ibid., 158.
3. Stuckey, *Slave Culture*, 299.
4. C. Eric Lincoln, *The Black Muslims in America* (3rd Edition, Trenton: Africa World Press, 1994), 11-15.
5. Hans A. Baer and Merrill Singer, *African-American Religion in the Twentieth Century* (Knoxville: University of Tennessee Press, 1992), 126.
6. Ibid., 147-148.
7. Robert Weisbrot, *Father Divine and the Struggle for Racial Equality* (Urbana: University of Illinois Press, 1983), unpaginated frontispiece.
8. Ibid., 221.
9. Stephanie Shaw, *What a Woman Ought to Be and Do: Black Professional Women Workers During the Jim Crow Era* (Chicago: University of Chicago Press, 1966), 174.
10. Jessie M. Rodrique, "The Black Community and the Birth Control Movement," in Hine et al., *'We Specialize in the Wholly Impossible,'* 508-509.
11. Gilmore, *Gender and Jim Crow*, 217.
12. Ibid.
13. Linda Gordon, "Black and White Visions of Welfare: Women's Welfare Activism, 1890-1945," in Hine et al., *'We Specialize in the Wholly Impossible,'* 466.
14. Gilmore, *Gender and Jim Crow*, 151.
15. Hine, *Speak Truth to Power*, 140.
16. Gerda Lerner, ed., *Black Women in White America* (New York: Random House, 1973), 580.
17. Nancy Weiss, *Farewell to the Party of Lincoln: Black Politics in the Age of FDR* (Princeton: Princeton University Press, 1983), 32.
18. Ibid., 33-34.
19. Robert S. McElvaine, *The Great Depression: America, 1929-1941* (New York: Times Books, 1984), 187.
20. Harvard Sitkoff, *A New Deal for Blacks: The Emergence of Civil Rights as a National Issue* (New York: Oxford, 1978), 36.
21. McElvaine, *Great Depression*, 189-190.
22. Weiss, *Farewell to the Party of Lincoln*, 37.
23. Ibid., 39.
24. Ibid., 42.
25. Sitkoff, *A New Deal*, 44.
26. Ibid., 55.
27. Pfeffer, *A. Philip Randolph*, 32-40.
28. McElvaine, *Great Depression*, 257.

Looking Outward: World War I to the Civil Rights Movement

Throughout the nineteenth century, a number of blacks endorsed emigration as one means of improving the condition of their people. Several thousand persons actually abandoned the United States for Liberia, Sierra Leone, Haiti, Canada, and elsewhere. Black Christian missionaries brought the gospel to several African countries and the Caribbean. Others who remained at home manifested an emotional identification with the peoples of African descent across the diaspora and subscribed to the emerging Pan-African movement. Burdened, but also politicized by their problems at home, and conscious of the difficulties that Africans and the peoples of African descent confronted everywhere, American blacks and West Indians played significant roles in illuminating the similarities in the black condition, in promoting a diasporan unity, and in articulating appropriate courses of action and remedies.

The colonization and partitioning of Africa by Europeans in the late nineteenth century starkly revealed the powerlessness of Africans and their brethren in the diaspora. Despite the fact that their enslavement had ended only in the 1860s, black Americans made rapid strides in improving their condition and benefited from a cadre of outstanding spokespersons such as Anna Cooper, W. E. B. Du Bois, and Bishop Henry McNeal Turner, who linked the struggle in America with that of oppressed blacks elsewhere. This internationalization of the black condition strengthened over time as an educated black elite expanded, black nationalist ideologies were popularized, and political consciousness heightened. Marcus Garvey's Universal Negro Improvement Association transcended national boundaries, spoke the language of an internationalized blackness, and enhanced popular understandings of the experiences of blacks across the diaspora. The highly educated Du Bois believed that if racial and class interests were joined, "a new unity of man" would emerge. Du Bois also believed, as Turner had articulated years earlier, that the improvement in the black condition in America was tied specifically to the destiny of Africans on the African continent. "I do not believe," he stated, "that it is possible to settle the Negro problem in America until the color problems of the world are well on the way toward settlement. I do not believe that the descendants of Africans are going to be received as American citizens so long as the peoples of Africa are kept by white civilization in semislavery, serfdom, and economic exploitation."[1]

The understanding that blacks had to unite in order to address the twin problems of colonialism and racism provided the impulse for the Pan-African movement. The first step in the formation of the Pan-African movement was taken in Chicago in 1893 with the convening of the Chicago Congress on Africa. It attracted blacks and whites, including Bishop Turner and Alexander Crummell. This was the first time that the term "Pan-African" was employed; a local newspaper characterized the gathering as such. The first international gathering of Pan-Africanists occurred in London in 1900. It was organized by the Trinidadian barrister Henry Sylvester Williams and attracted delegates from various parts of the African diaspora. Black Americans were represented by several persons, including Anna Cooper and Du Bois.

This pioneering congress was convened for the purpose of:

> First, to bring into closer touch with each other the peoples of African descent throughout the world; second to inaugurate plans to bring about a more friendly relation between the Caucasian and African races; third to start a movement looking forward to the securing to all African races living in civilized countries their full rights and to promote their business interests.[2]

The conferees established the Pan-African Congress movement and adopted resolutions calling for an end to racism and the economic exploitation of colonized peoples, as well as the granting of self-government to the British colonies in Africa and the Caribbean. One resolution called on the United States to grant blacks their civil rights, and another exhorted the imperial countries to respect the sovereignty of Haiti, Liberia, and Ethiopia. Du Bois wrote the conference's "Address to the Nations of the World." In it, he predicted that "the problem of the twentieth century is the problem of the color-line, the question as to how far differences of race–which show themselves chiefly in the color of the skin and the texture of the hair–will hereafter be made the basis to denying to over half the world the right of sharing to their utmost ability the opportunities and privileges of modern civilization."[3]

The conference did not change the black condition anywhere. Blacks were too powerless to implement their proposals, and the imperial powers and the American authorities paid little attention to the Pan-African gathering. But that was not the measure of its importance. The conference brought elite blacks from the diaspora together for the first time in a cause that signified unity of purpose and a willingness to challenge the bases of white supremacy. It was difficult, however, to maintain the energy that created this transnational movement in the face of financial difficulties and more immediate domestic concerns. Over the next several years, black Americans debated competing visions of the future, formed civil rights organizations, and launched self-help programs. Not until 1919 did Du Bois seize the initiative by calling the first Pan-African Congress.

The time for the congress seemed propitious, because the protagonists in World War I were meeting in Paris to construct peace and define a new world order. Since the principle of self-determination for all peoples was to be one of the guiding principles at the peace parley, Pan-Africanists wanted to use the occasion to promote the cause of racial justice and freedom for the colonized. Attended by representatives from several countries, the conclave met in Paris and endorsed humanitarian reforms in colonial administrations in Africa and urged the participation of Africans in their governments "as fast as their development permits, in conformity with the principle that the government exists for the natives, and not the natives for the government."[4] The conferees, including Du Bois, did not demand immediate independence for the African colonies but said it should be granted when they were deemed to be ready for it. In this regard, the Pan-Africanists accepted the notion of the White Man's Burden and the attendant claim that the colonial peoples needed European tutelage.

Du Bois organized Pan-African Congresses in 1921, 1923, and again in 1927. The issues the attendees discussed were generally similar to the ones on the agenda of the first two meetings. These conferences, as well as the one held in 1919, occurred at a time when the movement led by Marcus Garvey was raising the consciousness of blacks worldwide. Although Du Bois and the black elite in America distanced themselves from the UNIA, they were not blind to its universal appeal. Garveyism and its "race first" philosophy gave a certain urgency to the cause of Pan-Africanism and provided it with a potential mass base.

This did not occur, however. Interest in Pan-Africanism waned after the collapse of the Garvey movement and as the misery created by the Great Depression demanded more immediate attention in the 1930s. Preoccupied by local struggles, blacks in the diaspora lacked the requisite time, energy, and resources to give teeth to a transnational movement, however emotionally and politically compelling its cause. Moreover, only the elite could afford to attend the conferences. When the fifth Pan-African Congress was convened in Manchester, England, in 1945, Du Bois was the only black American representative. The delegates came primarily from Africa and the Caribbean. Their attendance and the anticolonial questions that dominated the congress reflected a rising nationalism that would culminate in political independence for many countries in the ensuing decades.

Pan-Africanism was only one expression of black America's developing embrace of Africa and the diaspora. Some persons had internalized negative images of Africa and Africans and had viewed the continent through a negative Western and American lens. For such persons, a secure embrace of their ancestral continent would not occur until after they had exorcised the negative constructions of African peoples and cultures and viewed them on their own terms. This process could be enhanced by a sensitive reinterpretation of the African past and the development of more sympathetic understandings of the present. Intellectuals such as Du Bois, Carter G. Woodson, and Paul Robeson knew that in liberating themselves, black Americans had to embrace Africa as well; the two processes were inextricably linked. For them, the immediate task was the eradication of the pejorative images of the continent, the recovery of its history, and the dissemination of the new knowledge. This daunting challenge placed unique burdens on black intellectuals. Not only were they trying to arrive at some elusive "truth," but they also confronted a body of existing scholarship—with few exceptions—replete with distortions, misunderstandings, and racist conceptualizations and conclusions about African peoples.

In *The Negro*, which he published in 1915, Du Bois observed that "racial prejudice" was so virulent in "so-called civilized centers" that a "judicial appraisement" of Africa was hampered.[5] His book reinterpreted the African past and broke with the racist conceptions of the continent's history. Woodson followed a similar conceptual path in *The Negro in Our History*, published in 1922.

Robeson celebrated the cultures of the African peoples by popularizing their songs. He learned various African languages and saw African cultures as forming "a treasure-store for the world."[6] Embracing the cause of the independence, Robeson joined and later served as director of the Council on African Affairs. Founded in London, the council developed strong roots in America, and during the 1940s and early 1950s it was the loudest voice in the country advocating an end to European colonial rule in Africa. As some had done before him, Robeson linked the black struggle in America with that of the African peoples. In denouncing the South African racial policies known as apartheid, he maintained in 1952 that "we simultaneously strike a blow at the reactionary forces in our own land who seek to preserve here, in South Africa, and everywhere else the super-profits they harvest from racial and national oppression."[7]

Those who linked the cause of blacks in America and Africa thought that black Americans had a special obligation to assist their African brethren. Robeson was quite insistent on this score:

> American Negroes have a real duty to our African brothers and sisters, a sacred duty. . . . Negroes who have not lost pride and dignity know that if we are at all serious about our full freedom here in America we must understand what the future of Africa means. . . . Should we not do all in our power to help people there. . . . Should we not arouse the youth in the universities? Should we not swing our churches, fraternal bodies, professional groups, women's organizations and civic clubs into action. . . . Not only is this a struggle in the interest of African people. Their freedom and dignity will be of immeasurable assistance in our final break-through here in these United States. New Africa in the end will mean . . . New Mississippi.[8]

There was nothing revolutionary about this stance, since black Americans had previously aided Africans in a variety of ways. Missionaries and teachers had gone to work in Africa, particularly after Reconstruction ended. During the early years of the twentieth century, Booker T. Washington sent graduates of Tuskegee Institute to Togo, Nigeria, and the Sudan to instruct the people in agricultural techniques, especially the cultivation of cotton. He also inspired the establishment of schools patterned after Tuskegee in several countries. John Dube, a South African nationalist, for example, met Washington when he was a student in the United States. Upon his return home, he founded the Ohlange Institute, which was devoted to vocational education in Natal in 1909. Dube was effusive in his praise of Washington. To him, Washington was his "guiding star."

> I have chosen this great man, firstly because he is perhaps the most famous and the best living example of our Africa's sons; and, secondly because, like him, I, too, have my heart centered mainly in the education of my race. Therein, me thinks, lies the shortest and best way to their mutual, moral, material and political betterment.[9]

Religious denominations such as the African Methodist Episcopal offered support to African students to attend colleges and universities in the United States. When the Eastern Cape Province of South Africa experienced a severe drought in the 1940s, the Council on African Affairs sent people money and food.

These and other forms of assistance that were pioneered by churches and secular organizations continued with ebbs and flows during the period being discussed. But the black Americans' interest in Africa became more overtly political after 1900 with their demanding an end to colonial exploitation, as evidenced by the Pan-African movement, the rise of Garveyism, the activities of the Council on African Affairs, and the pronouncements of Du Bois, Robeson, and a host of other lesser-known personages.

Black Americans were outraged when Italy, under the leadership of the Fascist dictator Benito Mussolini, massed on the Ethiopian border in the spring of 1935. This independent African state had repulsed an Italian invasion in 1896, a defeat that Mussolini sought to avenge. Italy's humiliation at the battle of Adowa had been welcomed at a time when almost all of Africa was under European rule. The *Savannah Tribune* spoke for many: "The Abyssinians [Ethiopians] are defending their homes and native land; they are perfectly right in expelling foreign aggressions. This overbearing spirit exercised by European nations over African nations should be stopped."[10] There was, however, much more at stake. Ethiopia had long played a symbolic role in black American life, particularly in religious terms. The biblical prophecy that Ethiopia would assist in the rejuvenation of Christianity and in black liberation retained a powerful appeal among them. Although Ethiopia was in this context a synonym for Africa, the distinction was frequently blurred in the popular imagination. The spectacle of the white Italians attacking a black African nation also racialized the conflict, leading black Americans to identify with the victims.

Black American interest in Ethiopia did not disappear after Italy's defeat in 1896, although it did wane. A small number of blacks immigrated there, often finding the problems of adjustment to be insurmountable. They faced language difficulties and inadequate job opportunities. Disillusioned, most eventually returned home. Sympathetic to Ethiopia and its peoples, a number of black Americans and Africans founded the Ethiopian Research Council in Washington, D.C., in 1934. Its objective was to promote the "assembling and disseminating" of information about the country. The organizers saluted Ethiopia as "one of the oldest living civilizations in the world." They emphasized that "in the Classical Age it was universally regarded as one of the greatest and most powerful nations of the earth."[11] Under the presidency of William Leo Hansberry, a Howard University history professor, the council increased the consciousness of blacks about Ethiopia and played a prominent oppositional role to Mussolini's invasion.

Italy's aggression aroused the passions of blacks throughout the diaspora. The first invasion of 1896 had not produced mass protests in the black world, but much had changed in the interim. A new generation of blacks in the diaspora had become vociferous in their denunciation of colonialism. By the 1930s, blacks in the United States had not only begun to challenge their oppression in new ways, but some also tied their cause, as we have seen, to that of the Africans. These internal developments in black America compelled an identification with Ethiopia and its travail.

Never before had black Americans been as emotionally involved in a foreign crisis as they were to become in the Ethiopian affair. This identification transcended class lines, uniting those who could speak learnedly about Ethiopia with those who could not locate it on a map. The invasion provided blacks with an opportunity to demonstrate to themselves, and to others, an embrace of their African homeland, even if almost no one could claim an Ethiopian ancestry. At another level, the conflict was interpreted in racial terms and as a part of the longer history of white exploitation of blacks. Accordingly, the obligation to defend Ethiopia was one that could hardly be avoided.

There were dissenting voices as well. While acknowledging emotional ties with African peoples, some persons believed that the most urgent struggle that blacks confronted was the one at home. In July 1935, the *Chicago Defender* derided those who wanted to travel "to far off Africa to repel an invasion of a country about which you know nothing and actually care less." "Why not fight at home?" enquired the newspaper. "Is there not enough here to fight for? Why don't you fight lynchings, peonage, bastardy, discrimination, segregation? Why don't you fight for jobs to which you are entitled? Why don't you fight for your own independence?"[12] Other papers, such as the *Pittsburgh Courier* and the *Atlanta Daily World*, expressed similar sentiments. The *Courier* would later change its position once it appreciated the wider implications of the invasion and the threat it posed to Ethiopian independence.

Italy's bellicose behavior on Ethiopia's border produced mass demonstrations by blacks in a number of American cities. Some persons expressed a desire to go to Ethiopia to fight the Italians. The United States government discouraged such plans, emphasizing that those who fought under another country's flag would lose their citizenship. Harlem emerged as one of the principal centers of pro-Ethiopian activity, as Garveyites, communists, civil rights organizations, churches, and others joined forces to oppose Mussolini's aggression. The leaders included Adam Clayton Powell, Jr., of the Abyssinian Baptist Church, James W. Ford of the Communist party, A. L. King of the UNIA, and J. A. Rogers, the writer and historian. These and other individuals, as well as a variety of groups, founded the Provisional Committee for the Defense of Ethiopia (PCDE).

The PCDE, and similar organizations in other cities, raised funds, and dispatched medical supplies to Ethiopia. But their activities were not confined to humanitarian assistance. The PCDE sent a representative to Geneva, Switzerland, to urge the League of Nations to aid the Ethiopians and deter the Italians. The representative, Willis N. Huggins, informed the League that the events in Ethiopia were being "viewed with righteous indignation by blacks in the western world who are bound by racial kinship to the ancient and illustrious Ethiopian people."[13] He hoped that the conflict could be resolved without a resort to arms.

The NAACP also worked to settle the crisis. Walter White, the executive secretary, appealed to Secretary of State Cordell Hull to use American influence to avert a war. "The pending dispute between Abyssinia and Italy is one . . . in which the people of the United States have an interest," he wrote, "and this Association appeals to you to assert this interest on behalf of the continuance of the status quo and the maintenance of peace."[14] The NAACP also urged the League of Nations "to restrain Italian aggression in Abyssinia."[15] The association was incensed when the Soviet Union failed to condemn Italy's behavior, particularly before a session of the League. "Has Russia abandoned its alleged opposition [to] imperialism and its much publicized defense [of] weaker peoples?" Walter White enquired. "Does your anti-imperialism stop at black nations?"[16]

The United States pursued a policy of neutrality in the conflict. Turning a deaf ear to the pleas of the Ethiopian emperor, Haile Selassie, for assistance, the European nations also failed to condemn Italy. The Ethiopians were no match for the Italians and their superior weaponry when the fighting began in the fall of 1935. Selassie fled the country, and he did not return to his throne until 1941 when Ethiopian and British troops expelled the Italians during the Second World War. The conflict had energized black Americans to participate more actively in international affairs and to help shape their country's foreign policy in those areas of immediate concern to them. Simultaneously, the crisis revealed the relative political powerlessness of blacks because they failed to influence American policy in the conflict in any significant way.

The invasion, Ethiopia's defeat, and the seeming indifference of the Europeans and white Americans to Italy's conduct exposed, yet again, serious racial fault lines. Colonel John Robinson, a black American who served as an aviator in Ethiopia, was disillusioned by European inattention to the conflict. He observed bitterly "that white people will all [sic] ways stick together in the end when it comes to the color question."[17] Justified or not, this was a sentiment that the handling of the Italo-Ethiopian crisis did little to destroy. Emperor Haile Selassie emerged from exile with enhanced prestige and much admiration for his tenacious defense of his people.

Although black Americans did not shape American and international policy on the Italo-Ethiopian question, they had a major and acknowledged impact on religious and political developments on the African continent. In Malawi, for example, the influence of ideas associated with black Americans was clearly evident in the Native Rising of 1915 against British colonial rule. Its leader, John Chilembwe, had studied in the United States, developed friendships with black Americans, and observed racial segregation firsthand. Upon his return to Malawi, he welcomed black American missionaries and established schools patterned after Booker T. Washington's Tuskegee Institute. The colonial authorities looked askance at the presence of black Americans, fearing that they were preaching a nationalist brand of Christianity–Ethiopianism–that was subversive of the political status quo. Chilembwe became increasingly critical of the colonial exploitation of his people and reinterpreted Christian dogma in such a way as to legitimize his protests. The unsuccessful revolt was rooted primarily in a local context, but it was animated also by black American nationalist ideas.

Similarly, the Kimbangu Movement in the Lower Congo in 1921 was not without black American influences. This messianic movement was led by Simon Kimbangu, who had been exposed to Garveyism and the nationalist writings of W. E. B. Du Bois. The publications of the Universal Negro Improvement Association were available in the urban areas of the Congo, such as Kinshasa. Some people believed that the UNIA's Black Star Line would arrive, bringing black Americans to settle, as well as to expel whites from the continent. Kimbangu infused Christianity with the ideas associated with black nationalism and Pan-Africanism. One colonial functionary thought Kimbangu's "so-called religion mixed elements of protestantism with the external practices of witchcraft. This is pure Garveyism," he asserted. Another official recommended that the authorities should "oppose Kimbangu since he has a tendency towards Pan-Africanism. The natives will say, 'We have found the God of the Blacks, the religion which suits the African,'" he said.[18] The politicoreligious implications of Kimbanguism led the Belgian colonial administration to suppress it. The movement certainly responded to the aspirations of some of the Congolese peoples, but there is no doubt that some of its impulses came from black America. Garvey was celebrated as the "king of the Americans" in one of the Kimbangu hymns. His expected arrival in the Congo, as this hymn suggests, would result in the liberation of the colonized and the restoration of their own king:

> If the King of the Americans comes
> To restore the King
> The chiefs of this world shall pass away.
> If the King of Americans comes,
> The troubles of this world shall pass away.
> If the King of the Americans comes,
> The King of the blacks will return.[19]

Although its extent is difficult to measure, there is no doubt that the black struggle in the United States had an impact on the rise and nature of African nationalisms. Kwame Nkrumah, the Ghanaian nationalist, and Nnamdi Azikiwe of Nigeria readily acknowledged a black American influence on the evolution of their political consciousness and on the strategies they employed to end colonial rule. In turn, black Americans were justifiably proud when the African colonies began to receive their political independence, Ghana being the first to do so in 1957. Andrew Young, who in 1977 became the U.S. ambassador to the United Nations, noticed:

> There was truly a new day dawning for the people of African descent around the world. We observed new African nations come into being and their leaders shed the yoke of European colonialism; Azikiwe in Nigeria, Nkrumah in Ghana, Kenyatta and Tom Mboya in Kenya. Africa's emergence from centuries of colonialism made us as African-Americans feel part of a world movement for the liberation and self-determination of a subjugated peoples.[20]

The consciousness to which Young referred led blacks to provide support, some of it symbolic, for the struggle against colonialism in Africa. Black intellectuals, journalists, and politicians were particularly vociferous in their demand for the end of colonial rule in Africa during World War II. The anti-colonial impetus waned in the aftermath of the war as blacks became more preoccupied with their struggles for social justice at home. At a time when the Cold War with the Soviet Union raged, blacks, with such notable exceptions as Paul Robeson, W. E. B. Du Bois, and the intellectual William Alphaeus Hunton, Jr., also feared being labelled and harrassed as Communists and subversives if they assaulted the Western European presence in Africa and acquiescence by the United States to it.

Still, an emotional identification with the cause of African freedom never died. Some blacks continued to link the struggles for civil rights at home with the liberation of oppressed peoples worldwide. Black organizations hosted visits by African dignitaries, and newspapers featured stories on their struggles. In April 1959, black New Yorkers celebrated African Freedom Day and the residents of Chicago's South Side honored their African brethren by celebrating African Freedom Week.[21] Many black women adopted African hairstyles and wore African prints. In Harlem, businesses carried live broadcasts of speeches made by Africans at the United Nations, so black patrons could hear, if not observe, the proceedings. Unable to hear a speech on one occasion, one black woman enquired what the African might be saying. The answer came from a man in the crowd: "Hell. He's just telling all the crackers in the world to kiss his black ass."[22]

In order to pressure the United States government to respond more affirmatively to developments in Africa, a group of prominent blacks founded the American Negro Leadership Conference on Africa (ANLC) in 1962. Its membership hailed from a coalition of civil rights, labor, women's, and other organizations and boasted such figures as A. Philip Randolph, Whitney Young of the National Urban League, Martin Luther King, Jr., of the Southern Christian Leadership Conference, Dorothy Height of the National Council of Negro Women, and James Farmer of the Congress of Racial Equality. According to Farmer, the organization wanted to have a voice "in the formation of American foreign policy regarding Africa" and also to interpret what was happening in Africa to Americans and vice versa.[23] Although the organization's leadership met with President John F. Kennedy shortly after its founding, its impact on the shaping of America's African policy was hardly significant. Still thinking of blacks as less than full citizens, the nation's leaders and much of the white public looked askance at any involvement by blacks in any policy issue except the domestic race problem. Consumed by their struggles for equality at home, black leaders lacked the time and resources to conduct a sustained and effective campaign to shape American foreign policy in areas of interest to them.

Although black Americans devoted most of their attention to the African struggles, they were not blind to developments elsewhere in the diaspora. Haiti was one of those countries that commanded special interest. The island state was of symbolic importance because it was the site of the only successful slave rebellion in the Americas. Haiti, as a black republic, faced the animus of the white nations who declined to recognize its independence or even to trade with it for many years. Possessing weak institutions and beset by seemingly insoluble internal problems, Haiti's survival as an independent state was never easy. In 1915, in order to stave off Germany's acquisition of the island for unpaid debts and in pursuit of its own economic interests, the United States occupied the island. The Wilson administration explained that it was intervening to restore order and to protect the lives and property of foreigners.

Some Haitians were not pleased with the arrival of the American marines and the violation of their sovereignty. The marines brought the American racial virus with them and were less than respectful of the black Haitians. The Americans introduced racial segregation in public places, exporting Jim Crow to the client state. A number of Haitians embraced Garveyism and used it as one basis for organizing opposition to the American invasion and the mistreatment of its citizens. Black American missionaries also complained about the conduct of the marines.

Although the NAACP was consumed by its domestic responsibilities, it did not ignore what was occurring in Haiti. Taking note of reports of American venality in Haiti, the *Crisis* thought that the American government should "help Haiti rid herself of thieves and not try to fasten American thieves on her."²⁴ The NAACP continued to criticize American policy on the island and called for an end to the occupation. Pressure from the organization produced some modification in the government's policies and mitigated some of the abuses, but the core features remained. Religious organizations, political groups, and the press joined in the opposition to American policy, signaling their identification with the black struggles beyond American borders. When the American occupation ended prematurely in 1934, the Haitian president thanked black Americans for their contribution to his nation's liberation.

There was also much support by blacks for the objectives of the successful 1959 Cuban Revolution. The young Cuban revolutionary Fidel Castro ousted the dictator Fulgencio Batista and began reconstructing his island and ultimately changing its dependent relationship with the United States. Castro's antiracist positions appealed to blacks, although some disliked his embrace of socialism. In 1960, when Castro came to the United States in order to address the General Assembly of the United Nations, he and his entourage booked accommodation at Harlem's Theresa Hotel after being allegedly mistreated at the posh Shelbourne Hotel. Not only did this gesture endear the Cuban leader to many blacks, but it also brought much national and international attention to Harlem. The *Pittsburgh Courier* expressed the widespread view:

> To say that Harlem was flattered is to put it mildly. She didn't give a continental as to whether the move of Castro to "uptown" was a smashing propaganda victory for the Cubans. She was happy to know that Castro and his party were thinking of them . . . one of the blacks quipped: "Why shouldn't we like him? He ended racial discrimination in Cuba and that's more than the United States has done in this matter. We're for him and we like him."²⁵

This emotional identification with Cuba and its revolution, as well as with the forces of change in Africa and elsewhere in the Third World, represented an awareness of the connection between the struggle for justice at home and the claims of other oppressed peoples for liberation and self-determination.

The involvement of blacks in international affairs was also reflected in their denunciations of Adolf Hitler and his espousal of Aryan superiority. Hitler angered black Americans in 1936 when he insulted Jesse Owens, the sprinter and winner of four gold medals at the Olympic games in Berlin. But it was his racist ideology that excited the most passion. When the fascist Francisco Franco, who shared many of Hitler's racist ideas, began his campaign to assume control of Spain in the late 1930s, seventy blacks fought with the Republican opposition. Paul Robeson, who visited Spain to lend his support to the Republican cause, was pleased that his fellow black Americans were fighting "against the new slavery." "It is to their eternal glory, " Robeson said, "that Negroes from America, Africa, and the West Indies are to be found fighting in Spain today on the side of the republican forces for democracy and against those forces of reaction which seek to land us back to a new age of darkness."[26] Walter Garland, one of the volunteer fighters, thought that the men's participation afforded them a chance to reclaim a personhood that had been diminished by racism at home. "You know, in a measure, we Negroes who have been in Spain are a great deal luckier than those back in America," he said. "Here we have been able to strike back, in a way that hurts, at those who for years have pushed us from pillar to post. I mean this—actually strike back at the counterparts of those who have been grinding us down back home."[27]

When the Europeans began fighting among themselves in 1939 as a consequence of Hitler's invasion of Poland, the United States remained neutral. The rapid successes of the Nazi troops, however, led to a reconsideration of American policy, particularly when it appeared that England faced defeat. America's imminent entrance into the war raised anew the question of segregation in the armed forces. As they had done in the war of 1914-18, blacks wanted the right to fight in the armed forces of their nation. But much had changed in black America during and since that war. Blacks had become more demanding of their rights and critical of the racial status quo. The racism that inspired the forces of fascism in Europe was as repugnant to blacks as the variant that circumscribed them at home.

Marginalized and oppressed but eager to demonstrate their patriotism nonetheless, blacks sat on the horns of a dilemma. There was, on the one hand, the desire to destroy Nazism, but on the other, this impulse was tempered by their intolerable domestic situation. The Rev. Adam Clayton Powell, Jr., a strong advocate for civil rights, explained the ambivalence of some blacks to the European war, noting, ". . . it is not because we don't recognize the monster Hitler. . . . We recognized him immediately, because he is like minor Hitlers here. . . . The Gestapo is like the Ku Klux Klan here."[28]

Powell and others were sensitive to the contradiction inherent in their nation's preparation to fight in a war to destroy fascism abroad, while racial discrimination remained officially untouched at home. Thurgood Marshall, the NAACP's legal counsel, confessed that he was not convinced by those who argued that "we must have national unity regardless of whether or not we have democracy at home."[29] The sociologist Horace Cayton demonstrated the profound difficulty of the issues that the war raised for black Americans. "Am I Negro first and then a policeman or soldier second?" Cayton enquired. "Or should I forget in an emergency situation the fact that . . . my first loyalty is to my race?" In the end, the war provided blacks with an opportunity to expose America's racism and to link their participation in it to improvements in their condition at home. Some embraced what was characterized as the

"Double-V Campaign," meaning a victory for the democratic cause overseas as well as for social justice at home. A. Philip Randolph predicted that "before the war ends [blacks will] want to see the stuffing knocked out of white supremacy and of empire over subject peoples."[30]

President Franklin D. Roosevelt was aware of the desire by blacks to end racial segregation in the armed forces. In response to the proposals made by Walter White, A. Philip Randolph, and others, the administration announced some reforms in military policy in September 1940. Henceforth, blacks were to be admitted into the army in proportion to their numbers in the general population. In addition, black units would be established in all branches of the army, and officer candidate schools would no longer refuse admission to black applicants. Racially segregated units remained, however, since the War Department believed that integration would pose a threat to troop morale.

Welcoming the opportunity to serve, about three million blacks registered by war's end. Of that number, over a million actually served. It is estimated that 909,000 blacks were inducted into the army, 167,000 in the navy, and 17,000 in the marine corps. They served in a variety of capacities but disproportionately in the service branches like the Transporation Corp. About 600 men saw service as fighter pilots, and 4,000 women were accepted into the Women's Army Corps. Overall, about 500,000 blacks served overseas. Regardless of whether they served in the army, navy, or marines, blacks confronted segregated facilities, faced dismal prospects for promotion, and experienced racial abuse. Off base, particularly in the South, black recruits were treated in accordance with the Jim Crow laws, producing occasions for brawls with white civilians.

In fighting the fascists and rescuing other peoples from their grip, blacks were indirectly fighting for themselves. Their presence overseas in segregated units, defending principles that were inapplicable to them at home, heightened their politicization as well as that of their civilian brethren. White enlistees and the army command in Europe refused social interaction with their black peers, often shocking the Europeans by the intensity of their feeling against their fellow Americans of a different hue. Such behavior embarrassed progressive whites, who defended the black troops, and it may have even led some of them to support an end to Jim Crow. When Senators James Eastland and Theodore Bilbo of Mississippi accused the black troops of cowardice, white Southern editors distanced themselves from such slander. In fact, General Douglas MacArthur commended the black soldiers for their "patience, their fortitude, their courage, and their complete devotion to their country." He noted that their actions "mark them as belonging to the nation's noblest citizens."[31]

Such high praise did not translate into equal rights for the soldiers or for other blacks. James Baldwin would later maintain, "The treatment accorded the Negro during the Second World War marks . . . a turning point in the Negro's relations to America. To put it briefly, and somewhat too simply, a certain hope died, a certain respect for white American faded."[32] The war, however, was a watershed in American life. It had unsettled the nation's life and altered it in significant ways. The wartime economy released new energies, accelerated the pace of industrialization, and brought more women into the labor force, reducing their economic dependence on men. The defense-related industries attracted untold numbers of people who abandoned farms, spurring urban growth. The mechanization of cotton farming, in particular, drove many black people away from sharecropping and agriculture. Unable to find jobs in the South, they went North.

The war left Jim Crow intact, but it helped to undermine the ideological bases of white supremacy and colonialism as no other event had done. American racism could not be shielded from the searchlight of international opinion, and Hitler's assertion of a vulgar racism and the terrible human consequences of its implementation offended and alarmed many whites who had hitherto remained indifferent to the mistreatment of black citizens. Several white citizens of the South joined organizations such as the Southern Regional Council, the Southern Conference Educational Fund, and its predecessor, the Southern Conference for Human Welfare, that were designed to promote interracial cooperation. Not all white members of these organizations either imagined or favored the dismantling of white supremacy as they knew it. In fact, many only contemplated an amelioration of the black condition, a limited but courageous stance in the context of the times. To advocate an improvement in race relations did not always signify an embrace of full civil equality for black citizens, the destruction of the color bar, and economic justice for all.

Although the United Nation's charter prevented its intervention in the domestic affairs of member states, black groups took their grievances to that body shortly after its creation in 1945. The first to do so was the National Negro Congress, a coalition of several black organizations that was formed in 1935. According to the petitioners, the racially inspired mistreatment of blacks by white Americans violated their human rights and therefore fell under the jurisdiction of the U.N. In making the case for U.N. intervention, the distinguished jurist Charles Houston concluded: "A national policy of the United States which permits disfranchisement in the South is just as much an international issue as elections in Poland or the denial of democratic rights in Franco Spain."[33] In 1947, the NAACP prepared and presented to the U.N. a "Statement on the Denial of Human Rights to Minorities in the Case of Citizens of Negro Descent in the United States of America. . . ." The U.S. government successfully opposed any consideration of the statement by the international body on this and other occasions.

The end of the war and the ensuing competition between the United States and the Soviet Union for international influence inaugurated the

Cold War. Frightened by the prospect of communist ascendancy and by any threat to the domestic racial, economic, and political status quo, many white Americans linked the struggle for equal rights with pro-communist activity. When the Democratic party included a civil rights plank in its 1948 platform, Strom Thurmond, the segregationist governor of South Carolina, said it was "made to order for Communist use in their designs upon national security."[34] Others characterized the opposition to Jim Crow as a communist-inspired plot designed to subvert society, and harassed the proponents of social justice. Such prominent blacks as Mary MacLeod Bethune, W. E. B. Du Bois, Paul Robeson, Langston Hughes, Ralph Bunche, and Charlotte Hawkins Brown were systematically harassed and had their patriotism challenged. Du Bois lost his passport and was arrested and charged as a foreign agent. The advocacy of full citizenship rights for blacks was seen as a subversive activity by those whose national claims were no more compelling or just. The embrace of a virulent anticommunism served conveniently to forestall any changes in the racial order and in power relationships.

In spite of their struggles for social justice at home and probably because of them as well, blacks identified with the cause of the colonized peoples and joined with others to promote the ideals of Pan-Africanism. Their impact on the international stage or even on their own government's foreign policy was not very significant, but their voices were never muted. They used their participation in World War II to highlight their disabilities at home and to generate changes in their condition. As Americans, they responded to their nation's call for service in the armed forces, acquitted themselves well, and many died on the battlefield. By looking outward, blacks expected that change would come at home, inevitably. The people's poet, Langston Hughes, said it well in "Jim Crow's Last Stand":

> Pearl Harbor put Jim Crow on the run.
> That Crow can't fight for Democracy
> And be the same old Crow he used to be–
> Although right now, even yet today,
> He tries to act in the same old way.
> But India and China and Harlem, too
> Have made up their minds Jim Crow is through . . .

Notes

1. Fredrickson, *Black Liberation*, 151.
2. P. Olisanwuche Esedebe, *Pan-Africanism: The Idea and Movement, 1776–1963* (Washington: Howard University Press, 1982), 45–49.
3. August Meier, Elliott Rudwick, and Francis L. Broderick, *Black Protest Thought in the Twentieth Century* (New York: MacMillan, 1971), 56.

4. Esedebe, *Pan-Africanism*, 83.
5. W. E. B. Du Bois, *The Negro*, (New York, 1915), preface.
6. Paul Robeson, *Here I Stand* (New York: Beacon Press, 1970), 34.
7. Stuckey, *Slave Culture*, 357.
8. Ibid., 413.
9. Peter Walshe, "Black American Thought and African Political Attitudes in South Africa," *Review of Politics*, 32 (1970), 54–55.
10. Elliott P. Skinner, *African Americans and U.S. Policy Toward Africa, 1850–1924* (Washington: Howard University Press, 1992), 279.
11. Joseph Harris, *African-American Reactions to War in Ethiopia, 1936–1941* (Baton Rouge: Louisiana State University Press, 1994), 20.
12. James Hunter Meriwether, "The African Connection and the Struggle for Freedom: Africa's Role in African-American Life, 1935–1963," (Unpublished Ph.D. dissertation, University of California-Los Angeles, 1995), 86.
13. William R. Scott, *The Sons of Sheba's Race: African-Americans and the Italo-Ethiopian War, 1935–1941* (Bloomington: Indiana University Press, 1993), 114.
14. Ibid., 123.
15. Ibid., 124.
16. Ibid.
17. Ibid., 213.
18. M. W. Kodi, "The 1921 Pan-African Congress at Brussels: A Background to Belgian Pressures," in Joseph Harris, *Global Dimensions of the African Diaspora* (2nd edition, Washington: Howard University Press, 1993), 271–273.
19. Ibid., 278.
20. Andrew Young, *An Easy Burden: The Civil Rights Movement and the Transformation of America* (New York: HarperCollins, 1996), 113.
21. Brenda Gayle Plummer, *Rising Wind: Black Americans and U.S. Foreign Affairs, 1935–1960* (Chapel Hill: University of North Carolina Press, 1996), 279.
22. Ibid., 285.
23. Ibid., 307.
24. Brenda Gayle Plummer, "The Afro-American Response to the Occupation of Haiti, 1915–1934," *Phylon*, 43 (1982), 131.
25. Plummer, *Rising Wind*, 290.
26. Martin Bauml Duberman, *Paul Robeson, A Biography* (New York: Ballantine Books, 1989), 212.
27. Robin Kelley, *Race Rebels: Culture, Politics, and the Black Working Class* (New York: Free Press, 1994), 138.
28. Clayton R. Koppes and Gregory D. Black, "Blacks, Loyalty, and Motion-Picture Propaganda in World War II," *Journal of American History*, 73:2 (1986), 385.
29. Ibid.
30. Ibid.
31. John Egerton, *Speak Now Against the Day: The Generation Before the Civil Rights Movement in the South* (Chapel Hill: University of North Carolina Press, 1995), 326.
32. Richard M. Dalfiume, "'The Forgotten Years' of the Negro Revolution," *Journal of American History*, 55:1 (1968), 90–106.
33. John Hope Franklin and Alfred Moss, Jr., *From Slavery to Freedom* (7th edition, New York: McGraw Hill, 1994), 459.
34. Jack Bloom, *Class, Race, and the Civil Rights Movement* (Bloomington: Indiana University Press, 1987), 94.

Claiming Equal Rights, 1917–1954

Unlike white men, and in some respects white women, blacks have had to wage relentless struggles to claim their basic rights. Taken together, the Thirteenth, Fourteenth, and Fifteenth Amendments should have eliminated all legal and social distinctions based on race, but this did not occur anywhere. The former Confederate states, particularly after 1890, introduced a body of legislation that contradicted the constitutional rights that blacks, as citizens, should have enjoyed. The rest of the nation did not go as far as the Southern states, but local ordinances severely limited the rights of blacks and segregation was omnipresent. Black citizens faced discrimination by the larger society in all areas of their public lives. Its intensity and pervasiveness varied in accordance with the local context, but no state was free from the ubiquitous racist virus.

The twentieth century has been characterized by aggressive and sustained campaigns by black citizens for their rights. The methods and styles of protest have been diverse, but the objective has remained constant. Those who have been the most aggressive in their pursuit of their constitutional rights have been frequently characterized, somewhat pejoratively, as radicals or militants. But a demand for a people's constitutional rights should never be characterized or dismissed as being radical and therefore frighteningly unacceptable or beyond the pale. Defenders of an unjust status quo see challenges to its foundations as being inherently radical, but those who want their legitimate rights recognized cannot share that loaded perception. Blacks, despite the desire of some to emigrate, have never really abandoned their faith in the possibilities of the nation. In demanding their rights, many emphasized their Americanness even as they called attention to their marginalization. Langston Hughes wrote:

> America never was America to me,
> And yet I swear, this oath—
> America will be
> An ever-living seed,
> Its dream
> lies deep in the heart of me.

The demand by blacks for justice and self-determination was nothing if not American to its core. The founding principles of the nation espoused liberty, justice, and egalitarianism. While these principles were inapplicable to blacks for much of the nation's history, blacks never acquiesced to being excluded. Addressing a Fourth of July gathering in 1852, Frederick Douglass asked with bitter irony, "Are the great principles of political freedom and of natural justice, embodied in that Declaration of Independence, intended to us?" Continuing, the former slave charged, "This Fourth of July is yours, not mine. You may rejoice, I must mourn. To drag a man into the grand illuminated temple of liberty, and call upon him to join you in joyous anthems, were inhuman mockery and sacrilegious irony."[1]

Blacks initiated or at least continued three principal types of challenges to the racial status quo after 1900. In the first place, they used the courts and the halls of the legislatures to undermine, if not destroy, discrimination and segregation. Secondly, some embraced ideologies such as socialism and communism, which promoted an alternative vision of America. Third, many people engaged in direct action such as strikes, boycotts, and mass demonstrations in an effort to force the larger society to concede their rights. Mass movements such as Marcus Garvey's Universal Negro Improvement Association were not aimed primarily at assaulting racist institutions and attaining the constitutional rights of blacks. Rather, the UNIA promoted a disengagement from white society and the development of autonomous institutions by and for blacks. This racial self-determination, if achieved, would have undermined the power of whites over blacks. If blacks became producers rather than consumers, created strong institutions, and managed their own affairs, they would enjoy a measure of independence beyond the reach of whites.

The legal challenges to discriminatory treatment and segregation were led by the National Association for the Advancement of Colored

People. Composed of blacks and whites, the organization subscribed to the belief that successful assaults on the legal foundations of racism would lead to an improvement in the black condition and the creation of a just social order. The organization chose its targets carefully, aiming its legal cannons against segregation in residential neighborhoods, racially separate schools, and the laws that disenfranchised black citizens.

The preparation of the legal challenges to racial segregation and discrimination required resources, time, and a cadre of committed lawyers. Black attorneys, in spite of their relatively small number, assumed important roles as researchers, strategists, and advocates. The Howard University Law School trained many of these attorneys, but some came from white law schools as well. Charles H. Houston played the most distinguished role in the training of these early civil rights attorneys and in the framing of the legal arguments against *de jure* segregation. Houston, born in 1895 in Washington, D.C., received a law degree from the Harvard University Law School in 1922. In 1929, he became vice dean of the Howard Law School, a position that allowed him to influence an entire generation of black attorneys. Houston was guided by the philosophy that "the Negro lawyer ought to be trained as a social engineer and group interpreter."[2]

Houston enjoyed tremendous success in raising the educational standards of the Howard Law School. In 1935, he left the university to become the special counsel for the NAACP, a position he held until 1938. By the time he died in 1950, the NAACP's civil rights litigation campaign had achieved notable successes. At his death, Erwin N. Griswold, dean of the Harvard Law School, observed: "It is doubtful that there has been a single important case involving civil rights during the past fifteen years in which Charles Houston has not either participated directly or by consultation and advice."[3] Houston, of course, did not work alone. His distinguished associates included Thurgood Marshall, William Hastie, and James M. Nabrit. Marshall became the head of the NAACP's legal team in 1938, replacing Houston.

Houston's assumption of the legal helm at the NAACP in 1935 was of enormous significance in the evolution of black America's most durable civil rights organization. It meant that blacks had begun to gain the ascendancy in policy making. Houston accelerated the process by adding a number of talented black attorneys to the organization's national legal staff. Focusing on discrimination in education, the NAACP won an important victory in 1938. The case, *Missouri* ex rel. *Gaines* v. *Canada,* concerned the failure of the state of Missouri to provide a law school for blacks in violation of the doctrine of separate but equal. When Lloyd Lionel Gaines was denied entry to the law school at the University of Missouri because of his race, he sued. In order to maintain racial segregation, Missouri, along with a number of other states, paid for blacks to attend professional schools in states that had segregated facilities or special institutions for blacks. In finding for Gaines, the Supreme Court held: "A state denies equal protection of the laws to a black student when it refuses him admission to its all-white school, even though it volunteers to pay his tuition at any law school in an adjacent state. By providing a law school for whites but not for blacks the state has created a privilege which one race can enjoy but the other cannot."[4] This decision was not a repudiation of *Plessy* v. *Ferguson*, but it required states to provide educational opportunities for black residents.

With determination and skill, the NAACP's attorneys, led by Thurgood Marshall and William Hastie, continued the struggle for civil rights throughout the 1940s and after. Speaking in 1944, Marshall recognized the urgency of the struggle:

> We must not be delayed by people who say "The time is not ripe." Nor should we proceed with caution for fear of destroying the "status quo." Persons who deny to us our civil rights should be brought to justice now. Many people believe the time is always "ripe" to discriminate against Negroes. All right then—the time is always "ripe" to bring them to justice. The responsibility for the enforcement of these statutes rests with every American citizen regardless of race or color. However, the real job has to be done by the Negro population with whatever friends of the other races are willing to join in.[5]

Three significant court challenges and decisions that the NAACP won deserve our attention. They are *Smith* v. *Allwright* (1944), *Shelley* v. *Kraemer* (1948), and *Brown* v. *Board of Education* (1954).

In *Smith* v. *Allwright*, the NAACP's lawyers challenged the exclusion of blacks from voting in Democratic party primaries in Texas. Blacks had been denied the right to participate by a statute adopted in 1923. Charging that this measure violated the Fourteenth and Fifteenth Amendments, the NAACP filed a suit with the Supreme Court after Texas courts had rejected various challenges to it. The Supreme Court agreed with the plaintiffs. Speaking for the majority, Justice Stanley Reed concluded that "the United States is a constitutional democracy. Its organic law grants to all citizens a right to participate in the choice of elected officials without restriction by any state because of race."[6] By extension, the Court had voided all white primaries, paving the way for additional assaults on other disfranchisement measures. The decision did not mean the removal of other barriers to black participation in the electoral process in the South, because the poll tax, literacy qualifications, and white violence remained.

The NAACP also challenged the enforcement of racially restrictive housing covenants in *Shelley* v. *Kraemer*. In 1945, a black resident of St. Louis, Missouri, J. D. Shelley, purchased a house, only to be sued by white residents Louis and Fern Kraemer on the grounds that the purchase violated a covenant that prevented the sale of the property to blacks. When the dispute finally reached the Supreme Court, the case was combined with similar ones from the District of Columbia and Michigan. As one indication that change was in the air, the U.S. Department of Justice filed an *amicus* brief, supporting the black litigants. In ruling in their favor, the Court found, "Because of the race or color of these petitioners they have been denied rights of ownership or occupancy enjoyed as a matter of course by other citizens of different race or color."[7] The Court's decision did not, in practice, eliminate discrimination in housing, but it was potentially significant in dismantling other forms of segregation. By associating itself with the case, the Justice Department could hardly decline to support similar challenges to segregation in the future.

The NAACP achieved its most far-reaching success in *Brown* v. *Board of Education,* a case decided in 1954. Starting in 1935, the attorneys had challenged segregated practices in schools. Not only did the organization find segregation morally repugnant, but its leaders were acutely sensitive to the fact that an inferior education sentenced blacks to a future of subordination to whites. There was also a developing body of literature suggesting that segregated education was psychologically harmful to black children. At first, the NAACP brought suits to obtain equal salaries for teachers, eliminate segregation in higher education, and provide access by blacks to graduate and professional schools. On June 5, 1950, the organization won the admission of Herman Sweatt to the University of Texas Law School, despite the fact that the state had established a separate law school for blacks. Texas, the justices found, violated the terms of the 1938 *Gaines* decision. In another decision handed down the same day, the Supreme Court upheld a challenge to racially separate facilities at the University of Oklahoma in a suit brought by George W. McLaurin, a black man. The Court, in a related judgment, also overturned segregation in interstate transportation. In *Henderson* v. *United States,* the justices held that racially based seating violated the Interstate Commerce Act. These decision did not overturn *Plessy,* as some had hoped, but the handwriting was on the wall.

Led by Thurgood Marshall, the NAACP's lawyers had come to the conclusion by about 1950 that a broad assault on the legal barriers of segregation in the schools, as opposed to discriminatory practices, had become essential. The NAACP's board of directors endorsed this position in October 1950, declaring that "pleadings in all educational cases . . . should be aimed at obtaining education on a non-segregated basis and . . . no other relief other than that will be acceptable. . . ."[8] This was an ominous resolution, since it presaged a challenge to all segregation statutes anywhere they existed.

The victories that the NAACP's attorneys had achieved boosted the organization's confidence that the entire citadel of racial segregation

Thurgood Marshall (center), George E. C. Hayes, and James Nabrit, attorneys who led the fight before the Supreme Court for the abolition of segregation in the public schools, as they leave the Court on May 17, 1954, after announcement of the Court's decision declaring segregation unconstitutional.

could be ultimately destroyed. But there was a deeper reason for its bold shift in strategy. By midcentury, most black Americans had developed a much more secure sense of their own possibilities and power, together with a strong belief in the rightness and urgency of their cause. Reflecting this mood, Thurgood Marshall exhorted a Virginia audience in 1954 that "we have nothing to fear except the belief by anyone that we can't win." Speaking for many, the gifted attorney proclaimed: "We demand freedom and we will take nothing less. As long as there is segregation, we are not free and we are not progressing."[9]

The NAACP's attorneys could not depend on the state and federal courts to uphold their suits. In cases heard in South Carolina, Kansas, Virginia, and elsewhere between 1950 and 1952, the NAACP's attorneys lost. Drawing upon recent social science research, the attorneys had begun to argue that segregation in the schools had a deleterious effect on black children. Had researchers studied its impact on whites, they would have undoubtedly concluded that white children were also damaged by racism's virus. Individual judges expressed sympathy with the NAACP's damage argument, but no court struck at the legal foundations of segregation.

The constitutionality of *de jure* racial segregation was, it became increasingly clear, the central question that had to be resolved. In 1951, the NAACP's attorneys brought five cases to the Supreme Court that they hoped would destroy the separate-but-equal doctrine. The cases dealt with desegregation in the schools and originated in Kansas, South Carolina, the District of Columbia, Virginia, and Delaware. Since the cases were related, they were combined under the name of Oliver Brown, the plaintiff from Kansas. Brown, a resident of Topeka, had filed a suit to enable his daughter to attend her neighborhood school, which was all white, instead of being forced to attend a black school a mile away.

Several organizations, including the American Civil Liberties Union, filed *amicus* briefs with the Supreme Court supporting the NAACP's position. The Justice Department also lent its support to this assault on *Plessy*. The federal government, the brief argued, was also sensitive to the image that the nation projected overseas. "Racial discrimination," the brief maintained, "furnishes grist for the Communist propaganda mills, and it raises doubts even among friendly nations as to the intensity of our devotion to the democratic faith." When oral arguments began in 1952, Thurgood Marshall argued that "the rights of the minorities . . . have been protected by our Constitution, and the ultimate authority for determining that is this Court. . . . As to whether or not I, as an individual, am being deprived of my right is not legislative, but judicial."[10]

The lawyers convinced the Court that it had an obligation to remedy the injustices that black citizens had endured in violation of the Fourteenth Amendment. Conscious of the political implications of undoing *Plessy*, the Court took its time to render a decision. When the unanimous decision was handed down in favor of the NAACP on May 17, 1954, Chief Justice Earl Warren concluded, "Segregation in public education is not reasonably related to any proper governmental objective."[11] The ruling also asserted that the separation of children "from others of similar age and qualifications solely because of their race generates a feeling of inferiority as to their status in the community that may affect their hearts and minds in a way unlikely to ever be undone."[12] A year after its decision, the Court revisited the issue, ordering "the parties to these cases" to desegregate their schools with "all deliberate speed."[13] Local federal judges were enjoined to set the pace at which desegregation occurred. This was a recipe for delay, a victory for the forces that either advocated a gradual approach to desegregation or wanted to obstruct the intent of the *Brown* decision.

The *Brown* decision marked the most important development in the acquisition of civil rights by blacks since Jim Crow replaced slavery as the signifier of racial oppression. The Court's repudiation of *Plessy*, at least in the schools, invigorated the black struggle even as it elicited an angry white resistance. The NAACP's victory was a testimony to the skill and tenacity of its lawyers and the willingness of the nation's highest court to recognize changing times. The Supreme Court noted that the country should not attempt to "turn the clock back to 1868 when the [Fourteenth] Amendment was adopted, or even to 1896 when *Plessy* v. *Ferguson* was written." Still, had blacks not challenged *Plessy*, it is certain that it would have remained entrenched.

Civil rights litigation did not constitute the only challenge that blacks leveled against Jim Crow and other forms of racial injustice. The NAACP worked within the judicial system, attempting to cleanse the nation's institutions of racial bias. Its approach in this context was gradualist, reasoned, and persistent. But the NAACP also joined with others in the accelerated campaign against lynching during and after the First World War. The organization believed that racial violence would be reduced if such incidents were publicized and the nation's conscience aroused. Marcus Garvey and the UNIA also denounced white violence against blacks. In 1920, Garvey sought to internationalize the issue, proclaiming, "This lynching and burning, and disrespect of Negroes is not confined to any one country. It is spreading all over the world; and it means that if we in this present age do not go out and do something to stop lynching, every inch of ground in the world will become unsafe for the negro in the next twenty years."[14]

Beginning in 1919, the NAACP campaigned to get a federal law passed outlawing lynching. The organization gave strong support to such a bill when it was introduced by Congressman Leonidas Dyer of Missouri in 1922. Although the bill passed the House, it was killed in the Senate by a filibuster led by Southern Democrats. The opponents of the bill argued that it violated states' rights, although much of their animus to it was racially inspired. Black women were particularly important in the antilynching campaign. They raised funds in support of the cause and tried to enlist white women as allies. At a meeting of the Council for Interracial Cooperation, an organization of black and white women formed to promote cooperation among the races, Charlotte Hawkins

Brown told the white women: "We all feel that you can control your men . . . that so far as lynching is concerned . . . if the white women would take hold of the situation . . . lynching would be stopped."[15]

But the cessation of lynching would take more than the efforts of white women. The politicians stood in the way, and many other whites in the affected areas remained silent in the face of the atrocities. The disappearance of lynching would have to await deeper changes in the social and political systems and in the racial zeitgeist of the nation. Still, blacks could hardly remain quiescent, and the struggle continued in the 1930s. Probably as a consequence of the misery caused by the Great Depression, the incidence of lynching began to increase in the early 1930s. The NAACP hoped that President Franklin D. Roosevelt would specifically denounce these assaults on black citizens, but to no avail. He condemned the practice on a couple of occasions but usually without any reference to race. The president feared, with good reason, that any aggressive support for antilynching legislation would alienate white Southerners, endangering the passage of his New Deal legislation. But blacks were citizens, too, and the president of the United States had a moral obligation to protect them from the violence of other citizens, or at the very least condemn the perpetrators unequivocally.

Led by its executive secretary, Walter White, the NAACP sought congressional support for antilynching legislation throughout the 1930s. In 1934, Senators Robert F. Wagner of New York and Edward P. Costigan of Colorado introduced a bill that was broadly similar to the one introduced by Congressman Dyer in 1922. Although the president refused to be publicly identified with it, Eleanor Roosevelt was most sympathetic and prodded her husband in private to take some action. Thousands of white women joined the cause, repudiating the claim of the apologists for lynching that it was designed to protect white womanhood. Churches, unions, and other organizations endorsed the bill, and many individuals signed petitions urging the president to support it.

When the country learned of the brutal lynching of Claude Neal in early 1935, public support for the bill increased. Neal had been lynched in October 1934 in Marianna, Florida. A mob of a hundred men snatched Neal from the jail where he was being held for murdering a white woman. He was slashed with knives, branded, and mutilated. Neal was forced to eat his penis and testicles, after which a knife was thrust through his heart. The spectacle was witnessed by thousands, and according to a report submitted to the NAACP, "little children . . . with sharpened sticks . . . drove their weapons deep into the flesh of the dead man."[16] The NAACP believed that the president would use this latest atrocity to declare his public support for the antilynching bill, but he did not do so. Southern Democrats led a successful filibuster against the measure when it came to the floor.

In 1937, Congressman Joseph A. Gavagan of New York and Senators Frederick Van Nuys of Indiana and Robert Wagner introduced a new bill. Although public opinion supported its adoption, Southern legislators fanned racial fears and succeeded in killing it. Opposing the bill, Senator Byron Harrison of Mississippi defended the oppression of black citizens in a speech to his colleagues:

> We see the people of the South confronted with the terrible situation of a Democratic majority betraying the trust of the Southern people, destroying the things that they have idolized and in which they believe. I read the other day that the Negro representative from Illinois has introduced a bill to abolish Jim Crow laws in the states, to abolish those laws which provide for the segregation of the races. The next thing, in all probability, will be a bill to provide that miscegenation of the races cannot be prohibited, and when that has been accomplished, they will come back here and seek the help of the majority party in power to take away from the states the right to say who shall vote in their elections, to say that every colored man in every Southern state should take part in the primaries of the state.[17]

In this rendering, blacks were not seen as Southerners; they were the perpetual "Other," foreigners in their native land.

In the end, Congress never passed an antilynching bill. A number of Southern states, however, legislated against the practice, hoping to keep the federal government at bay. Lynchings became infrequent by about 1940, although violence against blacks continued. Federal antilynching legislation did not fail primarily because it violated the acknowledged right of the states to control law enforcement in their boundaries; rather, the bills died because of the intransigence of whites who wanted to maintain the racial status quo. Lynching was, at bottom, a racial question. Thomas G. Corcoran, an adviser to Franklin Roosevelt, recalled that civil rights for blacks did not constitute "a primary consideration of the guy at the top. He does his best with it, but he ain't gonna lose his votes for it."[18]

Not only did blacks have to confront racist violence, but they faced a judicial system that was, in many places, palpably unfair. This was dramatized in a celebrated case that occurred in Scottsboro, Alabama. Nine young black men, ranging in ages from thirteen to twenty, had been arrested in 1931 for allegedly raping two white girls on top of a freight train. The white community demanded blood in the "nigger rape case." Although the evidence in the case was very weak, eight of the young men were quickly convicted by an all-white jury and sentenced to death. The verdict outraged many people as it gave the appearance of a judicial lynching. The young men's cause was championed by the International Labor Defense (ILD), an organization that was associated with the Communist party. In the appeal that the prisoners filed in April 1931, they pleaded:

We have been sentenced to die for something we ain't never done. Us poor boys have been sentenced to burn up on the electric chair for the reason that we is workers—and the color of our skin is black. We like any one of you workers is none of us older than 20. Two of us is 14 and one is 13 years old. What we guilty of? Nothing but being out of a job. Nothing but looking for work. Our kinfolk was starving for food. We wanted to help them out. So we hopped a freight—just like any one of you workers might have done—to go down to Mobile to hunt work. We was taken off the train by a mob and framed up on rape charges. . . . Working class boys, we asks you to save us from being burnt on the electric chair. We's only poor working class boys whose skin is black. We shouldn't die for that. . . . Help us boys. We ain't done nothing wrong.[19]

The Scottsboro case received international publicity because of what was perceived as a racially inspired miscarriage of justice. The NAACP and the communists feuded over whom should defend the young men. To the NAACP, the communists were exploiting the case for their political purposes. The ILD, in its turn, accused the NAACP of being overly timid and insensitive to the needs of poor blacks. On November 7, 1932, the Supreme Court ordered a new trial for the young men on the ground that the rights guaranteed them under the Fourteenth Amendment had been violated. Another all-white jury was empaneled for the retrial. In spite of the fact that one of the women recanted her earlier testimony about being raped, the jury found the defendants guilty. Once again they were sentenced to death. Upon appeal, the Supreme Court found that their Fourteenth Amendment rights had again been violated, since blacks had been excluded from the jury. The case was eventually resolved when the prosecution dropped the charges against four defendants and recommended the death penalty for one and imprisonment for the rest. The governor eventually commuted the death sentence, and all of them were released from jail between 1943 and 1950. The case left an indelible mark on the judicial system in Alabama and by extension the South as a whole. It embarrassed the nation, and the Scottsboro boys trial came to represent the institutionalized tyranny of the white majority and the complicity of the judicial system in the denial of justice to blacks.

Always perceiving a humorous angle to their situation, blacks told the story of a black man who was being tried by a white judge for the kicking of a "white man's behind":

Judge: John, what is this about you kicking someone?
John: Well, Captum, what would you do if someone called you a black son of bitch?
Judge: Well, John, nobody will ever call me that.
John: Well, Captum, spose they call you the kind of son of bitch you is?
Judge: Give him 30 days.[20]

The battle for civil rights was, of course, never confined to the courts or to the legislative halls. As we have seen, from time to time, blacks used the weapon of the boycott to protest their treatment. Between 1900 and 1906, for example, there were organized boycotts of segregated street cars in at least twenty-five cities in the South.[21] During the 1930s, an invigorated NAACP sponsored "Don't Buy Where You Can't Work" campaigns in several cities in the North. In 1943, the newly formed pacifist and interracial organization, the Congress for Racial Equality (CORE), inaugurated the "sit-in" strategy: blacks occupied public places, such as restaurants, from which they had been excluded on racial grounds. This would, in later years, become a highly effective strategy in the fight against segregation.

Perhaps the most dramatic expression of nonviolent protest was a march or demonstration or the threat of one. In Chapter 6, we discussed the great silent march that occurred in New York City in 1917. Other marches occurred elsewhere from time to time as the occasion warranted. Some of these were interracial. When the Scottsboro boys were sentenced to death, for example, several marches and demonstrations were held in various places to protest the decision. In New York, marchers carried banners proclaiming: "Down with Jim Crowism and Segregation," "Smash the Scottsboro Frameup," and "Death to Lynch Law."[22] Condemning police brutality in Chicago in 1931, thousands of blacks and whites took to the streets in a show of fragile unity.

The most effective peaceful demonstration in support of racial justice before the 1950s was one that did not actually occur. Upset by the failure of President Roosevelt to eliminate segregation in the armed forces and job discrimination in the growing defense industry, A. Philip Randolph decided to bring direct pressure on the administration. On January 15, 1941, Randolph issued a statement to the press:

> . . . Negro America must bring its power and pressure to bear upon the agencies and representatives of the Federal Government to exact their rights in National Defense employment and the armed forces of the country. . . . I suggest that TEN THOUSAND Negroes march on Washington, DC . . . with the slogan: WE LOYAL NEGRO AMERICAN CITIZENS DEMAND THE RIGHT TO WORK AND FIGHT FOR OUR COUNTRY. . . .[23]

Randolph's appeal received broad support from blacks. Encouraged, he raised the number of expected participants in the march to 100,000. "When 100,000 Negroes march on Washington, it will wake up Negro as well as white America," Randolph predicted. "Let the Negro masses march! Let the Negro masses speak!" the veteran trade unionist pleaded. Preempting the expected criticism that the march was certain to invite during a time when there was some support for the nation's entry into the conflict in Europe, Randolph emphasized the loyalty of blacks to their nation. Still, he believed that "if American democracy

A. Philip Randolph (right, seated), with Baynard Rustin, announcing plans for the March on Washington for Jobs and Freedom, 1963.

will not give jobs to its toilers because of race or color; if American democracy will not insure equally of opportunity, freedom and justice to its citizens, black and white, it is a hollow mockery and belies the principles for which it is supposed to stand."[24]

Randolph insisted that what he called the March on Washington Movement "be all-Negro and pro-Negro but not anti-white, or anti-semitic or anti-labor, or anti-Catholic. The reason for this policy is that all oppressed people must assume the responsibility and take the initiative to free themselves." But there were other reasons for it. Randolph thought that "the essential value of an all-Negro movement such as the March on Washington is that it helps to create faith by Negroes in Negroes. It develops a sense of self-reliance with Negroes depending on Negroes in vital matters. It helps to break down the slave psychology and inferiority-complex in Negroes which comes and is nourished with Negroes relying on white people for direction and support."[25] Randolph opposed the participation of communists in the march. He feared that their participation would be used by the march's detractors to discredit it and that the better organized and more disciplined communists might control and co-opt the protest.

The prospect of thousands of blacks in Washington seeking redress to their grievances alarmed the Roosevelt administration and a wide range of other white officials. Eleanor Roosevelt told Randolph that "your group is making a very grave mistake at the present time." Randolph resisted such pressure and continued to plan for the July 1 event. In a meeting with President Roosevelt on June 18, Randolph and his associates predicted that there would be 100,000 persons in the march, and he declined the president's invitation to cancel it. Forced to compromise in the face of such a challenge from blacks, the president issued Executive Order 8802 on June 25, announcing "that there shall be no discrimination in the employment of workers in defense industries or government because of race, creed, color or national origin." Roosevelt established, on a temporary basis, the Fair Employment Practices Committee to monitor the enforcement of the order. As a consequence of the president's action, Randolph canceled the march, much to the chagrin of some of its ardent supporters.

Recognizing that the forces that the potential march had unleashed should not be allowed to spend themselves, Randolph tried to give them an organizational voice. He founded the March on Washington Movement (MOWM), an organization rooted primarily in the urban areas of the North. The MOWM was committed to a strategy of nonviolent direct action to achieve social justice. As Randolph expressed it, "Freedom must be won by Negroes. It will not be granted. Justice must be exacted; it will not be given."[26] Many individuals who would become active in the civil rights movement of the 1950s and the 1960s, such as James Forman, Pauli Murray, and Bayard Rustin, attributed their political awakening to Randolph and the MOWM.

Although Executive Order 8802 represented a clear victory in the struggle for equal employment opportunities, it said nothing about segregation in the armed forces. Randolph continued his struggle to desegregate the military, an objective that eventually received the endorsement of President Harry Truman. In 1947, Truman received a report from his Presidential Committee on Civil Rights. This report, "To Secure These Rights," recommended "the elimination of segregation, based on race, color, creed, or national origin from American life." It maintained that discrimination undermined America's efforts to appear as "a positive influence for peace and progress" and allowed its critics to depict it as "a consistent oppressor of underprivileged people." Truman was evidently pursuaded by these arguments, declaring on February 2, 1948, that the nation needed to adopt measures "to secure for all our people their essential rights."[27]

In testimony to Congress on March 31, 1948, Randolph urged, in strong terms, the desegregation of the armed forces. He indicated that he had told the president, "Negroes are in no mood to shoulder a gun for democracy abroad so long as they are denied democracy here at home. In particular, they resent the idea of fighting or being drafted into another Jim Crow Army." Randolph announced that he would "advise Negroes to refuse to fight as slaves for a democracy they cannot possess and cannot enjoy." He felt "morally obligated to disturb and keep disturbed the conscience of Jim Crow America. In resisting the insult of Jim Crowism to the soul of black America, we are helping to save the soul of America." Randolph ended his testimony on a defiant note. "Negroes are just sick and tired of being pushed around and we just don't propose to take it, and we do not care what happens," he asserted.[28]

Prodded by statements such as these, sensitive to the claims by blacks, and concerned about the country's international image, Truman issued Executive Order 9981 on July 26, 1948, directing "equality of treatment and opportunity for all persons in the armed services without regard to race, color, religion, or national origin." The president also ordered an end to discrimination in the civil service. He affirmed that "the principles on which our Government is based require a policy of fair employment throughout the Federal establishment without discrimination because of race, color, religion, or national origin." Such sentiments were, to some extent, politically inspired. Truman wanted the support of black voters and racially progressive whites in the upcoming presidential election. Reportedly, the president assured an Alabama congressman: "I don't believe in this civil rights program any more than you do, but we've got to have it to win."[29] Southern segregationists were outraged by Truman's action. Senator James Eastland of Mississippi thought the president's program would "Harlemize the country" and demonstrated that the government was controlled by "an organized mongrel minority."[30]

Seemingly progressive decisions such as those by Truman notwithstanding, it is an unpleasant truth that black citizens have never obtained their basic constitutional rights without having to fight for them. They have had to struggle for a place under the national umbrella, symbolized by the transcendent and powerful concept of "we the people." Frequently, the measures that the nation embraced to correct racial injustice have been largely bereft of an animating moral core. They have been more the products of sustained pressure and political expediency and less the principled expression of a people's commitment to their nation's founding ideals. Not surprisingly, this has compromised the enforcement of these measures, prolonged divisive and acrimonious debate, and perpetuated the marginalization of black citizens.

The pursuit of civil rights by blacks did not follow a common script or a prescribed path. As a group, blacks were too heterogeneous to embrace a common strategy, and the modus operandi was often shaped by the local context and invariably reflected changing times as well. Blacks who resorted to violence to demonstrate their rejection of the social order were largely members of a dispossessed class, employing the only weapon available to them. More middle class in style, less confrontational, and enjoying greater access to white officialdom, the NAACP advanced the cause of blacks by other means. The goals of those who represented these two extremes were not dissimilar; each had a role to play in a very complex and difficult struggle.

The riot that occurred in Harlem in 1935 was a stark dramatization of the worsening tensions in urban America. The catalyst for the riot was the arrest of a boy, Lino Rivera, on a charge of shoplifting. As rumors spread that the boy had been killed, members of the community took to the streets. They targeted certain business establishments, usually those that refused to hire blacks, and destroyed them. Order was restored after two days as a consequence of the efforts of the mayor and a coalition of black leaders.

In order to understand the causes of the riots, the mayor appointed a commission of enquiry composed of distinguished black and white citizens. Among the many causes, the report identified a history of police brutality directed against black residents, employment discrimination, and economic distress. It concluded that "after five years of depression which had made them feel more keenly than ever the injustices of discrimination in employment, the aggressions of the police, and the racial segregation, [Harlemites] rioted against these intolerable conditions. This spontaneous outbreak . . . was symptomatic of pent-up feelings of resentment and insecurity."[31] This far-sighted report did not blame communists for the disorder, as others had done. Rather, it identified the structural roots of Harlem's problems. Seen in this light, the riot posed a moral challenge to the larger society to address the inequities that blacks endured. There were already other Harlems in existence and many more were in the making.

The nature of the Harlem riot should be distinguished from earlier ones. This was not a case of marauding white mobs invading black neighborhoods and of blacks defending their property and persons. Rather, the Harlem riot saw disenchanted and dispossessed blacks attacking and destroying the symbols of their oppression, namely the property of those who treated them unfairly. The riot was also a plea for racial justice, given the fact that its immediate cause was an allegation of police brutality. The police had become the most visible and hated symbols of an unjust social order. By destroying white-owned property and highlighting abuse by the police, the Harlem rioters presaged the strategy of those of the 1960s and later.

Eight years after the Harlem riot, there was a major outbreak of racially motivated violence in Detroit. The migration of large numbers of Southern blacks to Detroit and the resulting competition with whites for jobs produced intense racial tensions. Following the patterns of the racial disturbances before Harlem, a white mob assaulted black residents in June 1943. By the time the violence stopped, thirty-one persons had been killed and more than two hundred wounded. A white journalist who witnessed the frenzy wrote, "I thought that I had witnessed an experience peculiar to the Deep South. On the streets of Detroit I saw again the same horrible exhibition of uninhibited hate as they fought and killed one another–white against black–in a frenzy and homicidal mania, without rhyme or reason."[32]

Blacks who struggled to obtain their rights were expressing a profound confidence in the transforming capacity of the society. But there were others who believed that American capitalism was inherently racist and exploitative of workers. The system could not be redeemed and should be overthrown. Communism represented an attractive, alternative vision and gained a handful of adherents in the urban areas of the North in the 1920s, particularly in Harlem. The earliest sympathizers had been socialists and were disproportionately of West Indian ancestry. Cyril Briggs of Nevis and Richard Moore of Barbados were probably the two most prominent of these early black communists in Harlem. Harry Haywood, who would become one of the most influential black American communists, joined the party in 1925. Briggs and Moore and a few of the other communists in this early period were also members of a group of nationalists called the African Blood Brotherhood (ABB), founded in 1919. The ABB had chapters in a number of cities nationwide. Eclectic in its ideological streams, the ABB linked Marxism with a demand for autonomy for blacks. Briggs called for "a government of the Negro, by the Negro and for the Negro."[33] The organization supported the franchise for blacks in the South, opposed segregation, and endorsed retaliatory violence against white mobs. In 1921 when a white mob in Tulsa, Oklahoma, attacked blacks with bloody consequences, the Harlem chapter of the ABB was quick to invite "every Negro tired of lynching and peonage, jim crowism, and disfranchisement to come out and hear our plan of action to remove these injustices which we suffer with others. You have nothing to lose but your chains. You have your liberation to achieve."[34] Probably too radical for its times, the fledgling organization soon became moribund, however.

Small in number, but noisy and aggressive, Harlem's communists launched rent strikes, promoted employment opportunities for blacks, and tried to arouse and shape the political consciousness of the growing population. Capitalizing upon the nationalist fervor that had suffused the Garvey movement, the Communist International concluded in 1928 that blacks in the South constituted a national minority that should govern itself. It called for "self-determination for the black belt," and members of the party went to the South to organize blacks. They found some receptivity among industrial workers, domestics, sharecroppers, and tenant farmers. With the nation in the throes of the Great Depression, the party's appeal to the forgotten and dispossessed was strong. Its vigorous antiracism and defense of the Scottsboro boys further enhanced its attractiveness. On the other hand, blacks who embraced communism faced the loss of their jobs and other reprisals from fearful and disapproving whites. Party members also encountered the hostility and violence of whites who were upset at their denunciation of racism, their promotion of a nonracial society, and their challenge to the prevailing racial order. The vast majority of blacks, to be sure, never joined the party, but this did not mean that they found its cause objectionable.

Communism, on the other hand, held a strong appeal for many black intellectuals in the 1930s. With their political consciousness heightened by the Great Depression and capitalism's vulnerabilities starkly revealed, these intellectuals saw an opportunity to construct a different kind of world order. To them, the black struggle in the United States was part of a larger international movement to destroy capitalism, racism, and class-based oppression. Langston Hughes, the young writer Richard Wright, Paul Robeson, Ralph Bunche, Abram Harris, and W. E. B. Du Bois, among many others, found the theoretical principles of Marxism persuasive. For some, the appeal was shortlived, but for others like Robeson and Du Bois, it was no passing phase.

Sensitive to the cultural traditions of blacks, the Communist party shaped its strategy accordingly. This meant that it did not always follow the dictates of Moscow but responded pragmatically to the needs of the local situation. The creolization of party strategy made its message more palatable to blacks, even if it did not win majority support. Hosea Hudson, an early member and a leader of the Communist party in Alabama, recalled that its representatives were respectful of members:

> What the party was doing was taking this lower class like myself and making people out of them, took the time and they didn't laugh at you if you made a mistake. In other words, it made this lower class feel at home when they sit down in a meeting. . . . The Party made me know that I was somebody.[35]

Black and white communists did not succeed in overthrowing capitalism or in creating a nonracial society. But their commitment to transforming the lives of blacks in the nation was unmistakable and pursued with passion. As Carl Murphy of Baltimore's *Afro-American* newspaper declared in 1932: "The Communists appear to be the only party going our way. They are as radical as the NAACP were twenty years ago. Since the abolitionists passed off the scene, no white group of national prominence has openly advocated the economic, political, and social equality of black folks."[36] Angelo Herndon, a coal miner in Birmingham, explained why communism attracted him:

All my life I'd been sweated and stepped on and Jim-Crowed. I lay on my belly in the mines for a few dollars a week, and saw my pay stolen and slashed, and my buddies killed. I lived in the worst section of town, and rode behind the "colored" signs of street cars, as though there was something disgusting about me. I heard myself called "nigger" and "darky" and I had to say "yes, sir" to every white man. . . . I had always detested it, but I had never known anything could be done about it. And here, all of a sudden, I had found organizations . . . that weren't scared to come out for equality for the Negro people, and for the rights of the workers. The Jim-Crow system, the wage-slave system, weren't everlasting after all! It was like all of a sudden turning a corner on a dirty, old street and finding yourself facing a broad, shining highway.[37]

Men and women who shared Herndon's views were making a perfectly rational choice in supporting the Communist party. Pariahs in their native land, they were willing to abandon an oppressive and familiar system for one whose ideology seemed to promise a better life and human dignity.

The *Brown* v. *Board of Education* decision of 1954 encouraged many blacks that the struggle for equal rights would ultimately succeed. Few were totally prepared, however, for the intransigence of the opponents of social justice. Nor could anyone have predicted the dramatic emergence of a sustained mass movement against segregation a year later. Insistent in its demands, the movement would transform the nature of race relations in society and advance the process of including blacks under the umbrella of "we the people."

Notes

1. John Hope Franklin, "Race and the Constitutions of the Nineteenth Century," in John Hope Franklin and Genna Rae McNeil, eds., *African Americans and the Living Constitution* (Washington: Smithsonian Institution Press, 1995), 26.
2. Darlene Clark Hine, "Black Lawyers and the Twentieth Century Struggles for Constitutional Change," in Franklin and McNeil, *African Americans and the Living Constitution*, 38.
3. Ibid., 39.
4. See Mark V. Tushnet, *The NAACP's Legal Strategy Against Segregated Education, 1925–1950* (Chapel Hill: University of North Carolina Press, 1987).
5. Meier et al., *Black Protest Thought*, 260.
6. Mark V. Tushnet, *Making Civil Rights Law: Thurgood Marshall and the Supreme Court, 1956–1961* (New York: Oxford, 1994), 107. My account of the court challenges relies heavily on Tushnet.
7. Ibid., 95.
8. Ibid., 155.
9. Ibid., 232.
10. Ibid., 173, 181.
11. Ibid., 215.
12. Ibid., 214.

13. Ibid., 230.
14. Shapiro, *White Violence,* 165.
15. Giddings, *When and Where I Enter,* 178.
16. Weiss, *Farewell to the Party of Lincoln,* 108.
17. Sitkoff, *A New Deal,* 293.
18. Weiss, *Farewell to the Party of Lincoln,* 119.
19. Shapiro, *White Violence,* 207.
20. Watkins, *On the Real Side,* 461.
21. Meier et al., *Black Protest Thought,* 27.
22. Shapiro, *White Violence,* 210.
23. Anderson, *A. Philip Randolph,* 249.
24. Meier et al., *Black Protest Thought,* 223.
25. Ibid., 227.
26. For these issues, see Pfeffer, *A. Philip Randolph,* 45–88; 170.
27. Sean Dennis Cashman, *African Americans and the Quest for Civil Rights, 1900–1990* (New York: New York University Press, 1991), 100.
28. Meier et al., *Black Protest Thought,* 274–280.
29. Numan V. Bartley, *The New South, 1945–1980* (Baton Rouge: Louisiana State University Press, 1995), 78.
30. Ibid., 82.
31. Shapiro, *White Violence,* 265.
32. Ibid., 311.
33. Kelley, *Race Rebels,* 106.
34. Irma Watkins-Owens, *Blood Relations: Caribbean Immigrants and the Harlem Community, 1900–1930* (Bloomington: Indiana University Press, 1996), 103–104.
35. Nell Irvin Painter, *The Narrative of Hosea Hudson: His Life as a Negro Communist in the South* (Cambridge: Harvard University Press, 1979), 22.
36. Meier et al., *Black Protest Thought,* 147.
37. Ibid., 140.

Forcing Change: 1955–1965

The struggle for equal rights achieved its greatest successes in the 1950s and the 1960s. The impetus for the struggle, its style, and its energy must be located within a black society that was constantly transforming itself. The vigor of the assault on the racial status quo by the Generation of 1917 was primarily a function of the deeper structural changes that were taking place and continued to proliferate in black America. These changes accelerated during and after World War II and produced a greater intensity to the struggle. In turn, the battles that were won impacted upon these inner motions, further stimulating and shaping them as well. Accordingly, we cannot understand the nature of the assault on segregation and the struggle for civil rights between 1955 and 1965 without first appreciating these changes in the interior lives of black Americans and why the movement's spirit and tenacity were expressions of these inner transformations.

Any analysis of black life at midcentury must begin with the important demographic shifts that were in motion. In 1940, blacks constituted 9.8 percent of the general population, 10 percent in 1950, 10.5 percent in 1960, and 11.1 percent in 1970. According to the Bureau of the Census, there were 12,865,518 black Americans in 1940, 15,042,286 in 1950, 18,871,831 in 1960, and 22,580,289 in 1970. Not only did blacks constitute an increasing share of the population, but their spatial distribution changed significantly. As a result of natural increase, and more importantly, migration from the South, there was a dramatic increase in the proportion of blacks living in the North and West. In 1940, 23 percent of blacks resided in these regions; in 1960 the proportion increased to 40 percent, and in 1970, it stood at 47 percent. Put another way, only 53 percent of blacks resided in the South in 1970, a decrease from the 90 percent who lived there in 1910.

The pace of urbanization also accelerated in the North as well as the South. Such Northern cities as Chicago, Cleveland, New York, Detroit, and Philadelphia experienced spectacular increases in the black presence. The same was true of Atlanta, New Orleans, Charleston, Montgomery, Birmingham, and Baltimore. Between 1940 and 1960, these Southern cities experienced a growth of between 40 and 450 percent in the size of their black populations. Increasingly concentrated in cities, large and small, black residents provided critical support for mass-based challenges to Jim Crow in the South in the 1950s and the 1960s. In the North, they formed a growing share of the electorate in Michigan, Illinois, Pennsylvania, Ohio, and New York. Politicians for local and national offices could not ignore the black presence at election time, even if they later retreated from their promises.

The migration to the North and the wider distribution of blacks starkly dramatized the racial problem as a national one. Largely confined to ghettos and exposed to racial injustices in varying degrees everywhere, blacks recognized more than ever that theirs was a national struggle, although the principal battleground would be the South. Residence in an urban area and the exposure to racially based groups of different stripes had a politicizing effect on formerly rural peoples. The migrants and the children they produced were influenced by ideas espoused by Garvey and the Universal Negro Improvement Association, the Nation of Islam, the National Association for the Advancement of Colored People, and other organizations. World War II shook the ideological bases of white supremacy, generated a multitude of changes in American society, furthered the politicization of blacks, and enhanced the struggle for civil rights. The children and grandchildren of the Generation of 1917 had in the 1950s and 1960s become more insistent in their demands for social justice than the older generation had been. Influenced by the courage and examples of some members of the previous generations and shaped by the aforementioned black consciousness ideas, these persons became the leaders and footsoldiers in the social movement that engulfed the nation between 1955 and 1965.

The steady improvement in the educational attainment of blacks certainly made them more sensitive to the racially based obstacles in their path. While about 2 percent of blacks possessed college degrees in 1940, 5 percent did so in 1960, about 6 percent in 1970. Most of these students had been educated in the black colleges that proliferated during and after Reconstruction, chiefly in the Southern states. In response to court challenges, the movement for civil rights, and the softening of racial attitudes in higher education, many white colleges and institutions opened their doors to black students in the 1950s and the 1960s. By

1970, there were about 380,000 black students on those campuses. Black students on white and black campuses were particularly energetic in their support for civil rights and in organizing opposition to the racial order.

The changes, as well as the continuities in the economic condition of blacks after World War II, also help to explain the intensity of their support for civil rights in the 1950s and the 1960s. Blacks who were trapped in poverty and attributed their economic situation to racial discrimination strongly endorsed the movement for social change. In 1940, 87 percent of black families, as opposed to 48 percent of whites, lived below the poverty line. The robust economic growth after World War II reduced poverty levels so that by the 1960s, 36 percent of black families were considered by the federal government as poor in contrast to 9 percent of whites.

There were also notable changes in occupational patterns. While about 50 percent of black men had been employed in agriculture or related jobs in 1940, the percentage declined to 23.6 percent in 1950 and hovered around 3 percent in 1970. For women, the percentage decreased from 15.9 in 1940 to 9.1 in 1950. Blacks increased their presence in industrial and manufacturing jobs from 470,000 in 1940 to 1.3 million in 1970. In 1950, 8.3 percent of black men and 12.7 percent of black women filled white-collar jobs. In spite of an increasing diversity in the jobs that they were allowed to fill, black men were still represented disproportionately in unskilled and service jobs and women in domestic positions. With numerous options closed to them and their levels of unemployment remaining unacceptably high in a period of sustained economic growth, many had become eager to force the larger society to respond to their needs and remove the structural barriers to their progress.

The greater job opportunities that came in the wake of World War II contributed to the growth of a black middle class, although it remained disproportionately small up to the 1960s. Its slow but steady expansion also resulted from improvements in the levels of educational attainment and more job opportunities in the public sector. This growing black middle class had its own organizations, reflecting diverse professional interests and cultural tastes. Some belonged to the Prince Hall Masons, others were active in the National Medical Association, the National Bar Association, fraternities, sororities, and a host of other support, civic, and professional networks. The various black Christian denominations and the congregations they spawned transcended class lines in their appeal, to some extent, and remained the strongest institutions in black society. Statistics are imprecise, but the black denominations claimed a combined membership of about eight million in the early 1940s and twice that number in the 1980s. These estimates do not include the numerous black congregations that lacked denominational associations.

TABLE 12.1
Estimated Number of Blacks Registered to Vote in the South, 1940–1956

STATE	1940	1947	1952	1954	1956
Alabama	2,000	6,000	25,596	49,377	53,366
Arkansas	21,888	37,155	61,413	67,851	75,431
Florida	18,000	49,000	120,919	128,329	137,535
Georgia	20,000	125,000	144,835	?	163,389
Louisiana	2,000	10,000	120,000	118,183	152,378
Mississippi	2,000	5,000	20,000	19,367	20,000
North Carolina	35,000	75,000	100,000	?	135,000
South Carolina	3,000	50,000	80,000	?	99,890
Tennessee	20,000	80,000	85,000	?	90,000
Texas	30,000	100,000	181,916	?	214,000
Virginia	15,000	48,000	69,326	71,632	82,603
TOTAL	168,888	585,155	1,009,005	?	1,223,592

SOURCE: Steven Lawson, *Black Ballots: Voting Rights in the South, 1949–1969* (New York: Columbia University Press, 1976), p.134.

Despite the continued existence of a number of disfranchisement statutes in nine of the thirteen Southern states the number of blacks registered to vote showed a steady increase in the 1940s and the 1950s. According to the extant records, the percentage of eligible voters who were registered increased from 5 percent to 20 percent between 1944 and 1954. In 1940, there were an estimated 168,888 registered black voters in the South; this number increased to 1,009,005 in 1952 and to 1,223,592 in 1956. (See Table 12.1.)

The rate at which blacks registered to vote increased after the 1944 Supreme Court decision invalidating the white primary. Interestingly, the pace declined in a few states after the landmark *Brown* v. *Board of Education* decision in 1954. Fearing white harassment and violence, many blacks passed up the opportunity to register and vote. White hostility was usually greatest in counties where blacks formed a significant proportion of the eligible voters. One white resident expressed the fears that drove his people to intimidate potential black voters:

> The niggers would take over the county if they could vote in full numbers. They'd stick together and vote blacks into every office in the county. Why you'd have a nigger judge, nigger sheriff, a nigger tax assessor–think what the black SOBs would do to you![1]

Although black voters formed a small proportion of the electorate and generally were intimidated and harassed, they sometimes had an impact on the electoral outcome in several cities. Here and there blacks created organizations to enhance their political clout. In Durham, North Carolina, for example, they formed the Durham Committee on Negro Affairs, and in Atlanta, the Atlanta Negro Voters League represented the interests of the black constituency. This political energy achieved some modest local successes. By 1954, blacks had been elected to office in eleven municipalities in the South, although this trend was not always sustained.[2]

The spirit of black America was also reflected in the literary and cultural production of the times as much as it was shaped by it. Populated principally by members of the working class, the ghettos continued to manifest a cultural energy that belied their economic circumstances. Whatever else racism and economic deprivation did to black America, they did not silence the creative voices and may have even stimulated them. An urban idiom–hip talk–became ubiquitous; the zoot suit defined young men's desires to be brashly independent even in forms of attire, and dances such as the lindy hop were subject to constant stylistic recreations.

Much of the literature of the 1950s and 1960s epitomized the changing mood of black America. Lorraine Hansberry's prize-winning play, *A Raisin in the Sun* (1959), for example, was integrationist in tone, underscoring the human costs of racial discrimination. It was written and performed at a time when the civil rights movement was united behind the objectives of racial integration. By the mid-1960s, however, many had begun to question the emphasis on integration and the strategy of nonviolence upon which it was based. The poet and playright Amiri Baraka (LeRoi Jones) expressed this shifting mood in one of his works:

> We want "poems that kill."
> Assassin poems, Poems that shoot
> guns. Poems that wrestle cops into alleys
> and take their weapons leaving them dead
> with tongues pulled out and sent to Ireland.[3]

The protracted struggle for equal rights, along with the heightened political consciousness that characterized black America in the 1950s and the 1960s, the expanding appeal of the politics of black self-determination, and the imperative to define a people's cultural spaces produced the Black Arts Movement. Emerging around the mid-1960s, it was defined by writer Larry Neal in the following way:

> The Black Arts Movement is radically opposed to any concept of the artist that alienates him from his community. Black Art is the aesthetic and spiritual sister of the Black Power concept. As such, it envisions an

art that speaks to the needs and aspirations of black America. In order to perform this task, the Black Arts Movement proposes a radical reordering of the western cultural aesthetic. It proposes a separate symbolism, mythology, critique, and iconology. The Black Arts and the Black Power concept both relate broadly to the Afro-Americans desire for self determination and nationhood.[4]

The most ardent proponents of this move to redefine the Western cultural aesthetic included Baraka, Neal, the critic Addison Gayle, Jr., and the poets Sonia Sanchez, Nikki Giovanni, and Haki Madhubuti (Don L. Lee). These and other developments were a barometer of a people's inner transformations. As early as 1943, Roi Ottley, a journalist, had noticed these changes. "Listen to the way Negroes are talking these days!" he said of Harlem. ". . . [B]lack men have become noisy, aggressive, and sometimes defiant!"[5]

Under the circumstances, it can be maintained that by the mid-1950s blacks had created the religious and civic institutions that would help sustain their struggle; the sense of the justice of their cause had been well honed; a younger, gifted, and courageous set of leaders at national and local levels was available; and the timing appeared to be propitious. Divisions had begun to appear among whites, and racially progressive voices were no longer silent. The resulting freedom struggle that developed and defined the 1950s and the 1960s differed from previous ones, because blacks as a group were in a better position to provide strong and prolonged support for it, employ a multitude of strategies, and demonstrate the kind of fortitude that could only have come from a politically conscious, organized, and committed people.

The 1954 *Brown* decision certainly energized the mass-based struggle for justice, but it did not create it. In an address to the 1955 NAACP convention, Roy Wilkins, the newly appointed executive director, noted that *Brown* had inaugurated a new phase in the struggle, "an era where racial discrimination and segregation are to be not merely morally wrong but contrary to the law and the Constitution." He recognized that "destiny" had presented the NAACP–and by extension all blacks–"with new challenges, new responsibilities, new and more pressing calls to duty, to devotion, intelligence and skill." Taking note of the years of struggle, he told his listeners, "The people of 1903 had no such challenge and opportunity; nor did those of 1923, or 1943. This great day is ours. Upon us depend the speed, the order and the completeness of the victory." Wilkins promised that "in fashioning the new era we shall use all the weapons at our disposal." He welcomed the participation of whites "in the crusade which is one not alone for us, but for our nation as a whole. . . ." Ending on a determined note, Wilkins asserted, "We shall not–we cannot–fail. We shall, we will, be free men."[6]

This speech helped set the tone for the coming "crusade," as Wilkins characterized it. It affirmed the justice of the cause, proclaimed the "love" of blacks for "our country," and gave whites a place in the struggle. As the crusade evolved, it was not one driven by hate but largely by the redemptive power of human goodness and love. As James Baldwin, the novelist and essayist, expressed it, the nation's redemption resided in the transforming power of love, "not in the infantile American sense of being made happy but in the tough and universal sense of quest and daring and growth." Baldwin's essay, "The Fire Next Time," captured the promise of the crusade and the horror its failure portended:

> If we—and now I mean the relatively conscious whites and the relatively conscious blacks, who must, like lovers, insist on, or create, the consciousness of the others—do not falter in our duty now, we may be able, handful that we are, to end the racial nightmare, and achieve our country, and change the history of the world. If we do not dare everything, the fulfillment of that prophecy, re-created from the Bible in song by a slave, is upon us: *God gave Noah the rainbow sign, no more water, the fire next time!*[7]

WHITE RESISTANCE TO *BROWN*, AND BLACK RESPONSES

The legal victories achieved by the NAACP up to 1954 constituted important milestones on the road to full citizenship. Roy Wilkins thought that the *Brown* decision heralded "the death of all inequality in citizenship based upon race." While this was a sound judgment, blacks still confronted laws and local ordinances that either limited or nullified their citizenship rights and public and private institutions that openly discriminated against them. Racial segregation remained embedded in the societal landscape, but the ideology that gave it life had become slightly weakened. In September 1955, *Time* magazine characterized racial segregation as "a paralyzing sting" on America's conscience and "the ugliest blot upon its good name in the world." *Time* recognized, however, that change would not come readily because of those with "quite different . . . views."[8]

The magazine was right. More than three centuries of white supremacy could not be dismantled overnight; racist attitudes could not be easily transformed. When the *Brown* decision was rendered, some outraged and fearful whites attacked the NAACP and its lawyers venomously and vowed to resist the new racial order that they believed was on the horizon. Since the Supreme Court allowed states and school boards considerable latitude in the implementation of *Brown*, its opponents developed ingenious means of stymieing its enforcement and thwarting its intent. A few moderate white voices, however, urged compliance with the law, but they were soon overwhelmed by the more numerous and vocal proponents of resistance. Some saw the hand of communism in the decision. Senator John Eastland of Mississippi denounced *Brown* as "attempting to graft into the organic law of the land the teachings, preachments and social doctrines which can be traced to Karl Marx."[9]

White Southerners assaulted *Brown* on several fronts. There were voices that equated racial integration with miscegenation, igniting sexual fears. The Southern governors met in Virginia in the summer of 1954 and decided "not to comply voluntarily with the Supreme Court's decision against racial segregation in the public schools."[10] In March 1956, eighty-two Southern congressmen and all but three of the senators from the region issued the *Southern Manifesto*. Its signatories vowed "to use all lawful means to bring about a reversal" of the *Brown* decision, "which is contrary to the Constitution and to prevent the use of force in its implementation." The document denounced *Brown* as embodying the "personal, political, and social ideas" of the justices who had engaged in an "unwarranted" abuse of their power. The lawmakers praised "the motives of those states which have declared the intention to resist forced integration by any means."[11]

Opponents of *Brown* also founded the White Citizens' Council in Mississippi in July 1954. Dedicated to fighting school integration, the founding members were not the stereotypical "white trash" but were mostly highly educated, upper middle class citizens. The organization grew rapidly, and within three months, it boasted 25,000 members in the state. It expanded to other states as well. Reportedly, there were 60,000 members in Georgia, 40,000 in South Carolina, and 20,000 in Louisiana.

The study of white resistance to civil rights is, of course, not synonymous with the history of blacks. White intransigence and its impulses tell us a great deal about the currents within white America, but nothing about blacks. In order to understand the black freedom struggles, however, it is important to trace the course and nature of white resistance, because blacks had to develop strategies to deal with it. As whites more aggressively defended the status quo, blacks strengthened their resolve to transform it. There were some blacks, on the other hand, who had come to terms with the status quo and did not want to see it changed. Some, like the teachers who believed they would lose their jobs to whites if schools were integrated, opposed desegregation. Fearful of reprisals from the white power structure, others were too cowed to embrace the new order that beckoned. Some local ministers, even if they were not directly opposed to the developing movement, had to be prodded to participate in it. There were apparently no voices that endorsed white supremacy and segregation as the immutable and natural order of being.

With few exceptions, white-controlled school boards and legislatures were determined to preserve segregated schools. Local chapters of the NAACP usually took the initiative and petitioned the school boards to develop desegregation strategies. These boards were either unresponsive or prepared plans that sought to delay desegregation or evade and gut *Brown's* intent. Some states, such as North Carolina, devised a plan that allowed each community the option of determining whether it would desegregate its schools. Characterized as a form of popular sovereignty, this option was nothing more than an exercise in obfuscation and obstruction. Its designers sought to give this option the veneer of a democratic choice, but they knew full well that white communities were not likely to vote in favor of desegregation. Some school boards established cumbersome administrative procedures for assigning students to schools. The procedures were ostensibly color-blind and assigned students in accordance with what was deemed to be in their best interests. In practice, race was the only factor that determined these assignments.

In addition to such obstructions, some states such as Mississippi adopted constitutional amendments granting the legislatures the power to abolish their system of public education. In January 1956, Virginia's voters approved a referendum allowing state support for private schools. This measure was intended to encourage whites to abandon the public schools. Later that summer, the Virginia legislature gave the governor the authority to close schools that had been integrated either by choice or by court order. The governor was empowered to conduct an investigation to determine if the "tranquility" of the community were affected. If such was not the case, the schools could be reopened provided that no one objected to desegregation. In any event, schools that desegregated lost the state funding to which they had been entitled.

Virginians were particularly active in their opposition to *Brown*, overlooking nothing. In late 1955, the editor of the *Richmond News Leader* resurrected the dubious states rights theory known as "interposition." The theory, which went back to the 1790s, held that states had the legal right to nullify federal decisions they did not like by "interposing" their power between that of the national government and the people of the state. The Virginia legislature adopted this delaying strategy in early 1956, and some other states were not far behind.

In addition to such strategies, members of the Citizens Councils and others harrassed blacks who petitioned for *Brown's* implementation. Blacks lost their jobs and were denied loans. Others had their mortgages recalled, and many were assaulted and intimidated. Patients of black doctors who supported *Brown* were threatened with reprisals if they continued to seek medical assistance from them. Some states, such as Arkansas, Louisiana, Alabama, Virginia, Georgia, South Carolina, and Mississippi, tried to destroy the NAACP by either bringing spurious charges and lawsuits against the organization and its members or by investigating them.

The leadership exercised by most white politicians was myopic and undistinguished. Southern elected officials fanned the flames of resistance and appealed to some of the baser instincts in their constituency. President Dwight D. Eisenhower failed to demonstrate moral leadership by not publicly endorsing the *Brown* decision. In fact, the president demonstrated sympathy for white resistance, telling Chief Justice Earl Warren, "These are not bad people. All they are concerned about is to see that their sweet little girls are not required to sit in school alongside some big overgrown Negroes. . . ."[12] There was, of course, more to the opposition than Eisenhower implied, but his comment indicated that blacks could hardly count on their president to uphold and defend their cause.

Far from intimidating the NAACP and black citizens, white resistance to *Brown* fueled their resolve. The veteran civil rights organization was forced to spend much of its time and resources fending off legal attacks in several states. It could not always depend on the impartiality of the judiciary, as many judges were openly hostile to the organization and the cause it represented. The Supreme Court handed the NAACP many victories in its challenges to legal harrassment, but such litigation distracted the lawyers from their mission. In Alabama, the assault was so withering that the NAACP ceased to operate there between 1956 and 1964. Individual members of the NAACP were subjected to such harrassment that some had to flee the states in which they lived for sanctuaries in the North. Others left the organization and a few lost their lives. Still, the NAACP found courageous plaintiffs to bring desegregation suits in Virginia, North Carolina, Texas, and elsewhere.

White resistance to *Brown* received a profound setback in Little Rock, Arkansas, in 1957. The local chapter of the NAACP had petitioned for desegregation in 1954. In February 1956, Daisy Bates, president of the chapter, brought suit against the school board to desegregate Hall High School, a new school that was scheduled to admit students later that year. The NAACP lost the suit, but plans for the desegregation of the largely working-class Central High School proceeded, and this was to begin in September 1957. The stage was set for an ugly racial confrontation, since Governor Orval Faubus had promised that "there will be NO forced integration of public schools as long as I am governor."[13] On August 22, 1957, a rock thrown into Daisy Bates's living room bore the threatening note: "Stone this time, Dynamite Next." When nine black students reported for classes on the first day of school, a white mob blocked their path, and acting under the governor's orders, the National Guard barred their entrance to the school. After temporizing on the issue, President Eisenhower federalized the National Guard, sent in federal troops, and empowered them to protect the black students. This was a momentous decision because the government had forcefully responded to white defiance of the law. The fact that this was the first time that federal troops had been dispatched to the South since the end of Reconstruction was not lost on the defenders of the status quo.

Bowing to white pressure, the Little Rock school board asked the courts to allow it to delay desegregation for two years. The NAACP opposed the board and eventually triumphed in the Supreme Court. The justices affirmed the *Brown* decision and noted that segregation violated the intent of the Fourteenth Amendment. In a supporting opinion, Justice Felix Frankfurter observed that "local customs . . . are not decreed in heaven" and are able to "yield . . . to law and education."[14] Such strictures notwithstanding, the voters in Little Rock voted in September 1957 to close the public schools and lease them to a private corporation that would run them as segregated institutions. In spite of the fact that the federal Appeals Court ruled against the lease and ordered that the schools be reopened and desegregated, this did not occur until 1959. Even then, of the sixty blacks who applied for admission to the white schools, three were admitted to Central High and the same number to Hall High School.

Little Rock did not end the struggle over *Brown*. When the New Orleans schools were integrated in 1960, white opponents removed their children, and some engaged in violent protests. School desegregation exacerbated tensions between blacks and whites almost everywhere and precipitated a white flight to segregated private schools. Nationally, many whites moved to suburban and white enclaves to avoid sending their children to schools with blacks. *Brown*, however, had the potential to transform social relations in the nation, and its supporters as well as its opponents recognized this promise. For whites, the decision removed the boundaries that separated their children from the threatening and subordinate black "Other," inviting all manner of "undesirable" interactions among them. The school, as the extension of the home in the public sphere, had to remain racially inviolate. Blacks, on the other hand, saw segregated schools as part of the comprehensive arsenal of white supremacist behavior that had to be destroyed.

NONVIOLENT PASSIVE RESISTANCE

Beginning in 1955, the freedom struggle entered a new phase characterized by nonviolent passive resistance to segregation. It was a development that was neither planned nor foreseen. This struggle, along with the one driven by *Brown*, changed the participants in ways that were hardly predictable. Black children who grew to young adulthood while the struggle raged were transformed by the nonviolent war for their rightful place in society. Their elders, too, were changed, but it was a new, aggressive generation that would define and command the future. Whites were affected by the struggle as well; some came to embrace the promise of a new order in race relations. Others reluctantly accommodated themselves to it. Since they could not contain the changes, some whites frequently tried to control the pace and texture of the developments. There were also those who appeared not to change at all, clinging desperately to the old order and attempting to obstruct the nation's promise of equality for all of its peoples.

Chafing under the humiliating restrictions imposed upon them by the Jim Crow laws, individual blacks challenged them from time to time and suffered the penalties. Organized protest in the South was not unknown, but it was risky, and few were sustained for any period of time before 1955. Blacks in Orangeburg, South Carolina, organized a successful boycott of white businesses in early 1955, but this was more the exception than the rule. This would all change in Montgomery, Alabama, in December of that year.

The leaders among Montgomery's blacks were eager to challenge the city's ordinance permitting segregation on the buses. Although two blacks had been arrested for declining to vacate their seats for white passengers in the spring and early fall of 1955, their personal lives were not beyond reproach, so they were not deemed to be the ideal litigants. The opportunity came when Rosa Parks was arrested in December. Tired after working all day as a seamstress in a department store, Parks refused to give her seat to a white man when the bus driver ordered her to do so. She was duly arrested. "I was thinking that the only way to let them know I felt I was being mistreated was to do just what I did–resist the order,"she later explained.[15]

Rosa Parks was 42 years old when she was arrested. A woman of impeccable character, she had held office in the local NAACP chapter and had participated in campaigns to register black voters. E. D. Nixon, a former union organizer and past president of the NAACP chapter in Montgomery, put up bail for Parks and immediately recognized that she was a good candidate for the test case. After considering the issue, Parks agreed. "If you think it will mean something to Montgomery and do some good, I'll be happy to go along with it," she said.[16] The immediate challenge was to plan the defense as a basis for demanding fairer treatment for blacks on the buses.

There was a frenzy of activity as news of Parks's arrest spread. Attorney Fred Gray agreed to handle the defense. Jo Ann Robinson, an English professor and member of a civic group called the Women's Political Council, organized the members to disseminate information about the arrest. E. D. Nixon telephoned black spokespersons including Ralph Abernathy and Dr. Martin Luther King, Jr., two young Baptist ministers. As these people discussed the issues, considerable support developed for a boycott of the buses. They created the Montgomery Improvement Association (MIA) and elected King president. The twenty-six-year old, eloquent, and charismatic minister was the pastor of the Dexter Avenue Baptist Church. The son of a prominent Atlanta

Mrs. Rosa Parks sits in the front of a Montgomery, Alabama bus, December 21, 1955, as a Supreme Court ruling that banned segregation on the city's public transit vehicles took effect. Mrs. Parks's arrest on December 1, for sitting in a bus forward of white passengers, touched off the Montgomery boycott against the city's bus lines.

family, he attended Morehouse College in Atlanta and later received his Ph.D. in systematic theology from Boston University.

The demands that the MIA made as the price for ending the boycott were limited. Their intention was to nibble at the edges of segregation, not to end it. They had yet to test their strength or their will, nor could they anticipate the dimensions of the social movement they were about to launch. The three demands that gained popular approval included changes in the seating arrangements in the buses. Blacks would sit from the rear forward and whites from the front backward. The demeaning practice of blacks vacating their seats to whites would be eliminated. Black passengers would no longer have to stand while seats remained unoccupied. The second demand was that bus drivers should be respectful of their black passengers, and the third required that blacks should be hired as drivers.

Faced with these seemingly modest proposals for reform, the municipal authorities in Montgomery haughtily declined to consider them. The MIA's leadership met with the commissioners but to no avail. Even when the MIA softened its request that black drivers be hired, proposing instead that they should only be allowed to apply and be appointed when positions became available, the commissioners remained unmoved. The white representatives did not want to be perceived as making any concessions to blacks. Nor did they wish to create any cracks in Jim Crow's wall. The notion of whites negotiating with blacks was galling enough without the added complication of allowing them to claim any kind of victory over whites as a result of the boycott.

Blacks faced enormous challenges in sustaining the boycott. Most black workers depended on the buses for transportation, so a lengthy boycott presented considerable difficulties for them and the thousands who used that form of transportation daily. The MIA encouraged car pools, urging those with cars to volunteer to transport other blacks, and organized the black taxi cab companies to fill in where needed. The response was beyond the wildest expectations of the MIA, and the boycott was 99 percent effective. Members of the black working class, particularly the large number of women who worked as domestics and who often had to travel long distances to work, bore these sacrifices without complaint. This was one measure of the changes in the temper of blacks, manifesting the élan that would sustain the struggle for equal rights for a decade. Mother Pollard, an old woman who declined a ride and dismissed any suggestion that she end her boycott, said it well: "My feets is tired, but my soul is rested."[17] Women such as Mother Pollard formed the backbone of the protest, attending the meetings and performing the mundane and unspectacular chores that were needed.

As the boycott continued, whites tried to divide the movement and attempted to harass the participants into submission. Cars transporting black workers were ticketed by police on spurious charges. Martin Luther King was arrested for "speeding" as he stopped to pick up some passengers. The leaders of the MIA received threatening phone calls, and King's home was bombed on the night of January 30, 1956. Addressing the angry crowd of blacks who gathered in front of his damaged home, King set the tone for the movement he was chosen to lead:

> We are not advocating violence. We want to love our enemies. Be good to them. Love them and let them know you love them. . . . I want it to be known the length and breadth of this land that if I am stopped, this movement will not stop. If I am stopped, our work will not stop. For what we are doing is right, what we are doing is just.[18]

The movement could not be stopped, although the harrassment continued in a variety of ways. The success of the boycott created severe financial difficulties for the bus company, but the city commissioners still hoped that they could break the back of the movement. A number of white businessmen, alarmed at the impasse and fearful of the long-term economic implications of the boycott, recommended some compromises to the city but left intact the principle of reserved seats for whites at the front of the bus and for blacks at the rear. Blacks rejected the offer. Meanwhile, on February 21, a grand jury indicted a hundred members of the MIA for violating Alabama's antiboycott law.

The indictments steeled the resolve of the black citizens. It also brought national attention to the struggle, and reporters descended on Montgomery. Bayard Rustin, a Barbadian immigrant schooled in the strategies of nonviolent protest who would become a major theoretician of the movement, arrived from New York to provide help. Although there were moments when some doubted the outcome of the struggle, and despite dissension in the movement, few advocated surrender. More importantly, there were signs that the goals of the struggle were being expanded. King, and presumably some of the other participants, had experienced an epiphany in the midst of the prolonged fight. As he asserted in May:

> The key to the whole solution of the South's problem is the ballot. Through the ballot many of the other problems will be solved. Until the colored man comes to this point he will have a hard struggle. When he gets the ballot, he can wield political power and come into his own. . . . The chief weapon in our fight for civil rights is the vote.[19]

As the boycott continued and the months of weary protest passed, participants anxiously awaited the outcome of a suit opposing segregation in the buses that the MIA had filed with the Supreme Court. Roy Wilkins and the NAACP had given their support, linking the venerable civil rights organization with the new apostles of direct action. The Court's decision, handed down on November 13, 1956, was a bombshell. It declared Alabama's laws that sanctioned segregation on the buses to be unconstitutional. Blacks could now sit at the front of the bus, and at 5:45 A.M. on Friday, December 21, Martin Luther King, Rosa Parks, King's able lieutenant Ralph Abernathy, E. D. Nixon, and others did just that.

The success of the Montgomery boycott had national reverberations. It brought its leaders to national attention, and King emerged as one of the most influential voices in black America. During the course of the struggle, blacks in many other cities assumed leadership roles as they sought to change their own situations. The brash minister Fred Shuttlesworth became a dominant figure in the challenge to segregation in Birmingham; the Reverend Joseph Lowery tried to desegregate the buses in Mobile; and the Reverend C. K. Steele played a similar role in Tallahassee.

Women tended to be less visible in leadership positions in these struggles, suffering from a sexism that knew no organizational or state boundaries, yet several played prominent roles as the movement evolved. Despite her domestic obligations, Coretta Scott King, the wife of Martin Luther King, was an ardent supporter of the movement. Jo Ann Robinson was a principal architect in the formation of the Montgomery Improvement Association and its subsequent activities. Ella Baker, a former field organizer of the NAACP, brought her considerable organizational skills to the movement. The attorney Pauli Murray, a veteran of struggles to desegregate the University of North Carolina, offered legal advice. Fannie Lou Hamer, the daughter of a Mississippi sharecropper, served as field secretary to the Student Non Violent Coordinating Committee and distinguished herself in voter registration drives and in efforts to transform the segregated Mississippi Democratic party. Septima Clark was the Southern Christian Leadership Conference's director of education and teaching.

Women's contribution to the male-dominated movement cannot be measured only in terms of their leadership positions. As the movement developed, they formed its reliable foundation, the people whose numbers dominated the mass demonstrations, voter registration drives, and sit-ins. They kept the boycotts alive, made sure the activists to whom they gave shelter were comfortable, and led the freedom songs and hymns in churches that became the institutional bedrock of America's greatest social movement in the twentieth century. Profoundly religious, many of these women derived their strength to confront the challenges of the moment and bear their private pain from their Christian faith. Fannie Lou Hamer usually began mass meetings by leading the gathering in singing:

> Remember me
> Remember me
> Oh Lord, remember me.
>
> Father, I stretch
> My hands to thee
> No other help I know.
>
> You remembered my mother, remember me
> You remembered mother, remember me
> Oh Lord, remember me.[20]

Martin Luther King's philosophy of nonviolence was vindicated in the Montgomery boycott. Like the women, his animating ideology was firmly rooted in Christian traditions and principles and their expressions in the black church. The Reverend King employed the powerful Christian messages of suffering, sacrifice, forgiveness, and redemption to sustain himself and the movement. King spoke frequently of the cross that blacks had to bear before freedom came:

> The cross we bear precedes the crown we wear. To be a Christian one must take up his cross, with all of its difficulties and agonizing and tension-packed content and carry it until that very cross leaves its marks upon us and redeems us to that more excellent way which comes only through suffering.[21]

His faith sustained him in moments of despair. During the early stages of the boycott in January 1956, King confessed that "rationality" had left him but: "Almost out of nowhere I heard a voice saying to me, 'Preach the gospel, stand up for truth, stand up for righteousness.' Since that morning I can stand up without fear."[22]

King, of course, was a close student of the nonviolent philosophy of Mohandas Gandhi, A. J. Muste, Henry David Thoreau, and others, and he admitted their influence on him in his book, *Stride Toward Freedom*, published in 1958. But while these mentors strengthened his embrace of nonviolence and expanded King's philosophical horizons, they were not the principal architects of his ideological stances. King was, above all, a Christian who used the social message of the gospel to inspire the movement, enhance its appeal, and legitimize its strategies and demands. In a prayer that he offered in 1956, King expressed his faith in the sustaining power of Christianity, the gospel of forgiveness, and its call to social action:

> Help us never to let anybody or any condition pull us so low as to cause us to hate. Give us strength to love our enemies and to do good to those who despitefully use us and persecute us. We thank thee for thy Church, founded upon thy Word, that challenges us to do more than sing and pray, but go out and work as though the very answer to our prayers depended upon us and not upon thee. . . . Keep us, we pray, in perfect peace, help us to walk together, pray together, sing together, and live together until the day when all God's children, Black, White, Red, and Yellow will rejoice in one common band of humanity in the kingdom of our Lord and of our God, we pray. Amen.[23]

As a new generation joined the cause in increasing numbers in the 1960s, they were less animated by the language of Christianity and its social gospel and more by the secular constructions of power. Still, by situating the struggle in the black church and employing the teachings of the Bible to justify it, King not only guaranteed it a strong institutional base but mass support as well. This also meant that the struggle would be anchored in the bowels of black society in countless towns, cities, and villages. As a consequence, the movement was, for the most part, not one conducted by elites from afar but one that depended significantly upon local people striking at local targets and simultaneously participating in a larger movement to transform the nation. Martin Luther King's signal contribution was his remarkable ability to articulate the goals of the movement forcefully and eloquently to the nation, inspiring blacks to sustain the struggle and cajoling whites to respect America's promise and to honor its soul. He imbued the struggle with a moral fervor, compelling many to enlist. "To accept passively an unjust system is to cooperate with that system; thereby the oppressed become as evil as the oppressor," King maintained. "Noncooperation with evil is as much a moral obligation as is cooperation with good."[24]

Almost no one who enlisted in this extraordinary exercise in noncooperation realized the enormity of the struggle they were embracing, the sacrifices they would have to make, the acts of courage they would be called upon to demonstrate, and the private moments of doubt and pain. Andrew Young, a young clergyman who joined the Southern Christian Leadership Conference in 1961 and who would become one of the strategists of the movement, recalled a poignant moment after Fannie Lou Hamer lost her job and was mistreated as a result of her involvement in the struggle:

> This was perhaps the first time I felt deeply and personally how serious the business we were embarking upon would become. This was no play school, no play citizenship, no play freedom we were working for: people would pay with blood, with their lives, for doing what we maybe too comfortably were urging them to do. I had wanted to be part of this, and maybe now I was, but the responsibility was heavier than I by myself could handle. Never had I needed my faith more; for we knew, prophetically, that the sacrifices necessary to make change possible would be more than some could bear. As surely as the next few years portended accomplishments and a taste of victory, they also held promises of tragedy.[25]

King, who was arrested several times during the struggle and would become its martyr, had his moments of profound fear. Arrested in Georgia in 1960 on the charge of having violated the terms of a probation by driving without a license, King was suddenly removed from his jail cell late one night. The terrified preacher was put in a straitjacket, forced into a police wagon, and driven across the state. Not knowing his destination and acutely conscious of what his fate could be, King thought he "would never see anybody again." "That kind of mental anguish is worse than dying," he recalled, "riding for mile after mile, hungry and thirsty, bound and helpless, waiting and not knowing what you're waiting for, and all over a traffic violation."[26]

White supporters of the movement also faced their own difficulties. Beginning in the nineteenth century, a handful of Southern whites had dissented from the racial status quo, but their voices were ineffective. Nevertheless, a few whites joined the struggle in Montgomery from its earliest stage. They included the attorney Clifford Durr and his wife, Virginia, the Reverend Robert Graetz of the Trinity Lutheran Church, and the Reverend Glenn Smiley, a Methodist and a member of the Fellowhip of Reconciliation, a pacifist organization. Some quietly provided financial help. Other whites enlisted as the movement spread, some of the more moderate among them mediating between the defenders of the status quo and the black challengers. Businessmen who knew that boycotts and social disruptions threatened their economic well-being often urged compromise. Recognizing that these internal splits threatened white supremacy, the White Citizen's Council reminded Montgomery's whites in early 1957:

> There are only two sides in the Southern fight–those who want to maintain the Southern way of life or those who want to mix the races. . . . Whites must stand by whites just as Negroes are standing by Negroes. . . . There is no middle ground for moderation. . . . [T]hat middle ground has been washed away by the actions of the NAACP in seeking to destroy the freedoms of the Southern white man.[27]

There was, as subsequent events revealed, a white "middle ground for moderation" in most of the battlegrounds in the South. Some whites did not find compromise easy to embrace, and even those who accepted in principle the view that the racial order should change found it hard to accept in practice. Hodding Carter, the moderate and seemingly racially progressive editor of the *Delta-Democrat-Times* in Greenville, Mississippi, for example, was opposed "to putting into practice public school desegregation in the Deep South." He thought its advocates should "concentrate upon improving the mass level of morality rather than obtaining admission of a few Negro children to presently white schools."[28] William Faulkner, the celebrated Mississippi novelist, said in an interview in February 1956, "If I have to choose between the United States government and Mississippi, then I'll choose Mississippi. . . . As long as there's a middle road I'll be on it. But if it came to fighting I'd fight for Mississippi against the United States even if it meant going into the streets and shooting Negroes." Faulkner may have been inebriated when he made the comment, but its racist tone belied a history of support for the rights of blacks. He was disturbed by the disruptions that racial change produced and admonished blacks in March 1956, to "go slow now, stop for a time. You have the power now; you can withhold for a moment the use of it as a force."[29] For a people who had been subjugated since 1619 and whose basic rights remained largely unmet in 1956, this was the unwelcomed voice of delay and an endorsement of their continued oppression, if only temporarily.

Nationally, many white leaders of opinion remained relatively silent, at least in the early stages of the civil rights movement. In spite of the developing earthquake, progressive whites saw the race question as primarily a Southern problem that could be solved through increased interaction between blacks and whites. Racial fears and animus would be reduced as a result of this association, they reasoned. In 1956, the democratic candidate for the presidency, Adlai Stevenson, was criticized for observing, "You do not upset habits and traditions that are older than the Republic overnight." When Roy Wilkins of the NAACP condemned Stevenson for his remark, Eleanor Roosevelt characterized Wilkins's statement as "reckless," even suggesting that she might resign as a member of the NAACP board. Arthur Schlesinger, Jr., one of Stevenson's speech writers and a Harvard historian, thought the candidate should show greater passion on the civil rights question. As Schlesinger expressed it: "If we can communicate [deep] concern, then we can remain as responsible and uncommitted as we want when it comes to policy."[30]

With some exceptions, whites who were sympathetic to the freedom struggle could not readily understand the urgency of the demands. The black experience of unequal treatment had not been theirs, and none had been denied rights that their fellow citizens possessed. Interracial cooperation in the movement was possible, but it was fraught, understandably, with tensions. Both sides had to learn to deal with one another on the basis of equality. Blacks were sensitive to expressions of white condescension, and whites had to abandon any claims that blacks were their inferiors and in need of their tutelage and direction.

After the Montgomery boycott, King expressed the view that blacks had learned six lessons from the experience:

> (1) We have discovered that we can stick together for a common cause; (2) Our leaders do not have to sell out; (3) Threats do not necessarily intimidate those who are sufficiently aroused and non-violent; (4) Our church is becoming militant, stressing a social gospel as well as a gospel of personal salvation; (5) We have gained a new dignity and destiny; (6) We have discovered a new and powerful weapon–non-violent resistance.[31]

The victory in Montgomery, accordingly, energized the proponents of a mass-based, nonviolent, passive resistance. On the other hand, the national leaders of the NAACP were less than enthusiastic about the presence of these upstarts, people who were trying to employ strategies other than litigation to change their condition. Roy Wilkins also feared the emergence of a group that could compete effectively with the NAACP. In February 1957, ninety-seven blacks gathered in New Orleans to create the Southern Leadership Conference, later renamed the Southern Christian Leadership Conference (SCLC). The choice of the latter nomenclature occurred at King's insistence since he wanted to affirm the Christian base of the organization. King was elected president, and the other officers included the Reverend C. K. Steele of Tallahassee, the Reverend A. L. Davis of New Orleans, and Medgar W. Evers, an NAACP organizer from Jackson, Mississippi. Over the next several months, the fledgling organization groped for direction. But it still managed to conduct a voter registration campaign, and its officers traveled throughout the South to establish its foundations.

On May 17, 1957, the NAACP, the SCLC, and A. Philip Randolph sponsored a Prayer Pilgrimage for Freedom to the nation's capital. The pilgrimage was planned to coincide with the third anniversary of the *Brown* v. *Board of Education* decision. It was designed to emphasize the peaceful nature of the civil rights movement, involve a broad cross section of blacks in the struggle, prick the nation's conscience, and influence President Eisenhower and the Congress to support legislation to correct racial injustice. As many as 25,000 to 30,000 persons attended to hear King plead for the ballot:

> Give us the ballot and we will not longer have to worry the federal government about our basic rights. . . . Give us the ballot and we will no longer plead to the federal government for passage of an anti-lynching law. Give us the ballot and we will not longer plead—we will write the proper laws on the books. Give us the ballot and we will fill the legislature with men of good will. Give us the ballot and we will get the people judges who will do 'justly and love mercy.' Give us the ballot and we will quietly, lawfully, and nonviolently, without rancor or bitterness, implement the May 17, 1954, decision of the Supreme Court. . . . Give us the ballot and we will transform the salient misdeeds of the blood thirsty mobs into the calculated good deeds of orderly citizens.[32]

The cause of civil rights obtained a mild boost in September with the passage of the Civil Rights Act of 1957. It was the first such bill to obtain congressional approval in eight decades, and it passed only after its supporters defeated a filibuster by Southern segregationists. Senator Strom Thurmond of South Carolina spoke against the bill continuously for twenty-four hours. The measure created a Civil Rights Division in the Department of Justice empowered to seek injunctions against those who violated the voting rights of citizens. It also established a six-member Civil Rights Commission to investigate these infractions and report on them. Meanwhile, the SCLC had found its stride and expanded its agenda. King announced in November:

> The time has come for a broad, bold advance of the Southern campaign for equality. . . . Not only will it include a stepped-up campaign of voter registration, but a full-scale approach will be made upon discrimination

and segregation in all forms. . . . We must employ new methods of struggle involving the masses of our people.[33]

Encouraged by the turnout at the Prayer Pilgrimage, Randolph turned his attention to organizing two additional Washington marches, consisting primarily of students. The Youth March for Integrated Schools occurred on October 25, 1958, and attracted 9,500 black and white students. The march received the support of other civil rights leaders but was ignored by President Eisenhower. The second march took place on April 18, 1959, and this time 22,500 persons, mostly students participated. Although representatives of the demonstrators failed to get an appointment with the president, who was conveniently on vacation, they handed a petition urging integration in the schools to one of his assistants. The president would later write to thank the petitioners, promising that he would "take such action as in my best judgment will result in the most constructive progress towards equality of opportunity and the elimination of discrimination that it is possible to achieve."[34] President Eisenhower did not honor his promise.

DIRECT ACTION

The first half of the decade of the 1960s constituted a momentous period in the quest for justice. The assault on Jim Crow had developed into a vigorous battle for civil rights in its broadest sense. The movement embraced a mass-based strategy of direct action, becoming more aggressive and confrontational. A good deal of the energy came from young college students who entered the struggle in ever larger numbers, often shaping its strategy, particularly at the local levels. Most of these young people had come of age since 1954, growing up during the six-year campaign of passive resistance to segregation. They had been socialized by a tradition of protest, becoming impatient with the racial barriers that stood in their way. Unlike their elders, they had seen from a very early age what protest could accomplish, either by its threat or its exercise. After all, in their own times several cities had desegregated public transportation because of boycotts. A far lengthier list of cities–Charlotte, Greensboro, Durham, Little Rock, Pine Bluff, San Antonio, Knoxville, Dallas, and others–had done so to forestall social protests. Less willing to accept incremental changes than their parents had been, the students gave a greater immediacy to black demands.

On February 1, 1960, four college students in Greensboro, North Carolina, launched what became known as the "sit-in." They were Joseph McNeil, Izell Blair, Jr., Franklin McCain, and David Richmond of North Carolina Agricultural and Technical College. The students took their seats at a whites-only lunch counter at a Woolworth's store and were refused service. Ironically, the woman who declined to serve them

Greensboro sit-in: Students of North Carolina Agriculture and Technical College sit at an all-white lunch counter at the local Woolworth's.

was black. "You are stupid, ignorant!" she admonished. "You're dumb! That's why we can't get anywhere today. You know you are supposed to eat at the other end."[35] Probably steeled by the verbal assault, the young men remained seated until the store closed, promising to return the following day. Their goal was rather limited, the elimination of Jim Crow at this particular store. Not until July 25 did the protestors in Greensboro achieve the victory they sought after their ranks had been swelled by other students.

The Greensboro sit-in was not the first one that occurred in the South. There had been as many as sixteen within the previous three years. But unlike the others, Greensboro captured the imagination of other students and spawned protests all across the region. By the end of February, thirty-two cities had been touched and forty-one more in March. Sit-ins occurred in such cities as Nashville, Raleigh, Orangeburg, Montgomery, and Atlanta. Most were peaceful, but some provoked the violence of white mobs. By the end of 1961, about two hundred cities had agreed to desegregate.

The SCLC had given its support to the protests, and at executive secretary Ella Baker's insistence, a conference was held at Raleigh in mid-April. Student representatives attended, and Martin King told the gathering: "The youth must take the freedom struggle into every community in the South without exception. . . . Inevitably, this broadening of the struggle and the determination which it represents will arouse vocal and vigorous support and place pressures on the federal government that will compel its intervention." By the time the conference ended on April 18, the students had established the Student Non Violent Coordinating Committee (SNCC). Its founding statement emphasized the organization's commitment to a nonviolence rooted in "Judaic-Christian traditions."[36]

As the SNCC slowly evolved as an organization, it defined itself as one firmly rooted in local communities. The organization eschewed a "top down" philosophy, preferring to join with activists in each community and allowing the local milieu to shape their strategies. In time, the SNCC's members became the courageous "shock troops" of the movement, venturing into dangerous areas to provide assistance to the local people. But this only occurred after the organization had experienced the usual growing pains, found its voice, and defined its purpose. Along the way, the SNCC honed the leadership skills of numerous blacks. Its illustrious pantheon included Julian Bond, Stokely Carmichael, Cleveland Sellers, James Forman, Robert Moses, Anne Moody, Charles Sherrod, Diane Nash, John Lewis, Ruby Doris Robinson, Angela Davis, and Norma Collins. The SNCC also attracted white activists such as Bob Zellner, Casey Hayden, Tim Jenkins, and Allard Lowenstein.

The Freedom Rides that occurred in the spring of 1961 exposed the ugliness of white racism in the South, gained Northern sympathy for the protesters, and energized the struggle as a whole. Organized by James Farmer, one of the founders of the nonviolent and interracial Congress of Racial Equality, the purpose of the rides was to bring an end to discrimination in interstate travel. Two integrated busloads of riders left Washington on May 4, encountering their first violence on May 9 when two riders were assaulted as they tried to enter a whites-only waiting room at the bus terminal in Rock Hill, South Carolina. Later, a mob in Anniston, Alabama, burned one of the buses and beat the riders on both. The police responded slowly to these assaults, and press reports across the nation brought the victims much sympathy. The riders were again assaulted in Birmingham. When the rides resumed after being suspended for a while, the riders were arrested and later escorted out of town. They were attacked by another mob in Montgomery, and the police again provided little protection. U.S. Attorney General Robert Kennedy ordered an FBI investigation, and an outraged Martin King articulated the need to destroy segregation root and branch. He called for:

> . . . an intensified voter registration drive, a determined effort to integrate the public schools, lunch counters, public parks, theaters, etc. In

short, we will seek to mobilize thousands of people, committed to the method of non violence, who will physically identify themselves with the struggle to end segregation in Alabama. We will present our physical bodies to end segregation in Alabama. We will present our physical bodies to defeat the unjust system.[37]

The riders continued with police protection to Jackson but were arrested when they tried to use a whites-only restroom. Trying to keep the peace, Attorney General Kennedy urged the protesters to cease their activity, but this was to no avail. The civil rights organizations provided support, as several hundred protesters were jailed in Jackson. On September 22, the Interstate Commerce Commission banned segregation in interstate travel and in bus and train terminals, handing the forces of direct action the victory they sought.

Fortified by the struggle in the Freedom Rides where they had played a major role, some members of the SNCC turned their attention to a voter registration drive in Mississippi. Throughout the summer of 1961 the organization had debated its future strategy. Some members wanted to restrict the organization's activities to protest demonstrations and boycotts, while others argued that its energies should go into voter registration. Eventually, a compromise was reached, and the organization decided to pursue the two strategies simultaneously. The ensuing voter registration campaign in the Mississippi Delta tested the courage and fortitude of the young activists. They were subjected to persistent harassment and violence from white citizens. It was nothing less than a war zone as the law enforcement authorities joined with white reactionaries to crush the volunteers.

In the aftermath of the Freedom Rides, two SNCC staff members, Charles Sherrod and Cordell Reagon, also went to Albany, a town in southwest Georgia, to organize its 26,000 black citizens to demand their rights. Albany was reputed to be one of those areas where segregationists were stridently intransigent and thoroughly in control of the lives of black citizens. Despite the unease of some of the local blacks, the SNCC team began to organize students. Spurred by the activities of the SNCC staffers, whose number had grown to three, the disparate black groups met and formed the Albany Movement to promote their rights. The white authorities consistently refused any accommodation to the wishes of the protesters, and the police chief, Laurie Pritchett, responded to each challenge with mass arrests. When Martin King, Ralph Abernathy, and Wyatt Walker responded to an appeal for help and visited Albany, they were arrested along with hundreds of other demonstrators.

Under Chief Pritchett's leadership, the police refrained, for the most part, from brutalizing black citizens. The chief had learned much from the nonviolent strategy of the protesters and did not want to abuse them in such a way as to elicit national sympathy for them. As he put it, "We met 'non-violence' with 'non-violence,' and we are indeed proud of the outcome."[38] From November 1961 to the end of 1962, blacks continued their protest in Albany against segregation, and perhaps a thousand of them were jailed. But the opposing forces never cracked; the walls of segregation remained essentially intact, at least in Albany. The failure in Albany, King opined, was due to the fact that the movement "was centered on segregation in general, and no form of segregation in particular, and I think it would have been greater and would have been wiser, from a strategic and tactical point of view to say, 'now we are going to attack segregated lunch counters,' or 'we are going to attack segregated buses,' in other words, center it on something. . . ."[39]

If Albany could be said to represent a temporary setback for the movement, the assault on Birmingham was a major success. Chastened by the experience in Albany, King wanted to restore the movement's faith in the efficacy of nonviolence as well as boost the morale of its participants. The SCLC also wanted to force the federal government and the John F. Kennedy administration to become more forceful in its defense of black rights. In their strategy sessions, movement leaders agreed that they needed a crisis, so dramatic and so compelling in its moral force that the nation dared not refuse to take action.

Birmingham had the dubious distinction of being characterized as the most segregated city in America. Unlike the wily Pritchett of Albany, Birmingham's police chief was Bull Connor, a crude and belligerent racist. The movement's leaders, such as Fred Shuttlesworth, King, Walker, and Andrew Young, felt that they could provoke the chief into committing excesses in front of a national television audience and use the atrocities to their advantage.

The Birmingham campaign was to be distinguished by its focus on business establishments. In addition to sit-ins, the protesters would engage in boycotts of white-owned stores. They knew that if the businessmen suffered losses, they were likely to pursuade the politicians to accede to the desegregation goals of the movement. The SCLC also wanted the businesses to hire blacks. The sit-ins began on April 2, 1963, but the police did not immediately respond with the anticipated brutalities. But as demonstrations continued, Bull Connor unleashed dogs on the black citizens, and his men were unsparing in their use of their clubs. King and others were arrested for disobeying an injunction against marches and other forms of protest.

While the brutality of the police against black citizens shocked much of the nation, King claimed the moral high ground. As he waited in jail, he composed his "Letter from the Birmingham Jail." The nineteen-page document was a defense of the movement and an eloquent statement on the urgency of the cause. Taking issue with the white ministers who remained morally neutral in the struggle, King wrote: "I have heard numerous religious leaders in the South call upon their worship-

Police dog attacking a marcher in Birmingham's Kelly Ingram Park, May 1963.

pers to comply with a desegregation decision because it is the law, but I have longed to hear white ministers say, 'follow this decree because integration is morally right and the Negro is your brother.'" To those who advised the movement "to wait," King responded:

> I guess it is easy for those who have never felt the stinging darts of segregation, to say wait. But when you have seen vicious mobs lynch your mothers and fathers at will and drown your sisters and brothers at whim; when you have seen hate-filled policemen curse, kick, brutalize, and even kill your black brothers and sisters with impunity; when you see that vast majority of your twenty million Negro brothers smothering in an air-tight cage of poverty in the midst of an affluent society . . . when you are harried by day and haunted by night by the fact that you are a Negro, living constantly at tiptoe stance never quite knowing what to expect next, and plagued with inner fears and outer resentments; when you are forever fighting a degenerating sense of "nobodiness"–then you well understand why we find it difficult to wait.

King was certain, however, that the movement would prevail. He predicted:

> One day the South will recognize its real heroes. . . . One day the South will know that when these disinherited children of God sat down at lunch counters, they were in reality standing up for the best in the

American dream and the most sacred values in our Judeo-Christian heritage, and thusly, carrying our whole nation back to those great wells of democracy which were dug deep, by the founding fathers.[40]

Police brutality and the arrests merely stiffened black resistance. Upon King's release from jail, the SCLC's leaders, with his acquiescence, brought children into the demonstrations. Although this dramatic exposure of the very young to police violence was much criticized, it was a bold and ultimately successful gamble. The nation watched as Birmingham's police intimidated them with dogs, trained hoses on them, and beat some. About five hundred children were arrested and taken to jail as they prayed, sang, and clapped. The deeply moving and moral presence of the children and the barbarity of their treatment underscored to the world the ways in which many whites had been damaged by racism and revealed its corrosive effect on the nation's soul. Hundreds of adult protesters were also arrested, and the jails were literally filled. Alarmed by the bad publicity that their city was receiving and reeling from the economic effects of the boycott, some businessmen urged a settlement of the crisis. Outraged citizens across the nation asked President Kennedy to intervene.

The protest ended on May 10 when the Birmingham authorities accepted most of the demands of the protesters. King called the settlement "the most magnificent victory for justice we've ever seen in the Deep South."[41] The agreement called for the desegregation of washrooms, restrooms, lunchroom counters, and drinking fountains. Fitting rooms in stores were to be desegregated, and "a program of upgrading Negro employment will be continued."[42]

The successful Birmingham protest had a significant impact on other cities in the South. There were numerous marches, boycotts, and sit-ins in its wake. The Justice Department reported 758 demonstrations during the summer, as well as 14,000 arrests.[43] Segregation in public places collapsed in numerous cities. Embarrassed by the nature of white resistance in Birmingham and concerned about the unflattering international publicity it received, President Kennedy decided to submit a comprehensive civil rights bill to the Congress. He cautioned the nation, "The events in Birmingham and elsewhere have so increased the crisis for equality that no nation or state or legislative body can prudently choose to ignore them." The president believed that the country confronted a "moral issue," one that was "as old as the Scriptures and as clear as the American constitution."[44]

The culminating triumph of 1963 was the March on Washington, which occurred in August. The Birmingham success had raised expectations for an improvement in the black condition, and they could not be easily contained. King worried about the consequences of failed dreams. Acting upon a suggestion by A. Philip Randolph, the leaders of the civil

Dr. Martin Luther King, Jr., at the March on Washington (August 28, 1963), facing the crowd at the Lincoln Memorial for his "I Have a Dream" speech.

rights organizations, including King of the SCLC, Whitney Young of the National Urban League, James Farmer of CORE, and Roy Wilkins of the NAACP, began to plan to march on Washington to dramatize their cause. Randolph assumed the position of director of the march, and Bayard Rustin served as its talented organizer. The call for the march indicated an important tactical shift in the movement because it linked the struggle for equal rights with a demand for economic justice. Civil rights leaders had become aware of the need to reorder the economic structure of the nation so that marginalized peoples could share in its bounty. Legislative successes alone would not produce that end. Almost alone among the civil rights leaders, Randolph had long recognized that equal rights and economic justice walked hand in hand.

In their call to march on Washington, the organizers emphasized:

> In their historic nonviolent revolt for freedom, the Negro people are demanding the right to decent jobs. . . . [T]here is no way for Negroes to win and hold jobs unless the problems of automation, a stagnant economy, and discrimination are solved; therefore, the Federal government must establish a massive works program to train and employ all Americans at decent wages and at meaningful and dignified labor.[45]

In addition to the works program, movement leaders wanted an end to job discrimination in the public and private sectors, an end to police mistreatment of blacks, the passage of civil rights legislation, and the integration of public schools.

The march was an unqualified success. Two hundred and fifty thousand black and white marchers gathered on Wednesday, August 28, 1963, at the Lincoln Memorial to petition their government for full citizenship rights for the peoples of African descent. In opening the proceedings, A. Philip Randolph predicted that it was "not the climax to our struggle but a new beginning." Speaking on behalf of black citizens everywhere, the aging labor leader pleaded for a marriage between civil rights and economic opportunities:

> Yes, we want all public accommodations open to all citizens, but those accommodations will mean little to those who cannot afford them. Yes, we want a Fair Employment Practices Act, but what good will it do if profits geared to automation destroy the jobs of millions of workers, black and white? We want integrated public schools, but that means we also want Federal aid to education.[46]

Martin Luther King's speech epitomized the hopes of his constituency as much as it critiqued his country's treatment of blacks:

> I say to you today, my friends, so even though we face the difficulties of today and tomorrow, I still have a dream. It is a dream deeply rooted in the American dream. I have a dream that one day this nation will rise up and live out the true meaning of its creed—we hold these truths to be self-evident, that all men are created equal. I have a dream that one day on the red hills of Georgia, the sons of former slaves and the sons of former slave-owners will be able to sit down together at the table of brotherhood. I have a dream that one day, even the state of Mississippi, a

state sweltering with the heat of injustice, sweltering with the heat of oppression, will be transformed into an oasis of freedom and justice. I have a dream that my four little children will one day live in a nation where they will not be judged by the color of their skin but by the content of their character. I have a dream today! I have a dream that one day, down in Alabama, with its vicious racists, with its governor having his lips dripping with the words of interposition and nullification, one day, right there in Alabama, little black boys and little black girls will be able to join hands with little white boys and white girls as sisters and brothers. I have a dream today. I have a dream that one day every valley shall be exalted, every hill and mountain shall be made low, the rough places shall be made plain and the crooked places will be made straight and the glory of the Lord shall be revealed and all flesh shall see it together. This is our hope. This is the faith that I go back to the South with. With this faith we will be able to hew out of the mountain of despair a stone of hope. With this faith we will be able to transform the jangling discords of our nation into a beautiful symphony of brotherhood. With this faith we will be able to work together, to pray together, to struggle together, to go to jail together, to stand up for freedom together, knowing that we will be free one day.[47]

King spoke for many, but there were voices that wanted "freedom" to be obtained immediately, not delayed. In fact, the integrationist and nonviolent strategies that the civil rights movement promoted did not remain uncontested. Many nationalists, particularly members of the Nation of Islam, did not seek integration but economic autonomy, if not actual racial separation. Some persons questioned the efficacy of nonviolence as a means of effecting changes in the racial order. Malcolm X, who was a native of Detroit and was originally known as Malcolm Little, was one of the principal critics of the civil rights personages and their strategies. Largely self-educated, he became a member of the Nation of Islam while he served a jail sentence. Becoming a faithful disciple of Elijah Muhammad, Malcolm was named the principal minister of Temple Number Seven in New York City in 1954.

From his base in Harlem, Malcolm became an outspoken voice of the urban poor who flocked to hear him. Like Marcus Garvey before him, he proudly celebrated his blackness. "I'm black first," he asserted. "My sympathies are black, my allegiance is black, my whole objectives are black. . . . I am not interested in being American, because America has never been interested in me."[48] He derided the civil rights movement's integrationist stance, characterizing it as a "hypocritical approach." As he expressed it, "Any Negro trying to integrate is actually admitting his inferiority, because he is admitting that he wants to become a part of a superior society."[49]

While Martin King was an unabashed advocate of nonviolent strategies in the pursuit of justice, Malcolm X saw himself as the "field Negro"

Malcolm X (1925–1965)

who actively resisted his condition as a slave "by any means necessary."[50] In many respects, Malcolm X was a reincarnation of the plucky Jack Johnson, the "bad nigger" of boxing fame, except that he made his pronouncements from the mosque and the speaker's platform and not from the ring. "Yes, I'm an extremist," he said. "The black race in North America is in extremely bad condition. You show me a black man who is not an extremist and I'll show you one who needs psychiatric attention."[51] Malcolm moderated some of his positions before he was assassinated by opponents in the Nation of Islam in 1965, but he was an authentic voice of the people he represented, and at least for a time articulated an alternative vision for black America.

In addition to the competing vision associated with Malcolm X, the movement faced challenges that were both internal and external. Among other difficulties, it had to maintain the commitment of its supporters, contain those who would abandon nonviolence for other options, and keep the pressure on the administration to protect the rights of blacks and pass the appropriate civil rights legislation. President John Kennedy's assassination in November 1963, ironically, improved the chances of his civil rights bill being approved. In a message to Congress after that dreadful event, the new president, Lyndon Johnson, said:

> No memorial oration or eulogy could more eloquently honor President Kennedy's memory than the earliest possible passage of the civil rights bill for which he fought. We have talked long enough in this country about equal rights. We have talked for one hundred years or more. It is now time to write the next chapter—and to write it in the book of law.[52]

Although its opponents launched a filibuster against the bill, it was adopted by Congress and signed by the president on July 2, 1964. The measure outlawed racial discrimination in most forms of public accommodation and in government programs. It established the Equal Employment Opportunity Commission and banned discrimination by unions.

Inasmuch as these were signal achievements, the struggle was far from being over. Economic issues had to be addressed, and blacks had to enjoy unrestricted access to the franchise. Racist attitudes remained to be transformed, and racial violence was still a feature of the landscape. Medgar Evers, one of the stalwarts of the SCLC, had been murdered in Mississippi on June 12, 1963. Four girls lost their lives when their Birmingham church was bombed on September 15. This destruction of these young lives recalled the terrible incident in 1955 when a fourteen-year-old Chicago boy, Emmett Till, was lynched in Mississippi. Acting on a dare from his peers, Till had transgressed Southern racial etiquette by playfully asking a white store clerk for a date.

During 1964, the movement's emphasis was placed on voter registration campaigns. The impetus came primarily from the SNCC and from CORE. Their staffs organized the Summer Project, which attracted an integrated group of Northern students to register voters in Mississippi. White students were particularly welcomed, since the organizers believed this would "project an image of cooperation between Northern white people and Southern Negro people to the nation which will reduce fears of an impending race war."[53] Tragedy struck on June 21, when three workers—James Chaney, a black, and two whites, Michael Schwerner and Andrew Goodman—disappeared and were found dead on August 4. Three years later, seven white men were convicted for the horrible crime.

Unaccustomed to working together, blacks and whites in the Summer Project, popularly known as Freedom Summer, eventually were caught up in tensions. These tensions were exacerbated by cultural

Fannie Lou Hamer at the SNCC office in Greenwood, Mississippi, 1963.

differences, black resentment of white privilege, and concerns by some blacks about the commitment of white volunteers to the struggle. The hostile environment in which the volunteers worked did nothing to ease these misunderstandings. Although only 1200 black voters were registered, the Freedom Schools that the volunteers organized seem to have been successful.

The failure of the voter registration campaign and the harassment to which the volunteers were exposed underscored the degree to which white Mississippians would go to keep blacks disenfranchised. Determined to change the situation, thousands of blacks joined the newly created Mississippi Freedom Democratic party (MFDP) and sent delegates to the Democratic party's convention in Atlantic City, New Jersey. They tried unsuccessfully to unseat those delegates representing the segregationist Mississippi Democratic party. In an impassioned address to the convention, Fannie Lou Hamer declared that if the MFDP "is not seated now, I question America."[54] Malcolm X, who by then had developed into an influential leader with significant mass support, warned: "If they don't want to deal with the Mississippi Freedom Democratic Party, then we'll give them something else to deal with."[55]

As one expression of its increasing emphasis on voter registration and black political empowerment, the SCLC turned its attention to Selma, Alabama, in the fall of 1964. Dallas County, in which Selma was located, had an abysmal record for registering black voters, and King and his lieutenants saw it as an ideal place for forcing federal action on voting rights. When the demonstrations began in January 1965, the participants faced Sheriff James Clark, who responded with mass arrests and beatings. In full view of the television cameras, protesters were brutalized by the police as they tried to march across the Pettus Bridge from Selma to Montgomery to present their grievances to Governor George Wallace. Determined to continue the march to Montgomery, the SCLC appealed to a federal judge to enjoin the officials to allow it. Judge Frank Johnson surprised the civil rights leaders by enjoining both the officials and the marchers to cease their respective activities. Martin King responded:

> I have got to march. I do not know what lies ahead of us. There may be beatings, jailings, tear gas. But I would rather die on the highways of Alabama than make a butchery of my conscience.[56]

In the end, King led the demonstrators across the bridge, facing the armed state troopers. After praying and singing "We Shall Overcome," King, the apostle of nonviolence and the winner of the 1964 Nobel Peace Prize, led the crowd back to Selma. King had made his point, but angry voices, particularly members of the SNCC, denounced the retreat and accurately accused King of making a deal with white authorities.

The violence in Selma shocked the nation. President Lyndon Johnson addressed Congress and the nation on March 15 to urge passage of a voting rights bill. He said, "It is wrong–deadly wrong, to deny any of your fellow Americans the right to vote in this country" and invoked the movement's anthem, "We Shall Overcome," bringing tears to King as he watched the speech. The Texan, who had come to embrace the cause of racial justice unequivocally, told the country:

> the real hero of this struggle is the American Negro. His actions and protest, his courage to risk safety, and even to risk his life, have awakened the conscience of this nation. His demonstrations have been designed to call attention to injustice, designed to provoke change, designed to stir reform. He has called upon us to make good the promise of America. And who among us can say that we would have made the same progress were it not for his persistent bravery and his faith in American democracy?[57]

The administration's voting rights bill encountered the usual opposition from Southern legislators. The measure, which was adopted in August 1965, provided for federal intervention to protect the voting rights of citizens. It held that "no voting qualification or prerequisite to voting, or standard, practice or procedure shall be imposed or applied by any state or political subdivision to deny or abridge the right of any citizen of the United States to vote on account of race or color." The law allowed the attorney general to seek court approval to appoint federal examiners to "enforce the guarantees of the Fifteenth Amendment in any state or political subdivision." The Voting Rights Act was passed a century after Congress adopted the Thirteenth Amendment, which abolished slavery. Coming in response to a prolonged struggle, the act had the potential to enhance the political power of blacks. The vote could now be used as a weapon to force other changes upon a reluctant larger society.

Selma and the passage of the Voting Rights Act constituted watersheds in the civil rights movement and in the history of black America. They brought to an end the most dramatic and effective stage of the struggle for equal rights since Reconstruction. As one phase of the struggle ended, a new one was about to be inaugurated. Not only would King take the movement to the North, but he also broadened its scope and changed its emphasis. He now articulated the view that legislative victories "did very little to penetrate the lower depths of Negro deprivation, particularly in the North."[58] Along with some of the others in movement, King had come to believe that the nation had to undergo profound structural changes if the poor and marginalized were to share in its economic promise. Accordingly, he called for "a reconstruction of the entire society, a revolution of values."[59]

King's call for a fundamental restructuring of the economic order reflected the mood of the urban poor. Frustrated by the pace of change in their lives, suffering from official neglect, trapped in the ghetto, and short on hope, residents in Watts, a district of Los Angeles, rioted in August 1965. Thirty-four persons lost their lives and more than a thousand were wounded. The authorities estimated the damage to property at $40 million. Shocked by the intensity of the violence, King said, "Everyone underestimated the amount of rage Negroes were suppressing and the amount of bigotry the white majority was disguising."[60] This rejection of nonviolence as a strategy for change suggested a threatening phase in the struggle for justice and exposed deep ideological divisions in the civil rights movement. The NAACP and the NUL distanced themselves from such direct action, while their critics alleged that they were too committed to integration in the larger society, and too comfortably middle class in their protest styles and orientation. Representing a new generation of activists, Stokely Carmichael of the SNCC thought the proponents of integration believed "there was nothing of value in the Negro community, so the thing to do was to siphon off the 'acceptable' Negroes into the surrounding middle-class white community."[61]

Younger and more harshly critical of white Americans than their older counterparts, this new generation also wanted blacks to assume control of "the institutions within the black community," as Carmichael expressed it. He renounced "the dependent" and "the suppliant" posture of the older civil rights leaders. Known as "black power," the ideology of this new phase of protest had its spiritual roots in the black nationalism of David Walker and Marcus Garvey. In 1966, the SNCC urged "all black Americans to begin building independent political, economic, and cultural institutions that they will control and use as instruments of social change in the country."[62] The proponents of black power advocated deep changes in the structure of American society and promoted black autonomy and self-determination. Their chant, "We want black power," frightened many whites and led them to distance themselves from the movement. Martin King expressed his distaste for the new slogan and what it portended, but he was powerless to temper the mood of the times and the rhetoric of a new set of spokespersons.

As King observed the economic blight in urban and rural America, he became more insistent in demanding economic changes that would benefit the poor. Recognizing that the Vietnam War, which was then in progress, drained resources that could be used for the improvement of the black condition, King denounced the nature and conduct of the war in 1967. He charged that in prosecuting the war, America was allied with "the wealthy and the secure while we create a hell for the poor." The white press—and a few black newspapers—denounced the civil rights leader for linking the struggle for justice at home with the cessation of the war in Asia. Even his associates in the movement declined to endorse his position. "I knew that I could never again raise my voice against the violence of the oppressed in the ghettos without having first spoken clearly to the greatest purveyor of violence in the world today—my own government," the Baptist clergyman explained.[63]

Largely as a consequence of their own initiative and courage, blacks saw the legal barriers to full citizenship destroyed between 1955 and 1965. Writing years later, Andrew Young modestly assessed the role of the civil rights movement and its leaders in changing the place of blacks and the nation as a whole:

> We were flesh-and-blood human beings, men and women. We got involved with the most pressing issue of our day; we got our hands dirty with the labors of social change. We associated with racists and white supremacists. We negotiated and compromised with people who opposed everything we were trying to achieve. We were flawed and imperfect and we fell short of the glory of God. But we changed America. And we did it without harming anyone, except ourselves.[64]

These changes were as important as the ones that came in the wake of the emancipation of the slaves a century earlier. The elimination of *de jure* segregation and the adoption of civil rights legislation by the Congress raised expectations that relationships between blacks and whites would improve, opportunities would be open to all regardless of skin color, and social justice would prevail. The administration of President Lyndon Johnson introduced a series of programs to eliminate poverty and to construct what the president called the "Great Society."

But poverty was never eliminated, and since the 1960s the gap between the rich and the poor in the nation has widened. A disproportionate number of black Americans have remained mired in poverty, although there has been an expansion in the size of the middle class. The ghettos continue to symbolize the nation's failure to create an equal place for all of its citizens. Blacks have improved their presence in the legislative bodies of the land, but effective political power has eluded them. The racist ideology that legitimized the mistreatment of blacks still manifests itself in poisonous ways. Significantly, many of those who exercise political power have retreated from the promise of a just society, betraying the nation's ideals and reducing everyone in the process.

But black Americans have never been vanquished, as this account clearly indicates. They have consistently reminded the nation of its founding principles, while simultaneously creating the passageways for their survival and coping with the double consciousness that Du Bois identified. As a minority group, they have adhered–with some exceptions–to the possibilities of change within the nation but have remained ever conscious of the need to struggle to achieve it. Langston Hughes captured their sustaining spirit:

> Well, the poor old Negro's
> Had a hard, hard time–
> But he still ain't bowed his head.
> Yes, the poor old Negro's
> Had a hard time–
> Yet he sure ain't dead. . . .

Notes

1. James W. Vander Zander, *Race Relations in Transition* (New York: Random House, 1965), 28.
2. Bartley, *The New South*, 172–173.
3. Reprinted in Gates and McKay, *African American Literature*, 1327.
4. Larry Neal, "The Black Arts Movement," in Mitchell, *Within the Circle*, 184.
5. Kelley, *Race Rebels*, 164.
6. Meier et al., *Black Protest Thought*, 287.
7. James Baldwin, *The Fire Next Time* (New York: Dell, 1962), 141.

8. Meier et al., *Black Protest Thought*, 283; Tushnet, *Making Civil Rights Law*, 232-233.
9. Bloom, *Class, Race, and the Civil Rights Movement*, 95.
10. Ibid., 97.
11. Ibid., 108.
12. Ibid., 106.
13. Ibid., 111.
14. Tushnet, *Making Civil Rights Law*, 265.
15. David Garrow, *Bearing the Cross, Martin Luther King, Jr., and the Southern Christian Leadership Conference* (New York: Vintage, 1988), 12.
16. Taylor Branch, *Parting the Waters: America in the King Years, 1954-1963* (New York: Simon and Schuster, 1988), 130.
17. Ibid., 149.
18. Garrow, *Bearing the Cross*, 60-61.
19. Ibid., 77.
20. Bernice Johnson Reagon, "Women as Culture Carriers in the Civil Rights Movement: Fannie Lou Hamer," in Vicki L. Crawford, Jacqueline Anne Rouse, and Barbara Woods, eds., *Women in the Civil Rights Movement: Trailblazers and Torchbearers, 1941-1965* (Bloomington: Indiana University Press, 1993), 203.
21. Garrow, *Bearing the Cross*, unpaginated.
22. Ibid., 89.
23. James Washington, *Conversations with God: Two Centuries of Prayers by African-Americans* (New York: HarperCollins, 1994), 190.
24. Harvard Sitkoff, *The Struggle for Black Equality, 1954-1980* (New York: Hill and Wang, 1981), 61.
25. Young, *An Easy Burden*, 151.
26. Ibid., 175.
27. David Chappell, *Inside Agitators: White Southerners in the Civil Rights Movement* (Baltimore: Johns Hopkins University Press, 1994), 71.
28. John Dittmer, *Local People: The Struggle for Civil Rights in Mississippi* (Urbana: University of Illinois Press, 1995), 67.
29. Ibid., 69.
30. Walter A. Jackson, "White Liberal Intellectuals, Civil Rights and Gradualism, 1954-60," in Brian Ward and Tony Badger, eds., *The Making of Martin Luther King and the Civil Rights Movement* (New York: New York University Press, 1996), 96-114.
31. Branch, *Parting the Waters*, 195.
32. Sitkoff, *The Struggle for Black Equality*, 63-64.
33. Garrow, *Bearing the Cross*, 33.
34. Pfeffer, *A. Philip Randolph*, 184.
35. Clayborne Carson, *In Struggle: SNCC and the Black Awakening of the 1960s* (Cambridge: Harvard University Press, 1981), 9-10.
36. Carson, *In Struggle*, 23; Garrow, *Bearing the Cross*, 132.
37. Garrow, *Bearing the Cross*, 158.
38. Chappell, *Inside Agitators*, 131.
39. Garrow, *Bearing the Cross*, 226.
40. Martin Luther King, Jr., *Why We Can't Wait* (New York: Penguin Books, 1964), 76-95.
41. Sitkoff, *The Struggle for Black Equality*, 142.
42. Garrow, *Bearing the Cross*, 259.
43. Bloom, *Class, Race, and the Civil Rights Movement*, 177-178.
44. Bartley, *The New South*, 338.
45. Pfeffer, *A. Philip Randolph*, 246.
46. Ibid., 255.
47. Meier et al., *Black Protest Thought*, 349-350.
48. James H. Cone, *Martin and Malcolm and America: A Dream or a Nightmare* (Maryknoll, NY: Orbis Books, 1991), 38.

49. Ibid., 110.
50. Ibid., 116.
51. Ibid., 119.
52. Steven Lawson, *Black Ballots: Voting Rights in the South, 1944–1969* (New York: Columbia University Press, 1976), 298.
53. Carson, *In Struggle*, 110.
54. Ibid., 125.
55. Sitkoff, *The Struggle for Black Equality*, 185.
56. David Levering Lewis, "Martin Luther King, Jr., and the Promise of Nonviolent Populism," in Franklin and Meier, *Black Leaders of the Twentieth Century*, 291.
57. Sitkoff, *The Struggle for Black Equality*, 193.
58. Bartley, *The New South*, 341.
59. Lewis, "Martin Luther King," in Franklin and Meier, *Black Leaders of the Twentieth Century*, 292.
60. Bartley, *The New South*, 341.
61. Ibid., 342.
62. Ibid., 343.
63. Garrow, *Bearing the Cross*, 551–558.
64. Young, *An Easy Burden*, 332.

Further Reading

The following list of suggested readings is designed to introduce the reader to some of the major and more recently published secondary works on the history of black Americans. The emphasis is on the works that I found particularly useful, that pay significant attention to the evolution of black history, and to a much lesser extent the ones that describe the larger society's attitudes toward blacks. It is not intended to be exhaustive; I include only those works that should be readily accessible and that inform the themes that I have addressed in this volume.

GENERAL WORKS

There are few general works that address the historical experiences of blacks since 1863 exclusively. Most cover the entire span of black history with varying degrees of emphases. Some of the best ones are Rayford W. Logan, *The Negro in the United States* (New York, 1957); Lerone Bennett, *Before the Mayflower* (revised, Chicago, 1987); Benjamin Quarles, *The Negro in the Making of America* (New York, 1964); August Meier and Elliott Rudwick, *From Plantation to Ghetto*, 3rd edition (New York, 1976); Nathan Huggins, Martin Kilson, Daniel M. Fox, eds., *Key Issues in the Afro-American Experience*, vol. ii (New York, 1971); and Mary Frances Berry and John Blassingame, *Long Memory: The Black Experience in America* (New York, 1982). The most enduring and extensive coverage of the black past is John Hope Franklin and Alfred Moss, Jr.,

From Slavery to Freedom: A History of African Americans, 7th edition (New York, 1994). The three major works that emphasize the history of women are Jacqueline Jones, *Labor of Love, Labor of Sorrow: Black Women, Work, and the Family, From Slavery to the Present* (New York, 1985); Paula Giddings, *When and Where I Enter. The Impact of Black Women on Race and Sex in America*, 3rd edition (New York, 1988); and Darlene Clark Hine, Wilma King, Linda Reed, eds., *"We Specialize in the Wholly Impossible": A Reader in Black Women's History* (New York, 1995). Indispensable studies for understanding the lives of specific leaders include Leon Litwack and August Meier, eds., *Black Leaders of the Nineteenth Century* (Urbana, 1988); Howard Rabinowitz, ed., *Southern Black Leaders of the Reconstruction Era* (Urbana, 1982); and John Hope Franklin and August Meier, eds., *Black Leaders of the Twentieth Century* (Urbana, 1982).

There are a number of important books on aspects of black literary and cultural production. These include Lawrence Levine, *Black Culture and Black Consciousness: Afro-American Folk Thought from Slavery to Freedom* (New York, 1977); Eileen Southern, *The Music of Black Americans: A History* (Second Edition, New York, 1983); Mel Watkins, *On the Real Side: Laughing, Lying, and Signifying – the Underground Tradition of African-American Humor* (New York, 1994); Arnold Shaw, *Black Popular Music in America: The Singers, Songwriters and Musicians Who Pioneered the Sounds of American Music* (New York, 1986); Blyden Jackson, *A History of Afro-American Literature: The Long Beginning, 1746–1895*, vol. 1, (Baton Rouge, 1989); Henry Louis Gates, Jr., and Nellie Y. McKay, general eds., *The Norton Anthology of African American Literature* (New York, 1997).

CONSTRUCTING FREEDOM

The literature on the ways in which blacks organized their lives after freedom came is quite extensive. One of the best studies of the early years of freedom is Leon Litwack, *Been in the Storm So Long: The Aftermath of Slavery* (New York, 1979). Eric Foner, *Reconstruction: America's Unfinished Revolution, 1863–1877* (New York, 1988) is an excellent work that discusses the struggle by blacks to construct independent lives and the obstacles they confronted. An older but still valuable work is W. E. B. Du Bois, *Black Reconstruction in America* (New York, 1935). See also Eric Foner, *Nothing but Freedom: Emancipation and Its Legacy* (Baton Rouge, 1983). Two valuable historiographical essays are Armstead L. Robinson, "Beyond the Realm of Social Consensus: New Meanings of Reconstruction for American History," *Journal of American History*, 68 (September 1981): 276–297, and Eric Foner, "Reconstruction Revisited," *Reviews in American History*, 10 (December 1982): 82–100.

Among the works that address the economic status of blacks after emancipation and their efforts to improve their condition are Roger L. Ransom and Richard Sutch, *One Kind of Freedom: The Economic Consequences of Emancipation* (New York, 1977); Gerald D. Jaynes, *Branches Without Roots: The Genesis of the Black Working Class in the American South, 1862–1882* (New York, 1986); Claude F. Oubre, *Forty Acres and a Mule: The Freedmen's Bureau and Black Landownership* (Baton Rouge, 1973); Loren Schweninger, *Black Property Owners in the South, 1790–1915* (Urbana, 1990); Robert Higgs, *Competition and Coercion: Blacks in the American Economy, 1865–1914* (London, 1977); Carl Osthaus, *Freedmen, Philanthropy, and Fraud: A History of the Freedman's Savings Bank* (Urbana, 1976); Jay R. Mandle, *The Roots of Black Poverty: The Southern Plantation Economy after the Civil War* (Durham, 1978); Peter Rachleff, *Black Labor in Richmond, 1865–1900* (Urbana, 1984); Seymour Drescher and Frank McGlynn, *The Meaning of Freedom: Economics, Politics, and Culture after Slavery* (Pittsburgh, 1992); and Julie Saville, *The Work of Reconstruction: From Slave Labor to Wage Laborer in South Carolina, 1860–1870* (New York, 1994).

The political struggles after slavery ended have been much less studied, but some important works exist. The most outstanding is Thomas Holt, *Black Over White: Negro Political Leadership in South Carolina during Reconstruction* (Urbana, 1977). A good collection of essays on black leadership is Howard Rabinowitz, ed., *Southern Black Leaders of the Reconstruction Era* (Urbana, 1982). See also Charles Vincent, *Black Legislators in Louisiana during Reconstruction* (Baton Rouge, 1976); Elizabeth Balanoff, "Negro Leaders in the North Carolina General Assembly, July 1868–February 1872," *North Carolina Historical Review*, 49 (Winter 1972): 22–55; Alwyn Barr, "Black Legislators of Reconstruction Texas," *Civil War History*, 32 (December 1986): 340–352; William C. Hine, "Black Politicians in Reconstruction Charleston, South Carolina: A Collective Study," *Journal of Southern History*, 34 (May 1968): 200–213. For biographies of Robert Smalls, see Okon Edet Uya, *From Slavery to Political Service: Robert Smalls, 1839–1915* (New York, 1971); and Edward A. Miller, Jr., *Gullah Statesman: Robert Smalls from Slavery to Congress, 1839–1915* (Columbia, 1995).

The roles of the church in freedom are the focus of William E. Montgomery, *Under Their Own Vine and Fig Tree: The African-American Church in the South 1865–1900* (Baton Rouge, 1993). For a close examination of the ways in which Methodist clergymen helped the newly freed create new lives, see Reginald F. Hilderbrand, *The Times Were Strange and Stirring: Methodist Preachers and the Crisis of Emancipation* (Durham, 1995). Other significant studies are Clarence E. Walker, *A Rock in a Weary Land: The Methodist Episcopal Church during the Civil War and Reconstruction* (Baton Rouge, 1982); Joe M. Richardson, *Christian Reconstruction: The American Missionary Association and Southern*

Blacks, 1861-1890 (Athens, 1986); Robert L. Hall, "'Yonder Come Day': Religious Dimensions of the Transition from Slavery to Freedom in Florida," *Florida Historical Quarterly*, 65 (April 1987): 411-420; and J. Carleton Hayden, "After the War: The Mission and Growth of the Episcopal Church Among Blacks in the South, 1865-1877," *Historical Magazine of the Protestant Episcopal Church*, 42 (December 1973): 403-427. Two studies of efforts by the freed persons and others to promote literacy are Robert C. Morris, *Reading, 'Riting, and Reconstruction: The Education of Freedmen in the South, 1861-1870* (Chicago, 1976); and James D. Anderson, *The Education of Blacks in the South, 1860-1935* (Chapel Hill, 1988).

The movement of blacks within the South and ultimately to Kansas is discussed by William Cohen, *At Freedom's Edge, Black Mobility and the Southern White Quest for Racial Control, 1861-1915* (Baton Rouge, 1991). The exodus to Kansas is treated in Nell Irvin Painter, *Exodusters: Black Migration to Kansas after Reconstruction* (New York, 1977). See also Thomas Cox, *Blacks in Topeka, Kansas 1865-1915: A Social History* (Baton Rouge, 1982).

MAINTAINING WHITE SUPREMACY

The rise of segregation and the passage of Jim Crow laws represent important stages in the history of race relations. The literature is vast and controversial. An early attempt to trace the evolution of Jim Crow is C. Vann Woodard, *Origins of the New South, 1877-1913* (Baton Rouge, 1951); Woodward, *The Strange Career of Jim Crow*, rev. ed. (New York, 1965) is a more specialized and influential study of this question. Contrasting points of view are expressed in Howard Rabinowitz, *Race Relations in the Urban South, 1865-1890* (New York, 1978); John W. Cell, *The Highest Stage of White Supremacy: The Origins of Segregation in South Africa and the American South* (Cambridge, 1982); George M. Fredrickson, *White Supremacy: A Comparative Study in American and South African History* (New York, 1981); and Edward L. Ayers, *The Promise of the New South: Life After Reconstruction* (New York, 1992). An interesting and important study of the ideological underpinnings of white supremacy is Joel Williamson, *The Crucible of Race: Black-White Relations in the American South Since Emancipation* (New York, 1984). Jonathan Wiener, *Social Origins of the New South, 1880-1965* (Baton Rouge, 1978) addresses the problem as well but from a different perspective. Issues of gender are treated in Glenda Elizabeth Gilmore, *Gender and Jim Crow: Women and the Politics of White Supremacy in North Carolina, 1896-1920* (Chapel Hill, 1996). Segregation in the agencies of the federal government is analyzed by Desmond King, *Separate and Unequal: Black Americans and the US Federal Government* (Oxford,

1955). An impressive study of Jim Crow at the local level is Neil R. McMillen, *Dark Journey: Black Mississippians in the Age of Jim Crow* (Urbana, 1989).

SEARCHING FOR DIRECTION

The debates among blacks have received much scholarly attention. One of the earliest and best general studies is August Meier, *Negro Thought in America, 1880–1915: Racial Ideologies in the Age of Booker T. Washington* (Ann Arbor, 1963). In order to obtain Booker T. Washington's ideas of himself and his times, consult his *Up from Slavery: An Autobiography* (Garden City, 1901). See also Louis Harlan, ed., *The Booker T. Washington Papers* (Urbana, 1972–1985). Harlan has also written a fine two-volume biography of Washington. The first volume is *Booker T. Washington: The Making of a Black Leader, 1856–1901* (New York, 1972); and the second is *Booker T. Washington: The Wizard of Tuskegee, 1901–1915* (New York, 1983).

W. E. B. Du Bois was one of the most prolific writers of his times. His *The Souls of Black Folk, Essays and Sketches* (Chicago, 1903) and his autobiography, *Dusk to Dawn, An Essay Toward the Autobiography of a Race* (New York, 1940) provide his views on various issues. Du Bois has been the subject of several biographies. Francis L. Broderick published *W. E. B. Du Bois: Negro Leader in Time of Crisis* (Stanford, 1959); Arnold Rampersad focused on ideas in *The Art and Imagination of W. E. B. Du Bois* (Cambridge, 1976); and David Levering Lewis discussed the first half century of Du Bois's life in *W. E. B. Du Bois, Biography of a Race, 1868–1919* (New York, 1993).

The emigration issue is elucidated by Edwin S. Redkey, *Black Exodus: Black Nationalists and Back-to-Africa Movements 1890–1910* (New Haven, 1969). The life of Henry McNeal Turner, an ardent advocate of emigration, is treated in Stephen Ward Angell, *Bishop Henry McNeal Turner and African-American Religion in the South* (Knoxville, 1992). Emigrationism is also the subject of several essays in Okon Edet Uya, *Black Brotherhood: Afro-Americans and Africa* (Lexington, 1971). The odyssey of those who established independent settlements in the United States is detailed in Kenneth Marvin Hamilton, *Black Towns and Profit: Promotion and Development in the Trans-Appalachian West, 1877–1915* (Urbana, 1991).

The appeal of socialism is examined in Paula F. Pfeffer, *A. Philip Randolph: Pioneer of the Civil Rights Movement* (Baton Rouge, 1990). Populism and interracial alliances receive the attention of Margaret Carnavon, *Populism* (New York, 1981); and Lawrence Goodwyn, *Democratic Promise: The Populist Movement in America* (New York, 1976). There are also useful biographies of several lesser known but important personages. See Emma Lou Thornbrough, *T. Thomas Fortune: Militant Journalist* (Chicago, 1972); Stephen R. Fox, *The Guardian of Boston: William Monroe Trotter* (New York, 1971); and Wilson J. Moses, *Alexander Crummell: A Study of Civilization and Discontent* (New York, 1989).

UPLIFTING THE RACE

The most provocative study of the ideology of racial uplift is Kevin K. Gaines, *Uplifting the Race: Black Leadership, Politics, and Culture in the Twentieth Century* (Chapel Hill, 1996). Contemporary ideas on this question may be found in Anna Julia Cooper, *Voices from the South* (New York, reprint 1988); W. E. B. Du Bois, *The Philadelphia Negro* (New York, reprint 1967); William H. Ferris, *The African Abroad, or His Evolution in Western Civilization, Tracing His Development under Caucasian Milieu*, 2 vols. (New Haven, 1913).

The role of women in racial uplift has been fairly well studied. See Cynthia Neverdon-Morton, *Afro-American Women of the South and the Advancement of the Race, 1895–1925* (Knoxville, 1989); Evelyn Brooks Higginbotham, *Righteous Discontent: The Women's Movement in the Black Baptist Church, 1880–1920* (Cambridge, 1993); and Beverly Washington Jones, *Quest for Equality: The Life and Writings of Mary Eliza Church Terrell, 1863–1954* (Brooklyn, 1990).

Among the studies of organizations designed to enhance the welfare of blacks are Nancy Weiss, *The National Urban League, 1910–1940* (New York, 1974); Mary W. Ovington, *How the National Association of Colored People Began* (New York, 1914); Langston Hughes, *Fight for Freedom: The Story of the NAACP* (New York, 1962); and Charles F. Kellogg, *NAACP* (Baltimore, 1967).

The efforts to create economic and other forms of uplift are detailed in Willard B. Gatewood, *Aristocrats of Color: The Black Elite, 1880–1920* (Bloomington, 1990); Walter Weare, *Black Business in the New South: A Social History of the North Carolina Mutual Life Insurance Company* (Urbana, 1973); John Sibley Butler, *Entrepreneurship and Self-Help Among Black Americans: A Reconsideration of Race and Economics* (Albany, 1991). Useful studies of educational advancement include Vincent P. Franklin and James D. Anderson, eds., *New Perspectives on Black Educational History* (Boston, 1978); Vincent P. Franklin, *The Education of Black Philadelphia: The Social and Educational History of a Minority Community, 1900–1950* (Philadelphia, 1979); and James D. Anderson, *The Education of Blacks in the South, 1860–1935* (Chapel Hill, 1988).

CONSTRUCTING AN IDENTITY

There is no general study of the construction of a black racial identity, but information may be gleaned from several authorities and documentary collections. Ethiopianism is covered in J. Mutero Chirinje, *Ethiopianism and Afro-Americans in Southern Africa, 1883–1916* (Baton Rouge, 1987); George M. Frederickson, *Black Liberation: A Comparative History of Black Ideologies in the United States and South Africa* (New York, 1995); Albert Raboteau, *A Fire in the Bones: Reflections on African-American Religious History* (Boston, 1995); and James T. Campbell, *Songs of Solomon: The African Methodist Episcopal Church in the United States and South Africa* (New York, 1995). Black American missionary impulses and activities in Africa are discussed in Walter Williams, *Black Americans and the Evangelization of Africa, 1877–1900* (Madison, 1982); and St. Clair Drake, *The Redemption of Africa and Black Religion* (Chicago, 1970); Sylvia Jacobs, ed., *Black Americans and the Missionary Movement in Africa* (Westport, 1982).

Modern black nationalism is investigated in Wilson Jeremiah Moses, *The Golden Age of Black Nationalism, 1850–1925* (Hamden, 1978). An important analysis of black nationalist currents and the search for a black identity is Sterling Stuckey, *Slave Culture: Nationalist Theory and the Foundations of Black America* (New York, 1987); and Stuckey's *Going Through the Storm: The Influence of African American Art in History* (Oxford, 1994) is a fine collection of essays on the evolution of African-American culture. The Garvey movement remains a subject of much interest. An early but essentially unsympathetic treatment of Marcus Garvey and the movement is E. David Cronon, *Black Moses: The Story of Marcus Garvey and the Universal Negro Improvement Association* (Madison, 1955). An insider's view of the movement is presented in Amy Jacques Garvey, ed., *Philosophy and Opinions of Marcus Garvey*, 2 vols. (New York, 1969). A useful discussion of one aspect of Garveyism is Randolph Burkett, *Garveyism as a Religious Movement: The Institutionalization of a Black Civil Religion* (Methuen, 1978). Tony Martin places Garvey in the context of the African diaspora in *Race First: The Ideological and Organizational Struggles of Marcus Garvey and the Universal Negro Improvement Association* (Westport, 1976), while Judith Stein emphasizes class relations in *The World of Marcus Garvey: Race and Class in Modern Society* (Baton Rouge, 1986). An important study of Garveyism at the local level is Emory Tolbert, *The UNIA and Black Los Angeles: Ideology and Community in the American Garvey Movement* (Los Angeles, 1980). The most comprehensive collection of documents dealing with Garvey and the UNIA is in Robert A. Hill, ed., *The Marcus Garvey and Universal Negro Improvement Association Papers*, 10 vols. (Berkeley, 1983–1994). A shorter but very useful collection of the ideas of Washington, Du Bois, Garvey, and A. Philip Randolph can be found in Cary D. Wintz, ed., *African American Political Thought, 1890–1930* (New York, 1996).

THE GENERATION OF 1917

Two overviews of the history of violence in the United States are Paul A. Gilje, *Rioting in America* (Bloomington, 1996); and Herbert Shapiro, *White Violence and Black Resistance: From Reconstruction to Montgomery* (Amherst, 1988). For white violence directed at blacks, see Melinda Meek Hennessey, "Racial violence during Reconstruction: The 1876 riots in Charleston and Cainhoy," *South Carolina Historical Magazine*, 86:2 (1985): 100–112; and by the same author, "Race and Violence in Reconstruction New Orleans: The 1868 Riot," *Louisiana History*, 20:1 (1979): 77–91; Altina L. Waller, "Community, Class and Race in the Memphis Riot of 1866," *Journal of Social History*, 18 (1984): 233–246; and Bobby L. Lovet, "Memphis Riots: White Reactions to Blacks in Memphis, May 1865–July 1866," *Tennessee Historical Quarterly*, 38 (Spring 1979): 9–33. Admirable book-length accounts of specific riots include Roberta Senechal, *The Sociogenesis of a Race Riot: Springfield, Illinois, in 1908* (Urbana, 1990); Elliott M. Rudwick, *Race Riot at East St. Louis, July 2, 1917* (Carbondale, 1964); and William M. Tuttle, *Race Riot: Chicago in the Red Summer of 1919* (New York, 1970). Related studies are John D. Weaver, *The Brownsville Raid* (New York, 1970); and Garna L. Christian, *Black Soldiers in Jim Crow Texas, 1899–1917* (College Station, 1995). The best study of lynching is W. Fitzhugh Brundage, *Lynching in the New South: Georgia and Virginia, 1880–1930* (Urbana, 1993). See also George C. Wright, *Racial Violence in Kentucky, 1865–1940: Lynchings, Mob Rule, and 'Legal Lynchings'* (Baton Rouge, 1990). Resistance and responses by blacks are treated in Ann Lane, *The Brownsville Affair: National Crisis and Black Reaction* (Port Washington, 1971); August Meier and Elliott Rudwick, "The Boycott Movement against Jim Crow Street Cars in the South, 1900–1906"; and by the same authors, "The Origins of Non Violent Direct Action in Afro-American Protest: A Note on Historical Discontinuities," chapters in *Along the Color Line: Explorations in the Black Experience* (Urbana, 1976).

The attitude of blacks to World War I is discussed by Mark Ellis, "'Closing Ranks' and 'Seeking Honors': W. E. B. Du Bois in World War I," *Journal of American History*, 79:1 (1992): 96–124; William Jordan, "The Damnable Dilemma: African American Accommodation and Protest During World War I," *Journal of American History*, 81:4 (1995): 1562–1583; and Mark Ellis, "W. E. B. Du Bois and the Formation of Black Opinion in World War I: A Commentary on 'The Damnable Dilemma,'" *Journal of American History*, 81:4 (1995): 1584–1590. See also Arthur E. Barbeau and Florette Henri, *Unknown Soldiers: Black American Troops in World War I* (Philadelphia, 1971).

INTELLECTUAL AND CULTURAL LIFE

The historiography of the period is examined by Earl E. Thorpe, *Black Historians: A Critique* (New York, 1971); August Meier and Elliott Rudwick, *Black History and the Historical Profession, 1915–1980* (Urbana, 1986); and Darlene Clark Hine, ed., *The State of Afro-American History: Past, Present, and Future* (Baton Rouge, 1986). Three biographies of prominent historians are John Hope Franklin, *George Washington Williams: A Biography* (Chicago, 1985); Jacqueline Goggin, *Carter G. Woodson: A Life in Black History* (Baton Rouge, 1993); and Kenneth Janken, *Rayford W. Logan and the Dilemma of the African-American Intellectual* (Amherst, 1993).

The literary history of the period preceding the Harlem Renaissance is the subject of Dickson Bruce, *Black American Writing From the Nadir: The Evolution of a Literary Tradition, 1877–1915* (Baton Rouge, 1989). Hazel Carby discusses women writers in *Reconstructing Womanhood: The Emergence of the Afro-American Woman Novelist* (New York, 1987); Alain Locke, ed., *The New Negro: Voices of the Harlem Renaissance* (repr., New York, 1992) is the primary text of that literary movement. General but contrasting histories of the Renaissance include Nathan I. Huggins, *Harlem Renaissance* (New York, 1971); David L. Lewis, *When Harlem was in Vogue* (New York, 1981); and Cary D. Wintz, *Black Culture and the Harlem Renaissance* (Houston, 1988). The relationship between blacks and whites during the movement is ably addressed by George Hutchinson, *The Harlem Renaissance in Black and White* (Cambridge, 1995).

For studies of various aspects of the Renaissance, see Samuel A. Floyd, Jr., ed., *Black Music in the Harlem Renaissance: A Collection of Essays* (Knoxville, 1993); James Lincoln Collier, *The Making of Jazz: A Comprehensive History* (Boston, 1978); Marcia M. Mathews, *Henry Ossawa Tanner: American Artist* (Chicago, 1969); and Ann Douglas, *Terrible Honesty: Mongrel Manhattan in the 1920s* (New York, 1995). For firsthand accounts of the movement, consult Langston Hughes, *The Big Sea* (New York, 1940); James Weldon Johnson, *Black Manhattan* (New York, 1930); Arna Bontemps, ed., *The Harlem Renaissance Remembered* (New York, 1972); and Claude McKay, *A Long Way from Home* (New York, 1937). For excerpts from the literature of the period, see David Levering Lewis, *The Portable Harlem Renaissance Reader* (New York, 1994). Several luminaries of the Renaissance have been the subject of biographical studies. Among the best are Wayne F. Cooper, *Claude McKay: Rebel Sojourner in the Harlem Renaissance* (Baton Rouge, 1986);

Arnold Rampersad, *The Life of Langston Hughes, vol. 1: 1902–1941, I, Too, Sing America* and *The Life of Langston Hughes, vol. 2: 1941–1967, I Dream a World* (New York, 1986, 1988); Robert E. Hemenway, *Zora Neale Hurston: A Literary Biography* (Urbana, 1978); Blanche Ferguson, *Countee Cullen and the Harlem Renaissance* (New York, 1966); Cheryl A. Wall, *Women of the Harlem Renaissance* (Bloomington, 1995); Thadious Davis, *Nella Larsen, Novelist of the Harlem Renaissance: A Woman's Life Unveiled* (Baton Rouge, 1994); Amy Helene Kirschke, *Aaron Douglas: Art, Race, and the Harlem Renaissance* (Jackson, 1995); and Martin Bauml Duberman, *Paul Robeson: A Biography* (New York, 1989). A critical view of the Renaissance is presented in Harold Cruse, *The Crisis of the Negro Intellectual: A Historical Analysis of the Failure of Black Leadership* (New York, 1967).

A PEOPLE IN MOTION

The movement of black people within the country during the twentieth century has produced a distinguished historiography. For two collections of essays that treat aspects of the Great Migration, see Joe William Trotter, ed., *The Great Migration in Historical Perspective: New Dimensions of Race, Class and Gender* (Bloomington, 1991); and Alferdteen Harrison, ed., *Black Exodus: The Great Migration from the American South* (Jackson, 1991). Fine studies of migration include Peter Gottlieb, *Making Their Own Way: Southern Blacks' Migration to Pittsburgh, 1916–30* (Urbana, 1987); James R. Grossman, *Land of Hope: Chicago, Black Southerners, and the Great Migration* (Chicago, 1989); Carole Marks, *Farewell—We're Good and Gone: The Great Black Migration* (Bloomington, 1989); Earl Lewis, *In Their Own Interests: Race, Class and Power in Twentieth Century Norfolk* (Berkeley, 1991); and Nicolas Lemann, *The Promised Land: The Great Black Migration and How It Changed America* (New York, 1991).

Three early studies of the process of urbanization are Allan H. Spear, *Black Chicago: The Making of a Negro Ghetto, 1890–1920* (Chicago, 1967); Gilbert Osofsky, *Harlem: The Making of a Negro Ghetto: 1890–1920*, 2nd edition (New York, 1971); and Kenneth L. Kusmer, *A Ghetto Takes Shape: Black Cleveland, 1870–1930* (Urbana, 1976). More recent studies have employed the concept of proletarianization as opposed to ghettoization to describe the urbanization process. See two books by Joe William Trotter, Jr., *Black Milwaukee: The Making of an Industrial Proletariat, 1915–1945* (Urbana, 1988), and *Coal, Class, and Color, Blacks in Southern West Virginia, 1915-32* (Urbana, 1990). Richard W. Thomas, *Life for Us Is What We Make It: Building Black Community in Detroit, 1915–1945* (Bloomington, 1992) is another study employing this conceptual framework. For the experiences of women, see Gretchen

Lemke-Santangelo, *Abiding Courage: African American Migrant Women and the East Bay Community* (Chapel Hill, 1996).

The attempts at unionization are described by William H. Harris in *The Harder We Run: Black Workers Since the Civil War* (New York, 1982); and Julius Jacobson, ed., *The Negro and the American Labor Movement* (Garden City, 1968). The story of the Brotherhood of Sleeping Car Porters is told in William H. Harris, *Keeping the Faith: A. Philip Randolph, Milton P. Webster, and the Brotherhood of Sleeping Car Porters, 1925-1937* (Urbana, 1977). Two biographical studies of A. Philip Randolph are Jervis Anderson, *A. Philip Randolph: A Biographical Portrait* (New York, 1972); and Paula Pfeffer, *A. Philip Randolph: Pioneer of the Civil Rights Movement* (Baton Rouge, 1990).

Intellectual, literary, and scientific developments are discussed in Henry Allen Bullock, *A History of Negro Education in the South: From 1619 to the Present* (New York, 1970); Kenneth Janken, *Rayford W. Logan and the Dilemma of the African-American Intellectual* (Amherst, 1993); Angelyn Mitchell, ed., *Within the Circle: An Anthology of African American Literary Criticism From the Harlem Renaissance to the Present* (Durham, 1994); Jerry Gafio Watts, *Heroism and the Black Intellectual: Ralph Ellison, Politics, and Afro-American Intellectual Life* (Chapel Hill, 1994); David Leeming, *James Baldwin: A Biography* (New York, 1994); and William M. Banks, *Black Intellectuals: Race and Responsibility in American Life* (New York, 1996). Among the valuable studies of the lives of important scientific personages are Kenneth R. Manning, *Black Apollo of Science: The Life of Ernest Everett Just* (New York, 1983); Linda O. McMurry, *George Washington Carver: Scientist and Symbol* (New York, 1981); and Spencie Love, *One Blood: The Death and Resurrection of Charles R. Drew* (Durham, 1996).

Blacks in the cinema have been the subject of three important books: Thomas Cripps, *Slow Fade to Black: The Negro in American Film, 1900-1942* (repr. 1993, New York, 1977); Donald Bogle, *Toms, Coons, Mulattoes, Mammies, and Bucks: An Interpretive History of Blacks in American Films* (New York, 1989); Thomas Cripps, *Making Movies Black: The Hollywood Message Movie from World War II to the Civil Rights Era* (New York, 1993). For theatre, see Doris Abramson, *Negro Playwrights in the American Theatre, 1925-1959* (New York, 1969); Loften Mitchell, *Black Drama: The Story of the American Negro in the Theatre* (New York, 1967); Errol Hill, ed., *The Theatre of Black Americans: A Collection of Critical Essays* (repr. New York, 1987); and Jacqui Malone, *Steppin' on the Blues: The Visible Rhythms of African American Dance* (Urbana, 1996).

For blacks in sports, see especially Arthur Ashe, Jr., *A Hard Road to Glory: A History of the African-American Athlete, 1619-1945*, 2 vols. (New York, 1988). The experiences of blacks in boxing is described in Jeffrey T. Sammons, *Beyond the Ring, The Role of Boxing in American*

Society (Urbana, 1988). There are two major studies of Jack Johnson: Al-Tony Gilmore, *Bad Nigger: The National Impact of Jack Johnson* (Port Washington, 1975) and Randy Roberts, *Papa Jack: Jack Johnson and the Era of White Hopes* (New York, 1983). Jackie Robinson's story in baseball is told by Jules Tiegel, *Baseball's Great Experiment: Jackie Robinson and His Legacy* (New York, 1983).

BUILDING ORGANIZATIONS, WEATHERING STORMS

There are numerous studies of black organizations. The church has received its fair share of scholarly attention, and the best works include E. Franklin Frazier, *The Negro Church in America* (New York, 1974); Milton C. Sernet, *Black Religion and American Evangelicalism* (Metuchen, 1975); Gayraud S. Wilmore, *Black Religion and Black Radicalism* (Maryknoll, 1983); Gayraud S. Wilmore, ed., *African American Religious Studies: An Interdisciplinary Anthology* (Durham, 1989); Hans A. Baer and Merrill Singer, *African-American Religion in the Twentieth Century: Varieties of Protest and Accommodation* (Knoxville, 1992); C. Eric Lincoln and Lawrence H. Mamiya, *The Black Church in the African-American Experience* (Durham, 1990); and Cheryl J. Sanders, *Saints in Exile: The Holiness-Pentecostal Experience in African American Religion and Culture* (New York, 1996). Father Divine and the Peace Mission he founded are the subject of Robert Weisbrot, *Father Divine and the Struggle for Race Equality* (Urbana, 1983); and Jill Watts, *Harlem U.S.A.: The Father Divine Story* (Berkeley, 1992).

The Muslims have been ably treated by several scholars. Two of the earliest include E.U. Essien-Udom, *Black Nationalism: A Search for Identity in America* (Chicago, 1962); and C. Eric Lincoln, *The Black Muslims in America* (rev. ed., Boston, 1973). Three more recent works of varying depth are Clifton E. Marsh, *From Black Muslims to Muslims: The Transition from Separatism to Islam 1930–1984* (Metuchen, 1984); Martha E. Lee, *The Nation of Islam: An American Millenarian Movement* (Lewiston, 1988); and Mattias Gardell, *In the Name of Elijah Muhammad: Louis Farrakhan and the Nation of Islam* (Durham, 1996). A fine biography of Elijah Muhammad is Claude Andrew Clegg III, *An Original Man: The Life and Times of Elijah Muhammad* (New York, 1997).

The important roles that women played in building institutions is treated in several works already cited. See, however, Stephanie Shaw, *What A Woman Ought to Be and to Do: Black Professional Women Workers During the Jim Crow Era* (Chicago, 1996); Darlene Clark Hine, ed., *Black Women in United States History*, 16 vols. (Brooklyn, 1990); and Tera W. Hunter, *To 'Joy My Freedom: Southern Black Women's Lives and Labors after the Civil War* (Cambridge, 1997). Somewhat contrasting views of the impact of the Great Depression and black responses are presented in Howard Sitkoff, *A New Deal for Blacks: The Emergence of Civil Rights as a National Issue* (New York, 1978) and Nancy Weiss, *Farewell to the Party of Lincoln: Black Politics in the Age of F. D. R.* (Princeton, 1983). Other significant works include Raymond Wolters, *Negroes and the Great Depression: The Problem of Economic Recovery* (Westport, 1970); John H. Kirby, *Black Americans in the Roosevelt Era: Liberalism and Race* (Knoxville, 1980); Nancy L. Grant, *TVA and Black Americans: Planning for the Status Quo* (Philadelphia, 1980); and Patricia Sullivan, *Days of Hope: Race and Democracy in the New Deal Era* (Chapel Hill, 1996).

LOOKING OUTWARD

The best general study of black Americans and their impact on the foreign policy of the United States is Brenda Gayle Plummer, *Rising Wind: Black Americans and US Foreign Affairs, 1935-1960* (Chapel Hill, 1996). Three more specialized works are Sylvia M. Jacobs, *The African Nexus: Black American Perspectives on the European Partitioning of Africa, 1880-1920* (Westport, 1981); Elliott P. Skinner, *African Americans and US Policy Toward Africa, 1850-1924* (Washington, 1992); and Penny M. Von Eschen, *Black Americans and Anticolonialism 1937-1957* (Ithaca, 1997). Black American ties with and impact on African societies are explored in Okon Edet Uya, *Black Brotherhood: Afro-Americans and Africa* (Lexington, 1971); Hollis R. Lynch, *Black American Radicals and the Liberation of Africa: The Council on African Affairs, 1937-1955* (Ithaca, 1978); Sidney Lemelle and Robin Kelley, eds., *Imagining Home, Class, Culture and Nationalism in the African Diaspora* (New York, 1994); George Shepperson, "Notes on Negro American Influences on the Emergence of African Nationalism," *Journal of African History*, 1 (1960): 299-312; and Peter Walshe, "Black American Thought and African Political Attitudes in South Africa," *Review of Politics*, 32 (1970): 51-77. There are two major works on black responses to the Italian-Ethiopian War, namely William R. Scott, *The Sons of Sheba's Race: African Americans and the Italo-Ethiopian War, 1935-1941* (Bloomington, 1993); and Joseph E. Harris, *African-American Reactions to War in Ethiopia, 1936-1941* (Baton Rouge, 1994).

Pan-Africanism is addressed by George Padmore, *Pan-Africanism or Communism?* (London, 1956); P. Olisanwuche Esedebe, *Pan-Africanism: The Idea and the Movement, 1776-1963* (Washington, 1982); Joseph Harris, ed., *Global Dimensions of the African Diaspora*, 2nd edition (Washington, 1993); and Ronald W. Walters, *Pan Africanism in the African Diaspora: An Analysis of Modern Afrocentric Political Movements* (Detroit, 1993). Attitudes toward the U.S. occupation of Haiti are discussed by Brenda Plummer in "The Afro-American Response to the Occupation of Haiti, 1915–1934," *Phylon,* 43 (1982): 125–143.

CLAIMING EQUAL RIGHTS

There are several important studies of the prolonged struggle for equal rights. A sweeping account is Sean Dennis Cashman, *African-Americans and the Quest for Civil Rights, 1900–1990* (New York, 1991). The NAACP's campaign against lynching is detailed in Robert L. Zangrando, *The NAACP's Crusade Against Lynching, 1900–1950* (Philadelphia, 1980). Excellent studies of individual roles in the legal struggle for justice include Genna Rae McNeil, *Ground Work: Charles Hamilton Houston and the Struggle for Civil Rights* (Philadelphia, 1983); and Mark V. Tushnet, *Making Civil Rights Law: Thurgood Marshall and the Supreme Court, 1936–1961* (New York, 1994). Broader constitutional issues are treated in John Hope Franklin and Genna Rae McNeil, eds., *African Americans and the Living Constitution* (Washington, 1995); and A. Leon Higginbotham, Jr., *Shades of Freedom: Racial Politics and Presumptions of the American Legal Process* (New York, 1996).

The Scottsboro case is ably treated by Dan T. Carter, *Scottsboro: A Tragedy of the American South* (Baton Rouge, 1969). A human portrait of the case is presented in James Goodman, *Stories of Scottsboro* (New York, 1994). Efforts to end desegregation in the schools are detailed in Mark Tushnet, *The NAACP's Legal Strategy Against Segregated Education, 1925–1950* (Chapel Hill, 1988). The Brown decision is examined by Richard Kluger in *Simple Justice: The History of Brown v. Board of Education and Black America's Struggle for Equality* (New York, 1975). The record of the case is contained in Mark Whitman, ed., *Removing a Badge of Slavery: The Record of Brown v. Board of Education* (Princeton and New York, 1993); and its aftermath is the concern of Raymond Wolters, *The Burden of Brown: Thirty Years of Desegregation* (Knoxville, 1984); and Jennifer L. Hochschild, *Thirty Years after Brown* (Washington, 1985).

The story of those who embraced other strategies for change is found in Harry Haywood, *Black Bolshevik: Autobiography of an Afro-American Communist* (Chicago, 1978); Nell Irvin Painter, *The Narrative of Hosea Hudson, His Life as a Negro Communist in the South* (Cambridge, 1979); Wilson Record, *The Negro and the Communist Party* (Chapel Hill, 1951); Mark Naison, *Communists in Harlem during the Depression* (Urbana, 1983); and Robin Kelley, *Hammer and Hoe: Alabama Communists During the Great Depression* (Chapel Hill, 1990).

FORCING CHANGE

The civil rights movement is one of the best studied problems in black history. For two important historiographical essays, see Adam Fairclough, "Historians and the Civil Rights Movement," *Journal of American Studies*, 24:3 (December 1990): 387-398; and Steven F. Lawson, "Freedom Then, Freedom Now: The Historiography of the Civil Rights Movement," *American Historical Review*, 96:2 (April 1991): 456-471. General and highly useful studies of this social movement include Taylor Branch, *Parting the Waters: America in the King Years, 1954-1963* (New York, 1988); David J. Garrow, *Bearing the Cross: Martin Luther King, Jr. and the Southern Christian Leadership Conference* (New York, 1986); Robert Weisbrot, *Freedom Bound: A History of the American Civil Rights Movement* (New York, 1990); Jack M. Bloom, *Class, Race, and the Civil Rights Movement* (Bloomington, 1987); Charles W. Eagles, ed., *The Civil Rights Movement in America* (Jackson, 1986); Numan Bartley, *The New South, 1945-1980: The Story of the South's Modernization* (Baton Rouge, 1995); and Harvard Sitkoff, *The Struggle for Black Equality, 1954-1980* (New York, 1981). An important collection of articles, essays, theses, and so on treating various aspects of the movement is David J. Garrow, ed., *Martin Luther King, Jr. and the Civil Rights Movement*, 18 vols. (Brooklyn, 1989). The animating ideology for the struggle is described in Martin Luther King, *Why We Can't Wait* (New York, 1964); Haynes Walton, *The Political Thought of Martin Luther King, Jr.* (Westport, 1971); Kenneth Smith and Ira Zepp, Jr., *Search for the Beloved Community* (Valley Forge, 1974); and Richard H. King, *Civil Rights and the Idea of Freedom* (Athens, 1996).

There are several local studies of the movement. Some of the best are Aldon D. Morris, *The Origins of the Civil Rights Movement: Black Communities Organizing for Change* (New York, 1984); Robert J. Norrell, *Reaping the Whirlwind: The Civil Rights Movement in Tuskegee* (New York, 1985); William H. Chafe, *Civilities and Civil Rights: Greensboro, North Carolina, and the Black Struggle for Freedom* (New York, 1981); David J. Garrow, *Protest at Selma: Martin Luther King, Jr., and the Voting Rights Act of 1965* (New Haven, 1978); John Dittmer, *Local People: The Struggle for Civil Rights in Mississippi* (Urbana, 1995); and Charles M. Payne, *I've Got the Light of Freedom: The Organizing Tradition and the Mississippi Freedom Struggle* (Berkeley, 1995).

The civil rights organizations are the subjects of valuable studies, including Adam Fairclough, *To Redeem the Soul of America: The Southern Christian Leadership Conference and Martin Luther King, Jr.* (Athens, 1987); August Meier and Elliott Rudwick, *CORE: A Study in the Civil Rights Movement, 1942-1968* (New York, 1973); Howard Zinn, *SNCC: The New Abolitionists* (Boston, 1964); and Clayborne Carson, *In*

Struggle: SNCC and the Black Awakening of the 1960s (Cambridge, 1981). The roles of women in the movement deserve more attention. Existing studies include Jo Ann Gibson Robinson, *The Montgomery Bus Boycott and the Women Who Started It: The Memoir of Jo Ann Gibson Robinson*, ed., David Garrow (Knoxville, 1987); Vicki L. Crawford, Jacqueline Anne Rouse, and Barbara Woods, eds., *Women in the Civil Rights Movement: Trailblazers and Torchbearers, 1941–1965* (Bloomington, 1993); and Sara Evans, *Personal Politics: The Roots of Women's Liberation in the Civil Rights Movement and the New Left* (New York, 1979).

Biographies of Martin Luther King are numerous but are uneven in quality. The best studies are David L. Lewis, *King, A Critical Biography* (New York, 1970); and Stephen Oates, *Let the Trumpet Sound: The Life of Martin Luther King, Jr.* (New York, 1982). Several of the participants in the movement have written their memoirs. See, for example, Ralph David Abernathy, *And the Walls Came Tumbling Down* (New York, 1989); Coretta Scott King, *My Life with Martin Luther King, Jr.* (New York, 1969); James Forman, *The Making of Black Revolutionaries* (New York, 1972); James Farmer, *Lay Bare the Heart: An Autobiography of the Civil Rights Movement* (New York, 1985); Roy Wilkins, *Standing Fast: The Autobiography of Roy Wilkins* (New York, 1982); Cleveland Sellers with Robert Terrell, *The River of No Return: The Autobiography of a Black Militant and the Life and Death of SNCC* (New York, 1973); and Andrew Young, *An Easy Burden: The Civil Rights Movement and the Transformation of America* (New York, 1996). For useful studies of Malcolm X, see Peter Goldman, *The Death and Life of Malcolm X* (Urbana, 1979); John Henrik Clarke, ed., *Malcolm X: The Man and His Times* (Toronto, 1979); Benjamin Goodman, ed., *Malcolm X: The End of White World Supremacy* (New York, 1971); James H. Cone, *Martin and Malcolm and America: A Dream or a Nightmare* (Mary Knoll, 1991); Bruce Perry, *Malcolm: The Life of a Man Who Changed America* (New York, 1991). See also Alex Haley, ed., *The Autobiography of Malcolm X* (New York, 1965).

The resistance of Southern whites to the struggle against segregation and for equal rights is discussed by Numan Bartley, *The Rise of Massive Resistance: Race and Politics in the South during the 1950s* (Baton Rouge, 1969); Neil R. McMillen, *The Citizens Council: Organized Resistance to the Second Reconstruction, 1954–1964* (Urbana, 1971); and James W. Ely, *The Crisis of Conservative Virginia: The Byrd Organization and the Politics of Massive Resistance* (Knoxville, 1976). For a study of whites sympathetic to the movement, see David L. Chappell, *Inside Agitators: White Southerners in the Civil Rights Movement* (Baltimore, 1994).

Two accounts of the movement in the North are James R. Ralph, Jr., *Northern Protest: Martin Luther King, Jr., Chicago and the Civil Rights Movement* (Cambridge, 1993); and Alan B. Anderson and George W. Pickering, *Confronting the Color Line: The Broken Promise of the Chicago Civil Rights Movement* (Athens, 1987)

Photo Credits

26	Corbis-Bettmann
40	Corbis-Bettmann
51	The Granger Collection
55	New York Public Library, Schomburg Center
58	Moorland-Springarn Research Center, Howard University
69	Oberlin College Archives, Oberlin, Ohio
79	Culver Pictures, Inc.
80	Culver Pictures, Inc.
97	Corbis-Bettmann
108	New York Public Library, Schomburg Center
109	Photographer unknown. Reprinted by permission of the Schomburg Center for Research in Black Culture, New York Public Library.
114	Reprinted with permission, NAACP
133	Courtesy of Afro-American Newspapers Archives and Research Center
141	AP/Wide World Photos
146	The Yale Collection of American Literature, Beinecke Rare Book and Manuscript Library, Yale University
147	The Yale Collection of American Literature, Beinecke Rare Book and Manuscript Library, Yale University
162	Stock Montage/Historical Pictures Collection
188	Corbis-Bettmann
196	Reprinted from the collections of the National Archives
197	Reprinted from the collections of the National Archives
199	Moorland-Springarn Research Center, Howard University
224	AP/Wide World Photos
231	AP/Wide World Photos
251	Corbis-Bettmann
261	Photograph by Jack Moebes, News & Record
265	© Charles Moore/Black Star
267	AP/Wide World Photos
270	AP/Wide World Photos
272	Magnum Photos, Inc. © 1963 Danny Lyon

Literary Acknowledgments

"To Say That Harlem Was Flattered Was to Put it Mildly. . . ." Reprinted by permission of GRM Associates, Inc., Agents for *The Pittsburgh Courier*, from the issue of October 1, 1960, of *The Pittsburgh Courier*. Copyright © 1960 by *The Pittsburgh Courier*, copyright renewed 1988 by *The New Pittsburgh Courier*.

"Advice to Migrant Blacks" from *The Chicago Defender*. No portion of this text may be reprinted without permission.

James Baldwin, excerpt from *The Fire Next Time*, 1962, p. 141. Published by Dell, a division of Bantam Doubleday Dell. No portion of this text may be reprinted without permission.

Amiri Baraka, "A Poem for Black Hearts" from *Selected Poetry of Amiri Baraka*, 1979. Published by William Morrow & Co. No portion of this text may be reprinted without permission from Sterling Lord Literistic.

Gwendolyn Brooks, "The Sundays of Satin-Legs Smith" as it appeared in Gates & McKay, *African American Literature*, p. 1584. No portion of this text may be reprinted without permission from the author.

Gwendolyn Brooks, "We Knew How to Order." Excerpted from "Gay Chaps at the Bar" from *Annie Allen*, 1950. Appeared in *Selected Poems by Gwendolyn Brooks*, 1944, 1963. No portion of this text may be reprinted without permission from the author.

Sterling Brown, "Old Lem." Appeared in Michael S. Harper, *Collected Poems of Sterling Brown*. NY: Harper & Row, 1980, p. 170. No portion of this text may be reprinted without permission from the Estate of Sterling Brown.

Charles M. Christian, "Number of Black-Owned Business Enterprises, 1920" from *Black Saga*. Copyright © 1995 by Charles M. Christian. Reprinted by permission of Houghton Mifflin Company. All rights reserved.

Countée Cullen, "My Conversion" from *Black Brotherhood*, p. 196. Published by HarperCollins Publishers. No portion of this text may be reprinted without permission.

Countée Cullen, "Heritage" from *Black Brotherhood*. Published by HarperCollins Publishers. No portion of this text may be reprinted without permission.

Owen Dodson, excerpt from "Conversation on V" from *Powerful Long Ladder* by Owen Dodson. Copyright © 1946 and copyright renewed © 1973 by Owen Dodson. Reprinted by permission of Farrar, Straus & Giroux, Inc.

Thomas Dorsey, "Precious Lord." Published by Warner Brothers Publishing. No portion of this text may be reprinted without permission from Warner Brothers Publishing.

Reynolds Farley & Walter R. Allen, "Black Out-Migration from the South, 1870–1970" from *The Color Line and the Quality of Life in America*, 1987, p. 113. Copyright © 1987. No portion of this text may be reprinted without permission from the Russell Sage Foundation.

Fannie Lou Hamer, "Remember Me" from *Women in the Civil Rights Movement: Trailblazers and Torchbearers, 1941–1965* by Crawford, Rouse, & Woods, 1993, p. 203. Published by Indiana University Press. No portion of this text may be reprinted without permission.

Langston Hughes, ". . . Jim Crow's Last Stand" from *Collected Poems*, 1994, Alfred A. Knopf, Inc. No portion of this text may be reprinted without permission from the publisher.

Langston Hughes, "Negroes, Sweet and Docile. . ." from *Collected Poems*, 1994. Published by Alfred A. Knopf, Inc. No portion of this text may be reprinted without permission.

Langston Hughes, "America Never Was America to Me. . ." from *Collected Poems*, 1994. Published by Alfred A. Knopf, Inc. No portion of this text may be reprinted without permission.

Langston Hughes, "Well, The Poor Old Negro's Had a Hard, Hard Time–" (first two lines) from *Collected Poems*, 1994. Published by Alfred A. Knopf, Inc. No portion of this text may be reprinted without permission.

Langston Hughes, "Afro-American Fragment" from *Collected Poems* by Langston Hughes. Copyright © 1994 by the Estate of Langston Hughes. Reprinted by permission of Alfred A. Knopf, Inc.

Langston Hughes, "Negro" from *Collected Poems* by Langston Hughes. Copyright © 1994 by the Estate of Langston Hughes. Reprinted by permission of Alfred A. Knopf, Inc.

Langston Hughes, "I, Too" from *Collected Poems* by Langston Hughes. Copyright © 1994 by the Estate of Langston Hughes. Reprinted by permission of Alfred A. Knopf, Inc.

Langston Hughes, "Mother to Son" from *Collected Poems* by Langston Hughes. Copyright © 1994 by the Estate of Langston Hughes. Reprinted by permission of Alfred A. Knopf, Inc.

Georgia Douglas Johnson, "Wishes" from Cheryl Wall, *Women of the Harlem Renaissance*, 1995, p. 14. Published by Indiana University Press. No portion of this text may be reprinted without permission.

Martin Luther King, Jr., excerpts from speech given January 30, 1956, as reprinted from Garrow, *Bearing the Cross*, pp. 60–61, 77, 89, 133, 158, and unpaginated excerpt. No portion of this text may be reprinted without special permission from The Writer's House, as agents for the Heirs to the Estate of Martin Luther King, Jr.

Martin Luther King, Jr., prayer offered in 1956, as reprinted from James Washington, *Conversations With God: Two Centuries of Prayers by African-Americans*, 1994, p. 190. Published by HarperCollins Publishers. No portion of this text may be reprinted without special permission from The Writer's House, as agents for the Heirs to the Estate of Martin Luther King, Jr.

Martin Luther King, Jr., six lessons learned from the Montgomery Boycott. Appeared in Taylor Branch, *Parting the Waters*, p. 195. No portion of this text may be reprinted without special permission from The Writer's House, as agents for the Heirs to the Estate of Martin Luther King, Jr.

Martin Luther King, Jr., excerpt from Sitkoff, *The Struggle for Black Equality*, pp. 63–64. No portion of this text may be reprinted without special permission from The Writer's House, as agents for the Heirs to the Estate of Martin Luther King, Jr.

Martin Luther King, Jr., excerpts from "Letter from the Birmingham Jail" and "I Have a Dream" from *Why We Can't Wait*. No portion of this text may be reprinted without special permission from The Writer's House, as agents for the Heirs to the Estate of Martin Luther King, Jr.

Steven Lawson, "Estimated No. of Blacks Registered to Vote in the South, 1940– " from *Black Ballots* by Steven Lawson. Copyright © 1976, by Columbia University Press. Reprinted with permission of the publisher.

Larry Neal, excerpt from "The Black Arts Movement" in Angelyn Mitchell, *Within the Circle: Anthology of African American Criticism*, p. 184. No portion of this text may be reprinted without permission from the Estate of Larry Neal.

Melvin B. Tolson, "Dark Symphony" from *Rendezvous With America*, 1944, Dodd-Mead & Co. First appeared in *Atlantic Monthly*, 168: 3, September 1941, pp. 314–317. No portion of this text may be reprinted without permission.

"Our Fadder, Which Are in Heaben!" from Gayraud S. Wilmore, *Black Religion and Black Radicalism*, pp. 224–225, 1972. Copyright © 1972. Published by Doubleday, a division of Bantam Doubleday Dell. No portion of this text may be reprinted without permission.

Index

AAA. *See* Agricultural Adjustment Administration (AAA)
ABB. *See* African Blood Brotherhood (ABB)
Abernathy, Ralph, 250
  in Albany, 263
Abolitionists, protests by, 7
Abyssinia (musical), 152
Abyssinian Baptist Church, 76, 208
Abyssinians. *See* Ethiopia
Accommodation. *See* Racial accommodation
ACLU. *See* American Civil Liberties Union (ACLU)
"Address to the Nations of the World" (Du Bois), 203–204
Adowa, battle of, 207
AFL. *See* American Federation of Labor (AFL)
AFL-CIO, 165
Africa. *See also* Pan-Africanism; specific countries and movements
  black American help for, 90
  black Christianity and, 84, 86–93
  Du Bois on, 205
  emigration to, 57, 59–60, 202
  Garvey on, 96–99
  heritage from, 131
  impact of black Americans on, 209–211
  internationalization of black condition and, 202–214
  Pan-Africanism and, 204
  politicization of assistance to, 207
  religious traditions and, 86
  shared ancestry in, 89–90
  Western views of, 89
African, use of name, 91
African Blood Brotherhood (ABB), 235
African Freedom Day (New York), 211
African Freedom Week (Chicago), 211

African Methodist Episcopal (AME) Church. *See* AME Church
African Methodist Episcopal (AME) Zion Church. *See* AME Zion Church
Afro-American. *See also* Black Americans
  use of name, 90–91
"Afro-American Fragment" (Hughes), 91–92
Afro-American newspaper (Baltimore), 236
Agricultural Adjustment Administration (AAA), 196, 200
Agriculture. *See also* Farmers
  blacks in, 241
Alabama. *See also* specific cities
  integration and, 248
  Scottsboro case in, 228–229
Albany, Georgia, SNCC in, 263–264
Albany Movement, 263
Alexander, Alger, 150
Ali, Noble Drew. *See* Drew, Timothy (Noble Drew Ali)
Allen, Richard, 130
Allen University, 77
Alliance, between black and white workers, 61–62
Alpha Kappa Alpha, 190
AME Church, 24, 26, 27, 50, 187
  higher education and, 77
  nomenclature for blacks and, 91
AME Church *Review*, 148
Amendments. *See also* specific amendments
  equal rights and, 219
  Fifteenth, 122
  Fourteenth, 7–8, 122
  protecting black suffrage, 6
  Thirteenth, 1, 2
American Civil Liberties Union (ACLU), school segregation and, 225
American Colonization Society, 15
American Dilemma, An (Myrdal), 174

American Federation of Labor (AFL), 165
American Labor Congress, 165
American Missionary Association, 77
American Negro Academy (ANA), 137–138
American Negro Historical Society of Pennsylvania, 133
American Negro Leadership Conference on Africa (ANLC), 212
American Negro Theatre (ANT), 176–177
AME Zion Church, 26, 27, 77, 187, 194
Among the Pines (Gilmore), 134
Amos and Andy (radio show), 192
ANA. *See* American Negro Academy (ANA)
Anderson, Eddie "Rochester," 178
Anderson, Marian, 175
Andrews, Eliza Frances, 15
ANLC. *See* American Negro Leadership Conference on Africa (ANLC)
Annie Allen (Brooks), 172
ANT. *See* American Negro Theatre (ANT)
Anti-colonialism. *See* Colonialism
Antilynching legislation, 226–228
Apartheid, 205
Appeal (Walker), 135
Armed forces
  blacks in, 125–126, 215–216
  desegregation of, 233
  segregation in, 232–233
Armstrong, Louis "Satchmo," 150, 178
Armstrong, Samuel Chapman, 48
Arts, 130. *See also* Harlem Renaissance; Intellectual life; Poets and poetry
  in 1950s and 1960s, 243–244
  expressive, 174–178
  and societal change, 143–144
Aryan superiority, 213
ASNLH. *See* Association for the Study of Negro Life and History (ASNLH)
Association for the Study of Negro Life and History (ASNLH), 133–134, 168
Associations. *See* Organizations; specific associations
Astwood, C. C., 91
Athletics, 179–182
Atlanta, Georgia
  boycott against segregation in, 121
  race riot in, 117–118
Atlanta Compromise, of Washington, 50
Atlanta Daily World, 208
Augusta, Georgia, boycott against segregation in, 121

Autobiographies, 130
Autobiography of an Ex-Colored Man, The (Johnson), 136
Azikiwe, Nnamdi, 211

Bagnall, Robert, 101–102
Baker, Ella, 261
Baker, George. *See* Divine, Father
Baker, Josephine, 152, 178
Baker, Ray Stannard, 142
Baldwin, James, 173, 245
  on blacks in Second World War, 215–216
Baldwin, William H., 76–77
Baltimore Sun (newspaper), 168
Banks, Freedman's, 28
Banks, Nathaniel P., 20
Bannister, Edward Mitchell, 153
Baptists, 26, 27, 71, 90
  education and, 77
Baraka, Amiri, 243
Barnes, Mae, 150
Baseball, 181
Basketball, 181
Bates, Daisy, 248
Batista, Fulgencio, 213
Beauty-culture and hair-care business, 74
Belgium, Kimbanguism and, 210
Benevolent societies, 79
Bennett, Aaron, 144
Bethune, Mary McLeod, 169, 192, 198–200
  anti-communist harassment of, 217
Bethune-Cookman College, 198
Bibb, Henry, 130
Bilbo, Theodore, 215
Birmingham, Alabama, 253
  church bombing in, 271
  nonviolent protest in, 264–265
Birth control, 190
Birth of a Nation, The (film), 53
Black Americans
  attitudes of younger generation, 35–36
  businesses owned by, 75
  Compromise of 1877 and, 33
  demands for justice in Great Depression, 195–196
  economic conditions of, 72–76
  enlistment of free, 2
  in film, 177–178
  impact of Civil War on, 2
  impact on Africa, 209–211

internationalization of condition of, 202–214
legislation punishing, 6–7
Pan-Africanism and, 202–203
post-Reconstruction controls imposed on, 33–45
response to *Brown* decision by, 245–249
in Second World War armed forces, 215
suffrage for, 5–6
"Black-and-tan" conventions, 22
Black Arts Movement, 243–244
"Black Brain Trust," 198
"Black Cabinet," 199–200
Black Christianity, 83–93
Black Christian Nationalist Creed, 186–187
"Black church," 188
Black Codes, 6
Black communities, 60–61
Black Cross Nurses, 100
Black deity. *See* God
Blackface performers, 151–152
Black history, 132–135, 168–169
Black Holiness-Pentecostal Movement, 187
Black Jews, 85, 186
Black Man, The, The Father of Civilization (Webb), 132
Black Muslims. *See* Nation of Islam
Black nationalists, 82, 269–270
and *New Negro* anthology, 143
Black newspapers, 168. *See also* specific newspapers
Black power movement, 275
Black Reconstruction (Du Bois), 169
Blackson, Lorenzo D., 134
Black Star Line, 99
Congo and, 210
Blackwell, Annie, 191
Black women. *See also* Women
as property owners, 19
Blair, Izell, Jr., 260
Blake, James Hubert "Eubie," 150
Blanton, Jimmy, 175
Bledsoe, Jules, 152
Blues, 150
Bogle, Donald, 177
Boley, Oklahoma, 61
Bond, Julian, 262
Boney, Harrison N., 59
Bontemps, Arna, 154
Bottomland (musical), 152

Boxing, 179–181
Boycotts, 121, 230
of buses in Montgomery, 250–253
in Orangeburg, South Carolina, 250
Braddock, James, 180
Braithwaite, William Stanley, 140, 148
Brass bands, 150
Brawley, Benjamin, 132
Brazil, slavery in, 47
Breedlove, Sarah. *See* Walker, Madame C. J.
Briggs, Cyril, 95, 235
Britain. *See also* Colonialism
rising in Malawi and, 209–210
Brooks, Gwendolyn, 162, 172, 173
Brotherhood of Dining Car Employees, 164–165
Brotherhood of Sleeping Car Porters (BSCP), 165
Broughton, Virginia, 71
Brown, C. S., 89
Brown, Charlotte Hawkins, 191–192, 226–227
anti-communist harassment of, 217
Brown, Henry Billings, 41–42
Brown, Oliver, 225
Brown, Sterling, 154, 169, 170
Brown, William Wells, 130
Brown v. *Board of Education*, 223–226
black and white responses to, 245–249
voting rights after, 242–243
Bruce, Blanche K., 25
Brundage, W. Fitzhugh, 109
BSCP. *See* Brotherhood of Sleeping Car Porters (BSCP)
Buchanan v. *Warley*, 122
Bunche, Ralph, 198
anti-communist harassment of, 217
communism and, 236
Burleigh, Henry T., 152
Burns, Tommy, 180
Bus boycott, in Montgomery, 250–253
Business, 74–75. *See also* Economic entries
black-owned enterprises (1920), 75
Garvey and, 99

Cain, Richard A., 28, 59
Call-and-response style music, 150
Cameron, Lucille, 180
Cane (Toomer), 140–141
Cannon, Gus, 150
Capitalism, Randolph on, 62–63

Cardozo, Francis, 25
Caribbean region
　freedom of blacks in, 47
　missionaries to, 202
Carmichael, Stokely, 262, 274–275
Carter, Benny, 175
Carter, Hodding, 257
Carver, George Washington, 174
Castro, Fidel, 213
Cayton, Horace, 214
Central High School (Little Rock), integration of, 248–249
Chaney, James, 271
Charles, Robert, 116–117
Charleston, Oscar, 181
Chesnutt, Charles, 136
Chicago, Illinois, 158, 165
　African Freedom Week in, 211
　race riot in, 120–121
Chicago Congress on Africa, 203
Chicago Defender (newspaper), 108–109, 159, 160, 163, 168
　on assistance to Africa, 208
Chicago Whip (newspaper), 161
Children, as field workers, 21
Chilembwe, John, 209–210
Christian churches. *See* Christianity; Churches; specific churches
Christianity, 26–27, 186–189. *See also* Black Christianity; Churches; Religion; specific churches
　black, 83–93
　diversity in practice of, 188–189
　of King, Martin Luther, Jr., 255
　SCLC and, 259
Christian Methodist Episcopal, 187
Churches. *See also* Black Christianity; Religion; specific churches
　blacks in, 26–28
　education and, 77
　growth of, 241–242
　increase of, 161–162
　political organization and, 26
　women in, 189
Church of the Living God, 84–85
CIO. *See* Congress of Industrial Organizations (CIO)
Cities. *See also* Urbanization
　black impact on, 165–167
　black migration to, 158
　early segregation in, 38
　movement to, 14
Citizens Councils, resistance to integration and, 247

Citizenship, Fourteenth Amendment and, 7–8
Civilizing, by whites, 44
Civil rights. *See also* Equal rights; Racism
　Brown decision and, 226
　in Democratic platform (1948), 217
　increased demands for, 241
　Roosevelt, Franklin, and, 228
　Urban League and, 76
　Washington and, 52
　white resistance to, 246–249
　women and, 191
Civil Rights Act (1875), 10, 15
　unconstitutionality of, 41
Civil Rights Act (1957), 259
Civil Rights Act (1964), 171
Civil rights bill, 271
　of 1866, 7
　Kennedy and, 266
Civil Rights Commission, 259–260
Civil Rights Division, in Department of Justice, 259
Civil rights movement
　direct action by, 260–276
　integration and, 243
　nonviolent passive resistance and, 249–260
　in North, 274
　sit-ins and, 260–261
　Young's assessment of, 275–276
Civil rights organizations. *See also* Civil rights movement; Garvey, Marcus; Mass movements; specific organizations
　integration and, 248
　NAACP as, 56, 221–229
　Niagara Movement and, 56–57
Civil War, impact of, 2
Clark, James, 273
Clark, Septima, 254
Classes. *See also* Elites; Middle class; Working class
　black-white cooperation and, 61
　economic elite and, 73
　elite, 67–72
Clearview, Oklahoma, 61
Cleveland, Ohio, 158
Coker, Samuel, 57
Cold War, 211, 217
Collective action, 73–74
Collina, Norma, 262
Colonialism
　in Africa, 95

Communists and, 211
  denunciation of, 207–208
  in Malawi, 209–210
  Pan-Africanism and, 202, 203
  racism and, 44
  Second World War and, 216
Colored, use of term, 91
Colored American Magazine, 136, 148
Colored Farmers' National Alliance and Cooperative Union, 61
Colored Methodist Episcopal Church (CME), 27, 77
Colored Patriots of the American Revolution,... (Nell), 131
Colored Women's League, 69
Communism
  accusations of black involvement with, 217
  anti-colonialism and, 211
  appeal of, 235, 236–237
Communist International, 235
Communist party, ILD and, 228
Communities, establishment of black, 60–61
Composers, 152–153
Compromise of 1877, 11, 33
Confederacy. *See* South
Conferences, for collective action, 73–74
Congregationalists, 26
Congress. *See also* specific congresses
  antilynching legislation and, 226–228
  blacks from South in, 24–25
  De Priest in, 195
  Forty-Third and Forty-Fourth, 10
Congress for Racial Equality (CORE), 212, 262
  "sit-in" strategy of, 230
Congressional elections. *See* Elections
Congress of Industrial Organizations (CIO), 165
Connor, Bull, 264
Conservatives, white, 36
Constitution of the U.S. *See* Amendments; Laws; Supreme Court; specific cases
Constitutions
  Jim Crow provisions in, 39–41
  white supremacist, 39–40
Contending Forces (Hopkins), 136
Contraception information, 190
Contracts, labor, 20–21
Cook, Helen A., 69
Cook, Mary, 71–72
"Coon" songs, 151–152

Cooper, Anna Julia, 68, 69, 103, 108, 135, 202
Corbett, Maurice N., 90
Corcoran, Thomas G., 228
CORE. *See* Congress for Racial Equality (CORE)
Costigan, Edward P., 227
Cotton States and International Exposition, 49
Couch, W. T., 169–170
Council for Interracial Cooperation, 226
Council on African Affairs, 205
Courts, challenges in, 220–229
Cox, Ida, 150
Craft, William, 130
Crisis (magazine), 57, 144, 148, 176
  on Haiti, 212–213
Crummell, Alexander, 137–138, 203
Cuba. *See also* Cuban Revolution (1959)
  slavery in, 47
  white imperialism and, 44
Cuban Revolution (1959), 213
Cullen, Countée, 86, 91, 141, 153
  "Heritage" by, 92–93
Cultural life. *See also* Culture
  from emancipation to Harlem Renaissance, 130–182
  and intellectual life, 167–178
Culture. *See also* Arts
  of 1950s and 1960s, 243–244
  black impact on North, 165–167
  Crummell and, 138
  of ghettos, 167
  Harlem Renaissance and, 138–154
  movement of southern to North, 161
  New Deal and, 198
Cumming v. School Board of Richmond County, 122

Dabney, Virginius, 170
Dancy, John, 116
Dandridge, Dorothy, 178
Darker America (Still), 152
"Dark Symphony" (Tolson), 171
Davenport, Charlie, 14
Davis, A. L., 259
Davis, Angela, 262
Davis, John P., 195
"Declaration of Principles," Du Bois, Niagara Movement, and, 56
Deep Harlem (musical), 152
De jure segregation, 35, 37, 44
  constitutionality of, 225

imperialist racism and, 43–44
in railroad cars, 38
Delany, Martin, 57, 82, 130
Delta Sigma Theta, 190
De Mena, Madame M. L. T., 100
Democratic party
blacks and, 23
civil rights and, 217
elections of 1874 and, 10
MFDP and, 272–273
Reconstruction Act and, 9
Demography. *See also* Population
shifts in, 239–243
Demonstrations. *See* Civil rights movement; Protest demonstration
Denominations, 84. *See also* Churches; specific churches
De Priest, Oscar, 195
Desegregation. *See* Segregation
Detroit, 158
racial violence in, 234–235
Dett, Robert Nathaniel, 152
Detter, Thomas, 134
Diaspora, African, 202, 203
Direct action, civil rights and, 260–276
Discrimination. *See also* De jure segregation; Segregation
Civil Rights Act of 1875 and, 10
compared with segregation, 185
in executing government programs, 197
segregation in South and, 44–45
in unions, 271
Divine, Father, 187–188
Dixon-Carroll, Delia, 191
Dodds, Warren, 175
Dodson, Owen, 171
Domestic workers, 73
Domingo, W. A., 95
on Garvey, 102
Dorsey, Thomas A., 175
"Double-V Campaign," 215
Douglass, Frederick, 10, 28, 50, 54
autobiography of, 130
on emigration, 59
on equal rights, 220
on lynchings and mob violence, 110
Draft. *See also* Armed forces; First World War; Second World War
for First World War, 123–124
Dred Scott decision, 6, 42
Drew, Charles R., 174
Drew, Timothy (Noble Drew Ali), 85
Dube, John, 206

Du Bois, W. E. B., 48, 53–57, 55 (illus.), 141, 142
anti-communist harassment of, 217
on arts and social change, 143–144
on Atlanta riot, 117–118
Black Reconstruction by, 169
communism and, 211, 236
on equality, 169
as essayist, 135–136
First World War and, 124, 125–126
on Garvey, 100
historiography of, 132
Negro, The, of, 132, 205
at Pan-African Congress of 1945, 205
Pan-Africanism and, 202, 203–204
on race riots, 120
on self-determination of blacks, 95
on socialism, 62
"Talented Tenth" and, 67–68
theatre and, 176
Washington and, 50
on white mob violence, 111, 112
on white patrons, 145
on worship, 163
Dunbar, Paul Laurence, 134, 135, 136, 148
Durham, North Carolina, black-owned businesses in, 75
Durr, Clifford and Virginia, 257
Dyer, Leonidas, 226

Eastland, James, 215
Eastland, John, 246
East St. Louis, Illinois, race riot in, 119–120
Economic conditions, 72–76
Economic elite, 73
Economic issues
in Great Depression, 195–198
King on, 274
March on Washington (1963) and, 268
Economic nationalism, Garvey and, 99
Economy
civil rights demands and, 241
segregation and, 37
Education, 76–78, 167, 189–190. *See also* Higher education; Schools
of black elite, 67
in black history, 132
challenges to segregation in, 221–222, 223–226
improved attainment in, 240–241
levels of, 167–168

vocational vs. humanistic, 137-138
Washington and, 48, 49
Education of the Negro Prior to 1865
 (Woodson), 133
Eisenhower, Dwight D., integration and, 248, 260
Elected officials, 23-26
Elections
 of 1868, 9
 of 1872, 9-10
 1874 congressional, 10
 of 1876, 11
 of 1932, 192-193
Electoral rolls, removal of blacks from, 38-39
Eleventh National Woman's Rights Convention (1866), 13
Elites, 67-72
 attitudes toward other blacks, 68
 economic, 73
 Garvey and, 103
 women as, 68-72
Ellington, Edward "Duke," 150-151
Ellison, Ralph, 173, 174
Emancipation, life after, 47-65
Emancipation Proclamation, 2
Emigration, 57, 59-60, 202. *See also* Migration; Movement
Emperor Jones, The (film), 178
Employment, 163-165. *See also* Labor; Unemployment; Workers
 changes in, 241
 of freed slaves, 3-4
 shifts in patterns of, 164
England. *See* Britain
Enlistment. *See also* Armed forces; Draft; First World War; Second World War
 for First World War, 123-125
Entertainment. *See* Arts; Film; Music; Sports; Theatre
Entrepreneurs, 74-75
Eph, Uncle (former slave), 3
Equal employment opportunities, 232
Equal Employment Opportunity Commission, 271
Equality. *See also* Equal rights
 demands for, 169-170
 gender, 69
 social, 8-9
Equal protection clause, 122
Equal rights. *See also* Civil rights; Racism
 boycotts and, 230
 Du Bois and, 56-57
 in education, 221-226
 NAACP and, 57
 struggle for (1917-1954), 219-237
 struggle for (1955-1965), 239-276
Essays and essayists. *See also* Literature; Writers and writing
 on race, 169
Ethiopia
 impact of Italian invasion of, 207-208
 Italo-Ethiopian war in, 209
Ethiopianism, 87-89
Ethiopian Research Council, 207
Europe, lack of interest in Ethiopian conflict, 208-209
Evansville, Indiana, race riot in, 118
Evers, Medgar, 259
 murder of, 271
Executive Order 8802, 232
Executive Order 9981, 233
Exodus. *See also* Migration
 to Kansas, 30-31
Exodusters, 31
Extremists, white, 36-37

Family, reuniting of, 15-16
Fard, W. D. *See* Mohammed, Farrad
Farmer, James
 ANLC and, 212
 Freedom Rides and, 262
 March on Washington (1963) and, 267
Farmers. *See also* Agricultural Adjustment Administration (AAA)
 black-white alliance of, 61
 subsidies to, 196, 197
 tenant farming, sharecropping, and, 21
Fascism, 213-214
Faubus, Orval, 248
Faulkner, William, 257
Fauset, Jessie, 141, 142, 148, 153
 on middle class life, 145-146
Federal Art Project, 198
Federal Emergency Relief Administration (FERA), 196, 198
Federal government, segregation and, 43, 44
Federal Housing Administration (FHA), 196
Federal Music Project, 198
Federal Theatre Project, 176, 198
Federal Writers Project, 198
Feminism. *See also* Women
 Hurston and, 147

FERA. *See* Federal Emergency Relief Administration (FERA)
Ferris, William, 138
Fetchit, Stephin. *See* Perry, Lincoln
FHA. *See* Federal Housing Administration (FHA)
Fiction, 171–173
Fifteenth Amendment
　grandfather clause and, 122
　United States v. *Reese* and, 11
"Fifty Years" (Johnson), 136–137
Filibusters
　against antilynching legislation, 226, 227
　against Civil Rights Act (1957), 259
　against Civil Rights Act (1964), 271
Film, 177–178
　Birth of a Nation, The, 53
　Fire!!: A Quarterly Devoted to the Younger Negro Artists, 144
"Fire Next Time, The" (Baldwin), 245
First World War, 123–127
　Pan-Africanism and, 204
Fisk University, 48, 167
Fitzgerald, Ella, 175
Fitzhugh, George, 6
Football, 181
Ford, James, 208
Foreign policy
　toward Africa, 211–212
　toward Haiti, 212–213
Forman, James, 232, 262
Fort Brown, race riot in, 118
Fortune, T. Thomas, 48, 50, 61, 62, 88, 148
Forty-Fourth Congress, 10
Forty-Third Congress, 10
Fourteenth Amendment, 7–8
　Brown v. *Board of Education* and, 225
　equal protection clause of, 122
　Scottsboro case and, 220
Franchise
　grandfather clause and, 122
　restrictions on, 122
Franco, Francisco, 213
Frankfurter, Felix, 249
Franklin, James T., 90
Franklin, John Hope, 170
Fraternal organizations, 79
Frazier, E. Franklin, 195
Free blacks
　divisions between slaves and, 67
　enlistment in Civil War, 2
　institutions of, 66

Freedman's Bank, 28
Freedman's Saving and Trust Company, 28
Freedmen, reactions of, 3
Freedmen's Bureau, 5, 15, 78
　exploitive contracts and, 20–21
　protests by, 7
Freedom. *See also* Africa; Colonialism; Equal rights; Pan-Africanism
　decisions about future and, 3–4, 47–65
　granted to slaves, 1–2
　impact on Du Bois' beliefs, 54
　implementation of, 12–31
　limitations of, 6
Freedom Rides, 262–263
Freedom Summer, 271–272
Freed people
　movement of, 13–15
　needs of, 12–13
Free Speech and Headlight (newspaper), 110
From Slavery to Freedom (Franklin), 170
Future, debate over direction for, 47–65

Gaines, Lloyd Lionel, 221–222
Gaines decision, 221–222, 223
Gandhi, Mohandas, 255
Garland, Walter, 214
Garvey, Amy Jacques, 100–101
Garvey, Marcus, 83, 93–104, 97 (illus.), 148, 220, 275. *See also* Universal Negro Improvement Association (UNIA)
　on black deity, 85–86
　black institutions and, 186
　deportation of, 102
　on First World War, 127
　on links with mainland Africans, 96–99
　Pan-Africanism and, 203
Garveyism, 93–104
Garvin, Charles, 190
Gayle, Addison, Jr., 244
Gay life, 153
Gender
　equality of, 69
　search for black self and, 103
Generation of 1917, 123–127
　equal rights struggle by, 239
Germany. *See* Nazi Germany
Ghana, 211

Ghettos, 240, 276
  development of, 166-167
  Harlem as, 139
Gilmore, James Roberts, 134
Gilpin, Charles, 152
Giovanni, Nikki, 244
God. *See also* Religion
  black Christianity and, 83-93
  Garveyites and, 85-86
  Turner on, 83-84
Golf, 182
Gone With the Wind (film), 178
Goodman, Andrew, 271
Gospel music, 175
Government. *See also* Federal government
  of South after Civil War, 4
Government programs, in New Deal, 196-198
Graetz, Robert, 257
Grandfather clause, 39-40
  illegality of, 122
"Grandmother clause," 191
Grant, Abram, 50
Grant, Ulysses S., 9
Gray, Fred, 250
Great Britain. *See* Britain
Great Depression, 156-157, 194-201
  communism and, 236
  unionization and, 165
Great Society, 276
Greeley, Horace, 10
Greene, Lorenzo, 169
Greensboro, North Carolina, "sit-in" in, 260-261
Griggs, Sutton, 136
Grimké, Charlotte, 69
Grimke, Francis, 124
Griswold, Erwin N., 221
Guinn v. United States, 122
Guntharpe, Violet, 14

Hair-care business, 74
Haiti, 212
  status of blacks in, 47
Hamer, Fannie Lou, 254, 272
Hammon, Jupiter, 130
Hampton Institute, 77
Handy, William Christopher, 150
Hansberry, Lorraine, 243
Hansberry, William Leo, 207
Harding, Warren G., on segregation, 44
Harlan, John M., 42

Harlem, 165
  communists in, 235-236
  life in, 145
  pro-Ethiopian activity in, 208
  riot in (1935), 234
Harlem Renaissance, 138-154
  nomenclature for blacks and, 91
Harlem Shadows (Johnson), 140
Harper, Frances Ellen Watkins, 13, 28, 68, 103
Harris, Abram, 195
  communism and, 236
Harrison, Hubert, 95
Hart, William, 56
Hastie, William, 221, 222
Hawaii, annexation of, 43
Hayden, Casey, 262
Hayden, Robert, 171
Hayes, Roland, 175
Hayes, Rutherford B., 11
Haynes, Thomas, 61
Haywood, Anna Julia. *See* Cooper, Anna Julia
Haywood, Harry, 235
Health care, 190
Height, Dorothy, ANLC and, 212
Henderson v. United States, 223
"Heritage" (Cullen), 92-93
Herndon, Angelo, communism and, 236-237
Herskovits, Melville J., 142
Hierarchical society, 37
Higher education, 48, 77-78, 167. *See also* Education; Segregation; Universities and colleges
  black history courses in, 132
  challenges to segregation in, 223
  degrees and, 240
Hill, Abram, 176
History and historiography
  of black America, 131
  by black Americans, 132, 168-169, 170
History of the Negro Race from 1619 to 1880... (Williams), 131
Hitler, Adolf, black denunciation of, 213, 214
Hodges, Johnny, 175
Holliday, Billie, 175
Holy Qur'an. *See* Nation of Islam
Home improvement loans, 196
Home ownership, 165-166
Homesteader, The (film), 178
Home to Harlem (McKay), 145

Homosexuals and homosexuality, in arts, 153
Hope, Lugenia Burns, 189
Hopkins, Pauline, 132, 136, 148
Horne, Lena, 178
Horton, George Moses, 29, 130
Hose, Sam, 111–112
Hospitals, 190
House of Representatives. *See also* Congress
   De Priest in, 195
Housing
   discrimination in, 222–223
   in northern cities, 165–166
   segregation in, 122
Houston, Charles H., 216, 221
Houston Informer, 126
Howard University, 167
   Law School of, 221
Howes, Louis, 194
Hudson, Hosea, communism and, 236
Huggins, Willis N., 208–209
Hughes, Langston, 140, 142, 144, 149, 153, 154, 169, 172, 200–201, 276
   "Afro-American Fragment," 91–92
   anti-communist harassment of, 217
   communism and, 236
   Harlem and, 139
   "I, Too, Sing America," 93
   "Jim Crow's Last Stand," 217
   on marginal status, 220
Hull, Cordell, 209
Humanistic education, 137
Human rights statement, by NAACP, 216
Humphrey, Richard Manning, 61
Hunter, Alberta, 154
Hunton, William Alphaeus, Jr., communism and, 211
Hurston, Zora Neale, 86–87, 141, 144, 146–147, 153, 154

"I, Too, Sing America" (Hughes), 93
Ickes, Harold L., 194, 195
Identity, search for, 82–104
Ideologies
   alternative, 220
   racist, 37
"I Have a Dream" speech (King), 268–269
ILD. *See* International Labor Defense (ILD)
Imitation of Life (film), 178

Imperialism
   in Cuba and Philippines, 44
   racism and, 43–44
Imperium in Imperio (Griggs), 136
In Dahomey (musical), 152
Indianapolis Freeman, 53
Industrial proletariat, 164–165
Industry, blacks in, 241
Ingram, Rex, 178
Institutions, black, 186
Insurance business, 74–75
Integration, 8. *See also* Segregation
   white Southerners and, 246
Intellectual life
   and cultural life, 167–178
   from emancipation to Harlem Renaissance, 130–182
Intellectuals, communism and, 236–237
International Labor Defense (ILD), 228–229
International organizations, UNIA as, 98
Interracial cooperation, 216
   socialism and, 63
   among workers and small farmers, 61
Interstate Commerce Act, 223
Interstate transportation, segregation in, 223
Intimidation. *See also* Violence
   integration and, 247
Invisible Man (Ellison), 173
Iola Leroy (Harper), 68
Islam. *See* Nation of Islam
Italy, Ethiopian invasion by, 207–208

Jackman, Harold, 153
Jackson, Charlie, 150
Jazz, 150, 175
"Jazz Age," 150–151
Jeffries, Jim, 179–180
Jenifer, J. T., 91
Jenkins, Tim, 262
Jews. *See* Black Jews
Jim Crow, 37–45, 50, 107, 159
   in armed forces, 215, 232
   black women and, 191–192
   origins of name, 38
   after Second World War, 216
"Jim Crow's Last Stand" (Hughes), 217
Job opportunities, 72–73
   after Second World War, 241
Jobs
   black efforts toward creating, 195
   competition for, 193–194

John Kunering (ceremony), 151
Johnson, Andrew, 5
  and civil rights bill of 1866, 7
Johnson, Charles, 141, 148
Johnson, Frank, 273
Johnson, Georgia Douglas, 148
Johnson, Jack (John), 179–180, 270
Johnson, James Weldon, 103, 120, 124, 127, 136, 140, 142, 143
  on Harlem, 138–139
Johnson, Lyndon
  civil rights legislation and, 271
  Great Society programs of, 276
  voting rights bill and, 273–274
Johnson, Mordecai, 126
Johnson, Thomas, 89
Jones, Absalom, 87–88
Jones, Eugene, 198
Jones, LeRoi. *See* Baraka, Amiri
Joplin, Scott, 149
Journal of Negro History, 134, 168
Judicial system, 7. *See also* Courts; Supreme Court
  black resistance through, 121–122
Just, Ernest Everett, 174
Justice Department, Civil Rights Division in, 259

Kansas, migration to, 30
"Kansas Fever Exodus," 30
Keep Shuffling (musical), 152
Kellogg, Paul Underwood, 141
Kennedy, John F., 212, 264
  assassination of, 271
  civil rights bill and, 266
Kennedy, Robert, 262, 263
Kenya, 211
Kenyatta, Jomo, 211
Kimbangu, Simon, 210
Kimbangu Movement, 210
Kincannon, A. A., 78
King, A. L., 208
King, Coretta Scott, 254
King, Martin Luther, Jr., 250. *See also* Nonviolent protest
  in Albany, 263
  ANLC and, 212
  arrest of, 252
  in Birmingham, 264–265
  Christian principles and, 254–255
  as civil rights leader, 253–256
  "I Have a Dream" speech of, 268–269

"Letter from the Birmingham Jail," 264–266
  March on Washington (1963) and, 267–269
  Raleigh conference and, 261–262
  in Selma, Alabama, 273
  on Vietnam War, 275
King, Riley "B. B.", 175
Kinshasa, Congo, 210
Kraemer, Louis and Fern, 222–223
Krigwa Little Theatre, 176
Krigwa Playwriting Contest, 176
Ku Klux Klan, Garvey and, 101, 102

Labor, 19–21. *See also* Workers; Working class
  black, 6
  exploitive contracts for, 20–21
  of freed slaves, 3–4
  in North, 163–164
  Washington on, 49–50
Labor strike, race riot and, 119
Labor unions. *See* Unions
Lafayette Players, 176
Landownership, 17–19
Lane, Lunsford, 130
Langston, John Mercer, 30
Langston, Oklahoma, 61
Larsen, Nella, 146, 153
Laws. *See also* Courts; Legal challenges
  Jim Crow and, 37–45
  to separate races, 34
Law schools, 221
Leadership, 95. *See also* specific leaders
  by blacks, 253–254
League of Nations, aid for Ethiopia and, 208–209
Lee, Don L. *See* Madhubuti, Haki
Legal challenges, 220–229
Legislation. *See also* Civil Rights Act entries; Civil rights bill
  antilynching, 226–228
  Black Codes as, 6
  black support for, 25
Legislative assemblies, delegates to, 22–23
Legislators, black, 23–26, 26 (illus.)
Leigh, Frances Butler, 6
"Letter from the Birmingham Jail" (King), 264–266
Lewis, John, 262
Lewis, John Henry, 181

Lewis, Robert Benjamin, 131
Liberia, 90
　emigration to, 59
　movement to, 15, 29
Liberian Exodus Joint Stock Company, 59
Liberty League, 95
Life expectancy, 72
Lifestyle
　adjustment to North, 163–164
　African impact on, 211
　impact of migration on, 161
　transfer of southern to North, 163
"Lift Ev'ry Voice and Sing" (Johnson), 137
Light and Truth... (Lewis), 131
Lincoln, Abraham
　assassination of, 5
　Emancipation Proclamation and, 2
　pardon of rebels by, 4
Literacy, 23, 76–77, 78–79, 167. *See also* Education
　New Deal programs and, 198
　women's organizations and, 71
Literature, 130, 134–137. *See also* History and historiography
　of 1950s and 1960s, 243–244
　audience for, 134
　fiction, 172–174
　poetry, 171–172
　white patrons and publishers of, 144–145
Little Rock, Arkansas, school desegregation in, 248–249
Livingstone College, 77
Locke, Alain, 141, 142–143, 149, 153
Logan, Rayford, 170, 198
　anthology of, 169–170
Los Angeles, 158
　Watts riot in, 274
Louis, Joe, 180–181
Louisiana, 7
　grandfather clause in, 39–41
Love, Mary, 188
Lowenstein, Allard, 262
Lower Congo, Kimbangu Movement in, 210
Lowery, Joseph, 253
Lucky Sambo (musical), 152
Lynch, John Roy, 25, 61
Lynchings, 107, 108–111, 159
　legal challenges to, 226–228
　of Till, Emmett, 271

MacArthur, Douglas, commendation to black soldiers by, 215
Mackey, Raleigh "Biz," 181
Madhubuti, Haki, 244
Magazines. *See also* specific magazines
　Harlem Renaissance writers in, 148–149
　intellectual exchange in, 148
Malawi, 209–210
Malcolm X, 269–270, 272–273
Manly, Alex, 115–116
Mann Act, 180
Manufacturing, blacks in, 241
March, in New York City (1917), 230
March on Washington (1941), 230–232
March on Washington (1963), 266–269
March on Washington Movement (MOWM), 232
Marines. *See also* Armed forces
　in Haiti, 212
Marriage, formalizing of, 15
Marrow of Tradition, The (Chesnutt), 136
Marshall, Thurgood, 214, 221, 222
　school desegregation battle and, 223–226
Martin, Jane, 150
Mason, Charlotte Osgood, 145
Mass movements. *See also* Civil rights movement; Garvey, Marcus
　equal rights and, 220
　nonviolent protest and, 230–232
Maud Martha (Brooks), 173
Maynor, Dorothy, 175
Mboya, Tom, 211
McCain, Franklin, 260
McDaniel, Hattie, 178
McDougald, Elise Johnson, 143
McKay, Claude, 91, 122–123, 139–140, 144, 145, 153
McKinley, William, Spanish-Cuban-American War and, 44
McLaurin, George W., 223
McNeil, Joseph, 260
McQueen, Butterfly, 178
Meharry Medical College, 167
Memphis, Tennessee
　anti-black mob violence in, 113
　boycott against segregation in, 121
Merrick, John, 74
Messenger (magazine), 62, 63
Methodist Episcopal Church, South (ME), 27
Methodists, 26, 27

MFDP. *See* Mississippi Freedom Democratic party (MFDP)
MIA. *See* Montgomery Improvement Association (MIA)
Mial, Sallie, 191
Micheaux, Oscar, 178
Middle class
  Fauset on, 145–146
  participation in, 241
  women of, 189
Midwest, migration to, 157
Migrants, recruiting of, 159–160
Migration. *See also* Emigration; Movement
  church growth and, 161–162
  to Ethiopia, 207
  independence from whites and, 160
  intermediate moves and, 160–161
  after 1915, 157–167
  to North, 240
  out-migration from South, 157–158
  from South, 110, 138–139
Military. *See* Armed forces
Military districts, 8
Miller, Kelly, 76, 132
Miller, William "Rice," 175
Minstrelsy, 151–152
Mis-Education of the Negro, The (Woodson), 168
Missionaries, 26–27, 206
  black Christian, 202
Mississippi
  Black Codes in, 6
  Summer Project in, 271–272
  voter registration in, 263
  voting exclusion in, 39
Mississippi Democratic party, 254
Mississippi Freedom Democratic party (MFDP), 271–272
Missouri ex rel. *Gaines* v. *Canada*, 221–222
Mitchell, John L., Jr., 110
Mobile, Alabama, 253
  boycott against segregation in, 121
Mob violence. *See* Lynchings; Riots; Violence
Mohammed, Farrad, 185
Montgomery, Alabama
  bus boycott in, 250–253
  lessons of boycott in, 258
Montgomery, Bob, 181
Montgomery, Isaiah T., 61
Montgomery Improvement Association (MIA), 251–253

Moody, Anne, 262
Moore, A. M., 74
Moore, Richard, 235
Moorish Americans, 85
Moorish Science Temple of America (MST), 85
Morganfield, McKinley ("Muddy Waters"), 175
Morris Brown College, 77
Mortgages, 196, 197
Moses, Robert, 262
"Mother to Son" (Hughes), 140
Mound Bayou, Mississippi, 61
Movement, 29. *See also* Emigration; Migration
  end of Reconstruction and, 30
  of freed peoples, 13–15
Movies. *See* Film
MOWM. *See* March on Washington Movement (MOWM)
MST. *See* Moorish Science Temple of America (MST)
M Street High School (Washington), 69
Muhammad, Elijah, 185–186, 269
Muhammad Speaks (newspaper), 186
Mulattoes, 23
Murphy, Carl, 236
Murray, Pauli, 232, 254
Muse, Clarence, 176
Music, 175
  blues, 150
  composers of, 152
  gospel, 175
  Harlem Renaissance and, 149
  jazz, 150
  nightlife and, 149
  ragtime, 149–150
Musical theatre, 151–152
Muslims, 85. *See also* Nation of Islam
Mussolini, Benito, 207. *See also* Ethiopia
Muste, A. J., 255
Myrdal, Gunnar, 174
Myth of the Negro Past, The (Herskovits), 142

NAACP, 43, 56, 195
  antilynching efforts and, 226–227
  boycotts by, 230
  Du Bois and, 185
  equality movement and, 244–245
  Ethiopian crisis and, 209
  on Haiti, 212–213
  Houston and, 221–222

human rights statement of, 216
legal challenges by, 221-229
Montgomery bus boycott and, 253
protests against lynchings, 112-113
school desegregation and, 248-249
Scottsboro case and, 229
Supreme Court successes by, 122
Nabrit, James M., 221
NACW. *See* National Association of Colored Women's Clubs of America (NACW)
Names, of former slaves, 15
Nash, Diane, 262
National American Woman Suffrage Association, 191
National Association for the Advancement of Colored People. *See* NAACP
National Association of Colored Women, 68, 190, 198
National Association of Colored Women's Clubs of America (NACW), 69-71, 91
National Baptist Convention, USA, 71, 187
National Baptist Convention of America, 187
National Bar Association, 241
National Council of Negro Women, 189, 198, 212
National Federation of Afro-American Women, 69, 190
National Football League, 181
National Guard, school integration and, 248-249
Nationalism. *See also* Black nationalists; Economic nationalism
in Africa, 209-211
Nationalist organizations, Nation of Islam as, 185-187
National Medical Association, 241
National Negro Business League, 74, 75
National Negro Congress (NNC), 195, 196, 216
National Negro League, 181
National Recovery Administration (NRA), 196
National Urban League, 75-76, 195, 212
Opportunity magazine of, 148
National Youth Administration (NYA), Division of Negro Affairs, 198, 199
Nation of Islam, 185-187
Nation of Islam, Malcolm X and, 269, 270
Native Rising of 1915 (Malawi), 209-210
Native Son (Wright), 172-173
Nazi Germany, 213, 214

Neal, Claude, lynching of, 227
Neal, Larry, 243-244
Negro, The (Du Bois), 132, 205
Negro History Week, 134
Negro in American Life and Thought, The:... (Logan), 170
Negro in Colonial New England, The, 1620-1776 (Greene), 169
Negro in Our History (Woodson), 205
Negro Labor in the United States, 1850-1925 (Wesley), 169
"Negro National Anthem" (Johnson), 137
Negro Society for Historical Research, 133
Negro Southern League, 181
Negro Theatre, 176
Negro World (newspaper), 148
Neighborhood Union (NU), 189
Nell, William Cooper, 131
Nellie Brown or The Jealous Wife (Detter), 134
New Deal, 176, 195-201. *See also* Great Depression; Roosevelt, Franklin D.
benefits to blacks during, 198-200
government programs in, 196-198
New Mississippian, 37-38
"New Negro," concept of, 142
New Negro, The (Locke), 142, 143
New Negro, The (Pickens), 142
New Orleans
boycott against segregation in, 121
racial violence in, 113, 116-117
school integration in, 249
New South, 45
Newspapers, 168. *See also* specific newspapers
white violence against black-owned, 110
New West (journal), 30
New York Age (newspaper), 50, 168
Wells-Barnett and, 110
New York City, 158. *See also* Harlem
African Freedom Day in, 211
Harlem Renaissance and, 138-154
New York Times, on black landownership, 18
Niagara Movement, 56-57
Nicodemus, Kansas, 61
Nig, The (Wilson), 130
Nigeria, 211
Nightlife, 149
Nineteenth Amendment, 190-191
Nkrumah, Kwame, 211

NNC. *See* National Negro Congress (NNC)
Nobel Peace Prize, King and, 273
Nomenclature, for black Americans, 90–91
Nonviolent protest, 230–232
  passive resistance as, 249–260
North
  black population in, 239–240
  civil rights movement in, 274
  employment in, 163–165
  migration to, 15, 138–139, 157
  mob violence in, 118–119
  racial violence in, 113
  urbanization in, 240
North Carolina Mutual Life Insurance Company, 74
NRA. *See* National Recovery Administration (NRA)

Occupations
  of black elected officials, 23
  changing patterns, 241
Ohlange Institute, 206
Oklahoma
  black communities in, 60–61
  black Southerners in, 30
  grandfather clause in, 122
"Old Lem" (Brown), 170–171
Old people's homes, 190
Oliver, Joseph, 150
Olmsted, Frederick Law, 17
O'Neal, Frederick, 176
Opera, 175
Opportunity (journal), 141, 148
Orangeburg, South Carolina, boycott in, 250
Orchestras, 150
Organizations. *See also* Pan-Africanism; Religion; Unions; specific organizations; specific religious groups
  black history and, 133–135
  black women's, 190–191
  fraternal, 79
  of freed persons, 26
  labor, 164–165
  of middle class blacks, 241
  for migrants, 161
  nationalist, 184–185
  Nation of Islam as, 185–187
  for political power, 22
  social welfare, 79
  women and, 69–71, 189

Orphanages, 190
Ottley, Roi, 244
Owen, Chandler, 95, 101, 102
  socialism and, 62
Owens, Jesse, 213

Pacific region, expansion into, 43–44
Page, Walter Hines, 36
Paige, Leroy "Satchel," 181
Painting, 153
Pan-African Congresses, 204, 205
Pan African Congress movement, 203
Pan-Africanism, 95–96, 202–205
Parks, Rosa, 260, 261
Passing (Larsen), 146
Passive resistance, 249–260
Patriotism. *See also* First World War; Second World War
  First World War and, 123–125
Payne, Daniel Alexander, 28, 86
PCDE. *See* Provision Committee for the Defense of Ethiopia (PCDE)
Peace Mission, 187–188
Pearson, W. G., 74
Pennington, James W. C., 131
Performers. *See* Arts; specific performers
Perry, Lincoln (Stephin Fetchit), 177
Pettey, Charles, 42
Philadelphia, 158
  racial violence in, 113
Philadelphia Negro, The (Du Bois), 54, 68
Philanthropy, education and, 76–77
Pickens, William, 102, 142, 198
Pinchback, P. B. S., 24
Pittsburgh Courier, 208, 213
Plato, Ann, 130
Playwrights, 176. *See also* Theatre
Plessy v. *Ferguson*, 41–42, 122, 222, 226
Poets and poetry, 130, 170–172, 244. *See also* Harlem Renaissance; Intellectual life; specific poets and poems
  of Hughes, 140
Poitier, Sidney, 178
Poland, invasion of, 214
Police
  in Albany, 263–264
  in Birmingham, 264–266
  in Selma, 273
Political parties. *See also* Communism; Democratic party; Republican party
  black allegiance to, 192–193

Political power
 of blacks, 243
 organization for, 22
Political style
 of Du Bois, 53–57
 of Washington, 48–53
Politics
 black officials and, 23–26
 blacks in, 22–23
 literature and, 143–144
Pollard, Mother, 252
Poll tax, in Mississippi, 39
Population
 rural and urban, 72–73
 shifts in, 239–240
Populist party, 61
Porter, Benjamin F., 59
Poverty
 in cities, 166
 Great Society programs and, 276
Powell, Adam Clayton, Jr., 208, 214
Powell, Adam Clayton, Sr., 76
Prayer Pilgrimage for Freedom, 259
"Precious Lord" (Dorsey), 175
Presbyterians, 26
Presidential elections. *See* Elections
Presidents. *See* Elections; specific presidents
Price, Florence, 152
Primary elections, black exclusion from, 222
Primer of Facts Pertaining to the Early Greatness of the African Race (Hopkins), 132
Prince Hall Masons, 241
Pritchett, Laurie, 263
Private property, landownership and, 17–19
Professional organizations, 241
Professionals, increase in, 76–80
Professional schools, 221–222
Professions, 73
Progressive National Baptist Convention, 187
Progressives, white, 36
Proletariat, black industrial, 164–165
Property
 blacks as, 34–35
 landownership and, 17–19
 sales to blacks, 222–223
Protest demonstration
 in 1917, 106
 nonviolent, 230–232, 249–260
Providential role of blacks, 88

Provision Committee for the Defense of Ethiopia (PCDE), 208–209
Public assistance, 194
Public education. *See also* Education
 for blacks, 78
Public facilities, segregation of, 41
Public schools. *See* Education; Schools
Public welfare programs, black exclusion from, 189
Public Works Administration (PWA), 196
Pullman Company, 165
PWA. *See* Public Works Administration (PWA)

Quicksand (Larsen), 146
Qur'an. *See* Nation of Islam

Race, of God, 83–84
Race relations, 34–35
Race riots. *See also* Riots; Violence
 in Chicago, Illinois, 120–121
 in East St. Louis, Illinois (1917), 95
 in Tulsa, Oklahoma, 121
 in Watts, Los Angeles, 274
 whites' riots against blacks, 113–121
 in Wilmington, North Carolina, 115–116
Racial accommodation. *See also* Washington, Booker T.
 black elite and, 67–68
 education and, 77
Racial integration, 8
Racial stereotypes. *See* Stereotypes
Racism. *See also* Equal rights; Jim Crow
 Garvey and, 95
 in Haiti, 212
 imperialism and, 43–44
 of Nazis, 213–214
 poetry protesting, 171–172
 after Reconstruction, 35
 resistance to, 121–123
 Turner and, 60
 among whites, 257
Radicalism
 of *Fire!!* magazine, 144
 Locke's rejection of, 143
Radical Republicans, 7, 10
Radio, *Amos and Andy* on, 192
Ragtime music, 149–150
Railroad cars, segregation in, 38
Railway Men's International Industrial Benevolent Association, 164

Railway workers, organization of, 164–165
Rainey, Gertrude "Ma," 150, 152
Raisin in the Sun, A (Hansberry), 243
Raleigh conference, 261–262
Randolph, A. Philip, 44, 48, 95, 165, 195
  ANLC and, 212
  on blacks and Second World War, 215
  on Garvey, 102
  March on Washington (1941) and, 230–232
  March on Washington (1963) and, 266, 267
  Prayer Pilgrimage for Freedom and, 259
  socialism and, 62–63
  student marches and, 260
Rape
  anti-black violence and, 107
  Fort Brown riot and, 118
  Scottsboro case and, 228–229
Reactionary developments, after Reconstruction, 34
Reagon, Cordell, 263
Real estate. *See* Landownership
Reconstruction
  Johnson and, 5
  Lincoln and, 4
  segregation after, 35
  of Union, 4–12
  use of term, 12
Reconstruction Act of 1867, 8, 22
Redding, J. Saunders, 170
Red Moon, The (musical), 152
"Red Summer," 120
Reformers. *See also* Civil rights; Civil rights movement; Equal rights; Mass movements
  women as, 189–192
Religion. *See also* Churches; King, Martin Luther, Jr.
  African traditions and, 86–87
  black Christianity and, 83–93
  churches and, 186–189
  church growth and, 241–242
  of educated women, 71
  Garvey and, 85–86
  of Kimbangu, 210
  leaders and, 28
  National Baptist Convention, USA, and, 71
  Nation of Islam and, 185–186
  as source of comfort, 163
  support for African students and, 206

Republican party
  blacks in, 23
  black support for, 10
  Radicals and, 7
Republicans, in Spain, 213
Resistance
  to mob violence, 121–123
  by new generation, 122–127
Revels, Hiram, 24
Review (AME Church), 148
Richard Allen, Apostle of Freedom (Wesley), 169
Richardson, George, 118
Richmond, David, 260
Richmond News Leader, states rights theory of, 247
Rights. *See* Equal rights
Riots, 113–121, 114 (illus.). *See also* Race riots
  by blacks, 114
  in Harlem, 234
  over Johnson-Jeffries boxing match, 180
Rise and Progress of the Kingdoms of Light and Darkness;... (Blackson), 134
Rivera, Lino, 234
Robeson, Paul, 152, 175
  Africa and, 205–206
  anti-communist harassment of, 217
  communism and, 211, 236
  in film, 178
  and Republicans in Spain, 213–214
Robinson, Jackie, 181
Robinson, Jo Ann, 250, 254
Robinson, John, 209
Robinson, Ruby Doris, 262
Robinson, "Sugar Ray" (Walker Smith, Jr.), 181
Rogers, J. A., 190, 208
Roosevelt, Eleanor, 194, 195, 258
  anti-lynching issue and, 227
  March on Washington and, 232
Roosevelt, Franklin, and civil rights, 228
Roosevelt, Franklin D.
  black Americans and, 192, 193
  "Black Cabinet" and, 199–200
  lynching issue and, 227
  March on Washington and, 232
  policy toward blacks, 194–200
Roosevelt, Theodore, 118
Running Wild (musical), 152
Rural life, urban migration and, 159

Rural population, 72
Rural society
  black tenant farmers and, 21
  sharecropping and, 21–22
Russwurm, John, 57
Rustin, Bayard, 232, 253, 267

Sabbath schools, 78
"St. Louis Blues" (Handy), 150
Sanchez, Sonia, 244
Schlesinger, Arthur, Jr., 258
Schomburg, Arthur A., 132, 142
School boards, desegregation and, 245–246
Schools, 78. *See also* Education; Higher education
  black, 189–190
  boycotts against segregation in, 121
  challenges to segregation of, 223–226
  resistance to integration of, 246–249
Schwerner, Michael, 271
Sciences, 174
SCLC. *See* Southern Christian Leadership Conference (SCLC)
Scott, Emmett J., 52
Scott, Hazel, 178
Scott, James Sylvester, 149–150
Scottsboro case, 228–229
Second World War, 214–216
  colonial rule in Africa and, 211
  impact on sports, 181–182
  poetry and, 171–172
Segregation, 40 (illus.). *See also* Civil rights movement
  black protests against, 121
  boycotts against, 121
  desegregation in Birmingham and, 266
  Du Bois's support for, 185
  by federal government, 43
  fully established in South, 44
  in Haiti, 212
  in housing, 122
  in interstate transportation, 223
  NAACP challenges to, 221–226
  of public facilities, 41
  after Reconstruction, 34–37
  Supreme Court upholding of, 41–42, 122
  unconstitutionality on buses, 253
  Washington's endorsement of, 49–50
  under Wilson, 43
Selassie, Haile, 209

Self-determination
  communism and, 235–236
  Pan-Africanism and, 204
Self-help
  black elite and, 67–68
  programs, 184
  Washington and, 48
  women's organizations and, 71
Self-perception, freedom and, 2–3
Sellers, Cleveland, 262
Selma, Alabama, demonstrations in, 273
Senate. *See* Congress
"Separate but equal" doctrine, 41–42, 167. *See also* Education; Segregation
  legal challenges to, 225–226
Sex and sexuality. *See also* Homosexuals and homosexuality; Rape
  rumors of black male assaults and, 115–116
Sexism, 189. *See also* Gender; Women
  civil rights movement and, 254
Sexual abuse. *See also* Rape
  of black women, 108
Sexual assaults, 107
Sexual exploitation, by white men, 190
Sharecropping, 21–22
Share tenants, whites as, 21
Shelley, J. D., 222–223
Shelley v. *Kramer*, 222–223
Shephard, James E., 74
Sherman, William Tecumseh, 17
Sherrod, Charles, 262, 263
Shipping, Garvey and, 99
Short History of the American Negro (Brawley), 132
Shuffle Along (musical), 152
Shuttlesworth, Fred, 253, 264
Silent Protest Parade, 106
Simmons, Roscoe Conkling, 124
Singers, 175. *See also* Music
Singleton, Benjamin ("Pap"), 30
Sit-ins, 230, 260–261
  in Birmingham, 264
Slavery
  destruction of families by, 16
  impact on Washington's beliefs, 54
  white supremacy in South and, 6
Slaves, divisions with free blacks, 67
Smalls, Robert, 24–25
Smiley, Glenn, 257
Smith, Bessie, 150, 152, 154
Smith, Clara, 150
Smith, Harry Clay, 56

Smith, Lucy Wilmot, 71
Smith, Mamie, 150
Smith, Walker, Jr. *See* Robinson, "Sugar Ray"
Smith v. Allwright, 222
SNCC. *See* Student Non Violent Coordinating Committee (SNCC)
Socialists and socialism, 62-63
  in Cuba, 213
  New Negro anthology and, 143
Social Security Act, 197
  impact on blacks, 197
Social services
  black provision of, 189
  for migrants, 161
  of NACW, 71
Social welfare organizations, 79
Societal change, role of arts in, 143-144
Society
  barriers as cause of migration, 160
  black middle class in, 145-146
  black migration after 1915, 157-167
  black-white relations and, 45
  black women in, 191-192
  changes between 1915-1955, 156-182
  after Civil War, 4
  First World War and, 126
  hierarchical, 37
  integration and segregation of whites and blacks in, 34-35
  mistreatment of blacks and, 66-67
  place of blacks in, 45
"Song for the Emigrant" (Horton), 29
Sororities, 190
Souls of Black Folk, The (Du Bois), 54-55, 135
South
  black communities in, 60-61
  black migration from, 138-139, 157-158
  black population in, 239
  blacks registered to vote in, 242
  blacks remaining in, 159
  constitutional and judicial support for segregation in, 39-42
  impact on Washington, 48-49
  Johnson's policy toward, 5-6
  Lincoln's treatment of, 4
  military districts in, 8
  racial climate in, 39-40
  Reconstruction and, 4-12
  resistance to integration in, 246-249
  urbanization in, 240
  violence in, 159

voter registration in, 191
white supremacy in, 6
South Africa
  apartheid and, 205
  assistance to, 206
South Carolina, Black Codes in, 6
Southern Christian Leadership Conference (SCLC), 212, 258-259
  Birmingham and, 264
  direct action and, 261-262
Southern Conference Educational Fund, 216
Southern Conference for Human Welfare, 216
Southern Democrats, 9
Southern Negro League. *See* Negro Southern League
Southern Regional Council, 216
Soviet Union
  Cold War and, 211
  competition with, 216-217
  Italian invasion of Ethiopia and, 209
Spain
  anti-Franco Republicans in, 213-214
  Franco and, 213
Spanish-Cuban-American War, 44
Special Field Order Number 15, 17
Spelman College, 71
Sport of the Gods, The (Dunbar), 136
Sports, 179-182
Springfield, Illinois, race riot in, 118
Star of Zion (newspaper), 194
States, desegregation by, 245-246
States rights theory, 247
Status quo, challenges to, 220
Steele, C. K., 253, 259
Steelworkers, 164
Stereotypes
  of blacks, 192
  in films, 177-178
Stevens, Thadeus, 16-17
Stevenson, Adlai, 258
Still, William Grant, 131, 152
Storey, Moorfield, 125
Story of the Negro (Washington), 132
Stride Toward Freedom (King), 255
Student Non Violent Coordinating Committee (SNCC), 254, 262
  black power movement and, 275
  voter registration and, 263
Students
  marches on Washington by, 260
  SNCC organization of, 263
Subsidy, to farmers, 196, 197

Suffering, religion and, 88
Suffrage. *See also* Voting rights
  black, 5-6
  civil rights bill (1866) and, 7
  election of 1868 and, 9
  women's, 190-191
Summer Project, 271-272
"Sundays of the Satin-Legs Smith, The" (Brooks), 162
Suppression of the African Slave Trade to the United States of America, 1638-1870, The (Du Bois), 132
Supreme Court. *See also* specific cases
  challenges to segregation in, 222-226
  Dred Scott decision and, 6
  Scottsboro case and, 229
  segregation and, 41-42
  segregation upheld by, 122
  United States v. *Reese* and, 11
Survey Graphic, The (magazine), 141
Sweatt, Heman, 223

Talented Tenth, 67-68, 137
Tallahassee, Florida, 253
Tanner, Benjamin T., 59
Tanner, Henry Ossawa, 153
Taylor, Ralph W., 148
Tenant farmers, 21
Tennessee, segregation in, 38
Tennis, 182
Terrell, Mary Church, 57, 68, 69, 76
  protests against lynchings, 112
Territories, racism and, 44
Texas, 7
  blacks in, 30
Textbook of Negro History (Pennington), 131
Theatre, 151-153, 175-177
  Harlem Renaissance and, 149
Their Eyes Were Watching God (Hurston), 146-147
Third World, 213
Thirteenth Amendment, 2
  slavery ended by, 1
Thoreau, Henry David, 255
Thurman, Wallace, 141, 144, 153
Thurmond, Strom, 217, 259
Till, Emmett, lynching of, 271
Time magazine, 245
Tolson, Melvin, 171
Toomer, Jean, 139, 140-141
Trade Union Committee for Organizing Negro Workers, 165

Training. *See* Vocational training
Transnational movements, Pan-Africanism and, 202-204
Transportation, boycotts against segregation in, 121, 250-253
Troops, withdrawn from South, 11
Trotter, Monroe, 43, 56, 57, 124
Truman, Harry S., desegregation of armed services by, 233
Tulsa, Oklahoma
  mob attack in, 235
  race riot in, 121
Turner, Henry McNeal, 11-12, 23-24, 28, 48, 57-60, 58 (illus.), 82-83
  on anti-black violence, 114-115
  on black deity, 83-84
  Pan-Africanism and, 202, 203
  on providential role of blacks, 88
Tuskegee Institute, 48, 77
  as model for African development, 210
Tuskegee Machine, 52
Tuskegee Negro Farmers Conference, 73-74

UL. *See* National Urban League
Uncalled, The (Dunbar), 136
Uncle Tom character, in movies, 177
Underground Railroad, The (Still), 131
Unemployment. *See also* Employment; Jobs
  during Great Depression, 193
UNIA. *See* Universal Negro Improvement Association (UNIA)
Union, reconstructing after Civil War, 4-12
Union League, 22
Unions, 164-165
  attitudes toward blacks, 62
  discrimination outlawed in, 271
  Wagner Act and, 198
United Nations, black petitions to, 216
United States
  pressure to help Africa, 211-212
  Soviet competition and, 216-217
United States v. *Cruikshank,* 11
United States v. *Reese,* 11
Universal Negro Improvement Association (UNIA), 85, 94, 186, 203, 204, 220
  African development and, 99-100
  influence in Congo, 210
  as international organization, 98-99

Universities and colleges, 48, 77, 167. *See also* Higher education
  black enrollment in, 240–241
University of Texas Law School, 223
Unskilled workers, 73
Up from Slavery (Washington), 51–52
Urbanization, 240
Urban League (UL). *See* National Urban League
Urban population and society, 72, 74. *See also* Cities
  black migration and, 157, 158
  ghetto development and, 166–167

Vann, Robert, 198
Van Nuys, Frederick, 228
Vardaman, James K., 39, 79
Veterans, 125
Victim, rights of, 11
Vietnam War, 275
Villard, Oswald, 57
Violence. *See also* Lynchings; Race riots; Riots
  in Birmingham, 266
  black resistance to, 121–123
  against blacks, 35, 37
  as cause for migration, 159
  in Detroit, 234–235
  Freedom Rides and, 262–263
  in Harlem, 234
  legal challenges to, 226–227
  riots, 113–121
  Scottsboro case and, 228–229
  in Selma, 273
  by whites, 107–115
Virginia, school integration and, 247
Vocational education, 76–77, 137
Vocational training, Washington and, 48, 49
Voice from the South, A (Cooper), 68–69, 135
Voluntary associations, 69
Voter registration
  Freedom Summer and, 271–272
  in Mississippi, 263
  in Selma, Alabama, 273
  in South, 8
Voting rights. *See also* Suffrage; Voter registration
  blacks in electorate and, 242–243
  exclusion of blacks in Mississippi, 39
  limitations on, 41
  registration by black women, 191
  registration in South (1940-56), 242
  removal of blacks from electoral rolls, 38–39
  restrictions on, 34
  Smith v. *Allwright* and, 222
Voting Rights Act, 273–274

Wage labor, blacks and, 19–21
Wages. *See* Economic conditions; Job opportunities; Wage labor
Wagner, Robert F., 227, 228
Wagner Act, 198
Walker, David, 82, 88, 130, 135, 275
Walker, George, 151, 152
Walker, Madame C. J., 74, 103
Walker, Margaret, 171
Walker, Sidney, 181
Walker, Wyatt
  in Albany, 263
  in Birmingham, 264
Wallace, George, 273
Warren, Earl, 225–226, 248
Washerwomen, 73
Washington, Booker T., 13, 48–53, 51 (illus.)
  Africa and, 206
  autobiography of, 51–52
  black response to, 50–51
  on black-white cooperation, 49
  collective action and, 73, 74
  covert civil rights activities of, 52–53
  on emigration, 59
  on equal voting rights, 40
  impact of philosophy on Garvey, 94
  on lynchings, 110–111
  on "New Negro," 142
  Story of the Negro, 132
Washington, D.C. *See also* March on Washington entries
  Prayer Pilgrimage for Freedom to, 259
Washington, Fredi, 178
Washington Bee, 50
Waters, Ethel, 150, 154, 178
Watts riot, 274
Weaver, Robert C., 195, 198
Weaver, Sylvester, 150
Webb, James Morris, 132
Welfare. *See* Public assistance
Wells-Barnett, Ida, 57, 107
  protests against lynchings, 110, 112
  resistance to racism by, 121
"We Shall Overcome" (song), 273
Wesley, Charles Harris, 169

West
　black communities in, 60–61
　black population in, 239–240
　housing in, 165–166
　migration to, 157
West Africa, heritage from, 131
West Indians, 202
What the Negro Wants (anthology), 169–170
Wheatley, Phillis, 130
White, Clarence Cameron, 152
White, Elam, 68
White, George H., 61, 116, 195
White, Walter, 121, 168, 192–193, 209, 215
　anti-lynching legislation and, 227
Whitecaps (farmers), 37
White Citizen's Council, 257
"White man's burden," 44
"Whiteness" concept, 83
Whites. *See also* Lynchings
　anti-lynching efforts and, 226, 227, 228
　attitudes of younger generation, 35, 36
　as civil rights supporters, 257
　Compromise of 1877 and, 33
　conservative, progressive, and extremist views of, 36–37
　early civil rights movement and, 258
　migration as independence from, 160
　and Montgomery bus boycott, 252–253
　paternalistic attitudes of, 27
　as patrons of writers, 144–145
　in Peace Mission, 187–188
　post-Reconstruction controls over blacks by, 33–45
　protests against lynchings, 112
　resistance to integration by, 245–249
　riots against blacks by, 113–121
　sexual exploitation by, 190
　in SNCC, 262
　violence by, 107–115
　wage labor of, 19
　Washington and, 49–50
Whitesboro, New Jersey, 61, 116
White Slave Law. *See* Mann Act
White supremacy, 37, 38–39
　Second World War and, 216
　in South, 6
　Washington and, 49
Wilberforce University, 77
Wilkins, Roy, 169, 253, 258
　on *Brown* decision, 245
　on equality movement, 244–245
　March on Washington (1963) and, 267

Willard, Jess, 180
Williams, Egbert Austin, 151, 152
Williams, Fannie Barrier, 107–108
Williams, George Washington, 88, 131
Williams, Henry Sylvester, 203
Williams, Ike, 181
Wilmington, North Carolina, race riot in, 115–116
Wilson, Harriet E., 130
Wilson, Hawkins, 15–16
Wilson, Woodrow, 53
　on blacks in armed forces, 125
　segregation under, 43, 44
"Wishes" (Johnson), 148
Wizard of Tuskegee (Booker T. Washington), 52
Women. *See also* Gender; Sex and sexuality
　in anti-lynching campaign, 226–227
　in basketball, 181
　black self-help and, 189
　as blues singers, 150
　civil rights leadership and, 254
　as contributors to *New Negro* anthology, 143
　elite, 68–72
　employment in North, 164
　field work of, 7, 21
　fraternal organizations of, 79
　health care and, 190
　Hurston on, 146–147
　in literature and culture, 153
　in Montgomery bus boycott, 252
　in organizations, 189
　as property owners, 19
　search for identity and, 103
　social services and, 190–192
　status of, 28
　UNIA and, 100–101
　as writers, 139
Women's Political Council, 250
Women's rights. *See also* Women
　black elite women and, 68–69
　Eleventh National Woman's Rights Convention (1866) and, 13
Woodson, Carter G., 133, 168
　Africa and, 205
Woolworth's, sit-in at, 260–261
Workers. *See also* Employment; Labor; Working class
　industrial, 164–165
　loss of black, 159–160
　wage labor, 19–21
　Wagner Act and, 198

Working class, 61–62. *See also* Workers
    Randolph and, 62–64
    women of, 189
World War I. *See* First World War
World War II. *See* Second World War
Wright, Richard, 172
    communism and, 236
Writers and writing, 130–131. *See also* Harlem Renaissance; Literature; specific writers
    by black women, 68–69
    Federal Writers Project and, 198
    gay writers and, 153–154
Wyatt, Bayley, 17–18

Young, Andrew, 256
    in Birmingham, 264
    on civil rights movement, 275–276
    on Ghana, 211
Young, Robert, 82
Young, Whitney
    ANLC and, 212
    March on Washington (1963) and, 266
Youth March for Integrated Schools (1958), 260

Zellner, Bob, 262